THE CONFESSIONS

OF

NAT TURNER

THE
CONFESSIONS
OF
NAT TURNER

BY

WILLIAM STYRON

RANDOM HOUSE

• *New York* •

To

JAMES TERRY

to

LILLIAN HELLMAN

and to

MY WIFE ✦ *and* ✦ **CHILDREN**

In August, 1831, in a remote region of southeastern Virginia, there took place the only effective, sustained revolt in the annals of·American Negro slavery. The initial passage of this book, entitled "To the Public," is the preface to the single significant contemporary document concerning this insurrection—a brief pamphlet of some twenty pages called "The Confessions of Nat Turner," published in Richmond early in the next year, parts of which have been incorporated in this book. During the narrative that follows I have rarely departed from the *known* facts about Nat Turner and the revolt of which he was the leader. However, in those areas where there is little knowledge in regard to Nat, his early life, and the motivations for the revolt (and such knowledge is lacking most of the time), I have allowed myself the utmost freedom of imagination in reconstructing events—yet I trust remaining within the bounds of what meager enlightenment history has left us about the institution of slavery. The relativity of time allows us elastic definitions: the year 1831 was, simultaneously, a long time ago and only yesterday. Perhaps the reader will wish to draw a moral from this narrative, but it has been my own intention to try to re-create a man and his era, and to produce a work that is less an "historical novel" in conventional terms than a meditation on history.

WILLIAM STYRON

Roxbury, Connecticut
New Year's Day, 1967

CONTENTS

+ + + + + + + + + + + + +

TO THE PUBLIC

THE LATE INSURRECTION IN SOUTHAMPTON
has greatly excited the public mind and led to a thousand idle,
exaggerated and mischievous reports. It is the first instance in
our history of an open rebellion of the slaves, and attended
with such atrocious circumstances of cruelty and destruction,
as could not fail to leave a deep impression, not only upon the
minds of the community where this fearful tragedy was
wrought, but throughout every portion of our country in
which this population is to be found. Public curiosity has
been on the stretch to understand the origin and progress of
this dreadful conspiracy, and the motives which influence its
diabolical actors. The insurgent slaves had all been destroyed, or apprehended, tried and executed (with the exception of the leader) without revealing any thing at all satisfactory, as to the motives which governed them, or the means by
which they expected to accomplish their object. Every thing
connected with this sad affair was wrapt in mystery, until
Nat Turner, the leader of this ferocious band, whose name
has resounded throughout our widely extended empire was
captured. This "great Bandit" was taken by a single individual, in a cave near the residence of his late owner, on Sunday,
the thirtieth of October, without attempting to make the
slightest resistance, and on the following day lodged in the
jail of the County. His captor was Benjamin Phipps, armed
with a shot gun well charged. Nat's only weapon was a small
light sword which he immediately surrendered and begged
that his life might be spared. Since his confinement, by per-

mission of the Jailor, I have had ready access to him, and, finding that he was willing to make a full and free confession of the origin, progress and consummation of the insurrectory movements of the slaves of which he was the contriver and head, I determined for the gratification of public curiosity to commit his statements to writing and publish them, with little or no variation, from his own words. That this is a faithful record of his confessions, the annexed certificate of the County Court of Southampton, will attest. They certainly bear one stamp of truth and sincerity. He makes no attempt (as all the other insurgents who were examined did) to exculpate himself, but frankly acknowledges his full participation in all the guilt of the transaction. He was not only the contriver of the conspiracy, but gave the first blow toward its execution.

It will thus appear, that whilst every thing upon the surface of society wore a calm and peaceful aspect; whilst not one note of preparation was heard to warn the devoted inhabitants of woe and death, a gloomy fanatic was revolving in the recesses of his own dark, bewildered and overwrought mind schemes of indiscriminate massacre to the whites. Schemes too fearfully executed as far as his fiendish band proceeded in their desolating march. No cry for mercy penetrated their flinty bosoms. No acts of remembered kindness made the least impression upon these remorseless murderers. Men, women and children, from hoary age to helpless infancy, were involved in the same cruel fate. Never did a band of savages do their work of death more unsparingly. Apprehension for their own personal safety seems to have been the only principle of restraint in the whole course of their bloody proceedings. And it is not the least remarkable feature in this horrid transaction, that a band actuated by such hellish purposes, should have resisted so feebly, when met by the whites in arms. Desperation alone, one would think, might have led to greater efforts. Each individual sought his own safety ei-

ther in concealment, or by returning home, with the hope that his participation might escape detection, and all were shot down in the course of a few days, or captured and brought to trial and punishment. Nat has survived all his followers, and the gallows will speedily close his career. His own account of the conspiracy is submitted to the public, without comment. It reads an awful, and it is hoped, a useful lesson as to the operations of a mind like his, endeavoring to grapple with things beyond its reach. How it first became bewildered and confounded, and finally corrupted and led to the conception and perpetration of the most atrocious and heart-rending deeds. It is calculated also to demonstrate the policy of our laws in restraint of this class of our population, and to induce all those entrusted with their execution, as well as our citizens generally, to see that they are strictly and rigidly enforced. If Nat's statements can be relied on, the insurrection in this county was entirely local, and his designs confident but to a few, and these in his immediate vicinity. It was not instigated by motives of revenge or sudden anger, but the results of long deliberation, and a settled purpose of mind. The offspring of gloomy fanaticism, acting upon materials but too well prepared for such impressions, it will be long remembered in the annals of our country and many a mother as she presses her darling infant to her bosom, will shudder at the recollection of Nat Turner, and his band of ferocious miscreants.

Believing the following narrative, by removing doubts and conjectures from the public mind which otherwise must have remained, would give general satisfaction, it is respectfully submitted to the public by their ob't serv't,

T. R. GRAY

Jerusalem, Southampton County, Va., Nov. 5, 1831.

We the undersigned, members of the court convened at

Jerusalem, on Saturday, the fifth day of Nov., 1831, for the trial of Nat, alias Nat Turner a negro slave, late the property of Putnam Moore, deceased, do hereby certify that the confessions of Nat, to Thomas R. Gray, was read to him in our presence, and that furthermore, when called upon by the presiding Magistrate of the Court, to state if he had anything to say, why sentence of death should not be passed upon him, replied he had nothing further than he had communicated to Mr. Gray. Given under our hands and seals at Jerusalem, this 5th day of November, 1831.

JEREMIAH COBB,	[seal]
THOMAS PRETLOW,	[seal]
JAMES W. PARKER,	[seal]
CARR BOWERS,	[seal]
SAMUEL B. HINES,	[seal]
ORRIS A. BROWNE,	[seal]

Part

I

JUDGMENT

DAY

✦ ✦ ✦

*And God shall wipe away all tears from
their eyes; and there shall be no more
death, neither sorrow, nor crying,
neither shall there be any more pain:
for the former things are passed away.*

✦ ✦ ✦ ✦ ✦ ✦ ✦ ✦ ✦ ✦ ✦ ✦ ✦

ABOVE THE BARREN, SANDY CAPE WHERE the river joins the sea, there is a promontory or cliff rising straight up hundreds of feet to form the last outpost of land. One must try to visualize a river estuary below this cliff, wide and muddy and shallow, and a confusion of choppy waves where the river merges with the sea and the current meets the ocean tide. It is afternoon. The day is clear, sparkling, and the sun seems to cast no shadow anywhere. It may be the commencement of spring or perhaps the end of summer; it matters less what the season is than that the air is almost seasonless—benign and neutral, windless, devoid of heat or cold. As always, I seem to be approaching this place alone in some sort of boat (it is a small boat, a skiff or maybe a canoe, and I am reclining in it comfortably; at least I have no sense of discomfort nor even of exertion, for I do not row— the boat is moving obediently to the river's sluggish seaward wallow), floating calmly toward the cape past which, beyond and far, deep blue, stretches the boundless sea. The shores of the river are unpeopled, silent; no deer run through the forests, nor do any gulls rise up from the deserted, sandy beaches. There is an effect of great silence and of an even greater solitude, as if life here had not so much perished as simply disappeared, leaving all—river shore and estuary and rolling sea—to exist forever unchanged like this beneath the light of a motionless afternoon sun.

Now as I drift near the cape I raise my eyes to the promontory facing out upon the sea. There again I see what I know I will see, as always. In the sunlight the building stands white—stark white and serene against a blue and cloudless sky. It is square and formed of marble, like a temple, and is simply designed, possessing no columns or windows but rather, in place of them, recesses whose purpose I cannot imagine, flowing in a series of arches around its two visible sides. The building has no door, at least there is no door that I can see. Likewise, just as this building possesses neither doors nor windows, it seems to have no purpose, resembling, as I say, a temple—yet a temple in which no one worships, or a sarcophagus in which no one lies buried, or a monument to something mysterious, ineffable, and without name. But as is my custom whenever I have this dream or vision, I don't dwell upon the meaning of the strange building standing so lonely and remote upon its ocean promontory, for it seems by its very purposelessness to be endowed with a profound mystery which to explore would yield only a profusion of darker and perhaps more troubling mysteries, as in a maze.

And so again it comes to me, this vision, in the same haunting and recurrent way it has for many years. Again I am in the little boat, floating in the estuary of a silent river toward the sea. And again beyond and ahead of me, faintly booming and imminent yet without menace, is the sweep of sunlit ocean. Then the cape, then the lofty promontory, and finally the stark white temple high and serene above all, inspiring in me neither fear nor peace nor awe, but only the contemplation of a great mystery, as I move out toward the sea . . .

Never, from the time I was a child until the present—and I am just past thirty—was I able to discover the meaning behind this dream (or *vision;* for though it occurred mainly as I awoke from sleep, there would be random waking moments when, working in the fields or out trapping rabbits in the woods, or while I was at some odd task or other, the whole

scene would flash against my mind with the silence and clearness and fixity of absolute reality, like a picture in the Bible,
and in an instant's dumb daydream all would be re-created
before my eyes, river and temple and promontory and sea, to
dissolve almost as swiftly as it had come), nor was I ever
able to understand the emotion it caused me—this emotion of
a tranquil and abiding mystery. I have no doubt, however,
that it was all connected with my childhood, when I would
hear white people talk of Norfolk and of "going to the sea-
side." For Norfolk was only forty miles eastward from
Southampton and the ocean only a few miles past Norfolk,
where some of the white people would go to trade. Indeed, I
had even known a few Negroes from Southampton who had
gone to Norfolk with their masters and then seen the ocean,
and the picture they recalled—that of an infinite vastness of
blue water stretching out to the limit of the eye, and past that,
as if to the uttermost boundaries of the earth—inflamed my
imagination in such a way that my desire to see this sight
became a kind of fierce, inward, almost physical hunger, and
there were days when my mind seemed filled with nothing but
fantasies of the waves and the distant horizon and the groaning seas, the free blue air like an empire above arching eastward to Africa—as if by one single glimpse of this scene I
might comprehend all the earth's ancient, oceanic, preposter-
ous splendor. But since luck was against me in this regard,
and I was never allowed the opportunity of a trip to Norfolk
and the ocean, I had to content myself with the vision which
existed in my imagination; hence the recurring phantasm I
have already described, even though the temple on the
promontory still remained a mystery—and more mysterious
this morning than ever before in all the years I could reckon.
It lingered for a while, half dream, half waking vision as my
eyes came open in the gray dawn, and I shut them again,
watching the white temple dwindle in the serene and secret
light, fade out, removed from recollection.

I rose up from the cedar plank I'd been sleeping on and

sat halfway erect, in the same somnolent motion duplicating the instinctive mistake I'd made four times in as many mornings: swinging my legs sideways off the plank as if to plant them on the floor, only to feel metal bite into my ankles as the chain of the leg irons reached the limit of its slack, holding my feet suspended slantwise in midair. I drew my feet back and let them fall on the plank, then I sat upright and reached down and rubbed my ankles underneath the irons, aware of the flow of blood returning warm beneath my fingers. There was for the first time this year a wintry touch about the morning, damp and cold, and I could see a line of pale frost where the hard clay of the floor met the bottom plank of the jail wall. I sat there for several minutes, rubbing my ankles and shivering some. Suddenly I was very hungry, and I felt my stomach churn and heave. For a while all was still. They had put Hark in the cell next to me the evening before, and now through the planks I could hear his heavy breathing—a choked, clotted sound as if air were escaping through his very wounds. For an instant I was on the verge of waking him with a whisper, for we had had no chance to speak, but the sound of his breathing was slow and heavy with exhaustion. I thought, Let him sleep, and the words I had already formed on my lips went unspoken. I sat still on the board, watching the dawn light grow and fill the cell like a cup, stealthily, blossoming with the color of pearl. Far off in the distance now I heard a rooster crow, a faint call like a remote hurrah, echoing, fading into silence. Then another rooster crowed, nearer now. For a long while I sat there, listening and waiting. Save for Hark's breathing there was no sound at all for many minutes, until at last I heard a distant horn blow, mournful and familiar-sounding, a hollow soft diminishing cry in the fields beyond Jerusalem, rousing up the Negroes on some farm or other.

After a bit I manipulated the chain so that I could slide my legs off the board and stand up. The chain allowed my feet a yard or so of movement, and by shuffling to the length of the chain and then stretching myself forward I could see out the open barred window into the dawn. Jerusalem was waking. From where I was standing I could see two houses nearby, perched at the edge of the riverbank where the cypress bridge began. Through one house someone moved with a candle, a flickering light which passed from bedroom to living room to hallway to kitchen, where it finally came to rest on some table and stood still, yellow and wavering. Behind the other house, closer to the bridge, an old woman covered with a greatcoat came out with a chamber pot; holding the steaming pot before her like a crucible, she hobbled across the frozen yard toward a whitewashed wooden privy, the breath coming from her mouth in puffs of smoke. She opened the door of the privy, went in, and the sound of the hinges grated with a small shriek on the frosty air until abruptly and with a crack like that of a gun the door slammed shut behind her. Suddenly, more from hunger than anything else, I felt dizzy and closed my eyes. Tiny freckles of light danced across my vision and I thought for an instant I was going to fall but I caught myself against the sill of the window; when I opened my eyes again, I saw that the candle in the first house had gone out, and gray smoke was pluming upward from the chimney.

Just then from afar I heard a distant drumming noise, a plunging of hoofbeats in erratic muffled tattoo which grew louder and louder as it approached from the west across the river. I raised my eyes to the far riverbank fifty yards away, where the tangled forest wall of cypress and gum trees loomed high over waters flowing muddy and cold and sluggish in the dawn. A rent in the wall marked the passage of the county road, and now through this rent a horse at an easy gallop appeared, carrying a cavalryman, followed closely by another, then still another, three soldiers in all: like a collision of barrels they struck the cypress bridge in a thunderous uproar of hooves and squealing timber, passed swiftly across the river into Jerusalem, guns glinting in the pale light. I watched until they had galloped out of sight and until the noise of hoofbeats faded into a soft dim drumming behind me in the town. Then it was still again. I closed my eyes and rested my forehead against the window sill. The darkness was comforting to my eyes. It had for many years been my custom to pray at this hour of the day, or to read from the Bible; but during the five days that I had been made prisoner I had been refused the Bible, and as for prayer—well, it was no surprise to me any longer that I was totally unable to force a prayer from my lips. I still had this craving to perform a daily act which for the years of my grown-up life had become as simple and as natural as a bodily function, but which now seemed so incapable of accomplishment as to resemble a problem in geometry or some other mysterious science beyond my understanding. I now could not even recall when the ability to pray had left me—one month, two months, perhaps even more. It might have been some consolation, at least, had I known the reason why this power had deserted me; but I was denied even this knowledge and there seemed no way at all to bridge the gulf between myself and God. So for a moment, as I stood with my eyes closed and with my head pressed against the cold wood sill, I felt a terrible emptiness. Again I tried to pray but my mind was a void, and all that filled my consciousness was the still fading echo of plunging hoofbeats and roosters crowing far off in the fields beyond Jerusalem.

Suddenly I heard a rattling at the bars behind me and I opened my eyes, turning to see Kitchen's face in the lantern light. It was a young face, eighteen perhaps nineteen, pimpled and pockmarked and slack-jawed, quite stupid and so pitifully scared as to make me feel that I had perhaps wreaked upon him some irreversible mental change. For what had begun five days ago as apprehension had changed to constant fright, and this finally, it was plain to see, to a hopeless and demoralizing terror as each day passed and I slept and ate and breathed, still unclaimed by death. I heard his voice behind the bars, aquiver with dread. "Nat," he said. Then, "Hey, old Nat," in a skittish hesitant voice. "Nat, wake up!"

For a moment I wanted to shout out, yell "Scat!" and watch him fly out of his britches, but I said only: "I'm awake now."

He was obviously confounded to find me at the window. "Nat," he said quickly. "The lawyer's coming. Remember? He wants to see you. You awake?" He stammered a bit as he spoke, and by the lantern's glow I could see his white drawn young face with bulging eyes and a bloodless area of fright around the mouth. Just then I again felt a great empty aching in my stomach.

"Marse Kitchen," I said, "I'm hungry. Please. I wonder if you could fetch me a little bite to eat. Kindly please, young mastah."

"Breakfast ain't until eight," he replied in a croak.

I said nothing for a moment, watching him. Maybe it was hunger alone which stirred up a last breath, the ultimate gasp of a fury I thought I had safely laid to rest six weeks before. I looked back into the infantine slack-jawed face, thinking: Mooncalf, you are just a lucky child. You are the kind of sweet meat Will was after . . . And for no reason at all a vision of mad Will came back, and I thought in spite of myself, the moment's rage persisting: Will, Will. How that mad black man would have relished this simpleton's flesh . . . The rage shriveled, died within me, leaving me with a momentary sense of waste and shame and exhaustion. "Maybe you could fetch me just a little piece of pone," I said, pleading, thinking: Big talk will fetch you nothing but nigger talk might work. Certainly I had nothing to lose, least of all my pride. "Just a little bitty piece of pone," I coaxed, coarse and wheedling. "Please, young mastah. I'm most dreadful hungry."

"Breakfast ain't until eight!" he blurted in a voice too loud, a shout, his breath making the lantern flame tremble and flicker. Then he darted off and I was standing in the dawn, shivering, listening to the growling in my guts. After a moment I shuffled back over to the plank and sat down and thrust my head into my hands and closed my eyes. Prayer again hovered at the margin of my consciousness, prowling there restlessly like some great gray cat yearning for entry into my mind. Yet once again prayer remained outside and apart from me, banned, excluded, unattainable, shut out as decisively as if walls as high as the sun had been interposed between myself and God. So instead of prayer I began to whisper aloud: *"It is a good thing to give thanks unto the Lord, and to sing praises unto thy name, O most High. To show forth thy lovingkindness in the morning . . ."* But even these harmless words came out wrong, and as quickly as I had begun I ceased, the familiar diurnal Psalm foul and sour in my mouth and as meaningless and empty as all my blighted attempts at prayer. Beyond my maddest imaginings I had never known it possible to feel so removed from God—a separation which had nothing to do with faith or desire, for both of these I still possessed, but with a forsaken solitary apartness so beyond hope that I could not have felt more sundered from the divine spirit had I been cast alive like some wriggling insect beneath the largest rock on earth, there to live in hideous, perpetual dark. The chill and damp of the morning began to spread out like ooze through my bones. Hark's breathing came through the wall like the sound of an old dog dying, all gurgles and shudders and unholy vibrations, stitched together by a sickly thread of air.

A person who has lived as I have for many years—close to the ground, so to speak, in the woods and the swamp, where no animal sense is superior to another—eventually comes to own a supremely good nose; thus I smelled Gray almost before I saw him. Not that the odor that Gray put out de-

manded great sensiblity: suddenly the cold dawn was a May
morning, rank with the odor of apple blossoms, his sweet fragrance preceding him as he approached the cell. Kitchen was
carrying two lanterns this time. He put one down on the floor
and unlocked the door. Then he came in, holding both lanterns high, followed by Gray. The slop bucket was inside by
the door and Kitchen jarred it with one of his uncertain,
nervous feet, setting the whole bucket to gulping and slosh-
ing. Gray caught a hint of Kitchen's terror, because at that
instant I heard him say: "Calm yourself, boy, for pity's sake!
What on earth do you think he can *do* to you?" It was a
round, hearty voice, jovial even, booming with voracious
good will. At this hour I was unable to tell which I resented
more, that doughty voice or the honeyed, overpowering perfume. "Lawd amercy, you'd think he was going to eat you
alive!" Kitchen made no reply, set a lamp down on the other
plank which stuck out, like the one I was sitting on, at right
angles from the opposite wall, then picked up the slop bucket
and fled, banging the door behind him and throwing the bolt
home with a slippery chunking noise. For a moment, after
Kitchen was gone, Gray said nothing, standing near the door
and blinking slow, tentative blinks past me—I had already
noticed he was a bit near-sighted—then he eased himself
down on the board beside the lantern. We would not need
the lantern long: even as he seated himself morning was
pouring with a cool white glow through the window, and I
had begun to hear outside beyond the jail a slow-moving fuss
and clatter of creaking pumps and banging windows and
yapping dogs as the town came awake. Gray was a fleshy, red-
faced man—he must have been fifty or a little more—and his
eyes were hollow and bloodshot as if he needed sleep. He
stirred about to find a comfortable resting place on the plank,
then threw open his greatcoat abruptly, revealing beneath a
fancy brocaded waistcoat, now more grease-stained than
ever and with the lower button unloosened to accommodate
his paunch. Again he gazed toward me, blinking past me as if

still unable to see or find his focus; then he yawned and removed, finger by delicate pudgy finger, his gloves, which must once have been pink but now were seedy and begrimed. "Mornin', Reverend," he said finally. When I made no reply, he reached inside his waistcoat and took out a sheaf of papers, unfolding and flattening them against his lap. He said nothing more for a bit as he held the papers close to the lantern, shuffling them in and out, humming to himself, pausing from time to time to stroke his mustache, which was gray and indecisive, a faint shadow. His jaw was in need of a shave. With such an empty feeling in my stomach the oversweet smell of him almost made me puke as I sat there watching him, saying nothing. I was worn out from talking to him and seeing him, and for the first time—perhaps it was my hunger or the cold or a combination of both, or my general frustration about prayer—I felt my dislike of him begin to dominate my better nature, my equanimity. For although I had disliked him at the very beginning five full days before, disliked the mode and method of the trickery behind his very presence, despised his person and the mellifluous sugarplum stench of him, I quickly understood how foolish it would be not to yield, not to be acquiescent and blab everything now that it all was over—fully aside from his bribery and threat, what else had I to lose? Thus even at the outset I figured that hostility would avail me nothing and I managed if not completely to stifle my dislike (and dislike it was, not hatred, which I have only once felt for any single man) then to mask it, to submerge it beneath the general polite compliance which the situation demanded.

For I had said nothing when first I laid eyes on him, and he had slouched there in the yellow autumnal light (an afternoon, hazy with smoke; I recall the curled and brittle sycamore leaves drifting through the window bars), sluggish and sleepy-eyed, the words coming wearily deliberate while with pink-gloved fingers he scraped at his crotch: "Well now, looky-here, Reverend, ain't nothin' good goin' to come of you shuttin' up like a old walnut." He paused, but again I said nothing. "Except maybe—" And he hesitated. "Except maybe a pack of misery. For you and the other nigger." I remained silent. The day before, when they had brought me up by foot from Cross Keys, there had been two women—banshees in sunbonnets, egged on by the men—who had pricked my back deep with hatpins a dozen times, perhaps more; the tiny wounds along my shoulders had begun fiercely to itch and I yearned to scratch them, with a hopeless craving which brought tears to my eyes, but I was prevented from doing so by the manacles. I thought if I could get off those manacles and scratch I'd be able to think clearly, I'd be relieved of a great affliction, and for an instant I was on the verge of capitulating to Gray if he'd allow me this concession—nonetheless, I kept my mouth shut, saying nothing. This immediately proved wise. "Know what I mean by a pack of misery?" he persisted, deliberately, patiently, not unkindly, as if I were the most responsive of company, instead of a worn-out and beaten sack. Outside I could hear the thudding and clash of cavalry and a dull babble of hundreds of distant voices: it was the first day, the presence of my body in custody had been verified, and hysteria hung over Jerusalem like thunder. "What I mean about a pack of misery is this, Nat. Is two items. Now listen. Item in the first part: the con-tin-u-ation of the misery you already got. For example, all that unnecessary junk the sheriff got wound around you there, those chains there around your neck and them quadruple leg irons, and that big ball of iron they hung onto your ankle there. Lord God Almighty, you'd think they'd figured you was old Samson himself, fixing to break down the place with one big mighty jerk. Plain foolishness, I call it. That kind of rig, a man'd die settin' in his own, uh, ordure long before they got around to stretching his neck." He leaned forward toward me, sweat like minute pale blisters against his brow; in spite of his easy manner I could not help but feel that he exhaled eagerness and ambition. "Such things as that, what I might call, as I have already stated, the *con-tin-u-ation* of the misery you already got. Now then . . . Of two items, the item in the second part. Namely, the *pro-mul-gation* of *more* misery over and above and *in addition to* the misery you already got—"

"Excuse me." For the first time I spoke, and his voice abruptly ceased. He was of course working up to the idea that if I did not tell him everything, he would find a way of getting at me through some sort of villainous monkey business with Hark. But he had misjudged everything. He had at once misinterpreted my silence and unwittingly anticipated my most nagging, imminent need: to scratch my back. If I was to be hung come what may, what purpose could be served by withholding a "confession," especially when it might augment in some small way my final physical relief? Thus I felt I had gained a small, private initial victory. Had I opened up at the outset it would have been I who had to ask for indulgences, and I might not have gotten them. But by remaining quiet I had allowed him to feel that only by small favors could he get me to talk; now already he had expressed the nature of those favors, and we had each taken the first step toward getting me unwound from my cocoon of iron and brass. There is no doubt about it. White people often undo themselves by such running off at the mouth, and only God knows how many nigger triumphs have been won in total silence. "Excuse me," I said again. I told him there was no reason to go any further. And I watched his face flush and his eyes grow round and wide with sudden surprise, also with a glint of disappointment, as if my quick surrender had scattered all the beautiful possibilities of threat and cajolery and intimidation he was spoiling for in his tiresome harangue. Then I told him quite simply that I was most willing to make a confession.

"You *are?*" he said. "You mean—"

"Hark's the last one left, except for myself. They tell me he is mighty bad hurt. Hark and I growed up together. I wouldn't want anybody to hurt a hair on his head. No sir, not old Hark. But that ain't all—"

"Well sir," Gray broke in, "that's a right intelligent decision, Nat. I thought you'd come round to that decision."

"Also, there's something else, Mr. Gray," I said, speaking very slowly. "Last night, after they carried me up here from Cross Keys and I sat here in the dark in these chains, I tried to sleep. And as I tried to sleep, the Lord seemed to appear to me in a vision. For a while I didn't feel it was the Lord, because long ago I thought the Lord had failed me, had deserted me. But as I sat here in these chains, with this neck iron and these leg irons and these here manacles eating at my wrists, as I sat here in the hopeless agony of the knowledge of what was going to befall me, why, Mr. Gray, I'll swear that the Lord came to me in a vision. And the Lord said this to me. The Lord said: *Confess, that all the nations may know. Confess, that thy acts may be known to all men.*" I paused, gazing at Gray in the swarming, dusty fall light. For a brief instant I thought the falsity of these words would reveal itself, but Gray was lapping it up, intent now, even as I spoke scrabbling at his waistcoat for paper, groping for the walnut writing box at his knee, all fussy anxiety now, as if he risked being left in the lurch. "When the Lord said that to me," I continued, "Mr. Gray, I knowed there was no other course. Now sir, I'm a tired man, but I'm ready to confess, because the Lord has given this nigger a sign."

And already the quill pen was out, the paper laid flat on the lid of the writing box, and the sound of scratching as Gray hastened to get down to business. "What'd the Lord say to you again, Nat? 'Confess your sins, that'—what?"

"Not confess your sins, sir," I replied. "He said confess. Just that. Confess. That is important to relate. There was no *your sins* at all. *Confess, that all nations may know . . .*"

"*Confess, that all nations may know,*" he repeated beneath his breath, the pen scratching away. "And what else?" he said, looking up.

"Then the Lord told me: *Confess, that thy acts may be known to all men.*"

Gray paused, the quill in midair; still sweating, his face wore a look of such pleasure that it verged on exaltation, and for an instant I almost expected to see his eyes water. He let the pen fall slowly to the writing box. "I can't tell you, Nat," he said in a voice full of emotion, "I honestly can't tell you what a splendid—what a really splendid decision you've made. It's what I call an honorable choice."

"What you mean by honorable?" I said.

"To make a confession, that is."

"The Lord commanded me," I replied. "Besides, I ain't got anything to conceal any more. What have I got to lose by telling all I know?" I hesitated for a moment; the desire to scratch my back had driven me to the edge of a kind of tiny, separate madness. "I'd feel like I could say a whole lot more to you though, Mr. Gray, if you'd get them to take off these here manacles. I itch up along my neck somethin' powerful."

"I think that can be arranged without too much trouble," he said in an amicable voice. "As I have already intimated at some length, I have been authorized by the court to, within reason, ameliorate any such continuation of present misery that might obtain, providin' you cooperate to a degree as would make such amelioration, uh, mutually advantageous. And I am happy—indeed, I might say I am *overpowered* with delight—to see that you feel that cooperation is desirable." He leaned forward toward me, surrounding the two of us with the smell of spring and blossoms. "So the Lord told you: *Confess, that all nations may know?* Reverend, I don't think you realize what divine justice lies in that phrase. For near about onto ten weeks now there's been a mighty clamor

to *know*, not only in the Virginia region but all over America.
For ten weeks, while you were a-hidin' out and a-scamperin'
around Southampton like a fox, the American people have
been in a sweat to know how come you started a calamity like
you done. All over America, the North as well as the South,
the people have asked theirselves: How could the darkies get
organized like that, how could they ever evolve and promulgate not to say coordinate and carry out such a *plan*? But the
people didn't know, the truth was not available to them.
They were in the profoundest dark. Them other niggers didn't
know. Either that or they were too dumb. Dumb-assed!
Dumb! *Dumb!* They couldn't talk, even that other one we ain't
hung yet. The one they call Hark." He paused. "Say, I've
been meanin' to ask. How'd he ever get a name like that?"

"I believe he was born Hercules," I said. "I think Hark is
short for that. But I ain't sure. Nobody's sure. He's always
been called Hark."

"Well, even him. Brighter than most of the others, I
reckon. But stubborn. Craziest nigger I ever saw in my life."
Gray bent closer to me. "Even *he* wouldn't say anything. Had
a load of buckshot in his shoulder that would of felled an ox.
We nursed him along—I'll be frank with you, Nat, frank and
level. We thought he'd tell where you were hidin' out at.
Anyway, we nursed him along. He was tougher'n rawhide, I'll
have to hand him that. But ask him a question and he'd set
there right here in this jail, he'd set there crackin' chicken
bones with his teeth and just rare back and laugh like a hoot
owl. And them other niggers, they didn't know nothin'." Gray
drew back for an instant, silent, wiping his brow, while I sat
there listening to the humming and murmuration of people
outside the jail—a boy's call, a whistle, a sudden thudding of
hooves, and beneath it all a rise and fall of many voices like
the distant rushing of water. "No sir," he resumed, slower,
softer now, "Nat and Nat alone had the key to all this ruction." He paused again, then said in a voice almost a whisper:

"Don't you see how you're the key, Reverend?"

Through the window I watched the curled and golden sifting of sycamore leaves. The immobility in which I had sat for so many hours had caused oblong shadowy images to flutter across the margin of my consciousness like the dim beginning of hallucinations. I began to get these mixed up with the leaves. I didn't reply to his question, finally saying only: "Did you say there was a trial for the others?"

"Trial?" he said. "Trials, you mean. Hell, we had a million trials. Had a trial pretty near every day. September and this past month, we had trials runnin' out our ears."

"But trials? Then you mean—" An image came to mind like an explosion of light: myself, the day before, hurried toward Jerusalem along the road from Cross Keys, the booted feet thudding into my back and behind and spine and the fierce sting of the hatpins in my shoulders, the blurred infuriated faces and the dust in my eyes and the gobs of their spit stringing from my nose and cheek and neck (even now I could feel it on my face like an enormous scab, dried and encrusted), and, above all, one anonymous wild voice high and hysterical over the furious uproar: "Burn him! Burn him! Burn the black devil right here!" And through the six-hour stumbling march my own listless hope and wonder, curiously commingled: I wish they would get it over with, but whatever it is they're going to do, burn me, hang me, put out my eyes, why don't they get it over with right now? But they had done nothing. Their spit seemed everlasting, its sourness a part of me. But save for this and the kicks and the hatpins, I had come out unharmed, wondrously so, thinking even as they chained me up and hurled me into this cell: The Lord is preparing for me a special salvation. Either that, or they are working up to some exquisite retribution quite beyond my power of comprehension. But no. I was the key to the riddle, and was to be tried. As for the rest—the other Negroes, as for *their* trials—suddenly as I gazed back at Gray it became more or less clear. "Then it was to separate the wheat from the chaff," I said.

"Bien sure, as the Frenchies put it. You couldn't be more correct. Also you might say it was to protect the rights of property."

"Rights of property?" I said.

"Bien sure again," he replied. "You might say it was a combination of both." He reached into the pocket of his waistcoat and drew out a fresh plug of dark brown tobacco, examined it between the tips of his fingers, then gnawed off a cheekful. "Offer you a chaw," he said after a moment, "except I imagine a man of the cloth like you don't indulge in Lady Nicotine. Very good idea too, rot the tongue right out of your head. No, I'll tell you somethin', Nat, and that somethin' is this. Speakin' as a lawyer—indeed, speakin' as *your* lawyer, which to some degree I am—it's my duty to point out a few jurisprudential details which it might be a good idea to tuck under your bonnet. Now, of two items, item in the first part is this. Namely: rights of property."

I stared at him, saying nothing.

"Allow me to put it crudely. Take a dog, which is a kind of a chattel. No, first take a wagon—I want to evolve this analogy by logical degrees. Now let's take some farmer who's got a wagon—a common, ordinary dray wagon—and he's got it out in the fields somewhere. Now, this farmer has loaded up this wagon with corn shucks or hay or firewood or somethin' and he's got it restin' on a kind of slope. Well, this here is a rickety old wagon and all of a sudden without him knowin' it the brake gives way. Pretty soon that old wagon is careerin' off down the road and across hill and dale and before you can say John Henry—*kerblam!*—it fetches up against the porch of a house, and there's a little girl peaceably settin' on the porch—and *kerblam!* the wagon plows right on across the porch and the poor little girl is mashed to death beneath the wagon wheels right before her stricken mother's eyes. Matter of fact, I heard of this very thing happenin' not long ago, somewhere up in Dinwiddie. Well, there's a lot of boo-hooin' around, and a funeral, and so on, but pretty soon thoughts inevitably turn back to that old wagon. How come it happened? How come little Clarinda got mashed to death by that old wagon? Who's responsible for such a horrible dereliction? Well, who do you think's responsible?"

This last question was addressed to me, but I didn't choose to answer. Perhaps it was boredom or exasperation or exhaustion, or all three. At any rate, I didn't reply, watching him shift the quid in his jaws, then send a coppery jet of tobacco juice to the floor between our feet.

"I'll tell you what," he went on. "I'll tell you where responsibility lies. Responsibility lies clean and square with the farmer. Because a wagon is an *in-an-i-mate* chattel. A wagon can't be held culpable for its acts. You can't punish that old wagon, you can't take it and rip it apart and throw it on a fire and say: 'There, that'll teach you, you miserable misbegotten wagon!' No, responsibility lies with the unfortunate *owner* of the wagon. It's *him* that's got to pay the piper, it's *him* that's got to stand for whatever damages the court adjudicates against him—for the demolished porch and the deceased little girl's funeral expenses, plus possibly whatever punitive compensation the court sees fit to award. Then, poor bugger, if he's got any money left, he fixes the brake on the wagon and goes back and minds his land—a sadder but a wiser man. Do you follow me?"

"Yes," I said. "That's clear."

"Well then, now we come to the heart of the matter—which is to say, *an-i-mate* chattel. Now, animate chattel poses a particularly tricky and subtle jurisprudential problem when it comes to adjudicating damages for loss of life and destruction of property. I need not say that the problem becomes *surpassin'* tricky and subtle in a case like that of you and your cohorts, whose crimes are unprecedented in the annals of this nation—and tried in an atmosphere, I might add, where the public passions are somewhat, uh, inflamed to say the least. What're you fidgetin' for?"

"It's my shoulders," I said. "I'd be mighty grateful if you could get them to ease off these chains. My shoulders pain something fierce."

"I told you I'd have them take care of that." His voice was impatient. "I'm a man of my word, Reverend. But to get back to chattel, there are both similarities and differences between animate chattel and a wagon. The major and manifest *similarity* is, of course, that animate chattel *is* property like a wagon and is regarded as such in the eyes of the law. By the same token—am I speakin' too complex for you?"

"No sir," I said.

"By the same token, the major and manifest *difference* is that animate chattel, unlike inanimate chattel such as a wagon, *can* commit and may be tried for a felony, the owner being absolved of responsibility in the eyes of the law. I don't know if this seems a contradiction to you. Does it?"

"A what?" I said.

"Contradiction." He paused. "I guess you don't comprehend."

"Oh yes." Actually, I simply hadn't heard the word.

"Contradiction. That means two things that mean one and the same thing at the same time. I reckon I shouldn't be quite so complex."

I didn't reply again. There was something about the tone of his voice alone—the wad of tobacco had thickened it, making it sound moist and blubbery—that had begun to grate on my nerves.

"Well, nem'mine that," he went on, "I ain't even goin' to explain it. You'll hear all about it in court. The point is that *you* are *animate* chattel and animate chattel is capable of craft and connivery and wily stealth. You ain't a wagon, Reverend, but chattel that possesses moral choice and spiritual volition. Remember that well. Because that's how come the law provides that animate chattel like you can be tried for a felony, and that's how come you're goin' to be tried next Sattidy."

He paused, then said softly without emotion: "And hung by the neck until dead."

For a moment, as if temporarily spent, Gray took a deep breath and eased himself back away from me against the wall. I could hear his heavy breathing and the juicy sound his chewing made as he regarded me through amiable, heavy-lidded eyes. For the first time I was aware of the discolored blotches on his flushed face—faint reddish-brown patches the same as I had seen once on a brandy-drinking white man in Cross Keys who had rapidly fallen dead with his liver swollen to the size of a middling watermelon. I wondered if this strange lawyer of mine suffered from the same affliction. Sluggish autumnal flies filled the cell, stitching the air with soft erratic buzzings as they zigzagged across the golden light, mooned sedulously over the slop bucket, crept in nervous pairs across Gray's stained pink gloves, his waistcoat, and his pudgy hands now motionless on his knees. I watched the leaves merging with the shadow shapes swooping and flutter-ing at the edge of my mind. The desire to scratch, to move my shoulders had become a kind of hopeless, carnal obses-sion, like a species of lust, and the last of Gray's words seemed now to have made only the most dim, grotesque im-pression on my brain, the quintessence of white folks' talk I had heard incessantly all my life and which I could only compare to talk in one of my nightmares, totally implausible yet somehow wholly and fearfully real, where owls in the woods are quoting price lists like a storekeeper, or a wild hog comes prancing on its hind legs out of a summer corn-field, intoning verses from Deuteronomy. I looked steadily at Gray, thinking that he was no better, no worse—like most white men he had a lively runaway mouth—and Scripture leaped to my mind like a banner: *He multiplieth words without knowledge, whoso keepeth his tongue keepeth his soul.* But finally I said again only: "It was to separate the wheat from the chaff."

"Or, to switch around the parable," he replied, "to separate the chaff from the wheat. But in principle you're dead right, Nat. Point is this: some of the niggers, like yourself, were up to their eyes in this mess, guilty as sin itself with nothin' to mitigate their guilt whatsoever. Pack of the other niggers, however—and I guess I don't have to *drive home* this melancholic fact to you—was either youngly and innocently dragooned or mere tagalongs or they out-and-out *balked* at this crazy scheme of your'n. It was the owners of *them* niggers these assizes were designed to protect . . ."

He was still talking now, and as he talked he removed a sheet of paper from his pocket, but I was no longer listening, attending rather to a sudden miserable, corrosive bitterness in my heart which had nothing at all to do with this jail or the chains or my aching discomfort or that mystifying, lonesome apartness from God which was still a bitterness almost impossible to bear. Right now I had this other bitterness to contend with, the knowledge which for ten weeks I had so sedulously shunned, buried in the innermost recesses of my mind, and which Gray had casually fetched up ugly and wriggling right before my eyes: *them other niggers, dragooned, balked.* I think I must have made a quick choked noise of distress in the back of my throat, or perhaps he only sensed this new anguish, for he looked up at me, his eyes narrowing again, and said: "It was them other niggers that cooked your goose, Reverend. That's where you made your fatal error. Them others. You could not dream of what went on in their philosophy—" And for a moment I thought he was going to continue, to elaborate and embellish this idea, but instead now he had flattened the paper against the plank and was bending down above it, flattening and smoothing the document as he went on in his bland, offhand garrulous way: "So like I say, you can get a good idea from this list how little chaff there was amongst all that wheat. Now listen—Jack, property of Nathaniel Simmons. Acquitted." He slanted an eye up at me—a questioning eye—but I didn't respond.

"Stephen," he went on, "property of James Bell, acquitted. Shadrach, property of Nathaniel Simmons, acquitted. Jim, property of William Vaughan, acquitted. Daniel, property of Solomon D. Parker, discharged without trial. Ferry and Archer, property of J. W. Parker, ditto. Arnold and Artist, free niggers, ditto. Matt, property of Thomas Ridley, acquitted. Jim, property of Richard Porter, ditto. Nelson, property of Benjamin Blunt's estate, ditto. Sam, property of J. W. Parker, ditto. Hubbard, property of Catherine Whitehead, discharged without trial . . . Hell, I could go on and on, but I won't." He peered up at me again, with a knowing, significant glance. "If that don't prove that these trials were fair and square right down the line, I'd like to know what does."

I hesitated, then spoke. "All it proves to me is that—a certain observance. The rights of property, like you done already pointed out."

"Now wait a minute, Reverend," he retorted. "*Wait* a minute! I want to advise you not to *get impudent* with me. I still say it proves we run a fair series of trials, and I don't need none of your lip to show me the contrary. You set here givin' me a line of your black lip like that and you'll wind up draggin' more iron ruther than less." The idea of even more restraint being unsettling to me, I immediately regretted my words. It was the first time Gray had shown any hostility, and it didn't rest too well on his face, causing his lower lip to sag and a trickle of brown juice to leak from one corner of his jaws. Almost instantly, though, he had composed himself, wiped his mouth, and his manner again became conversational, casual, even friendly. Somewhere outside the cell, somewhere distant beneath the sparse November trees, I could hear a prolonged shrill woman's cry, uttering jubilant words of which only one I could understand: my own name, *N-a-a-t*, the single syllable stretched out endlessly like the braying of a mule across the tumult and the hubbub and the liquid rushing of many voices. "Sixty-odd culprits in all," Gray was saying. "Out of sixty, a couple dozen acquitted or discharged, another fifteen or so convicted but transported. Only fifteen hung—plus you and that other nigger, Hark, *to be* hung—seventeen hung in all. In other words, out of this whole catastrophic ruction only round one-fourth gets the rope. Dad-burned mealy-mouthed abolitionists say we don't show justice. Well, we do. Justice! That's how come nigger slavery's going to last a thousand years."

Gray fussed with his lists and his papers. Then I said: "Mr. Gray, sir, I know I ain't in much of a position to ask favors. But I fears I'm goin' to need a little time to collect my thoughts afore I make that confession. I wonder if you'd be so kind as to let me alone here for a short time. I needs that time, sir, to collect my thoughts. To reconcile some things with the Lord."

"Why sure, Nat," he replied, "we got all the time in the world. Matter of fact, I could use that time too. Tell you what, I'll take this opportunity to go see Mr. Trezevant, he's the Commonwealth's attorney, about all those shackles and irons they got on you. Then I'll be back and we'll get down to work. Half an hour, three-quarters do?"

"I'm most grateful to you. Also, I hope I don't pressure too much, but, Mr. Gray, I've done got powerful hungry since last night. I wonder if you could get them to fetch me a little bite to eat. I'll be in a better fix for that confession if I had a little somethin' on my stomach."

Rising, he rattled the bars, calling for the jailor, then turned back to me and said: "Reverend, you just say the word and it's your'n. Sure, we'll get you somethin' to eat. Man can't make a proper confessional 'thout some pone and bacon in his guts."

When he had gone and the door had closed me in again, I sat there motionless in my web of chain. The midafternoon sun was sinking past the window, flooding the cell with light. Flies lit on my brow, my cheeks and lips, and buzzed in haphazard elastic loopings from wall to wall. Through this light, motes of dust rose and fell in a swarmy myriad crowd and I began to wonder if these specks, so large and visible to my eye, offered any hindrance to a fly in its flight. Perhaps, I thought, these grains of dust were the autumn leaves of flies, no more bothersome than an episode of leaves is to a man when he is walking through the October woods, and a sudden gust of wind shakes down around him from a poplar or a sycamore a whole harmless, dazzling, pelting flurry of brown and golden flakes. For a long moment I pondered the condition of a fly, only half listening to the uproar outside the jail which rose and fell like summer thunder, hovering near yet remote. In many ways, I thought, a fly must be one of the most fortunate of God's creatures. Brainless born, brainlessly seeking its sustenance from anything wet and warm, it found its brainless mate, reproduced, and died brainless, unacquainted with misery or grief. But then I asked myself: How could I be sure? Who could say that flies were not instead God's supreme outcasts, buzzing eternally between heaven and oblivion in a pure agony of mindless twitching, forced by instinct to dine off sweat and slime and offal, their very brainlessness an everlasting torment? So that even if someone, well-meaning but mistaken, wished himself out of human misery and into a fly's estate, he would only find himself in a more monstrous hell than he had even imagined—an existence in which there was no act of will, no choice, but a blind and automatic obedience to instinct which caused him to feast endlessly and gluttonously and revoltingly upon the guts of a rotting fox or a bucket of prisoner's slops. Surely then, that would be the ultimate damnation: to exist in the world of a fly, eating thus, without will or choice and against all desire.

I recall one of my former owners, Mr. Thomas Moore, once saying that Negroes never committed suicide. I recollect the exact situation—hog-killing time one freezing autumn (maybe it was this juxtaposition of death against death's cold season that made such an impression), and Moore's puckered, pockmarked face purple with cold as he labored at the bloody carcass, and the exact words spoken to two neighbors while I stood by listening: "Every hear of a nigger killin' hisself? No, I figger a darky he might want to kill hisself, but he gets to thinkin' about it, and he keeps thinkin' about it, thinkin' and thinkin', and pretty soon he's gone off to sleep. Right, Nat?" The neighbors' laughter, and my own, anticipated, expected, and the question repeated—"*Right*, Nat?" —more insistent now, and my reply, with customary chuckling: "Yes sir, Marse Tom, that's right, sure enough." And indeed I had to admit to myself, as I thought more deeply about it, that I had never known of a Negro who had killed himself; and in trying to explain this fact I tended to believe (especially the more I examined the Bible and the teachings of the great Prophets) that in the face of such adversity it must be a Negro's Christian faith, his understanding of a kind of righteousness at the heart of suffering, and the will toward patience and forbearance in the knowledge of life everlasting, which swerved him away from the idea of self-destruction. *And the afflicted people thou wilt save, for thou art my lamp, O Lord; and the Lord will lighten my darkness.* But now as I sat there amid the sunlight and the flickering shadows of falling leaves and the incessant murmur and buzz of the flies, I could no longer say that I felt this to be true. It seemed rather that my black shit-eating people were surely like flies, God's mindless outcasts, lacking even that will to destroy by their own hand their unending anguish . . .

For a long while I sat motionless in the light, waiting for Gray to return. I wondered if he would get them to bring me some food, after they took off the manacles and chains. I also wondered if I could persuade him to bring me a Bible, which I had begun to hunger for far down inside me with a hunger that made me ache. I shut out the clamor of the crowd from my mind, and in the stillness the flies buzzed round me with an industrious, solemn noise, like the noise of eternity. Soon I tried to pray, but again as always it was no use. All I could feel was despair, despair so sickening that I thought it might drive me mad, except that it somehow lay deeper than madness.

When dawn broke on that first morning, and cool white light began to fill the cell, Gray blew the lantern out. "Mercy, it's gotten cold," he said, shivering, buttoning his greatcoat. "Anyway—" And he paused, gazing at me. "You know, first thing today after the trial's over I'm going to try to requisition you some winter clothes. 'Tain't right for a body to set in a cell like this and freeze half to death. I didn't pay it any nem'mine before, them clothes of your'n, it being so warm until now. But what you've got on there—what's left of it— that's plain old summer issue, ain't it? Cotton? Osnaburg cloth? Pity, rags like that in this kind of weather. Now, about the confession, Nat, I got everything down that's important; worked durn near all night on it too. Well, like I already hinted, this confession will, I'm afraid, comprise the evidence for the prosecution and there won't be any other issue or issues at stake. I expect that I or Mr. W. C. Parker—that's your defense attorney—will get up and make some kind of formal statement, but under the circumstances it can't be much more than a plea that the judges carefully consider the evidence placed before them—in this case your full, free, and voluntary confession. Now, as I've already told you, before you sign it this mornin' I wanted to read it out to you—"

"You mean, this Mr. Parker—" I put in. "You mean *you're* not my lawyer?"

"Why sure. He's my what you might call associate."

"And I ain't even seen him? And you tell me today?" I paused. "And you're taking this all down for the *prosecution*?"

Impatience flashed across his face, curtailing a yawn. "E-yaw! The prosecutor's my associate too. What difference does it make, Reverend? Prosecution, defense—it don't make a hair's difference one way or the other. I thought I made that perfectly clear to you—that I am a, uh, delegate of the court, empowered to take down the confession. Which I've gone and done. But your goose is cooked already." He looked at me intently, then spoke in a cajoling, hearty voice: "Come on now, Reverend. Let's be realistic about this matter! I mean— well, to call a spade a spade—" He halted. "I mean—Hell, you know what I mean."

"Yes," I said. "I know I'm going to be hung."

"Well, since this is a priori and foregone there's not too much use standing on the legal niceties of the matter, is there?"

"No sir," I said, "I reckon not." And there wasn't. I even felt a kind of relief that logic, at last, had flown completely out of the window.

"Well then, let's get down to business, because I want to have this written out as sensible as I can before ten o'clock. Now, as I said, I'm going to read the whole thing out to you here. You'll sign it, and then it'll be read out again in court as evidence for the prosecution. But while I recite the entire thing out, there are a few items that I haven't gotten entirely straight in my own mind and I want you to clarify them for me if you can. So while I read I'll probably have to stop every now and then and make one or two minor amendments. Ready?"

I nodded, convulsed with a shivering cold.

" 'Sir—you have asked me to give a history of the motives which induced me to undertake the late insurrection, as you call it. To do so I must go back to the days of my infancy, and even before I was born . . .' " Gray had begun to read slowly and with deliberation, as if relishing the sound of each word, and already he interrupted himself, glancing up at me to say: "Of course, Nat, this ain't supposed to represent your exact words as you said them to me. Naturally, in a court confession there's got to be a kind of, uh, dignity of style, so this here's more or less a reconstitution and *recomposition* of the relative crudity of manner in which all of our various discourses since last Tuesday went. The essence—that is, all the quiddities of detail are the same—or at least I hope they are the same." He turned back to the document and resumed: " 'To do so,' et cetera, 'before I was born.' Hem. 'I was thirty-one years of age the second of October last, and born the property of Benjamin Turner of this county. In my childhood a circumstance occurred which made an indelible impression on my mind, and laid the groundwork of that enthusiasm which has terminated so fatally to many, both white and black, and for which I am about to atone at the gallows. It is here necessary to relate—' " And he broke off again, saying: "Do you follow me so far?"

I was cold, and my body felt drained of all energy. I could only look back at him and murmur: "Yes."

"Well then, to go on: 'It is here necessary to relate this circumstance; trifling as it may seem, it was the commencement of that belief which has grown with time and even now, sir, in this dungeon, helpless and forsaken as I am, I cannot divest myself of. Being at play with other children, when three or four years old, I was telling them something, which my mother, overhearing, said had happened before I was born. I stuck to my story, however, and related some things which went, in her opinion, to confirm it. Others, being called on, were greatly astonished, knowing that these things had happened, and caused them to say in my hearing: I surely would be a prophet, as the Lord had shown me things that had happened before my birth. And my mother strengthened me in this my first impression, saying in my presence that I was intended for some great purpose . . .' " He halted again. "Fair enough so far?"

"Yes," I said. And this was true; at least the essence, as he put it, of what I had told him seemed to be no wrench of the truth. "Yes," I repeated. "That's fair."

"All right, to continue—I'm glad you feel I've done justice to your own narrative, Nat: 'My mother, to whom I was much attached, my master—who belonged to the church, and other religious persons who visited the house, and whom I often saw at prayers, noticing the singularity of my manners, I suppose, and my uncommon intelligence for a child— remarked that I had too much sense to be raised, and if I was, I would never be of any service to anyone, as a slave . . .' " As he continued to read, I heard a muffled clatter of rattling chains and shackles on the other side of the wall, and then a voice, also muffled, bubbling with phlegm—Hark's: "Cold in here! Watch-man! I'se cold! Cold! He'p a poor nigger, watch-man! He'p a poor freezin' nigger! Watch-man, fetch a poor freezin' nigger somep'n to kivver up his bones!" Gray, unperturbed by the racket, continued to read. Hark kept up his hollering, and at that moment I slowly rose from the plank, stamping my feet to keep warm. "I'm listenin'," I said to Gray, "don' mind me, I'm listenin'." I moved my shackled feet toward the window, paying less attention to Gray now than to Hark's howls and moans beyond the wall; I knew he had been hurt, and it was cold, but I also knew Hark: this was bogus suffering, Hark at his rarest. The voice of the only Negro in Virginia whose wise flattery could gull a white man out of his very britches. I stood at the window, not listening to Gray but to Hark. The voice grew faint, weak, aquiver with the most wretched suffering: he seemed ready to expire, his voice would have melted a heart of brass. "Oh, somebody come he'p this pore sick freezin' nigger! Oh, massah watchman, jes' one little rag to kivver up his bones!" Presently, behind me, I heard Gray get up and go to the door, calling out to Kitchen. "Get some kind of a blanket for that other nigger," he ordered. Then I heard him sit down again, resume reading, while beyond the wall I was certain I heard Hark's voice trail off in something like a stifled laugh, a gurgle of satisfaction.

"'I was not addicted to stealing in my youth, nor have ever been. Yet such was the confidence of the Negroes in the neighborhood, even at this early period of my life, in my superior judgment, that they would often carry me with them when they were going on any roguery, to plan for them. Growing up among them, with this confidence in my superior judgment, and when this, in their opinions, was perfected by divine inspiration, from the circumstances already alluded to in my infancy, and which belief was ever afterward inculcated by the austerity of my life and manners, which became the subject of remark by white and black. Having soon discovered to be great, I must appear so, and therefore studiously avoided mixing in society, and wrapped myself in mystery, devoting my time to fasting and prayer . . .'"

The voice droned on. For a long while I ceased listening. It had begun to snow. The tiniest, most fragile flakes flew past like springtime seed, dissolving instantaneously as they struck the earth. A cold wind was blowing up. Above the river and the swamp beyond, a white rack of cloud hovered, covering the heavens, impermeable, its surface crawling with blackish streaks of mist like tattered shawls. Jerusalem had burst awake. Four more cavalrymen came at a canter over the cypress bridge, filling the air with a noisy cobbling of hooves. Singly, in pairs, in clusters, men and women bundled against the cold had commenced to hurry up the road toward the courthouse. The road was rutted, brittle with frost, and as they picked their way along they murmured together and their feet made a crunched and crusty sound. It seemed early for such a procession, but then I realized what it was, thinking: They are going to make sure of getting seats, they don't want to miss anything this day. I gazed across the narrow sluggish river to the forest wall: a long mile of swamp, then the flat fields and woods of the county. It would be the time of year now to lay up firewood: my thoughts moved, as in a daydream, out across cold space to some coarse thicket of beech or chestnut where already in the chill morning light a pair of slaves would be out with ax and wedge; and I could hear the *chuck, chuck* of the ax and the musical *chink* of the wedge and see the Negroes' breaths steaming on the frosty air, and hear their voices ahowl as they labored against the timber, blabbery voices forever innocently pitched to be heard by someone a mile away: "Ole mistis, she say she kain't find a sartin' fat turkey pullet!" And the other: "Don' look at me, brother!" And the first: "Who I goin' look at, den? Ole mistis, she fine out, she break ev'y bone in yo' black head!" And then their big-mouthed laughter, childishly loud and heedless in the morning, echoing from the dark woods, from bog and marsh and hollow, and a final silence save for the *chuck, chuck* of the ax and the *chink* of the wedge and, far off, a squalling of crows in wheeling descent over cornfields blurred with specks of flying snow. For a moment, despite myself, something wrenched painfully at my heart, and I had a brief blinding flash of recollection and longing. But only for an instant, for now I heard Gray say: "That's the first item I'm curious about, right there, Reverend. I wonder if you might not clarify that a bit."

"Which one is that?" I said, turning back to him.

"It's that part right there in the passage I just read. See, now we're windin' up out of the groundwork material and into the insurrection proper and I want to get this part straight especially. I'll repeat: 'It was intended by us to have begun the work of death on the fourth of July last. Many were the plans formed by us,' et cetera, et cetera. Les'see: 'And the time passed without our coming to any determination how to commence. Still forming new schemes and rejecting them, when the sign appeared again, which determined me not to wait longer,' et cetera, et cetera. Now then: 'Since the commencement of 1830, I had been living with Mr. Joseph Travis, who was to me a kind master, and placed the greatest confidence in me; in fact, I had no cause to complain of his treatment to me . . .' " I saw Gray stir uncomfortably, then raise one haunch up off a fart, trying to slide it out gracefully, but it emerged in multiple soft reports like the popping of remote firecrackers. Suddenly he seemed flustered, discomfited, and this amused me: Why should he feel embarrassed before a nigger preacher, whose death warrant he was reading? He began to speak in a kind of roar, compounding his fluster and stew: " *'I had been living with Mr. Joseph Travis, who was to me a kind master, and placed the greatest confidence in me; in fact, I had no cause to complain of his treatment to me!'* That's the item! That's the item, Reverend!" I found him staring at me. "How do you explain that? That's what I want to know, and so does everyone else. A man who you admit is kind and gentle to you and you butcher in cold blood!"

For a moment I was so surprised that I couldn't speak. I sat down slowly. Then the surprise became perplexity, and I was silent for a long time, saying finally even then: "That— That I can't give no reply to, Mr. Gray." And I couldn't—not because there was no reply to the question, but because there were matters which had to be withheld even from a confession, and certainly from Gray.

"For see here, Reverend, that's another item the people can't understand. If this was out and out tyranny, yes. If you was maltreated, beaten, ill-fed, ill-clothed, ill-housed—yes. If any of these things prevailed, yes. Even if you existed under the conditions presently extant in the British Isles or Ireland, where the average agricultural peasantry is on an economic level with a dog, or less—even if you existed under these conditions, the people could understand. Yes. But this ain't even Mississippi or Arkansas. This is *Virginia* in the year anno Domini 1831 and you have labored under civilized and virtuous masters. And Joseph Travis, among others, you butcher in cold blood! That—" He passed his hand across his brow, a gesture of real lament. "*That* the people can't understand."

Again I had the impression, dim and fleeting, of hallucination, of talk buried deep in dreams. I stared long and hard at Gray. Little different from any of the others, nonetheless it was a matter of wonder to me where this my last white man (save one with the rope) had come from. Now, as many times before, I had the feeling I had made him up. It was impossible to talk to an invention, therefore I remained all the more determinedly silent.

Gray looked at me narrowly. "All right, if you won't open up about that, I'll skip ahead to this other item. Then I'll come back and read the whole thing." He thumbed through the papers. Watching him, I again felt dizzy from hunger. Off in the town, the courthouse clock dropped eight jangling chimes on the morning and the stir and bustle, the sound of hoofbeats and voices, became louder and louder. Somewhere I heard a Negro's voice, a woman's, shrill with mock fury: "I gwine knock you to yo' knees directly!" And then a little black girl's young laughter, ashiver with equally mock panic and fright. Then a second's stillness, then the hoofbeats and voices again. I began to nurse and coddle the pain of my hunger, folding my arms over my belly, standing guard over its emptiness like a sentinel. "Here we are," said Gray. "Now listen to this, Reverend. It's right after you've left the Bryants' place—remember, you yourself haven't killed anybody yet—and gone to Mrs. Whitehead's. I quote: 'I returned to commence the work of death, but they whom I left had not been idle: all the family were already murdered but Mrs. Whitehead and her daughter Margaret. As I came round to the door I saw Will pulling Mrs. Whitehead out of the house, and at the step he nearly severed her head from her body with his broadax. Miss Margaret, when I discovered her, had concealed herself in the corner formed by the projection of the cellar cap from the house; on my approach she fled but was soon overtaken, and after repeated blows with a sword I killed her by a blow on the head with a fence rail.' Unquote. Right so far?"

I said nothing. I felt a prickling at my scalp.

"Very well, we now skip down, oh, maybe ten, fifteen sentences, and what I have written here is this. Now listen careful, because this is more or less the sequence you told me it. I quote: 'I took my station in the rear, and as it was my object to carry terror and devastation wherever we went, I placed fifteen or twenty of the best armed and most to be relied on, in front, who generally approach the houses as fast as their horses could run; this was for two purposes, to prevent their escape and strike terror to the inhabitants.' Now listen careful: '*On this account I never got to the houses, after leaving Mrs. Whitehead's, until the murders were committed.* I sometimes got in sight in time to see the work of death completed, viewed the mangled bodies as they lay, in silent satisfaction, and immediately started in quest of other victims. Having murdered Mrs. Waller and ten children, we started for Mr. William Williams's; having killed him and two little boys that were there,' et cetera, et cetera. Now of course, Nat, this here like all the rest is a rough paraphrase of your actual words, and subject to your own correction. But the main point is this, which you didn't tell me in so many words, but which I'm going to bring out now by deductive reasoning, as it were. The main point is that in this whole hellish ruction involving dozens upon dozens of the slain, you, Nat Turner, were personally responsible for *only one death*. Am I right? Right? Because if I'm right it seems passin' strange indeed." He halted, then said: "How come you only slew one? How come, of all them people, this here particular young girl? Reverend, you've cooperated with me right down the line, but this here line of goods is hard to buy. I just can't believe you only killed one . . ."

Foot-thuds and a rattling at the bars and Kitchen entered, carrying cold cornmeal mush on a plate, along with a tin cup of water. With jittery hands he put plate and cup down on the plank beside me, but for some reason now I was no longer very hungry. My heart had begun to pound, and I felt sweat in rivulets beneath my arms.

"Because it ain't as if you had been *disinvolved* in these proceedings—a field general runnin' the whole show from way behind the lines, like the Little Corporal standin' aloof and pompous on the heights above Austerlitz." Gray halted, slanting an eye at Kitchen. "Ain't you got any bacon for the Reverend?" he said.

"The niggers over to Mrs. Blunt's place fix it," the boy replied. "The one that fetched it over here said they done run out of bacon."

"Pretty pissy kewzine for a distinguished prisoner, I'll vow, cold mush like that." The boy hurried from the cell, and Gray turned back to me. "But you *wasn't* disinvolved from the very beginning. Yes—You have to look at—this reluctance. Videlicet . . . Les'see . . ."

There was a shuffling of pages. I sat motionless, sweating, aware of the pounding of my heart. His words (mine? ours?) came back in my brain like a somber and doleful verse from Scripture itself: . . . *came round to the door I saw Will pulling Mrs. Whitehead out of the house, and at the step he nearly severed her head from her body with his broadax.* So easy in the telling, why now, uttered by Gray, did it cause me such panic and discomfort? Suddenly, savage lines crashed against my memory: *After this I saw in the night visions, and behold a beast, dreadful and terrible, and strong exceedingly; and it had great iron teeth: it devoured and brake in pieces. I beheld then because of the voice of the great words: I beheld even till the beast was slain, and his body destroyed, and given to the burning flame.* For an instant I saw Will's skinny self, Will's hatchet face black as night with bulging eyes, mashed-in nose, loose pink minutely creviced lips, and white teeth flashing a smile murderously fixed, dim-brained, remorseless, pure; I felt myself shudder, not from the day's cold but as if from chill fever coursing through the marrow of my bones.

"An overall reluctance. Videlicet . . . And I quote from back near the beginning, which has to do with the murder of none other than your late owner—the aforesaid and, I might add, the benevolent Mr. Joseph Travis. 'It was then observed that I must spill the first blood. On which, armed with a hatchet and accompanied by Will, I entered my master's chamber, it being dark I could not give a deathblow, the hatchet glanced from his head, he sprang from the bed and called his wife; it was his last word, *Will* laid him dead with a blow of his ax,' and so on." He paused again, regarding me gloomily out of his flushed face with blotches and spidery veins. "Why?" he said. " 'Twarn't any less dark in there for Will than for you, less'n he was a cat. All I mean is this, Reverend. You haven't come out and so much as stated it, but the implication here, as I have said, is that you personally killed only one person. Furthermore, the implication if I read it rightly is that the act of killing or trying to kill got you so rattled that Will had to come in and do all the dirty work. Now, it is curious indeed, but Will was one of the few niggers actually slain during the course of this ruction. So it is your word alone I've got to take. And that you killed only one and were reluctant to kill more is a line of goods mighty hard to buy. Come on, Reverend, after all, you were the *leader* . . ."

I thrust my head into my hands, thinking: *Then I would know the truth of this beast, which was diverse from all the others, exceeding dreadful, whose teeth were of iron and his nails of brass; which devoured, brake in pieces* . . . And barely listening now to Gray, who was saying: "Or this, Reverend, later on that night after the Travises and the Reeses and old Salathiel Francis. You've gone on across the fields and now: 'As we approached, the family discovered us and shut the door. Vain hope! Will, with one stroke of his ax, opened it, and we entered and found Mrs. Turner and Mrs. Newsome in the middle of a room, almost frightened to death. Will immediately killed Mrs. Turner with one blow of his ax. I took Mrs. Newsome by the hand, and with the sword I had when I was apprehended, I struck her several blows over the head' —now listen careful—'*but not being able to kill her.* Will, turning around and discovering it, dispatched her also . . .' "

Suddenly I was on my feet in front of Gray, stretched to the limit of the chain. "Stop!" I yelled. "Stop! We done it! Yes, yes, we done it! We done what had to be done! But stop recitin' about me and Will! Leave off studyin' about all this! We done what had to be done! So stop it!"

Gray had drawn back in alarm, but now as I relaxed and grew limp, my knees rattling in the cold, and as I looked at him as if to regret this sudden fury, he too composed himself, settling himself on the plank and saying finally: "Well, if that's the way you feel about it. It's your funeral. Figger I can't get blood from a turnip noways. But I got to read it and you got to sign it. That's the edict of the court."

"I'm sorry, Mr. Gray," I said. "I truly didn't mean to get impudent. It's just that I don't think you understand about this business, and I don't know but whether it's too late to make it all plain."

I moved slowly over to the window again and gazed out into the morning. After a silence Gray commenced to read once more in a subdued, monotonous voice; he shuffled pages in mild confusion. "Hem. '. . . Viewed the mangled bodies as they lay, *in silent satisfaction*.' My emphasis. Well, that last item—gildin' the lily, maybe?" I made no reply. Off in the other cell I could hear Hark chuckling, muttering jokes to himself. The fragile dustlike snow was still falling; it had begun to cling to the earth, the thinnest film of white like hoarfrost, no more substantial than breath blown frosty against a pane of glass.

"Encore, as the Frenchies put it," Gray was saying, "meaning, that is, *re*-peat: '. . . and immediately started in quest of other victims.' But let's skip ahead now . . ." The voice droned on.

I raised my eyes toward the river. Across the stream, beneath the trees on the far bank, I saw the procession I had seen each morning, though this time it was late for them— the children usually came at dawn. As always there were four of them, four black children; the oldest could not have been older than eight, the smallest was younger than three. Dressed in shapeless clothing which some troubled mammy had fashioned for them out of cotton sacking or the poorest odds and ends, they picked their way along beneath the trees on the far bank, gathering twigs and fallen branches for some cabin fireplace. Pausing, stooping down, suddenly scampering forward, they moved with quick and sprightly motions beneath the clumsy flapping of their formless little sacks, piling twigs and sticks and fagots high in their arms against their bodies. I heard them call out to each other. I couldn't make out their words, but on the cold air their voices were shrill and bright. Black hands and feet and faces, bobbing, swooping, dancing shapes silhouetted like lively birds against the white purity of the forest and the morning. I watched them for a long time as they moved, all unknowing doomed and hopeless, across the clean space of snow and finally vanished with their burdens, still sweetly chattering and shrill, upriver past the limit of my sight.

Suddenly I thrust my face into my hands, thinking of Daniel's beast again in the burning visions of the night, thinking of Daniel's cry: *O my Lord, what shall be the end of these things?*

But the answer was not the Lord's. It was Gray's. And in the imprisoned space of my mind it seemed to come back amid a tumult and murmuration of flowing waters, wild waves, rushing winds. *Justice. Justice! That's how come nigger slavery's going to last a thousand years!*

Hark always declared that he could distinguish between good white people and bad white people—and even white people who lay between good and bad—by their smell alone. He was very solemn about all this; over the years he had worked out many subtleties and refinements upon his original philosophy, and he could talk endlessly as we worked alongside each other—advising me at the top of his voice, assigning exact, marvelous odors to white people like Moses handing down the law. About much of this he was deadly serious, and as he jabbered away his broad, bold face would become furrowed in the most worrisome thought; but Hark's nature was basically humorous, outward-going, beneficent, serene, and he could not long sustain a somber mood, even though many horrible things had happened to him.

Finally something connected with a white person and a certain smell would tickle some interior nerve: against all restraint the giggles would begin to well up from his belly and in an instant he would have broken down, clutching himself in helpless, wheezing, rich, delirious laughter. "Now, Nat, maybe it jes' *me*," he would begin seriously, "but dis yere nose of mine she jes' get better ev'y day. Like I was comin' roun' de side of de barn yestiddy evenin' and dere's ole Miss Maria a-feedin' the chickens. She seed me afore I could take off. 'Hark!' say she. 'Hark! Come right yere!' So I come, an' awready my nose begin twitchin' like a mushrat pokin' up

out'n de swamp. 'Hark!' say she. 'Whar de corn?' 'Why, what
corn, Miss Maria?' say I, de ole smell gittin' strong now. 'De
corn in de shed for de chickens!' de ole bitch say. 'You suppose' to have a couple bushels shelled fo' my chickens and dere
ain't a cupful lef'! Dis de fo'th time in a month! You a shiftless black nigger scoundrel and I pray to see de day my
brother sells you off to Mississippi! *Git* dat corn shelled right
now, you shiftless nigger!' Jesus jumpin' Judas, de smell, Nat,
comin' out dat woman, if it water 'twould have drown' me in
my shoes. What it like? 'Twas like an ole catfish somebody
lef' three days up on a stump in July." And he would begin to
giggle softly, already clutching at his midriff. "Stink! Even de
buzzards fly away from ole pussy like dat!" And glorious
laughter.

But not all of them had smells like this, according to
Hark. Mr. Joseph Travis, our master, had "a right honest
stench about him," said Hark, "like a good horse what worked
him up a sweat." Joel Westbrook, the boy whom Travis employed as an apprentice, was an uncertain, gawky lad, given
to temper fits but amiable, even generous when in the mood;
hence to Hark his smell had a changing, fitful quality:
"Sometime dat boy smell right pretty, like hay or somethin',
other time he smell up a storm." This offensive Miss Maria
Pope was to Hark, however, in every way consistent in her
smell. She was Travis's half sister, who had come down from
Petersburg to live with Travis and his family after her mother's death. A bony, angular woman, she suffered from blocked
sinuses which caused her to breathe through her mouth; as a
result her lips were always peeling to the quick and sometimes bled, which necessitated a poultice of lard, and this
gave her ever-parted mouth a blanched appearance altogether ghostly and strange. Her eyes wandered distantly, and
she was given to stroking her wrists. She hated us Negroes,
who were at her beck and call, with a kind of profound and
pointless hatred which was all the more burdensome to us

because she was not really of the family, and therefore her attitude had a harsh, remote, despotic quality. On summer nights, from the windows of the upstairs room where she slept, I could hear her sobbing hysterically and crying out for her departed mother. She was about forty, I suspect a virgin, and she read aloud from the Bible incessantly with a kind of hollow-eyed, mesmeric urgency, her favorite passages being John 13, which deals with humility and charity, and the sixth chapter of I Timothy, beginning: *Let as many serv-ants as are under the yoke count their own masters worthy of all honour, that the name of God and his doctrine be not blasphemed.* Indeed, according to Hark, she once flattened him up against the porch wall and made him repeat this homily until he had committed it to memory. I have no doubt that she was more than a little cracked, but this did not diminish my intense dislike of Miss Maria Pope, though oc-casionally I felt myself feeling sorry for her against my better judgment.

But Miss Maria is, in a manner of speaking, only inci-dental to a man I am trying to get at in a roundabout fashion —namely, Mr. Jeremiah Cobb, the judge who was about to sentence me to death, and into whose earlier acquaintance I was led by a complicated series of transactions which I must here try briefly to describe.

As I told Mr. Gray, I was born the property of Benjamin Turner, about whom I remember only a little. Upon his abrupt death when I was around eight or nine (a miller and dealer in timber, he was killed while felling a cypress tree, having turned his back on the monster at an improvident moment), I passed by bequest into the possession of his brother, Samuel Turner, whose property I remained for ten or eleven years. These years, and those preceding them, I shall return to in due course. Eventually Samuel Turner's fortunes declined, and there were other problems; at any rate, he was unable to continue to operate the sawmill he inherited, along with me, from his brother, and so for the first time I was sold, to Mr. Thomas Moore—a sale which a weakness for irony impels me to remark was effected at the moment I reached my manhood, during my twenty-first year. I was the property of Mr. Moore, who was a small farmer, for nine years until his death (another bizarre misadventure: Moore broke his skull while presiding at the birth of a calf. It had been a balky delivery, and he had wrapped a cord around the calf's protruding hooves in order to yank it out; as he sweated and tugged and as the calf mused at him soulfully from the damp membranes of its afterbirth, the cord snapped, catapulting him backward and fatally against a gatepost. I had very little use for Moore, and my grief was meager, yet at the time I could not but help begin to wonder if ownership of me did not presage a diminution of fortune, as does the possession, I am told, of a certain kind of elephant in India), and upon Mr. Moore's demise I became the property of his son, Putnam, who was then fifteen. The following year (that is to say, last year) Mr. Moore's widow, Miss Sarah, married Joseph Travis, a childless widower of fifty-five desirous of offspring, who lived in this same country region of Cross Keys, an expert wheelwright by trade and the last person so luckless as to enjoy me in the pride of ownership. For although under law I was Putnam's by title, I belonged also to Travis, who had the right to exercise full control over me until Putnam reached his majority. Thus when Miss Sarah wed Joseph Travis and became domiciled beneath his roof, I turned into a kind of twofold property—not an unheard-of arrangement but additionally unsatisfying to property already half deranged at being owned even once.

Travis was moderately prosperous, which is to say that like a few of the other inhabitants of this backwater, he managed to eke out slightly more than a living. Unlike the hapless Moore, he was adept at that which the Lord had him cut out to do, and it was a great relief for me to be able to help him at his trade after the long years at Moore's and the monotony of toting his water and sopping his feverish, languishing pigs and alternately baking and freezing in his cornfield and his cotton patch. In fact, because of the circumstances of my new employment—which was to act as a general handyman around the wheel shop—I had a sense of well-being, physical at least, such as I had not felt since leaving Samuel Turner's nearly ten years before. Like most of the other property owners of the region, Travis was also a small farmer, with fifteen acres or so in corn, cotton, and hay, plus an apple grove whose principal function it was to produce cider and brandy. Since the relative success of the wheel shop, however, Travis had cut back on his farm holdings, leasing out his acreage to others, and retaining just the apple orchard, and a small produce garden and patch of cotton for his own use. Besides myself, Travis owned only two Negroes—a number, however, not unusual in its smallness, inasmuch as few white people in the region could any longer afford to support more than five or six slaves, and it was rare indeed to find a citizen prosperous enough to own as many as a dozen. Travis himself had recently owned seven or eight, not counting several unserviceable children, but as his acreage diminished and his solitary craft flourished, he had no need for this obstreperous pack, indeed found so many fat mouths to feed a burden on his capital, and thus, three years before, with great moral misgivings (or so I heard) sold off the whole lot—all but one—to a trader specializing in labor for the Mississippi delta. The one left was Hark, who was my age lacking a year. Born on a vast tobacco plantation in Sussex County, he had been sold to Travis at the age of fifteen after the tobacco sucked the soil dry and the land went to rack and ruin. I had known him for years and had come to love him like a brother. The other Negro, acquired subsequent to the Mississippi sale, was Moses, a husky, tar-black, wild-eyed boy of twelve or thereabouts whom Travis, finding himself belatedly short-handed, had bought at the Richmond market several months before my arrival. He was strong and strapping for his age, and bright enough, I think; but he never quite got over the separation from his mammy; it left him bereft, stuporous, and he cried a lot and peed in his pants, sometimes even when he was at work, and all in all was a nuisance, becoming a great trial to Hark especially, who had a mother's soul in the body of a bull, and felt compelled to soothe and nurse the foundling.

This then was the population of our household at the time when I first encountered Jeremiah Cobb, almost one year to the day before he sentenced me to death: three Negroes—Hark, Moses, myself—and six white people—Mr. and Mrs. Travis and Putnam, Miss Maria Pope, and two more besides. The last were the previously mentioned Joel Westbrook, fifteen years old, a budding wheelwright whom Travis had apprenticed to himself; and Travis's child by Miss Sarah, an infant boy of two months born with a purple blemish spreading across the center of his tiny face like the single shriveling petal of a blighted gentian. The white people, of course, lived in the main house, a modest, plain but comfortable two-storied structure of six rooms which Travis had built twenty years before. He had hewn the beams himself, planed the timbers, made it all weather-tight with pine gum and mortar, and had been wise enough to leave standing round it several enormous beech trees which offered shade from any angle against the summer sun. Adjacent to the house, separated from it only by the pigpen and a short path through the vegetable garden, was the wheel shop, converted from a one-time barn: here was the center of activity on the farm, here were the stores of oak and ashwood and iron, the forge and anvils, the bending frames, the modeling hammers and tongs and vises and the rows of chisels and punches and all the other equipment which Travis employed in his demanding craft. Doubtless at least in part because of my repute (decent albeit somewhat ambiguous and suspect in a way that I will soon explain) as a kind of harmless, runabout, comic nigger minister of the gospel, I was later made custodian of the shop; in fact, prompted by Miss Sarah's avowal of my integrity, Travis gave into my keeping one of two sets of keys. I had plenty enough to do, but I cannot honestly say that my work here was toilsome; unlike Moore, Travis was no taskmaster, being by nature unable, I think, to drive his servants unreasonably and already having been well provided with willing help in the person of his stepson and the Westbrook boy, who was an eager apprentice if there ever was one.

Thus my duties, compared to what I had been used to, were light and fairly free of strain: I kept the place clean and added my shoulder to a job when extra strength was needed, such as bending a wheel rim, and frequently I spelled Hark as he pumped at the bellows of the forge, but generally speaking (and for the first time in years), the tasks I encountered were those calculated to tax not my muscles but my ingenuity. (For instance, the loft of the shop since its conversion from the status of a barn had still been infested by bats, tolerable enough when the place was the abode of cattle but an insufferable plague of drizzling bat shit to humans laboring daily below. Travis had tried half a dozen futile measures to rid himself of the pests, including fire and smoke, which nearly burned the place down; whereupon at this point I went out into the woods to a certain nest I knew of and plucked a blacksnake out of hibernation, wrenching it from the tail-end of its winter's sleep and installing it in the eaves. When spring came a week later the bats quickly vanished, and the blacksnake continued in friendly, satisfied residence, slithering benevolently around the circumference of the shop as it gobbled up rats and field mice, its presence earning me, I know, quiet admiration in Travis's regard.) So, all things being equal, from the beginning of my stay with Travis, I was in as palmy and benign a state as I could remember in many years. Miss Maria's demands were annoying, but she was a small thorn. Instead of the nigger food I was accustomed to at Moore's, fat pork and corn pone, I got house food like the white people—a lot of lean bacon and red meat, occasionally even the leavings from a roast of beef, and often white bread made of wheat—and the lean-to shed adjoining the wheel shop where Hark and I shared housekeeping was roomy enough, with the first bed elevated above the ground that I had slept on since the old days with Samuel Turner; and I constructed, with my owner's blessing, an ingenious wooden vent leading through the wall from the forge, which was always banked with charcoal: the vent could be shut off in the summer, but in the winter its constant warmth made Hark and me (the poor boy Moses slept in the house, in a damp kitchen closet, where he could be available for errands night and day) as snug as two grubs beneath a log. Above all, I had quite a bit of time on my hands. I could fish and trap and do considerable Scriptural reading. I had for going on to several years now considered the necessity of exterminating all the white people in Southampton County and as far beyond as destiny carried me, and there was thus available to me more time than I had ever had before to ponder the Bible and its exhortations, and to think over the complexities of the bloody mission that was set out before me.

The particular November day I met Jeremiah Cobb is clear in my memory: an afternoon of low gray clouds scudding eastward on a gusty wind, cornfields brown and sere stretching toward the distant woods, and the kind of stillness which comes with that time of autumn, the buzz and hum of insects having flickered out, the songbirds flown south, leaving the fields and woods to dwell in a vast gray globe of silence; nothing stirs, minutes pass in utter quiet, then through the smoky light comes the sound of crows cawing over some far-off cornfield, a faint raucous hullabaloo which swiftly dwindles off in the distance, and silence again,

broken only by the scratching and scrabble of dead wind-
blown leaves. That afternoon I heard dogs yapping in the
north, as if they were coming down the road. It was a Saturday, Travis and Joel Westbrook had driven that morning to
Jerusalem on an errand, and only Putnam was at work in the
shop. I was outside at the corner of my shed cleaning some
rabbits from my trapline, when in the midst of this deep and
brooding silence I heard the dogs yapping up the road. They
were foxhounds, but not enough of them for a hunt, and I
recall being puzzled, my puzzlement vanishing just as I rose
and looked up the road and saw a whirlwind of dust: out
of the whirlwind came a tall white man in a pale beaver
hat and gray cloak, perched on the seat of a dogcart
drawn by a frisky jet-black mare. Behind and below the seat
were the dogs, three flop-eared hounds yapping at one of
Travis's yellow cur dogs who was trying to get at them
through the spokes of the wheels. It was, I think, the first
time I ever saw a dogcart with dogs. From where I stood I
saw the dogcart draw up to a halt in front of the house, then
saw the man dismount; I thought he came down clumsily,
seeming for an instant to falter or to stumble as if weak in the
knees, but then, instantly regaining control of himself, he
muttered something half aloud and at the same time aimed a
kick at the yellow dog, missed wildly, his booted foot fetching up against the side of the carriage with a clatter.

It was comical to watch—a white man's discomfiture,
observed on the sly, has always been a Negro's richest delight
—but even as I felt the laughter gurgling up inside me the
man turned and my laughter ceased. I was now able to observe him for the first time straight on: the face I beheld was
one of the most unhappy faces I had ever seen. It was
blighted, ravaged by sorrow, as if grief had laid actual hands
on the face, wrenching and twisting it into an attitude of in-
eradicable pain. Now too I could see that the man was a little
drunk. He stared somberly at the dog howling at him from

the dust of the road, then raised his hollow eyes briefly to the gray clouds scudding across the heavens. I thought I heard a groan pass his lips; a spasm of coughing seized him. Then with an abrupt, clumsy gesture he drew the cloak about his gaunt and bony frame and proceeded with fumbling gloved hands to fasten the mare to the tethering post. Just then I heard Miss Sarah call from the porch. "Judge Cobb!" I heard her cry. "Sakes alive! What are you doin' down this way?" He shouted something back to her, the cadence of his words obscure, muffled against the gusty wind. The leaves whirled around him, all the dogs kept yapping and howling, the pretty little mare chafed and tossed her mane and stamped. I managed to make out the words: a hunt in Drewrysville, he was taking his dogs there, a grinding noise in the spindle box of his wheel. He thought the axle broke, split, something; being nearby he had come here for repairs. Was Mr. Joe to home? Downwind came Miss Sarah's voice from the porch, loud, buxom, cheerful: "Mr. Joe's done gone to Jerusalem! My boy Putnam's here, though! He'll fix that wheel for you, Judge Cobb, straightaway! Won't you come in and set a spell!" Thank you no ma'am, Cobb hollered back; he was in a rush, he'd get that axle fixed and be on his way. "Well, I 'spect you know where the cider press is," Miss Sarah called. "Right next to the shop. They's some brandy too! Just help yourself and drink your fill!"

I went back to the corner of the shed, attending to my rabbits, and paid no more mind to Cobb for the moment. Travis had allowed me to have the trapline, and in fact encouraged me in the enterprise since by arrangement he was to get two out of every three rabbits I caught. Such an agreement was satisfactory to me, inasmuch as this game was plentiful in the countryside and the two or three rabbits a week left for Hark and me were as much as we cared to eat, and more; nor did it matter to me that Travis sold most of the rabbits in Jerusalem and retained the money, which was clear profit, since if he was to earn interest on the capital which, body and brain, I represented anyway, I was glad to be capitalized upon in one small way which I myself took pleasure in. For after all of the dull drudgery at Moore's, it was the greatest delight to me to be able to make use of some actual indwelling talent, to fashion the traps myself—box traps which I made out of scrap pine from the shop, sawing and planing the wood with my own hands, carving the pegs and the notched pins which tripped the doors, and uniting one after another of the neat miniature coffins into a single smoothly operating, silent, lethal assembly. But this was not all. As much as manufacturing the traps I enjoyed walking the trapline at daybreak in the silence of the countryside, when frost crackled on the ground and the hollows overflowed as if with milk in the morning mists. It was a three-mile hike through the woods along a familiar pine-needled path, and I devised a sort of cloth pouch to take along with me, in which I carried my Bible and my breakfast—two apples and a piece of streak-of-lean pork already cooked the night before. On my return, the Bible shared the pouch with a couple of rabbits, which I brained bloodlessly with a hickory club. A multitude of squirrels preceded me on these walks, in rippling stop-and-go motion; with some of them I became quite familiar and I bestowed names upon them, prophetic Hebrew names like Ezra and Amos, and I numbered them among God's blest since unlike rabbits they could not by nature be easily trapped and could not by law be shot (at least by me, Negroes being denied the use of guns). It was a silent, gentle, pristine time of day, and as the sun shone pale through the dews and the mists and the woods hovered round me gray and still in the autumnal birdless quiet, it was like the morn of Genesis with the breath of creation fresh upon it.

Near the end of my trapline there was a little knoll, surrounded on three sides by a thicket of scrub oak trees, and here I would make my breakfast. From this knoll (though hardly taller than a small tree, it was the highest point of land for miles) I could obtain a clear and secret view of the countryside, including several of the farmhouses which it had already become my purpose eventually to invade and pillage. Thus these morning trapping expeditions also served to allow me to reconnoiter and to lay plans for the great event which I knew was in the offing. For at such times it seemed that the spirit of God hovered very close to me, advising me in this fashion: *Son of man, prophesy, and say, Thus saith the Lord; Say, a sword, a sword is sharpened, and also furbished: it is sharpened to make a sore slaughter* . . . Of all the Prophets it was Ezekiel with his divine fury to whom I felt closest by kinship, and as I sat there these mornings, the pork and apples devoured, the bag of brained cottontails at my side, I would for a long time ponder Ezekiel's words because it was through his words that the wishes of the Lord concerning my destiny (even more so than through the words of the other Prophets) seemed most clearly to be revealed: *Go through the midst of Jerusalem, and set a mark upon the foreheads of the men that sigh and that cry for all the abominations that be done in the midst thereof* . . . *Slay utterly old and young, both maids and little children, and women: but come not near any man upon whom is the mark* . . . Often as I brooded over these lines, I wondered why God should wish to spare the well-meaning and slay the helpless; nonetheless, it was His word. Great mornings, filled with hints, auguries, portents! I find it hard to describe the exaltation which seized me at such times when, crouched upon my secret knoll in gray momentous dawns, I saw in the unfolding future—fixed there as immutably as Saul or Gideon—myself, black as the blackest vengeance, the illimitable, devastating instrument of God's wrath. For on these mornings as I looked down upon the gray and somber and shriveling landscape it seemed as if His will and my mission could not be more plain and intelligible: to free my people I must one day only commence with the slumbering, mist-shrouded dwellings below, destroying all therein, then set forth eastward across the swamps and fields, where lay Jerusalem.

But to get back to Cobb, rather meanderingly I'm afraid, and again by way of Hark. Hark had a flair for the odd, the off-center: had he been able to read and write, been white, free, living in some Elysian time when he was anything but negotiable property worth six hundred dollars in a depressed market, he might have been a lawyer; to my disappointment, Christian teachings (my own mainly) had made only the shallowest imprint upon his spirit, so that being free of spiritual rules and restraints he responded to the mad side of life and could laugh with abandon, thrilling to each day's new absurdity. In short, he had a feeling for the crazy, the unexpected; all in all, this caused me mild envy. There was for instance the time when our shed behind the wheel shop was still uncompleted, and our master paid us a visit during a roaring thunderstorm, gazing skyward at the water cascading through the roof. "It's leaking in here," he said, to which Hark replied: "Nawsuh, Marse Joe, hit leakin' outside. Hit *rainin'* in here." Likewise, it was Hark who gave expression to that certain inward sense—an essence of being which is almost impossible to put into words—that every Negro possesses when, dating from the age of twelve or ten or even earlier, he becomes aware that he is only merchandise, goods, in the eyes of all white people devoid of character or moral sense or soul. This feeling Hark called "black-assed," and it comes as close to summing up the numbness and dread which dwells in every Negro's heart as any word I have ever known. "Don' matter who dey is, Nat, good or bad, even ol' Marse Joe, dey white folks dey gwine make you feel *black-assed.* Never seed a white man smile at me yet 'thout I didn' feel just about twice as black-assed as I was befo'. How come dat 'plies, Nat? Figger a white man treat you right you gwine feel *white-assed.* Naw *suh!* Young massah, old massah sweet-talk me, I jes' feel *black-assed* th'ough an' th'ough. Figger when I gets to heaven like you says I is, de good Lord hisself even *He* gwine make old Hark feel black-assed, standin' befo' de golden throne. Dere He is, white as snow, givin' me a lot of sweet talk and me feelin' like a *black-assed* angel. 'Cause pretty soon I know His line, yas *suh!* Yas *suh,* pretty soon I can hear Him holler out: 'Hark! You dere, boy! Need some spick and span roun' de throne room. Hop to, you *black-assed* scoundrel! Hop to wid de mop and de broom!'"

It is impossible to exaggerate the extent to which white people dominate the conversation of Negroes, and it is with certainty I can record that these were the words that Hark (who had come out of the shed to help me dress and clean the rabbits) had been speaking on this gray November day when, like the most vaguely discernible shadow, we felt simultaneously a presence at our crouched backs and again, half startled, looked upward to see the distressed and ravaged face of Jeremiah Cobb. I don't know whether he overheard Hark's words, it would hardly have mattered if he had. Both Hark and I were taken unawares by the man's magisterial, sudden, lofty figure looming above us, swaying slightly against the smoky sky; so abruptly and silently had he come upon us that it was a long instant before the face of him actually registered, and before we were able to let slip from our hands the bloody rabbits and begin to move erect into that posture of respect or deference it is wise for any Negro to assume whenever a strange white man—always a bundle of obscure motives—enters upon the scene. But now, even before we had gotten up, he spoke. "Go on," he said, "go on, go on," in a curiously rough and raspy voice—and with a motion of his hands he bade us to continue at our work, which we did, easing back slowly on our haunches yet still gazing up into the unsmiling, bleak, tormented face. Suddenly a hiccup escaped his lips, a sound incongruous and unseemly and even faintly comical emanating from that stern face, and there was a long moment of silence all around; he hiccuped again, and this time I was sure I sensed Hark's huge body beginning to shudder with—with what? Laughter? Embarrassment? Fear? But then Cobb said: "Boys, where's the press?"

"Yondah, massah," Hark said. He pointed to the shed several yards away, directly at the side of the shop, where the cider barrels lay in a moist and dusty rank in the shadows past the open door. "Red bar'l, massah. Dat's de bar'l fo' a gennleman, massah." When the desire to play the obsequious coon came over him, Hark's voice became so plump and sweet that it was downright unctuous. "Marse Joe, he save dat red bar'l for de *fines'* gennlemens."

"Bother the cider," Cobb said, "where's the brandy?"

"Brandy in de bottles on de shelf," said Hark. He began to scramble to his feet. "I fix de brandy fo' you, massah." But again Cobb motioned him back with a brisk wave of his hand. "Go on, go on," he said. The voice was not pleasant, neither was it unkindly; it had rather a distant, abstracted quality, yet somehow it remained tinged with pain as if the mind which controlled it struggled with a preoccupying disquiet. He was abrupt, aloof, but there was nothing one might call arrogant about him. Nonetheless, something about the man offended me, filled me with the sharpest displeasure, and it wasn't until he limped unsteadily past us through the crackling brown patch of weeds toward the cider press, saying not another word, that I realized that it wasn't the man himself who annoyed me so much as it was Hark's manner in his presence—the unspeakable bootlicking Sambo, all giggles and smirks and oily, sniveling servility. Hark had slit open a rabbit. The body was still warm (on Saturdays I often collected my game in the afternoon), and Hark was holding it aloft by the ears to catch the blood, which we saved to bind stews. I can recall my sudden fury as we crouched there, as I looked up at Hark, at the bland, serene glistening black face with its wide brow and the grave, beautiful prominences of its cheekbones. With dumb absorption he was gazing at the stream of crimson blood flowing into the pan he held below. He had the face one might imagine to be the face of an African chieftain—soldierly, fearless, scary, and resplendent in its bold symmetry—yet there was something wrong with the eyes, and the eyes, or at least the expression they often took on, as now, reduced the face to a kind of harmless, dull, malleable docility. They were the eyes of a child, trustful and dependent, soft doe's eyes mossed over with a kind of furtive, fearful glaze, and as I looked at them now—the womanish eyes in the massive, sovereign face mooning dumbly at the rabbit's blood—I was seized by rage. I heard Cobb fumbling around in the cider press, clinking and clattering. We were out of earshot. "Black toadeater," I said. "Snivelin' black toadeatin' white man's bootlickin' scum! You, Hark! Black *scum!*"

Hark's soft eyes rolled toward me, trusting yet fearful. "How come—" he began in an abrupt startled voice.

"Hush your face, man!" I said. I was furious. I wanted to let him have the back of my hand flush in the mouth. "Just hush, man!" I began to mimic him, hoarsely, beneath my breath. " 'Red bar'l, massah! Dat's de bar'l wid de *gennlemen's* cidah! I fix de brandy fo' you, massah!' How come you make with that kind of talk, bootlickin' nigger suckup? It was enough to make me plain ordinary *sick!*"

Hark's expression grew hurt, downcast; he moped disconsolately at the ground, saying nothing but moving his lips in a moist, muttering, abstracted way as if filled with hopeless self-recrimination. "Can't you see, miserable nigger?" I persisted, boring in hard. "Can't you see the *difference?* The difference betwixt plain politeness and bootlickin'? He didn't even say, 'Get me a drink.' He said just, 'Where the press?' A *question,* that's all. And there *you* is, already: scramblin' and scroungin' like a bitch pup, massah this and massah that! You enough to make a man chuck up his dinner!" *Be not hasty in thy spirit to be angry: for anger resteth in the bosom of fools.* Ashamed suddenly, I calmed myself. Hark was a vision of dejection. More gently I said: "You just got to *learn*, man. You got to learn the difference. I don't mean you got to risk a beatin'. I don't mean you got to be uppity and smart. But they is some kind of limit. And you ain't a *man* when you act like that. You ain't a man, you is a fool! And you do this all the time, over and over again, with Travis and Miss Maria and Lord help you even with them two *kids*. You don't learn nothin'. You a fool! *As a dog returneth to his vomit, so a fool returneth to his folly.* You a *fool*, Hark. How'm I goin' to teach you?"

Hark made no reply, only crouched there muttering in his hurt and dejection. I was seldom angry at Hark, but my anger when it came had the power to grieve him. Loving him as I did, I often reproved myself for my outbursts and for the misery they caused him, but in certain ways he was like a splendid dog, a young, beautiful, heedless, spirited dog who had, nonetheless, to be trained to behave with dignity. Although I had not yet told him of my great plans, it was my purpose that when the day came to obliterate the white people, Hark would be my right arm, my sword and shield; for this he was well endowed, being quick-witted and resourceful and as strong as a bear. Yet the very sight of white skin cowed him, humbled him, diminished him to the most fawning and servile abasement; and I knew that before placing my ultimate trust in him I must somehow eliminate from his character this weakling trait which I had seen before in Negroes who, like Hark, had spent most of their early lives on big plantations. Certainly it would not do to have a chief lieutenant who was at heart only an abject nigger, full of cheap grins and comic shufflings, unable to gut a white man and gut him without a blink or qualm. In short, Hark was for me a necessary and crucial experiment. Though it is a painful fact that most Negroes are hopelessly docile, many of them are filled with fury, and the unctuous coating of flattery which surrounds and encases that fury is but a form of self-preservation. With Hark, I knew I must strip away and destroy that repulsive outer guise, meanwhile encouraging him to nurture the murderous fury which lay beneath. Yet somehow I did not think it would take too much time.

"I don' know, Nat," Hark said finally. "I tries and tries. But hit seem I cain't git over dat black-assed feelin'. I tries, though." He paused, ruminating, nodding his head ever so slightly over the bloody carcass in his hands. " 'Sides, dat man he look so sad an' mou'nful. Never seed such a sad an' mou'nful man. Kind of felt sorry fo' de man. What you reckon made him so sad-lookin' anyways?"

I heard Cobb returning from the press through the weeds, unsteadily, stumbling slightly, with a brittle crackling sound of underbrush being trampled underfoot. "Feel sorry for a white man and you wastin' your sorrow," I said in a low voice. Then even as I spoke I made a sudden connection in my mind, remembering how a few months before I had over-heard Travis speaking to Miss Sarah about this man Cobb, and the terrors which had beset him grisly and Job-like within the space of a single year: a merchant and banker of property and means, chief magistrate of the county, master of the Southampton Hounds, he lost his wife and two grown daughters to typhoid fever on the coast of Carolina, whither, ironically, he had sent his ladies to recuperate from winter attacks of the bronchial ailments to which all three were prone. Shortly afterward his stable, a brand-new structure on the outskirts of Jerusalem, burned to the ground in one horrid and almost instantaneous holocaust, incinerating all therein including two or three prize Morgan hunters and many valuable English saddles and harnesses, not to mention a young Negro groom. Subsequently, the unfortunate man, having taken heavily to the bottle to ease his affliction, fell down some stairs and broke his leg; the limb failed to mend properly, and although ambulatory, he was plagued by a hectic, mild, irresistible fever and by unceasing pain. When I first heard of all this adversity I could not help but feel a spasm of satisfaction (do not consider me altogether heartless—I am not, as you shall surely see; but the contentment a Negro takes in a white man's misery, existing like a delicious tidbit among bleak and scanty rations, can hardly be overestimated), and I must confess that now as I heard Cobb behind me toiling back through the noisy weeds I experienced anew the same sense of gratification. (*For the thing which I greatly feared is come upon me, and that which I was afraid of is come unto me. I was not in safety, neither had I rest, neither was I quiet; yet trouble came . . .*) A small thrill of pleasure coursed through my flesh.

I thought he was going to walk past us to the shop or perhaps the house. Certainly I was taken by surprise when, instead, Cobb halted next to us with his boots practically atop one of the skinned rabbits. Again Hark and I started to rise, again he motioned for us to continue work. "Go on, go on," he repeated, taking a huge gulp from the bottle. I heard the brandy vanish with a froglike croak in the back of his gullet, then the long aspirated gasp of breath, the final wet smacking of lips. "Ambrosia," he said. Above us the voice was self-confident, sturdy, stentorian; it had an unmistakable vigor and force, even though the tired undertone of sorrow remained, and I felt the residue of an emotion, ever so faint, which I must confess was only the fear I was born and brought up with. "*Am-ba-ro-sia*," he said. My fear receded. The yellow cur dog came snuffling up and I hurled into his face a slippery blue handful of rabbits' guts, which he made off with into the cotton patch, groaning with pleasure. "A Greek word," Cobb went on. "From *ambrotos*, that is to say, immortal. For surely the gods were conferring upon us poor humans a kind of immortality, no matter how brief and illusory, when they tendered us this voluptuous gift, made of the humble and omnipresent apple. Comforter to the lonely and outcast, an anodyne for pain, a shelter against the chill wind of remorseless, oncoming death—surely such an elixir must be touched by the hand of something or someone divine!" Another hiccup—it was like a species of shriek, really prodigious—racked his frame, and again I heard him take a swig from the bottle. Intent upon my rabbits, I had not as yet looked up, but I had caught a glimpse of Hark: transfixed, with bloody glistening hands outstretched, he was gazing open-mouthed at Cobb with a look of absolute attention, a kind of ignorant and paralyzed awe affecting to behold; straining to understand, he moved his lips silently in unison with Cobb's, chewing upon the gorgeous syllables as if upon air; droplets of sweat had burst forth from his black brow like a spray of quicksilver, and for an instant I could almost have sworn that he had ceased breathing. "Aaa-h," Cobb sighed, smacking his lips. "Pure delight. And is it not remarkable that to his already estimable endowments—the finest wheelwright in the Southside of Virginia—your master Mr. Joseph Travis should add another supreme talent, that of being the most skillful distiller of this ineffable potion within the span of a hundred miles? Do you not find that truly remarkable? Do you *not* now." He was silent. Then he said again, ambiguously, in a voice which seemed—to me at least—touched with threat: "Do you *not* now?"

I had begun to feel uncomfortable, disturbed. Perhaps I was oversensitive (as always) to the peculiar shading of a white man's tone; nonetheless, there seemed to be something pointed, oppressive, sardonic about this question, alarming me. It has been my usual exprience that when a strange white man adopts this florid, familiar manner, and when his listener is black, the white man is out to have a little fun at the black man's expense. And such had been my developing mood of tension during the recent months that I felt I must avoid at all costs (and no matter how harmless the by-play) even the faintest premonition of a *situation*. Now the man's wretched question had deposited me squarely upon a dilemma. The trouble is: a Negro, in much the same way as a dog, has constantly to interpret the *tone* of what is being said. If, as was certainly possible, the question was merely drunken-rhetorical, then I could remain humbly and decently mute and scrape away at my rabbit. This (my mind all the while spinning and whirling away like a water mill) was the eventuality I preferred—dumb nigger silence, perhaps a little scratching of the old woolly skull, and an illiterate pink-lipped grin, reflecting total incomprehension of so many beautiful Latinisms. If on the other hand, as seemed more likely from the man's expectant silence, the question was drunken-surly-sarcastic and demanding of an answer, I would be forced to mutter the customary Yassuh—Nawsuh being impermissible in view of the simple-minded nature of the question. What was so disturbing about this moment was my fear (and these fears, one may be assured, are neither vagrant nor inconsequential) that the Yassuh might very well be followed by something like this: "Ah, you do now. You *do* find it remarkable? Am I to understand then that you consider your master a dummox? That because he can make wheels he can't make brandy? You darkies don't have much regard for your owners these days, do you? Well, I want to tell you something, Pompey, or whatever your ludicrous name is, that . . ." et cetera. The changes on this situation are endless, and do not think me overly cautious: motiveless nigger-needling is a common sport. But at this point it was not the possibility of humiliation I wanted to avoid so much as the possibility that having recently vowed that humiliation would never again be a constraint upon me, or a repression, I would be forced to surmount it by beating the man's brains out, thus completely wrecking all my great designs for the future.

I had begun to shake, and I felt a stirring, a kind of

watery weakness in my bowels; just then, however, came a fortunate distraction: nearby in the woods there arose the sound of a crashing in the undergrowth, and we all three turned to see a tawny mud-streaked wild sow lumber out of a thicket, snorting and grunting, trailed by her squealing brood; now as quickly as they appeared pig and piglets seemed to dissolve back into the sere and withered forest, the space of sky above silent and gray and desolate with low-hanging, tattered, wind-driven clouds like smudged cotton through which faint sunlight seeped yellowish and wan. Distracted, our eyes lingered on the scene for a moment, and then came a slamming noise, very close, as the door of the shop opened suddenly, and caught by the wind, hurled itself on screaming hinges backward against the wall. "Hark!" a voice called. It was my boy owner, Putnam. "Where you, Hark?" The child was in a foul mood; I could tell this from the blotches on his pale white face: they grew prominent and rosy whenever he became exercised or harassed. I should add that Putnam had more or less had it in for Hark ever since the preceding year when, out hunting hickory nuts on a balmy afternoon, Hark had innocently but clumsily ambushed Putnam and Joel Westbrook in some tangled carnal union by the swimming pond, both of the boys naked as catfish on the muddy bank, writhing about and skylarking with each other in the most oblivious way. "Never seed such foolishness," Hark had said to me, "But 'twarn't like I was gwine pay it no never mind. Nigger don' care 'bout no white boys' foolishness. Now dat daggone Putnam he so mad, you'd think it was *me* dat *dey* caught jackin' off de ole bird." I sympathized with Hark but in the end I couldn't take it too seriously, as it simply typified an uncorrectable condition: white people really see nothing of a Negro in his private activity, while a Negro, who must walk miles out of his path to avoid seeing everything white people do, has often to suffer for even the most guileless part of his ubiquitous presence by being called a spy and a snooping black scoundreL

"Hark!" the boy called again. "Get in here straight away! What do you think you're doin' out there, you no-account nigger! Fire's gone plumb out! Get in here, God durn you lazy wretch!" The boy wore a leather apron; he had a coarse-featured, sullen, pouty-mouthed face with flowing dark hair and long side whiskers: as he shouted at Hark, I felt a brief, fleeting spasm of rage and I longed for the day to arrive when I might get my hands on him. Hark scrambled to his feet and made off for the shop as Putnam called out again, this time to Cobb: "I think you have someways broke a axle, Judge, sir! My stepdad will fix it! He should be here afore too long!"

"Very well," Cobb called back. Then so abruptly that for an instant I thought he was still talking to the boy, he said: "*As a dog returneth to his vomit, so a fool returneth to his folly.* That of course is most familiar, but for the life of me I am unable to place it within the Scriptures. I suspect however that it is one of the Proverbs of King Solomon, whose delight it was to rail at fools, and to castigate human folly . . ." As he went on talking, a queasy sensation crept over me: the customary positions were reversed, the white man this time had caught the nigger at *his* gossip. How did I know that my own black blabbermouth would betray me, and that he would overhear every word I had said? Humiliated, ashamed of my humiliation, I let the sticky wet rabbit corpse fall from my fingers and braced my spirit, preparing for the worst. "Was it not Solomon who said the fool shall be the servant to the wise? Was it not he too who said a fool despiseth his father's instruction? And is not the instruction of the father, through Paul the Jew of Tarsus, manifest even to the fools of this great dominion, to wit: *Stand fast therefore in the liberty wherewith Christ hath made us free, and be not entangled again with the yoke of bondage!*" As he continued to speak I slowly stood erect, but even at my full height he towered over me, sickly, pale, and sweating, his nose, leaking slightly in the cold, like a great scimitar protruding from the stormy and anguished face, the brandy bottle clutched in one

huge mottled hand against his breast as he stood there in a
limping posture, swaying and perspiring, speaking not so
much to me as through and past me toward the scudding
clouds. "Yes, and to this comes the reply, to this mighty and
manifest truth we hear the response"—he paused for an instant, hiccuping, and then his voice rose in tones of mockery
—"to this irresistible and binding edict we hear the Pharisee
cry out of that great institution the College of William &
Mary, out of Richmond, from the learned mountebanks
abroad like locusts in the Commonwealth: 'Theology must
answer theology. Speak you of liberty? Speak you of the yoke
of bondage? How then, country magistrate, do you answer
this? Ephesians Six, Five: *Servants, be obedient to them that
are your masters according to the flesh, with fear and trembling, in singleness of your heart, as unto Christ.* Or this, my
hayseed colleague, how answer you to this? One Peter, Two,
Eighteen: *Servants, be subject to your masters with all fear;
not only to the good and gentle, but also to the froward.*
There, friend—*there*—is not that divine sanction for the
bondage of which you rave and prattle?' Merciful God in
heaven, will such casuistry never end! Is not the handwriting
on the wall?" For the first time he seemed to look at me,
fixing me for a moment with his feverish eyes before upend-
ing the bottle, thrusting its neck deep into his throat, where
the brandy gulped and gurgled. "*Howl ye,*" he resumed,
"*Howl ye: for the day of the Lord is at hand: it shall come as
a destruction from the Almighty.* You're the preacher they
call Nat, are you not? Tell me then, preacher, am I not right?
Is not Isaiah only a witness to the truth when he says *howl
ye*? When he says the day of the Lord is at hand, and it shall
come as a destruction from the Almighty? Tell me in the
honesty of truth, preacher: is not the handwriting on the wall
for this beloved and foolish and tragic Old Dominion?"

"Praise God, mastah," I said, "that sure is true." My words
were evasively meek and humble, with a touch of ministerial

sanctimony, but I uttered them mainly to cover up my sudden alarm. For now I was truly afraid that he had identified me; the fact that this strange and drunken white man knew who I was smote me like a blow between the eyes. A Negro's most cherished possession is the drab, neutral cloak of anonymity he can manage to gather around himself, allowing him to merge faceless and nameless with the common swarm: impudence and misbehavior are, for obvious reasons, unwise, but equally so is the display of an uncommon distinction, for if the former attributes can get you starved, whipped, chained, the latter may subject you to such curiosity and hostile suspicion as to ruinously impair the minute amount of freedom you possess. As for the rest, his words had spilled from his lips so rapidly and wildly that I was as yet unable to get the exact drift of his thought, which seemed nonetheless mighty precarious for a white man; and I still could not get over the sensation that he was trying to bait me, or lead me into some kind of trap. To conceal my dismay and confusion, again I mumbled, "That sure is true," and I chuckled idiotically, gazing toward the ground while I slowly wagged my head—as if to indicate that this poor darky understood precious little if indeed he understood anything.

But now, bending down slightly, his face drifted nearer to me, the skin close up not flushed and whiskey-pink as I had imagined but pale as lard, utterly bloodless and seeming to grow even whiter as I forced myself to return his gaze. "Don't play dumb with me," he said. There was no hostility in his voice, its sound was more request than command. "Your mistress pointed you out to me just now. Even so, I would have known, I could have distinguished between you two. The other Negro, what's his name?"

"Hark," I said. "That's Hark, mastah."

"Yes, I would have known you. I would have known even had I not overheard you. 'Feel sorry for a white man and the sorrow is wasted.' Is that not what you said?"

A shiver of fear, old and habitual and humiliating, passed through me, and despite myself I averted my eyes and blurted: "I'm sorry I said that, mastah. I'm dreadful sorry. I didn't mean it, mastah."

"Poppycock!" he exclaimed. "Sorry that you said you're *not* sorry for a white man? Come, come, preacher, you don't mean that. You don't mean that, do you?" He paused, waiting for an answer, but by now my distress and embarrassment had so unsettled me that I couldn't even force a reply. Worse, I had begun to despise and curse myself for my own slow-witted inability to deal with the situation. I stood there licking my lips as I gazed out toward the woods, feeling suddenly like the most squalid type of cornfield coon.

"Now don't play dumb with me," he repeated, the voice edged with a tone almost gentle, curiously ingratiating. "Your reputation precedes you, as it were. For several years now there has come to my attention wondrous bruit of a remarkable slave, owned at different times by various masters here in the vicinity of Cross Keys, who had so surpassed the paltry condition into which he had been cast by destiny that— *mirabile dictu*—he could swiftly read, if called upon to demonstrate, from a difficult and abstract work in natural philosophy, and in a fair hand inscribe page after page of random dictation, and had mastered his numbers as far as a comprehension of simple algebra, and had so attained an understanding of Holy Scripture that such of those few adepts in the science of divinity as had examined his knowledge of the Bible came away shaking their heads in wonder at the splendor of his erudition." He paused and belched. My eyes moved back again toward his, and I saw him wipe his mouth with his sleeve. "Rumor!" he resumed quickly. Now his voice had risen to a kind of impassioned runaway sing-song, his eyes were wild and obsessed. "Astounding rumor to emerge from the backwoods of Old Virginny! Astounding as those rumors which in olden times came back from the depths of Asia—that at the source of the River Indus, I believe it was, dwelt a species of mammoth rat, six feet long, which could dance a lively jig while accompanying itself on a tambourine, and when approached would sprout heretofore invisible wings and fly to the topmost branch of the nearest palm tree. Rumor almost impossible to entertain! For to believe that from this downtrodden race, the very laws governing which bind it to an ignorance more benighted and final than death, there could arise one single specimen capable of spelling *cat* is asking rational intelligence to believe that balmy King George the Third was not a dastardly tyrant or that the moon is made of clabber cheese!" He had begun to jab his finger at me as he spoke, a long bony finger with hairy joints, sending it forth into my face in quick thrusts like a snake's darting neck. "But beyond this, mind you, beyond this—to imagine this . . . this prodigy, this *paragon*, a Negro *slave*—oh, perish the vile word!—who had acquired the lineaments not just of literacy but of knowledge, who it was rumored could almost speak in the accents of a white man of breeding and cultivation; who, in short, while still one of this doomed empire's most wretched minions, had transcended his sorry state and had become not a thing but a *person*—all this is beyond the realm of one's wildest imagination. No. No! The mind boggles, refuses to accept such a grotesque image! Tell me, preacher, how do you spell *cat*? Come now, prove to me the reality of this hoax, this canard!" He kept jabbing his finger at me, the voice cajoling, amiable, the eyes still wintry-wild and obsessed. The smell of applejack was around him like a sweet vapor. "Cat!" he said. "Spell *cat*. Cat!"

I had begun to feel surely that he was not being sarcastic, that he was somehow trying to express mad, hulking, terrifying feelings beyond anyone's surmise. I felt blood pounding at my temples and the cold sweat of fear and anxiety clammy beneath my arms. "Don't mock me, mastah, I pray you," I breathed in a whisper. "Kindly please, mastah. Don't mock me." Time crept past and we were both silent, gazing at each other, and the November wind boomed behind us in the forest, crashing like giant, diminishing footfalls across the graying waste of cedar and cypress and pine; for a moment my compliant lips trembled on a broken wisp of air, faltering—"Ca-, Ca-"—and a grief-haunted sense of futility, childish, lifelong, nigger-black, welled up in me like a sigh of pain. I stood there sweating in the blustery wind, thinking: So this is the way it is. Even when they care, even when they are somehow on your side they cannot help but taunt and torment you. The palms of my hands slimy, and my mind roaring, thinking: I do not want to, but now, now if he forces me to spell the word I will have to try to kill him. I lowered my eyes again, saying more distinctly: "Don't mock me, mastah, please."

Yet now Cobb, adrift in his brandy haze, seemed to have forgotten what he had said to me and turned away, staring madly toward the forest where the wind still thrashed and flayed the distant treetops. He clutched the bottle as if with desperation at a lopsided angle against his chest, and a trickle of brandy oozed out against his cloak. With his other hand he began to massage his thigh, holding the leg so tightly that above the knuckles the flesh grew bone-white. "Almighty God," he groaned, "this everlasting mortal ache! *If a man live many years and rejoice in them all, yet let him remember the days of darkness, for they shall be many.* God, God, my poor Virginia, blighted domain! The soil wrecked and ravaged on every hand, turned to useless dust by that abominable weed. Tobacco we cannot any longer raise, nor cotton ever, save for a meager crop in these few southern counties, nor oats nor barley nor wheat. A wasteland! A plump and virginal principality, a cornucopia of riches the like of which the world has never seen, transformed within the space of a century to a withering, defeated hag! And all to satisfy the demand of ten million Englishmen for a pipeful of Virginia leaf! Now even that is gone, and all we can raise is horses! Horses!" he cried as if to himself now, stroking and kneading his thigh. "Horses and what else, *what else*? Horses and pickaninnies! *Pickaninnies!* Little black infants by the score, the hundreds, the thousands, the tens of thousands! The fairest state of them all, this tranquil and beloved domain—what has it now become? A *nursery* for Mississippi, Alabama, Arkansas. A monstrous breeding farm to supply the sinew to gratify the maw of Eli Whitney's infernal machine, cursed be that blackguard's name! In such a way is our human decency brought down, when we pander all that is in us noble and just to the false god which goes by the vile name of *Capital!* Oh, Virginia, woe betide thee! Woe, thrice woe, and ever damned in memory be the day when poor black men in chains first trod upon thy sacred strand!"

Groaning in pain now, fiercely stroking his thigh with one hand while with the other he elevated the bottle to his lips and drained it to the dregs, Cobb seemed, for once, oblivious of me, and I recall thinking that wisdom dictated my stealing out of his presence, if only I could find a decent way to do it. In scattered, disordered riot, all manner of emotions had run through me as he had spoken; not in years having heard a white man talk in this crazy fashion, I would not be honest if I did not admit that what he said (or the drunken gist of it, stealing in upon my consciousness like some unreal ghostly light) caused me to feel a shiver of awe and something else, dim and remote, which might have been a thrill of hope. But for some reason I cannot explain, both awe and hope swiftly retreated in my mind, dwindled, died, and even as I looked at Cobb, I could only smell the musky scent of danger—flagrant, imminent danger—and feel a sense of suspicion and mistrust such as I had rarely ever known. Why? It is perhaps impossible to explain save by God, who knows all things. Yet I will say this, without which you cannot understand the central madness of nigger existence: beat a nigger, starve him, leave him wallowing in his own shit, and he will be yours for life. Awe him by some unforeseen hint of philanthropy, tickle him with the idea of hope, and he will want to slice your throat.

Yet now before I could make any kind of move, a cracking noise sounded behind us as once again the shop door opened, swung wide, and drove itself with windy force against the wall. And as we turned then, Hark emerged with shirttail flying, scrambling away from the shop, plunging in panicky headlong flight toward the fields and the woods beyond. Legs churning, his great black body moved at a furious gallop; his eyes rolled white with alarm. Scant yards behind him now came Putnam, his leather apron flapping as he brandished a stick of lightwood, bawling at the top of his voice. "You, Hark, come back here! Come back here, you dad-dratted no-good an'mal! I'll get hold of you at last, black bastard!" Fleet as a deer, Hark scampered across the open lot, bare black feet sowing puffs of dust, the barnyard cat fleeing his approach, goose and gander too, cumbersomely flapping their flightless wings, emitting dismal honking sounds as they waddled from his path. On he came past us, looking neither left nor right, eyes round and white as eggshells, and we could hear the voice panting *ah-ah-ah* as he sprinted for the woods, moving now with such nimble-footed speed that he seemed whisked forward like a sail on the wind. Far behind, losing ground each second, came the pimpled boy, still howling. "Stop! You, Hark! Black wretch! Stop!" But Hark's great legs were churning as if propelled by steam; vaulting the pump trough, he soared through the air in a gigantic leap like something suspended by wire or wings, struck the earth with a thumping sound, and without breaking stride, bounded on toward the distant forest, the inside of his bare soles flashing splendidly pink. Then all of a sudden it was as if he had been felled by a cannon ball: his head snapped back, and the rest of him including his pinwheeling legs sailed out and forward, and he came down flat on his back with a bladdery, sacklike thud, directly beneath the clothesline which, at gullet level, had intercepted his flight. But as Cobb and I stood watching, watched him shake his head and try to rise up on his elbows, we saw now not one but two forces, though equally sinister and somber, converging on Hark from opposite directions: Putnam, still waving his lightwood stick, and Miss Maria Pope, who had appeared as if from nowhere like some augury of frustrate bitchery and vengeance, bearing down upon Hark with a hobbled spinster's gait amid black snapping yards of funereal gingham. Blown back on the wind, her voice already was hysteric with shrill malevolence. "It's up the tree for you, nigger!" she screeched. "Up the tree!"

"Now," I heard Cobb murmur, "now we are about to witness a ritual diversion indigenous to this Southern clime. We are about to witness two human beings whipping another."

"No, mastah," I said. "Marse Joe don't 'low his niggers to be beaten. But there's ways around that, as you will surely see. You about to witness something else, mastah."

"Not a speck of charcoal in the shop!" Putnam was shouting in a kind of wail.

"And not a drop of water in the kitchen pail!" Miss Maria shrilled. As if vying with each other to be the chiefest victim of Hark's enormity, they surrounded him, encompassed the prostrate form, squawking like birds. Hark staggered to his feet, shaking his head with the slow, stunned, dizzy bewilderment of an about-to-be-slaughtered ox that has received a faulty glancing blow. "It's up the tree with him this time, impudent black scoundrel!" Miss Maria cackled. "Putnam, get the ladder!"

"Hark's most dreadful feared of heights," I found myself explaining to Cobb. "This for him is worse than a hundred beatings."

"A fantastic specimen!" Cobb breathed. "A regular *gladia-*

tor, a veritable black Apollo. And swift as a race horse!
Where did your master get him?"

"From up Sussex way," I said, "about ten, eleven years
ago, mastah, when they broke up one of the old plantations."
I paused for a moment, half wondering to myself why I was
proffering all this information. "Hark's all forlorn now," I
went on, "heartsick and forlorn. On the outside he's very
cheery, but inside he's just all torn up. He can't keep his mind
on anything. That's how come he forgets his chores, and how
come he gets punished. Poor old Hark . . ."

"Why is that, preacher?" said Cobb. Putnam had fetched
a ladder now from the barn, and we watched the procession
as it made its way across the windswept lot, bleak and gray in
the fading autumnal light—Miss Maria in the lead, grim,
hands clenched, her back stiff and straight as a poker, Putnam behind with the ladder, and between them Hark in his
dusty gray denim, shuffling along with his head bent in total
dejection, looming over the two of them like some huge
Goliath, a giant towering above a pair of vengeful, hurrying
dwarfs. In Indian file, straight as an arrow, they made their
way toward an ancient and enormous maple whose lowermost branch, leafless now, stretched across the pale sky like a
naked arm twenty feet above the earth. I could hear Hark's
bare feet scuffing across the ground, scuffing like the feet of a
reluctant child. "Why is that?" Cobb said again.

"Well, mastah, I'll tell you," I said. "Couple years ago,
afore I became Marse Joe's property, Marse Joe had to sell off
most all of his niggers. Sell them off down to Mississippi,
where you know they are planting considerable cotton. Hark
told me Marse Joe was in a misery about this, but he just
couldn't do anything else. Well, amongst these niggers was
Hark's wife and Hark's child—little boy about three or four
years old he was then. Hark cared for that little boy almost
more than anything."

"Yah, yah, yah," I could hear Cobb murmur, making little
clucking sounds beneath his breath.

"So when that little boy was gone, Hark near about went mad with grief, couldn't think about anything else."

"Yah, yah, yah, yah."

"He wanted to run away and follow them all the way down to Mississippi, but I talked him out of it. See, he'd already run off once years ago and hadn't gotten anywhere. Besides, it's always been my idea that a nigger should follow all the rules and regulations so far as he was able."

"Yah, yah, yah."

"Anyway," I went on. "Hark ain't been quite right ever since then. You might say he's just been distracted. That's why he does things—or doesn't do things—that get him punished. And I'll be quite truthful with you, mastah, he *doesn't* do his chores, but I tell you he just can't help it."

"Yah, yah," Cobb muttered, "yah, great God, the logical outcome . . . *the ultimate horror!*" He had begun to hiccup again and the sound came forth in intermittent gasps, almost like sobs. He started to say something else, thought better of it, turned away, whispering over and over again: *"God, God, God, God, God."*

"Now about this here," I explained. "Like I say, Hark's most dreadful feared of high places. Last spring the roof leaked and Marse Joe sent Hark and me up to fix it. But Hark got halfway up and he just froze there. Begun to whimper and mumble to hisself and wouldn't go an inch further. So I had to fix that roof myself. Anyway, Marse Putnam and Miss Maria caught ahold of this fear of Hark's—you might say they found out his weak spot. Like I said, Marse Joe won't tolerate anyone to mistreat his niggers, to beat them or anything like that. So whenever Marse Joe's away, and Marse Putnam and Miss Maria figger they can get away with it, why, they run old Hark up a tree."

Which is what they were doing even as I spoke, their voices muffled, remote, indistinct now on the blustery wind. Putnam propping the long ladder against the tree trunk, then jerking his arm furiously upward as he bade Hark to climb.

And Hark began climbing, reluctantly, at the third rung turning his frightened face imploringly back as if to see whether they might not have had a change of heart, but this time Miss Maria's arms jerked upward—*up, nigger, up*—and again Hark continued his climb, knees quaking beneath his trousers. At last arrived at the lowermost branch, Hark swung himself off the ladder, clutching the tree so tightly that I could see even from this distance the veins standing out against the muscles of his arms, then with a sort of scrounging, sliding motion of his rump, deposited himself in the crotch formed by trunk and branch, and sat there embracing the tree with his eyes squeezed shut—dizzy, windy yards above the earth. Then Putnam removed the ladder and laid it flat on the ground beneath the tree.

"Five, ten minutes will go by, mastah," I said to Cobb, "and then old Hark will commence crying and moaning. Just wait and see. Then pretty soon he'll start swaying. Crying and moaning and swaying there on that branch like he's about to fall off. Then Marse Putnam and Miss Maria'll set that ladder up against the tree and Hark'll climb down. I reckon they get scared Hark will fall off and break his neck, and they wouldn't want that to happen. No, they just want to give old Hark a poor time for a while."

"Yah, yah, yah," Cobb murmured, distantly now.

"And that for Hark is a poor time indeed," I said.

"Yah, yah, yah," he replied. I don't know whether he was listening to me or not. "Great God! Sometimes I think . . . sometimes . . . *it is like living in a dream!*"

Then suddenly, without another word, Cobb was gone, limping in gaunt strides toward the house, the empty brandy flask still clutched in his hand, cloak flapping, shoulders hunched against the wind. I crouched down again above my rabbits, watching Cobb limp and sway across the lot and up to the front porch, his voice faint and weary as he called out: "Hallo, Miz Travis, think I'll come in and set a spell after all!"

And Miss Sarah's voice way off within, high and full of cheer, and the sound of the door slamming as Cobb vanished inside the house. I stripped the white translucent inner skin from a rabbit, separating it from the pinkish flesh, and plunged the corpse into the cool water, feeling the guts squirming wet and slimy beneath my fingers. Blood mingled with the water, turning it a muddy crimson. Gusts of wind swept through the cotton patch, whistling; an army of dead withered leaves marched along the edge of the barn, rolled with a husky scrabbling noise across the vacant yard. I gazed down into the bloody water, thinking of Cobb. *Go through the midst of Jerusalem, and set a mark upon the foreheads of the men that sigh and that cry for all the abominations, that be done in the midst thereof . . . Slay utterly old and young, both maids and little children, and women: but come not near any man upon whom is the mark . . .*

Suddenly I found myself thinking: It is plain, yes, plain, plain. When I succeed in my great mission, and Jerusalem is destroyed, this man Cobb will be among those few spared the sword . . .

Across the roof of the woods the wind rushed in hissing, majestic swoop and cadence, echoing in far-off hollows with the thudding sound of footfalls. Gray and streaked, boiling, in ponderous haste, the clouds fled eastward across the lowering heavens, growing darker now in the early dusk. After a bit I heard Hark begin to moan, a soft disconsolate wordless wail, filled with dread. For long minutes he moaned, swaying high in his tree. Then I heard the *tap-tap-tapping* of the ladder as they set it against the tree trunk and let him down.

It is curious how sometimes our most vivid dreams take place when we are but half asleep, and how they occupy the briefest space of time. In the courtroom this day, dozing off for several seconds at the oaken table to which I had been bound by a length of chain, I had a terrifying dream. I seemed to be walking alone at the edge of a swamp at nightfall, the light around me glimmering, crepuscular, touched with that greenish hue presaging the onslaught of a summer storm. The air was windless, still, but high in the heavens beyond the swamp thunder grumbled and heaved, and heat lightning at somber intervals blossomed against the sky. Filled with panic, I seemed to be searching for my Bible, which strangely, unaccountably I had left there, somewhere in the depths and murk of the swamp; in fear and despair I pressed my search into the oncoming night, pushing now deeper and deeper into the gloomy marshland, haunted by the ominous, stormy light and by a far-off pandemonium of thunder. Try desperately as I might, I could not find my Bible. Suddenly another sound came to my ears, this time the frightened outcry of voices. They were the voices of boys, hoarse and half grown and seized with terror, and now instantly I saw them: half a dozen black boys trapped neck-deep in a bog of quicksand, crying aloud for rescue as their arms waved frantically in the dim light and as they sank deeper and deeper into the mire. I seemed to stand helpless at the edge of the bog, unable to move or to speak, and while I stood there a voice echoed out of the sky, itself partaking of that remote sound of thunder: *Thy sons shall be given unto another people and thine eyes shall look, and fail with longing for them all the day long, so that thou shalt be mad for the sight of thine eyes* . . . Screaming their mortal fright, black arms and faces sinking beneath the slime, the boys began to vanish one by one before my eyes while the noise of a prodigious guilt overwhelmed me like a thunderclap . . . *"The prisoner will . . ."* The sharp rapping of a mallet interrupted the horror, and I snapped awake with a start.

"If the court please . . ." I heard the voice say, "it is a crying outrage. Sech behavior is a *crying outrage!*"

The mallet cracked down again. "The prisoner is cautioned to stay awake," said another voice. This time the voice was more familiar: it was that of Jeremiah Cobb.

"If the court please," the first voice continued, "it is a disgrace to these assizes that the prisoner goes to sleep, and in the full view of this honorable court. Even if it is true that a nigger can't stay awake any longer than—"

"The prisoner has been duly cautioned, Mr. Trezevant," Cobb said. "You may proceed with the reading of the deposition."

The man who had been reading my confessions aloud now paused and turned to stare at me, obviously relishing the pause, his own sparkling gaze, the total effect. His face was filled with hatred and disgust. I returned his gaze without faltering, though with no emotion. Smooth-featured, bull-necked, squinty-eyed, he now turned back to the papers, leaning forward aggressively on thick haunches and poking the air with a stubby finger. " 'The aforementioned lady fled and got some distance from the house,' " he recited, " 'but she was pursued, overtaken, and compelled to get up behind one of the company, who brought her back, and after showing her the mangled body of her husband, she was told to get down and lay by his side, where she was shot dead. I then started for Mr. Jacob Williams's . . .' " I ceased listening.

There must have been two hundred people in the jammed courtroom: in holiday finery, the women in silk bonnets and tasseled shawls, the men in black morning suits and patent leather shoes, stern, aggrieved, blinking and blinking, they crowded together on the straight-backed benches like a congregation of owls, silent now and attentive, breaking the steaming stillness with only a sneeze or a strangled, rattling cough. The round iron stove sizzled and breathed in the quiet, filling the air with the scent of burning cedar; the room grew stifling warm and vapor clung to the windowpanes, blurring the throng of people still milling outside the courthouse, a row of tethered gigs and buggies, distant pine trees in a scrawny, ragged grove. Somewhere in the back of the courtroom I could hear a woman sobbing softly, but hoarsely and bitterly and with that particular rhythmic scratchy persistence of a female close to hysteria. Someone tried to shush her up, to no avail; the sobs continued, heartbroken, rhythmic, unceasing.

For many years it had been my habit, when situated in a position where time grew heavy on my hands, to pray— often not so much beseeching God for special favor (for I had long since come to believe that He must surely frown upon too many pesky requests) as simply out of some great need to stay in touch with Him, making sure that I never strayed so far away that He would be beyond hearing my voice. The Psalms of David I knew by heart, almost all of them, and many were the times each day when I would stop in the midst of work and recite a Psalm half aloud, feeling that by so doing I did not bother or harass the Lord yet magnified Him all the same by adding one voice to the choir of ascending praise. Yet again as I sat in the courtroom, listening to the restless stir and fidget of bodies on the benches, the hacking and coughing, the woman's persistent sobbing like a single thread of hysteria, the same feeling of apartness from God which I had felt early that morning, and for past days in numbers beyond counting, washed over me in a chill, desolating gush of anguish. Beneath my breath I tried to murmur a Psalm, but the words were flat, ugly, without meaning. The sense of His absence was like a profound and awful silence in my brain. Nor was it His absence alone which caused me this renewed feeling of despair, absence itself might have been endurable: instead it was a sense of repudiation I felt, of denial, as if He had turned His back on me once and for all, vanished, leaving me to mouth prayers, supplications, psalms of praise which flew not upward but tumbled hollow, broken, and meaningless into the depths of some foul dark hole. As I sat there I felt again almost overwhelmed by weariness, the weariness of hunger, but I forced my eyes to stay open and my gaze drowsed across the room toward Gray, still scribbling at his writing box, pausing now and then only to splash tobacco juice, with a dull pinging sound, into the brass spittoon at his feet. Nearby in the crowd an old hatchet-faced man sneezed enormously, again and again, the sneezes exploding violently from his nose in a shower of mist. My mind turned inward upon my abandonment. I found myself thinking of some lines from Job: *Oh that I were as in months past, as in the days when God preserved me; when his candle shined upon my head, and when by his light I walked through darkness* . . .

Then suddenly, and for the first time, with the same kind of faint shivery chill at my spine and shoulders that announces the commencement of a fever—a prickle at my neck as if from the lighest passing touch of icy fingers—I began to fear the coming of my own death. It was not terror, it was not even panic; it was rather an apprehension and a faint one at that, an airless mounting sense of discomfort and uneasiness as if, knowing that I had eaten a piece of tainted pork, I was awaiting the cramps and the griping flux to come, the sweats and the gut-sickness. And somehow this sudden fear of death, or rather this tremulous and hesitant emotion which was more like a dull worry than fright, had less to do with death itself, with the fact that I must soon die, than with my inability to pray or make any kind of contact with God. I mean, it was not that I had wanted to beseech God because I was afraid of dying; it was rather that my own failure in praying to Him had caused me now this troublesome fear of death. I felt a trickle of sweat worm its humid way down the side of my forehead.

Now I could tell that the man they called Trezevant was approaching the end of my confessions, the voice at once slowing its pace and rising in tone on a note of dramatic finality: "'. . . I immediately left my hiding place, and was pursued almost incessantly until I was taken a fortnight afterwards by Mr. Benjamin Phipps, in a little hole I had dug out with my sword, for the purpose of concealment, under the top of a fallen tree. On Mr. Phipps's discovering the place of my concealment, he cocked his gun and aimed at me. I requested him not to shoot and I would give up, upon which he demanded my sword. I delivered it to him forthwith. During the time I was pursued, I had many hairbreadth escapes, which your time will not permit me to relate. I am here loaded with chains and willing to suffer the fate that awaits me . . .' "

Trezevant let the paper slip from his hand onto the table beside him and wheeled toward the six magistrates at the long bench, speaking quickly, almost without a pause, his next words surprisingly quiet but coming in such a rush that they seemed almost a continuation of my confessions: "If it may please this honorable court, the Commonwealth rests its case. All this here is self-evident and self-explained. It would be very unseemly to indulge in a prolixity of words after the simple fact of sech a document—each bloody and horrifying phrase of which reveals the prisoner setting here as a fiend beyond any parallel, a hell-born and degenerate mass-murderer the likes of which has been unknown to Christendom. Now, this is no elaboration on the truth; this is truth itself, your Honors. Search the annals of all time, uh-huh, pry into the darkest and obscurest chronicles of human bestiality and you will search in vain for the equal of sech villainy. Attila the Hun that they aptly called the Scourge of God—him that ransacked Rome and held the very Pope in thrall—the Chinese Khan, nicknamed Genji, that with his rapacious Mongol hordes laid waste to the great empires of the Orient; the nefarious General Ross, all too well known to most of those older people here still living, the cruel Englishman that in the conflict of 1812 devastated our capital of Washington, D.C.— *vipers* in human clothing *all,* yet not a man amongst them that does not tower as a pillar of virtue and rectitude along--

side the monster setting here this day, right here, in this court
of law . . ."

Bemused, the grand names tolling in my brain like
chimes, I felt a kind of horrible, silent laughter welling up
within me as the stupid-looking, bull-necked man propelled
me thus into history. He again turned and gazed at me,
squinty eyes filled with scorn and hatred. "Yeah, uh-huh,
those men, your Honors, abominable as their deeds may have
been, was yet capable of a certain magnanimousness. Even
their vengeful and ruthless code demanded that they spare
the lives of the young, the helpless, the old and the frail, the
pitifully weak. Even *their* hard rules allowed them a smidgen
of human charity; and wanton in their cruelty as they was,
some spark of grace, some quality of mercy compelled them
oftentimes to withhold the sword when it come to shedding
the blood of helpless innocence, babies and so on. Your
Honors—and I shall be brief, for this case needs no clamorous protestation—the prisoner here, unlike his bloody prede-
cessors in evil, can lay hold on to no mitigation by reason of
charity or mercy. No compassion, no memory of past kindnesses or of gentle and paternal care deviated him from the
execution of these bleak deeds. Tender innocence and feeble
old age—sech alike fell victim to his inhuman lust. A fiend
incarnate, self-confessed, his diabolical actions now stand revealed in all their hideous lineaments. Your Honors! Your
Honors! The people cry out for swift retribution! He must
pay the supreme penalty with all due speed, that the stink of
his depraved and hateful flesh be erased from the nostrils of a
shocked humanity! . . . Commonwealth rests its case." He was
finished. Suddenly I was aware that his eyes were spilling
over with tears. He had made a prodigious effort.

Dabbing at his eyes with the back of his hand, Trezevant
sat down beside the whispering stove; there was no great
sound in the courtroom—only a subdued mumbling and a
shuffling of feet, a renewed outburst of hacking and coughing

through which that solitary noise of hysterical female weeping rose and rose in a soft despondent wail. Across the room I saw Gray murmuring behind his hand to a cadaverous man in a black frock coat, then he quickly arose and addressed the bench. And immediately, with no shock, I realized he was now speaking in tones that he always reserved for court, not for a nigger preacher.

"Honorable Justices," Gray said, "Mr. Parker and I, speaking as counsel for the defendant, wish to commend our colleague Mr. Trezevant both for his persuasive and fluent reading of the prisoner's confession and also for his splendid summation. We heartily concur and submit the defendant's case to the court without argument." He paused, turned to glance at me impassively, then continued: "However, one or two items, if it pleases your Honors—and I too shall try to be brief, agreeing with the able prosecutor that this case needs no *clamorous protestation*. Felicitous phrase! I would like to make it clear that Mr. Parker and I submit these items not by way of argument, nor out of the desire for mitigation or extenuation for the prisoner, who to our minds is every bit as black—no play on words intended!—as he has been painted by Mr. Trezevant. Yet if these assizes have been convened to apportion justice to the principals in this conspiracy, they have also been held in the spirit of inquiry. For this terrible event has given rise to grave questions—crucial and significant questions the answers to which involve the safety and the well-being and peace of mind of every white man, woman, and child within the sound of my voice, and far beyond, yes, throughout every inch and ell of this Southern empire where the white race and the black race dwell in such close propinquity. Not a few of these questions, with the capture and confinement of the prisoner here, have been answered to our considerable satisfaction. The widespread fear —nay, conviction—that this uprising was no mere local event but was part of a larger, organized scheme with ramifications spreading out octopus-like throughout the slave population universally—this terror has been safely laid to rest.

"Yet other questions perforce remain to trouble us. The rebellion was put down. Its maniacal participants have received swift and impartial justice, and its leader—the misguided wretch who sits before us in this courtroom—will quickly follow them to the gallows. Nonetheless, in the dark and privy stillness of our minds there are few of us who are not still haunted by worrisome doubts. Honesty, stark reality —naked fact!—compel us to admit that the seemingly impossible did, in truth, eventuate: benevolently treated, recipients of the most tender and solicitous care, a band of fanatical Negroes did, in truth, rise up murderously and in the dead of night strike down those very people under whose stewardship they had enjoyed a contentment and tranquillity unequaled anywhere among the members of their race. It was not a fantasy, not a nightmare! It was an actual happening, and its awful toll in human ruin and heartbreak and bereavement can be measured to this very day by the somber pall of mourning which hangs like a cloud here—here in this courtroom, two months and more after the hideous event. We cannot erase these questions, they refuse to dissolve like a mist, as the Bard put it, leaving not a rack behind. We cannot wish them away. They haunt us like the specter of a threatening black hand above the sweetly pillowed head of a slumbering babe. Like the memory of a stealthy footstep in a murmurous and peaceful summer garden. How did it happen? From what dark wellspring did it flow? Will it ever happen again?"

Gray paused and again turned toward me, the square ruddy face impassive, bland, regarding me as ever without hostility. I had grown only mildly surprised by his voice, filled as it was with eloquence and authority, free of the sloppy patronizing half-literate white-man-to-a-nigger tones he had used in jail. It was obviously he—not the prosecutor Trezevant—who was in charge of things. "How did it happen?" he repeated in a slow, measured voice. "From what dark wellspring did it flow? Will it ever happen again?" And he paused once more, then with a flourish toward the papers on the table, said: "The answer lies here, the answer lies in the confessions of Nat Turner!"

Again he turned to address the bench, his words momentarily drowned out as an ancient toothless Negro woman fumbled with a clattering noise at the stove door, hurled in a cedar log; blue smoke fumed outward, and a popping shower of sparks. The door clanged shut, the woman shuffled away. Gray coughed, then resumed: "Honorable Justices, as briefly as I can I want to demonstrate that the defendant's confessions, paradoxically, far from having to alarm us, from sending us into consternation and confusion, should instead give us considerable cause for relief. Needless to say, I am not suggesting that the prisoner's deeds mean that we must not enforce stricter and more stringent laws against this class of the population. Far from it: if anything, this dreadful insurrection shows that stern and repressive measures are clearly indicated, not only in Virginia but throughout the entire South. Yet, your Honors, I will endeavor to make it plain that all such rebellions are not only likely to be exceedingly rare in occurrence but are ultimately doomed to failure, and this as a result of the basic weakness and inferiority, the moral deficiency of the Negro character."

Gray picked up the confessions from the table, shuffled through the pages briefly, and continued: "Fifty-five white people went to a horrible death in this insurrection, your Honors, yet of this number Nat Turner was personally responsible for only one murder. *One murder*—this being that of Miss Margaret Whitehead, age eighteen, the comely and cultivated daughter of Mrs. Catherine Whitehead—also a victim of the insurrection—and sister to Mr. Richard Whitehead, a respected Methodist minister known to many of those in this courtroom, who likewise met a cruel fate at the hands of this inhuman pack. One murder alone, it seems plain, was all that Nat Turner committed. A particularly foul and dastardly murder it was, to be sure—taking the fragile life of a young girl in all her pure innocence. Yet I am convinced that this was the defendant's sole and solitary victim. Convinced, your Honors, only after much preliminary skepticism. For indeed—perhaps like your honorable selves—skepticism nagged at, nay, overwhelmed me when I pondered close the evidence I transcribed from the prisoner's own lips. Would not the admission of a single slaying—a single slaying alone —be tantamount to a sly plea for clemency? Thoroughly in key with the malingering nature of the Negro character, would not such an admission be typical of the evasiveness which the Negro perennially employs to cloak and disguise the base quality of his nature? I thereupon resolved upon a sturdy confrontal of the defendant with my strictures and doubts, only to discover that he was adamant in his refusal to admit a greater involvement in the actual slayings. And at this moment—if the court will permit me the levity—I had begun durn well to doubt my doubts. For why should a person, knowing full well that he must die for his deeds anyway, having already owned to one ghastly murder, and having displayed otherwise a remarkable candor in terms of the extent of his crimes—why should he not own *all*? 'The man hath penance done,' quoth the poet Coleridge in his immortal rhyme, 'and penance more will do.' What availed the defendant any further reticence?" Gray halted, then resumed: "Thus, not without some reluctance, I concluded that in terms of this *beaucoup* important item—the killing of one individual, and one individual alone—the prisoner was speaking the truth . . .

"But why?" Gray continued. "*Why* only one? This was the next question to which I addressed myself, and which caused me a severe and worrisome perplexity. Cowardice alone may well have served to explain this oddity. Certainly, pure Negro

cowardice would find its quintessential expression in this base
crime—the slaying not of a virile and stalwart man but of a
fragile, weak, and helpless young maiden but a few years out
of childhood. Yet once again, your Honors, logic and naked
fact compel us to admit that this insurrection has caused us
to rearrange, at least provisonally, some of our traditional
notions about Negro cowardice. For certainly, whatever the
deficiencies of the Negro character—and they are many,
varied, and grave—this uprising has proved beyond any
captious argument that the ordinary Negro slave, faced with
the choice of joining up with a fanatical insurgent leader
such as Nat Turner or defending his fond and devoted master, will leap to his master's defense and fight as bravely as
any man, and by so doing give proud evidence of the benevolence of a system so ignorantly decried by the Quakers and
other such moralistically dishonest detractors. 'Whatever is
unknown is magnified,' quoth Tacitus in *Agricola!* So *much*
for Northern ignorance. To be sure, Nat Turner had his misguided adherents. But the bravery of those black men who at
their good masters' sides fought faithfully and well cannot be
gainsaid, and let it be so recorded to the everlasting honor of
this genial institution . . ."

Now as Gray spoke, the same sense of misery and despair
I had felt that first day when, in the cell, Gray had tolled off
the list of slaves acquitted, transported, but not hung—*them
other niggers, dragooned, balked, it was them other niggers
that cooked your goose, Reverend*—this same despair suddenly rolled over me in a cold and sickening wave, mingled
with the dream I had had, only a few minutes before, of the
Negro boys screaming their terror in the swamp, sinking out
of sight beneath the mire . . . Sweating, the sweat rolling in
streams down my cheeks, I felt an inward, uncontrollable
wrench of guilt and loss, and I must have made a sound in my
throat, or moved in my rattling chains, uncontrollably again,
for Gray suddenly halted and turned and stared at me, as did

the six old men at the bench, and I could feel the eyes of the
spectators on me, blinking and blinking, watching. Then I
slowly relaxed, with a kind of icy interior shudder, and gazed
out through the steaming windows at the ragged grove of
pine trees far off beneath the wintry sky—of a sudden then,
for no particular reason other than that once more I had
heard her name, thinking of Margaret Whitehead in some
fragrant, summery context of dappled light and shade, dust
blooming up from a baked and rutted summer road, and her
voice clear, whispery, and girlish beside me on the carriage
seat as I gaze at the mare's clipclopping hooves beneath the
coarse and flourishing tail: *And he came himself—the Governor, Nat! Governor Floyd! All the way down to Lawrenceville he came! Isn't that just the most glorious thing you ever
heard?* And my own voice, polite, respectful: *Yes, missy, that
must indeed be something grand.* And again the breathless
and whispery girl's voice: *And we had a big ceremony at the
Seminary, Nat. And it was the most splendiferous thing! And
I'm the class poet and I wrote an ode and a song that the
little students sang. And the little girls presented the Governor with a wreath. Want to hear the words of the song,
Nat? Want to hear them?* And again my own voice, solemn
and polite: *Why yes, missy. I'd sure love to hear that song.*
And then the joyous and girlish voice in my ear above the
jogging, squeaking springs, mountainous white drifting
clouds of June sending across the parched fields immensities
of light and dark, dissolving patterns of shade and sun:

> *We'll pull a bunch of buds and flowers,*
> *And tie a ribbon round them;*
> *If you'll but think, in your lonely hours,*
> *Of the sweet little girls that bound them.*
> *We'll cull the earliest that put forth,*
> *And those that last the longest,*
> *And the bud that boasts the fairest birth,*
> *Shall cling to the stem the strongest . . .*

Gray's voice swam back through the courtroom above the restless shuffle, the hiss and hum and torment of the stove, panting like an old hound: ". . . was not Negro cowardice in this case, honorable Justices, which was at the root of the defendant's egregious and total failure. Had it been pure cowardice, Nat would have conducted his operation from a vantage point allowing him but little if any propinquity with the carnage, the bloody proceedings themselves. But we know from the prisoner's own testimony, and from the testimony of the nigger . . . Negro Hark and the others—and we have no clear reason to doubt any of it—that he himself was intimately involved in the proceedings, striking the first blow toward their execution, and repeatedly attempting to wreak murderous acts of violence upon the terrified and innocent victims." Gray paused for an instant, then said with emphasis: "But note well, your Honors, that I say *attempting*. I stress and underline that world. I put that word in *majuscules!* For save in the inexplicably successful murder of Margaret Whitehead—inexplicably motivated, likewise obscurely executed—the defendant, this purported bold, intrepid, and resourceful leader, was unable to carry out a *single feat of arms!* Not only this, but at the end his quality of leadership, such as it was, utterly deserted him!" Gray paused again, then went on in a soft, somber, deliberate voice: "I humbly submit to this court and your Honors the inescapable fact that the qualities of irresolution, instability, spiritual backwardness, and plain habits of docility are so deeply embedded in the Negro nature that any insurgent action on the part of this race is doomed to failure; and for this reason it is my sincere plea that the good people of our Southland yield not, succumb not to the twin demons of terror and panic . . ."

But listen, Nat, listen to the rest . . .

Yes, missy, I'm listening. That's a very fine poem, Miss Margaret . . .

> *We've run about the garden walks*
> *And searched among the dew, Sir,*
> *These fragrant flowers, these tender stalks,*
> *We've plucked them all for you, Sir.*
> *Pray, take this bunch of buds and flowers,*
> *Pray, take the ribbon round them;*
> *And sometimes think, in your lonely hours,*
> *Of the sweet little girls that bound them.*

There! That's the end of it! What do you think of it, Nat? What do you think?

That's a very beautiful poem, missy. The mare's rump tawny and glistening, and slower now clipclopping past green hayfields busy with the cricketing stitch of insects; slowly I too turn, eying her face with a nigger's tentative, cautious, evasive glance (some old black mammy's warning ever a watchword, even now: *Look a white folks in de eye you prayin' for trouble*), catching a glimpse of the cheekbone's lovely swerve and the fine white skin, milky, transparent, the nose uptilted and the shadow of a saucy dimple in a round young chin. She is wearing a white bonnet, and beneath it glossy strands of hair the color of chestnut have become unloosened, which all unconsciously lends to her demure and virginal beauty the faintest touch of wantonness. Sheathed in white Sunday linen, she is sweating, and I am close enough to smell her sweat, pungent and womanly and disturbing; now she laughs her high, giggly girlish laugh, wipes a tiny bubble of perspiration from her nose, and suddenly turning to gaze straight in my eyes, takes me off guard with a look joyous, gay, and unwittingly coquettish. Confused, embarrassed, I swiftly turn away. *You should have seen the Governor, Nat. Such a fine-looking man! And oh yes, I almost forgot. There was an account of it in the Southside Reporter, and it mentions my poem, and me! I have it right here, listen.* For a moment she is silent as she gropes in her handbag, then reads rapidly, the voice breathless and excited above the drumming hooves. *The Governor was then conducted into the Academical Apartment where upwards of a hundred pupils were handsomely arranged to receive him, and where a brilliant circle of ladies had previously assembled to witness the scene. After being introduced, an address was delivered by the Principal, to which Governor Floyd made a feeling and appropriate reply. An original ode for the occasion was then sung by the young ladies, accompanied by Miss Timberlake on the piano, to the air of Strike the Cymbal. Miss Covington then delivered the committee's address in behalf of the school, in a style of pathos and eloquence which could not easily be surpassed . . .* (*Now listen, Nat, this is about me . . .*) *Miss Margaret Whitehead's ode then followed, at the close of which the youngest pupils sang, in the most charming manner, Buds and Flowers, as a sequel to the ode, and at the same time presented a wreath. The effect was electrical, and almost every eye was in tears. We doubt whether the Governor has anywhere witnessed a more interesting scene, than this one in our own Seminary, dedicated to the highest principles of Christian female education . . .*

What do you think of that, Nat?

That's mighty fine, missy. That's mighty fine and grand. Yes, yes, that's just grand.

There is a moment's silence, then: *I thought you would like the poem. Oh, I knew you would like it, Nat! Because you—oh, you're not like Mama or Richard. Every weekend I've come over from school you've been the only one I could talk to. All Mama cares about is the crops—I mean the timber and the corn and those oxen and all—and making money. And Richard is just as bad almost. I mean he's a preacher and all but there's nothing, oh, spiritual about him at all. I mean they don't understand anything about poetry or spiritual things or even religious things. I mean the other day I said something to Richard about the beauty of the Psalms and he said, with that sort of scrunched-up sour look: What beauty?*

*I mean can you imagine that, Nat? From your own brother
and a preacher, too! What is your favorite Psalm, Nat?*

For a moment I am silent. We are going to be late to
church, and I urge the mare along at a canter, tapping her
rump with the whip as the dust swarms and billows around
her prancing feet. Then I say: *That's right hard to tell, Miss
Margaret. There's a whole slew of Psalms I dearly love. I
reckon though I love the best the one that begins: Be merciful unto me, O God, be merciful unto me: for my soul trust-
eth in thee: yea, in the shadow of thy wings will I make my
refuge, until these calamities be overpast.* I pause, then say: *I
will cry unto God most high; unto God that performeth all
things for me.* And then I say: *That's the way it begins. That
is number Fifty-seven.*

Yes, yes, she says in her whispery voice. *Oh yes, that's the
one that has the verse in it that goes: Awake up, my glory;
awake, psaltery and harp: I myself will awake early.* As she
speaks, I feel her closeness, oppressive, disturbing, almost
frightening, the flutter and tremble of her linen dress against
my sleeve. *Oh yes, it is so beautiful I could just weep. You're
so good at remembering the Bible, Nat. And you have such a
knowledge of, oh, spiritual things. I mean it's funny, you
know, when I tell the girls at school they just don't believe
me when I say I go home on weekends and the only person I
can talk to is a—is a darky!*

I am silent, and I feel my heart pounding at a great rate,
although I do not know the reason for this.

*And Mama said you were going. Going back to the
Travises. And that makes Margaret so sad, because she won't
have anyone to talk to all summer. But they're only a few
miles away, Nat. You will come by sometime, won't you, on a
Sunday? Even though you won't be carrying me to church
any more? I'll just feel lost without your society—I mean
reciting to me from the Bible, I mean really knowing it so
deeply and all . . .* On she prattles and chirrups, her voice

joyful, lilting, filled with Christian love, Christian virtue, Christ-obsessed young awe and discovery. Did I not think that Matthew was of all the Gospels the most *sublime*? Was not the doctrine of temperance the most *noble, pure,* and *true* contribution of the Methodist Church? Was not the Sermon on the Mount the most *awe-inspiring* message in the entire world? Suddenly, my heart still pounding uproariously, I am filled with a bitter, reasonless hatred for this innocent and sweet and quivering young girl, and the long hot desire to reach out with one arm and snap that white, slender, throbbing young neck is almost uncontrollable. Yet—strange, I am aware of it—it is *not* hatred; it is something else. But what? What? I cannot place the emotion. It is closer to jealousy, but it is not even that. And why I should feel such an angry turmoil over this gentle creature baffles me, for save for my one-time master Samuel Turner, and perhaps Jeremiah Cobb, she is the only white person with whom I have experienced even one moment of a warm and mysterious and mutual confluence of sympathy. Then all at once I realize that from just that sympathy, irresistible on my part, and unwanted—a disturbance to the great plans which this spring are gathering together into a fatal shape and architecture—arises my sudden rage and confusion.

Why are you going back to the Travises, Nat, so soon? she says.

Well, missy, I was just hired out for two months by Marse Joe. It's what they call trade-fair-and-square.

What's that? she says. *Trade . . . what?*

Well, missy, that's why I've been working for your mama. Marse Joe he needed a yoke of oxen to pull stumps and Miss Caty she needed a nigger to work on her new barn. So Marse Joe traded me for two months for a yoke of oxen. That's what they call trade-fair-and-square.

She makes a thoughtful humming noise. *Hm-m. A yoke of oxen. I mean, and you . . . That seems so very strange.* She is silent for a moment. Then: *Nat, why do you call yourself a nigger like that? I mean it sounds so—well, so sad somehow. I much prefer the word darky. I mean, after all, you're a preacher . . . Oh, look yonder, Nat, the church! Look at how Richard has gotten one whole side whitewashed already!*

Now again, the soft reverie flowing away in my mind like smoke, I heard Gray's voice as he addressed the court: ". . . are doubtless familiar, perhaps actually conversant, with an even more important work by the late Professor Enoch Mebane of the University of Georgia at Athens, a study of still more commanding stature and exhaustive research than the opus by Professors Sentelle and Richards just quoted. For whereas Professors Sentelle and Richards have demonstrated, from a theological standpoint, the innate and inbred, indeed the *predestined* deficiency of the Negro in the areas of moral choice and Christian ethics, it remained the achievement of Professor Mebane to prove beyond the iota of a doubt that the Negro is a *biologically* inferior species. Certainly this court is aware of Professor Mebane's treatise, therefore I shall refresh your honorable minds of its contents only in the barest outlines: videlicet, that all the characteristics of the nigger head—the deeply receding jaw, measurable by what Professor Mebane has termed the gnathic index; the sloping, beetle-browed cranium, with its grotesque and brutelike width between ear and ear and its lack of vertical lobal areas that in other species allow for the development of the most upwards-reaching moral and spiritual aspirations; and the extraordinary thickness of the cranium itself, resembling not so much that of any human but of the lowest beasts of the field—that all these characteristics fully and conclusively demonstrate that the Negro occupies at best but a middling position amongst all the species, possessing a relationship which is not cousin-german to the other human races but one which is far closer to the skulking baboon of that dark continent from which he springs . . ."

Gray halted, and as if pausing for a moment's breath, leaned forward with both hands against the table top, resting his weight there as he contemplated the magistrates at the bench. The courtroom was silent. Quiet, blinking in the steamy air, the people seemed to attend Gray's every word, as if each syllable was atingle with the promise of some revelation which would assuage their fright and their anxiety and even the grief which stitched them together, one and all, like the hysteric thread of that woman's sobbing anguish still persisting in the back of the courtroom, a single noise in the stillness, out of hand now, inconsolable. The manacles had made my hands numb. I flexed my fingers, felt no sensation. Gray cleared his throat, then continued: "Now then, honorable Justices, I beg to be permitted a philosophical leap. I beg to be permitted to connect these unassailable biological theories of Professor Mebane with the concepts of an even greater figure in human thought, namely, the great German philosopher Leibnitz. Now, you are all acquainted with Leibnitz's concept of the monad. The brains of all of us, according to Leibnitz, are filled with monads. These monads, millions and billions of them, are nothing but tiny, infinitesimal mental units *striving for development* according to their pre-established nature. Now, whether one takes Leibnitz's theory at its face value or more or less in a symbolical fashion, as I myself am wont to do, the fact remains—and it seems indisputable—that the spiritual and ethical organization of a single mind may be studied and understood from not alone a *qualitative* standpoint but from a *quantitative* standpoint likewise. That is to say, that this *striving for development*—and I emphasize and underline that phrase—may in the end be only the product of the number of monads that a single mind is physically capable of accommodating."

He paused, then said: "And here, your Honors, is the crux of the issue which, I submit, if we now examine it closely, can lead only to the most optimistic of conclusions. For with his

unformed, primitive, almost rudimentary cranium, the Negro
suffers from a grave insufficiency of monads, so grave indeed
that this *striving for development*—which in other races has
given us men like Newton and Plato and Leonardo da Vinci
and the sublime inventive genius of James Watt—is unalter-
ably hampered, nay, mutilated, in the severest degree; so that
on the one hand we have the glorious musicianship of Mozart
and on the other, pleasant but childish and uninspired croon-
ings, on the one hand the magnificent constructions of Sir
Christopher Wren and on the other the feeble artifacts and
potsherds of the African jungle, on the one hand the splendid
military feats of Napoleon Bonaparte and on the other—" He
broke off again, with a gesture toward me. "On the other the
aimless and pathetic and futile slaughter of Nat Turner—
destined from its inception to utter failure because of the
biological and spiritual inferiority of the Negro character!"
Gray's voice began to rise. "Honorable Justices, again I do
not wish to minimize the prisoner's atrocious deeds, nor the
need for stricter controls upon this portion of the population.
But if this trial is to illumine us, it must also give us room for
hope and optimism! It must show us—and I submit that the
defendant's confessions have done so already—that we must
not run in panic before the Negro! So crudely devised were
Nat's plans, so clumsily and aimlessly put into effect . . ."

Again his words fade away on my ears, and I briefly shut
my eyes, half drowsing, and again I hear her voice, bell-clear
on that somnolent dusty Sunday half a year past: *Oh me oh
my, Nat, too bad for you. It's Mission Sunday. This is Richard's day that he preaches to the darkies!* Alighting from the
buggy, she casts me a sweet, rueful look. *Poor Nat . . .* And
she is gone ahead of me through the dazzling clear light, the
white linen swishing as she runs on tiptoe, disappearing into
the vestibule of the church, where I too now enter, cautiously, quietly, stealing up the back ladder to the balcony set
off for Negroes, hearing as I climb Richard Whitehead's voice

nasal and high-pitched and effeminate as always even as he exhorts that black sweating assembly among whom I will take my seat: *And think within yourselves what a terrible thing it would be, after all your labors and sufferings in this life, to be turned into hell in the next life, and after wearing out your bodies in service here to go into a far worse slavery when this is over, and your poor souls be delivered over into the possession of the devil, to become his slaves forever in hell, without any hope of ever getting free from it . . .* High above the white congregation, beneath the church roof where heat as if from an oven blooms stifling and damp amid a myriad swarming motes of dust, the Negroes, seventy or more from the surrounding countryside, sit on dilapidated back-less pine benches or squat helter-skelter on the gallery's creaking floor.

I cast a quick glance over the crowd and glimpse Hark and Moses, and I exchange looks with Hark, whom I have not seen for nearly two months. Intent, absorbed, some of the women fanning themselves with thin pine-bark shingles, the Negroes are gazing at the preacher with the hollow-eyed fixity of scarecrows, and as I regard them I can tell whom they belong to by what they wear: the ones from Richard Porter and J. T. Barrow and the Widow Whitehead, owners who are fairly rich, dressed cleanly and neatly, the men in cotton shirts and freshly laundered trousers, the women in printed calico and scarlet bandannas, some with cheap ear-rings and pins; the ones from poorer masters, Nathaniel Francis and Levi Waller and Benjamin Edwards, in dingy rags and patches, a few of the crouched men and boys with-out shirts, picking their noses and scratching, sweat stream-ing off their black backs in shiny torrents, the lot of them stinking to heaven. I sit down on a bench near the window in an empty space between Hark and an obese, gross-jowled, chocolate-colored slave named Hubbard, owned by the Widow Whitehead, who sports a white man's cast-off frayed multicolored vest over his flabby naked shoulders, and whose thick lips wear even now, as he meditates conscientiously upon the sermon from below, a flatterer's avid smirk. Beneath us, from a pulpit elevated above the assembled whites, in black suit and black tie, pale and slender, Richard Whitehead raises his eyes toward heaven and remonstrates to those of us squatting beneath the roof: *If therefore you would be God's free men in paradise, you must strive to be good, and serve him here on earth. Your bodies, you know, are not your own; they are at the disposal of those you belong to, but your precious souls are still your own, which nothing can take from you if it is not your own fault. Figure well then that if you lose your souls by leading idle, wicked lives here, you have gained nothing by it in this world and you have lost your all in the next. For your idleness and wickedness are generally found out and your bodies suffer for it here, and what is far worse, if you do not repent and alter your ways, your unhappy souls will suffer for it hereafter . . .*

Black wasps soar and float through the windows, drowsily buzzing as they lurch against the eaves. I but barely listen to the sermon; from these same lips I have heard these same sour and hopeless words half a dozen times in as many years: they do not change or vary, nor do they even belong to the one who speaks them, having been composed rather by the Methodist Bishop of Virginia for annual dispensation by his ministers, to make the Negroes stand in mortal fear. That they have a profound effect on some of us, at least, I cannot doubt: even now as Richard Whitehead warms up to his subject, and his pale face dampens and begins to flush as if from the glow of promised hellfire, I can see around me a score of faces popeyed with black nigger credulity, jaws agape, delicious shudders of fright coursing through their bodies as they murmur soft *Amens*, nervously cracking their knuckles and making silent vows of eternal obedience. *Yes, yes!* I hear a high impassioned voice, then the same voice croons *Ooooo-h yes, so right!* And I shift my glance and see that this is Hubbard: obscenely he sways and wiggles on his thick buttocks, his eyes squeezed tightly shut in a trance of prayerful submission. *Ooooh yes!* he groans, a fat house nigger, docile as a pet coon. And now I feel Hark's big hand on mine, firm and and friendly and warm, and I hear his voice in a whisper: *Nat, dese yere niggers goin' git to heaven or bust dey britches. How you been, Nat?*

Eat high off the hog at ole Widow Whitehead's, I whisper back. Afraid that Hubbard might overhear, I keep my voice pitched low: *There's a gun room there, Hark, it's something enormous. She's got fifteen guns locked up behind glass. And powder and shot enough to fill a shed. We get them guns and Jerusalem belongs to the niggers.* Last March, a month before leaving the Travises' for the Widow Whitehead's, I told Hark of my plans—Hark and three others. *Where's Henry and Nelson and Sam?*

Dey all here, Nat, Hark says. *I knowed you'd be here, so I got dem to come too. Funniest daggone thing, Nat, lissen . . .* Already he has begun to chuckle, and I start to shush him up, but he continues: *You know dat Nelson, his white folks is Baptists and goes to church down Shiloh way. So Nelson didn' have no business goin' to no Meth'dist meetin', specially when dey was preachin' to de niggers like now. So his massah —you know dat mean ol' Marse Jake Williams what has one leg—he say: "Nelson, how come you want to go to a Meth'dist meetin' where they's exhortin' the niggers?" So Nelson he say: "Why, massah, dear massah, I feels right sinful. I feels I done bad things to you, and jes' needs the fear of God in me so's I can be your faithful nigger from now on!"* For a moment Hark shakes and trembles with silent laughter, I fear that he might give us away. But then he is whispering: *Now dat Nelson is a caution, Nat! Ever I seed a black man wanted to stick a knife in some white foks it's dat ole Nelson. Dere he is, Nat, over yondah . . .*

I have acquired the strongest faith in Hark, during the past six months slowly undermining his soppy childish esteem for white people, his confidence in them and his reliance upon them, digging in hard on the matter of the sale of his wife and little boy, which, I have insisted, was an irredeemable and monstrous act on the part of our master, no matter how helpless Marse Joe has claimed to be in the transaction; I have battered down Hark's defenses, playing incessantly, almost daily, upon his sorrow and loss, coaxing and wheedling him into a position where he too must grasp, firmly and without qualm, one of the alternatives of freedom or death-in-life, until at last—revealing my plans for a bloody sweep through the countryside, the capture of Jerusalem, and a safe flight into the bosom of the Dismal Swamp where no white man can follow us—I see that my campaign has borne fruit: on a winter day in Travis's shop, harassed to the breaking point by one of Putnam's yowling, peevish harangues, he turns on the boy, brandishing in one hand a ten-pound crowbar, and with the glint of murder in his eye, saying nothing but presenting such an aspect of walled-up rage breaking loose that even I am alarmed, faces his quaking tormenter down once and for all. It is done, it is like once when I watched a great glorious hawk burst free from a snare into the purity of a wide blue sky. Hark is exuberant. *Dat l'il sonabitch never run me up a tree again.* Thus Hark becomes the first to join me in this conspiracy. Hark, then Henry and Nelson and Sam: trustworthy, silent, without fear, all men of God and messengers of His vengeance, these have shared already in the knowledge of my great design.

I see Nelson now across the packed gallery: an older man, fifty-four or fifty-five or fifty-six—as is common among Negroes, he himself is not quite sure—he sits oval-faced and impassive amidst this addled, distraught, intimidated throng, heavy-lidded eyes making him appear half asleep, a presence of unconquerable patience and calm, yet like a placid sea beneath which lie boiling vast convulsions of fury. A slick and shiny, elevated "S" the ragged length and width of a small garter snake, souvenir of old-time branding days, winds its way through the sparse gray hairs of his black chest. He can read a few simple words—where or how he has learned them I do not know. Weary and sick—close to madness—of bondage, he has had more than a half a dozen masters, the last and present one an evil-tempered, crippled woodcutter his same age who dares not whip him after his one adventure in this area (with no more emotion than if he had been slapping a gnat, Nelson struck him back full in the face, and said that if he tried it again he would kill him) but now in frightened retaliation and hatred works him like two, and feeds him on the nastiest kinds of leavings and slops. Nelson had a wife and family once but can hope no longer to see them either together or often, scattered as they are all over three or four counties of the Tidewater. Like Hark he has little religion—and like Hark is often foul of mouth, which generally causes me some distress—but this does not really trouble me; to me he is a man of God: shrewd, slow-moving, imperturbable, his slumbrous eyes conceal a maddened defiance, and he will be a strong right arm. *Nigger life ain't worth pig shit,* he once said to me; *mought make a nigger worth somethin' to hisself, tryin' to git free, even if he don't.* And his counsel about strategy is many times inspired: *Rock de places what's got horses first, horses'll git us a-moverin' fast.* Or: *Rock on a Sunday night, dat's a nigger's night for huntin'. Dem white cocksuckers hears a commotion and figger hit's some niggers out treein' a possum.* Or: *Us jes' gots to keep de niggers out'n dem cider presses. Let dem black bastids get at dat cider an' brandy and us done lost de war* . . . I look at Nelson and he looks back at me with sleeping, impassive eyes, betraying no recognition . . .

Now again I hear Hark's voice in my ear: *After church dey's some kind of doin's at de graveyard dat de niggers ain't suppose to go to* . . .

. Yes, I say, *I know.* I feel a growing excitement, for I sense that on this day I may be able at last to outline and enlarge upon the details of my plans. *I know. Where we goin' to meet?*

See, dey's dem two logs over de creek down behin' de church. I tol' Henry and Nelson and Sam to meet us dere while de white foks was at de graveyard . . .

Yes, good, I say, then *sssh-h,* squeezing his hand, fearing that we will be overheard, and we both turn then, faking pious attention to the words rising toward us through the swarming wasps, up across the creaking and snapping rafters: *Poor creatures! You little consider when you are idle and neglectful of your masters' business, when you steal and waste and hurt any of their substance, when you are saucy and impudent, when you are telling them lies and deceiving them, or when you are stubborn and sullen and will not do the work you are told to do without chastisement—you do not consider, I say, that what faults you are guilty of towards your masters and mistresses are faults done against God Himself, who has set your masters and mistresses over you in His own stead, and expects that you would do for them just as you would do for Him. Do not your masters, under God, provide for you? And how shall they be able to do this, to feed and to clothe you, unless you take honest care of everything that belongs to them? Remember that God requires this of you. And if you are not afraid of suffering for it here, you cannot escape the vengeance of Almighty God, who will judge between you and your masters, and make you pay severely in the next world for all the injustice you do them here. And though you could manage so cleverly as to escape the eyes and hands of man, yet think what a dreadful thing it is to fall into the hands of the living God, who is able to cast both soul and body into hell . . .*

And now through the soft moaning of the black crowd, through Hubbard's fat sighs of pleasure and the murmur and fidget and the *Amens* gently aspirated in gasps of dumb rapture and desire, I hear another voice behind me and very near, almost at my shoulder, a harsh rapid low muttering, almost incoherent, like that of a man in the clutch of fever: *... me some of dat white stuff, yas, get me some of dat white stuff, yas ...* And without turning—suddenly unsettled and afraid to turn; rather, afraid to confront that obsessed and demented face, the mashed-in nose and deformed and jutting jaw and bulging eyes with their gaze murderous, fixed, dim-brained, pure—I know whose voice it is: Will's. I am seized with a quick displeasure. For although like Nelson he has been driven half crazy by slavery, Will's madness is not governed by silence and some final secret control, but has the frenzied, mindless quality of a wild boar hog cornered hopelessly in a thicket, snarling and snapping its brutish and unavailing wrath. Age twenty-five or a little more, a chronic runaway, he once got nearly to Maryland, sustained in his flight not so much by intelligence as by the same cunning and endurance of those little animals native to the swamps and woods in which he roamed for six weeks, before being overhauled and delivered to his present master, a nigger-breaker named Nathaniel Francis who has beaten him into some kind of stunned and temporary submission. He crouches behind me now, muttering to whom it is impossible to tell—to himself, to no one, to anyone at all. *Ole white cunt,* he whispers, and in a sort of demented litany repeats it over and over.

Will's presence disturbs me, for I want no part of him, either now or in my future plans. And I am afraid that he will discover what's afoot. Rather than finding any value in his fractiousness, his rage and rebellion, I am filled with distrust, instinctively put off by the foaming and frenzied nature of his madness. Besides, there is one other thing, evident enough now in that obsessive incantation: I know from hearsay that he broods constantly upon rape, the despoliation of white women masters his dreams night and day. And already—and Hark and Nelson and the others have sworn to obey—I have forbidden this kind of violation. It is God's will, and I know it, that I omit such a vengeance: *Do not unto their women what they have done to thine* . . .

I banish Will from my mind and as my eyes rove around the gallery I see the other two in whom I have placed my trust. Owned like Will by Nathaniel Francis, Sam is a mulatto, a wiry muscular young field hand with freckles and ginger-colored hair. He is intractable and high-strung, also many times a runaway, and his yellow skin is knobbed and striped by the lash. I value him for his intelligence but also for his color: he is light of hue and his presence thus commands considerable respect among many of the Negroes, especially the simple-minded, and I feel that when my scheme achieves momentum Sam's appearance will be useful in gaining new recruits. He is skillful in quiet, furtive intrigue and has already won for the cause Henry, who sits beside him now, eyes shut, rocking slightly, with a look of beatitude and calm. So far as I can tell, he is sound asleep. Short, square in shape, very black, he alone among my group is of a religious nature. He is owned by Richard Porter, a devout and kindly master who has never raised a hand against him. At forty, Henry lives among Biblical fancies, in a shadowland of near-silence, almost completely deaf from boyhood by a blow on the head from a drunken overseer whose name or face he can no longer remember. It is the recollection of that blow that feeds his calm fury . . .

The sound of organ music fills the air. The sermon is ended. Down below, the white people have risen, joining together in song.

> "Can we, whose souls are lighted
> With wisdom from on high,
> Can we to men benighted
> The lamp of life deny?"

The black people do not sing but stand respectfully in the hot gallery, mouths agape or with sloppy uncomprehending smiles, shuffling their feet. Suddenly they seem to me as meaningless and as stupid as a barn full of mules, and I hate them one and all. My eyes search the white crowd, finally discover Margaret Whitehead, her dimpled chin tilted up as, with one arm entwined in her mother's, she carols heavenward, a radiance like daybreak on her serene young face. Then slowly and softly, like a gentle outrush of breath, my hatred of the Negroes diminishes, dies, replaced by a kind of wild, desperate love for them, and my eyes are wet with tears.

> "Salvation, O Salvation!
>   The joyful sound proclaim,
> Till each remotest nation
>   Has learnt Messiah's name . . ."

And later that afternoon—after the hurried secret parley by the creek—driving the carriage back home through the parched and windless fields, I hear behind me two voices now, Margaret Whitehead's and her mother's, fondly:

I do think Boysie's sermon was most inspiring, don't you, little Miss Peg?

There is a short space of silence, then her bright laughter: *Oh, Mother, it's the same old folderol, every year! Just folderol for the darkies!*

Margaret! What an expression to use! Folderol indeed! I'm simply appalled! If your sainted father were here, to hear you talk like that about your own brother. Shame!

Then suddenly, to my surprise, I realize that Margaret is close to tears. *Oh, Mother, I'm sorry, I just don't know.* And she is quietly sobbing now. *I just don't know. I just don't know . . .*

. And I hear the woman draw Margaret to her with a rustle. *There, there, dear. I understand. It must be a bad time of the month. We'll be home soon and you can just go lie down and I'll make you a nice cup of tea . . .*

High over the flat land thunderheads loom, their undersides churning, promising a storm. I feel the sweat rolling down my back. After a bit I let my eyes close, and I smell the rich odor of horse droppings as I make a silent prayer: *Forsake me not, O Lord: O my God, be not far from me. Make haste to help me, O Lord my salvation, for the hour of my battle comes near . . .*

"Nat Turner! Stand up!"

I rose to my feet in the courtroom. It was hot and very still, and for a long time as I stood clumsily in my chains leaning against the table there was no interruption to the silence save for the panting and roaring of the stove. I turned to face Jeremiah Cobb. As I did so, regarding him for the first time straight on, I saw that his face was as white as tallow; drawn and almost fleshless, it was the face of a cadaver, and it trembled and nodded as if with palsy. He looked down at me, the eyes sunk deep within their sockets, so that the effect was that of a gaze from some immeasurable distance, profound as all eternity. Then all of a sudden I realized that he too was close to death, very close, almost as close as I myself, and I felt a curious pang of pity and regret.

Cobb spoke again. "Have you anything to say why sentence of death should not be pronounced against you?" His voice was tremulous, feeble, dead.

"I have not," I replied. "I have made a full confession to Mr. Gray and I have nothing more to say."

."Attend then to the sentence of the court. You have been arraigned and tried before this court and convicted of one of the highest crimes in our criminal code. You have been convicted of plotting in cold blood the indiscriminate destruction of men, of helpless women, and of infant children . . . The evidence before us leaves not a shadow of doubt but that your hands were imbrued in the blood of the innocent, and your own confession tells us that they were stained with the blood of a master—in your own language, *too indulgent.* Could I stop here your crime would be sufficiently aggravated

. . . But the original contriver of a plan, deep and deadly, one that never could be effected, you managed so far to put it into execution as to deprive us of many of our most valuable citizens, and this was done when they were asleep under circumstances shocking to humanity . . . And while upon this part of the subject, I cannot but call your attention to the poor misguided wretches who have gone before you." He paused for an instant, breathing heavily. "They are not few in number—they were your bosom associates, and the blood of all cries aloud, and calls upon you as the author of their misfortune. Yes. You forced them unprepared from time to eternity . . . Borne down by this load of guilt, your only justification is that you were led away by fanaticism."

He paused again, gazing at me from the awful and immeasurable distances where not alone his eyes but his dying flesh and spirit seemed to dwell, remote as the stars. "If this be true," he concluded slowly, "from my soul I pity you, and while you have my sympathies I am nevertheless called upon to pass sentence of the court . . . The time between this and your execution will necessarily be very short, and your only hope must be in another world. The judgment of the court is that you be taken hence to the jail from whence you came, thence to the place of execution, and on Friday next, November eleventh, at sunrise, be hung by the neck until you are dead! dead! *dead!*—and may the Lord have mercy upon your soul."

We gazed at each other from vast distances, yet close, awesomely close, as if sharing for the briefest instant some rare secret—unknown to other men—of all time, all mortality and sin and grief. In the stillness the stove howled and raged like a tumultuous storm pitched in the firmament between hell and heaven. A door flew open with a clatter. Then we ceased looking at each other, and outside a human roar went up like thunder.

That evening as Hark talked to me through the cracks of the jail wall, his voice came pained and laborious and with a sort of faint gurgle or croak, like a frog's. Only Hark could have lived so long.

He had been shot through the chest on that day in August when they broke us up. Time after time they had carried him to court on a litter and they were going to have to hang him roped to a chair. The two of us would be the last to go.

Dusk was coming on: as the cold day lengthened, light began to drain away from the cell as from a vessel, turning the corners dark, and the cedar plank I was lying on grew as chill as a slab of stone. A few leaves clung to the branches outside and through the gray twilight a cold wind whispered sharply, and often a leaf would flicker to earth or scuttle through the cell with a dry rattling sound. Every now and then I listened to Hark, but mainly I waited on Gray. After the trial he had said that he would come again this evening, and he promised to bring me a Bible. The idea of a Bible kept me in a greedy suspense, as if after a day's long thirst in some parched and burning field someone was about to fetch me brimming pails of cool clear water.

"Oh yes, Nat," I heard Hark say beyond the wall, "yes, dey was lots and lots of niggers kilt afterwards, w'ile you was hid out. And warn't our niggers neither. Dey tells me roun' about a hundred, maybe lots mo'. Yes, Nat, de white folks come down like a swarm of golly-wasps and plain long stomped de niggers ev'ywheres. You didn' know about dat, Nat? Oh yes, dey was plain long *stomped*. White folks dey come fum all over ev'ywheres. Dey come a-gallopin' down from Sussex an' Isle of Wight and all dem other counties an' run de niggers clean into de groun'. Didn' make no nem'mine dat dey didn' fight fo' Nat Turner. If'n he had a black ass, dey fill hit full of lead." Hark was silent for a while and I could hear his thick, tortured breathing. "After you was hid out I heerd tell of some ole free nigger dat was standin' in a field up somewheres aroun' Drewrysville. Dese white folks rode up an' stop dere. 'Is dis yere Southampton?' dey holler. Nigger he say, 'Yassuh, boss, you done jes' passed de county line over yondah.' 'Pon my soul, Nat, dem white folks shot him dead." Again he was silent, then he said: "I heerd tell of a nigger name of Statesman livin' down aroun' Smith's Mill what ain't even heerd of de ruction, bein' slow in de head, you know? Anyways, his massah he *powerful* exercise' an' mad an' he take ole Statesman out an' tie him to a tree an' shoot him so full of holes you could see de sun shine th'ough. Oh me, Nat. Some sad stories I done heerd all dese months in jail . . ."

I watched the wintry gray light stealing softly away from the cell, thinking: *O Lord, hear; O Lord, forgive; O Lord, hearken and do; defer not, for thine own sake, O my God, forgive me the blood of the innocent and slain* . . . But it was not a prayer at all, there was no echo, no understanding that it had reached God's almighty hearing, only the sense of its falling away futile on the air like a wisp of smoke. A shudder passed through my bones and I clasped my arms around my legs, trying to still their shaking. Then as if to blot out this new knowledge, I broke in upon Hark, saying: "Tell me, Hark, tell me. Nelson. Tell me about Nelson. How did he die? Did he die brave?"

"Why sho he die brave," Hark said. "Hung ole Nelson back in September. Him and Sam together, standin' up straight as you could pray for, both dem. Dey tells me ole Sam wouldn' die right off, flew off'n dat hangin' tree an' jes' jiggle dere like a turkey gobbler a-jumpin' and a-twitchin'." Feebly, softly, Hark began to laugh. "Reckon dat li'l ole yellow nigger was too light fo' de rope. Dem white folks had to yank on old Sam's feet afore he'd give up de ghost. But he died brave, though, him an' Nelson. Didn' hear no mumblin' nor groanin' when dem two niggers died." He paused and sighed, then said: "Onliest thing ole Sam was sad about was dat we didn' cotch dat mean sonabitch Nat Francis dat

owned him. Cotched his overseer and two chillun but not Nat
Francis. Dat's what give Sam a misery. I seed Nat Francis in
de cou'troom de day dey tried ole Sam. Jesus jumpin' Judas!
Talk 'bout a mad white man! Oo-ee, Nat, he let out a howl
and jump straight over de railin' an' like to strangle dat Sam
befo' dey could haul him off. I heerd tell Nat Francis like to
went clean out'n his head after we finished de ruction. Got
him a gang of folks an' rode from Cross Keys to Jerusalem,
shootin' down ev'y nigger in sight. Dey was a free nigger
woman name Laurie, wife to old John Bright live up Cloud
School way, you know? Well, dey took dat woman an' leant
her up 'longside a fence and druv a three-foot spike right up
her ole pussy like dey was layin' out a barbecue. Oh me, Nat,
de tales I heerd tell dese months and days! Dey was two white
mens I heerd about, come up from Carolina, has actual got
dem a real bunch of black nigger heads all nailed to a pole
and was out to git dem some mo' till de troops grabbed holt
'em an' run 'em back to Carolina—"

"Hush," I broke in. "*Hush,* Hark! That's enough. I can't
bear no more of that. I can't bear such talk no more." I tried
not to think, yet even as I tried could not help thinking, scraps
of prayer afloat turbulent and spinning in my brain like twigs
upon a flood: *O spare me, that I may recover strength. Before
I go hence. And be no more.*

I heard footsteps in the passageway, and suddenly Gray
appeared at the door with the boy Kitchen, who noisily threw
open the latch. "I can't stay but a minute, Reverend," he said
as he stepped into the cell and sat himself down across from
me slowly, with a soft weary grunt. He looked exhausted and
unstrung. I noticed that he was carrying nothing with him,
and I felt my heart sink like a stone; even before I could start
to protest, though, he had begun to speak: "I know, I know,
that durn Bible! I know I promised to fetch you one—I'm a
man of my word, Reverend—but I run into a patch of difficulty, all unforeseen. The vote was five to one agin it."

"What do you mean, Mr. Gray?" I exclaimed. "What vote? Mr. Gray, I ain't asked for much—"

"I know, I know," he put in. "By all rights any man condemned to death should have the fullest spiritual comfort, be he black or white. And this afternoon when I petitioned the court for a Bible for your own personal use, I brought this fact out in the strongest terms. But like I say, Reverend, I run into a bit of difficulty. The majority of the Justices didn't cotton to this idea in any way, shape, nor form. In the first place, they felt very strongly about the moot point *in*—and the general tenor *of*—the community feeling as it stands, namely, that no nigger is to be allowed to read or write anyhow. In the second place, and on account of this, since no nigger about to be hung in this county has ever been allowed to have a Bible, why then, they couldn't make an exception in your case. So they took a vote. Five to one against your havin' a Bible, with only the Chief Magistrate in favor—Mr. Jeremiah Cobb, who's about to cash in hisself, so I guess he's got good reason to be soft on matters pertainin' to spiritual comfort."

"I'm sorry," I said. "I'm sorry about that, Mr. Gray. It'll be right tough on me without a Bible."

Gray was silent for a while, a queer quizzical look on his face. Then he said: "Tell me, Reverend, you ever heard tell of a galaxy?"

"A what?" I said. I was barely listening. I cannot describe my misery and desolation.

"A galaxy. G-a-l-a-x-y. Galaxy."

"Well, sir," I replied finally, "I may have heard that word used, but I can't rightly say I know what it exactly means."

"Well, you know what the sun is," he said. "The sun don't move around the earth, a great big ball up there. The sun is a star. You know about that, don't you?"

"Yes," I said, "it seems to me I did hear about that. There was a white man in Newsoms told some of the Negroes that, long time ago. He was one of those Quaker men."

"And you believe it?"

"I used to think it was right hard to believe," I said, "but I've come to believe it. By the Lord's grace all things can be believed."

"Well, you know the sun is a star, but you don't exactly know what a galaxy is. That right?"

"No, I don't know," I replied.

"Well now, in England there's a great astronomer name of Professor Herschel. Know what an astronomer is? Yes? Well, there was a big write-up on him not long ago in the Richmond newspaper. What Professor Herschel has found out is that this here star of our'n that we call the sun is but one of not thousands, not millions, but *billions* of stars all revolvin' around in a great big kind of cartwheel that he calls a galaxy. And this sun of our'n is just a piddlin' little third-rate star swimmin' around amongst millions of other stars on the edge of the galaxy. Fancy that, Reverend!" He leaned forward toward me, and I could smell the sudden apple-sweet perfume of his presence. "Fancy that! Millions and even billions of stars all floatin' around in the vastness of space, separated by distances the mind can't even conceive of. Why, Reverend, the light we see from some of these stars must of left there long before man hisself ever dwelt on earth! A million years before Jesus Christ! How do you square that with your Christianity? How do you square that with God?"

I pondered this for a moment, then I said: "As I told you, Mr. Gray, by the Lord's grace all things can be believed. I accept the sun and the stars, and the galaxies too."

"Hogwash!" he exclaimed. "Christianity is finished and done with. Don't you know that, Reverend? And don't you realize further that it was the message contained in Holy Scripture that was the cause, the *prime mover,* of this entire miserable catastrophe? Don't you see the plain ordinary *evil* of your dad-burned Bible?"

He fell silent, and I too said nothing. Though I was no longer either as hot or cold as I had been that morning—indeed, for the first time that day I felt a tolerable comfort—my throat had gotten dry and I found it difficult to swallow. I closed my eyes for a second, opened them again: in the cold, pale, diminishing light Gray seemed to be smiling at me, though perhaps it was only the dimness of the twilight which blurred and made indistinct the configurations of his heavy round face. I felt that I had only faintly understood what Gray had said—grasped the barest beginnings of it; finally I replied in a dry voice, the frog still in my throat: "What do you mean, Mr. Gray? I fear I don't quite follow. *Evil?*"

Gray leaned forward, slapping his knee. "Well, *Jehoshaphat*, Reverend, look at the record! Jes' look at it! Look at your own words! The words you rattled off to me for three days runnin'! *The divine spirit! Seek ye the kingdom of heaven! My wisdom came from God!* All that hogwash, what I mean. And what's that line you told me the heavenly spirit said to you when you were about to embark on this bloody course of your'n? *For he who knows*—What?"

"*For he who knoweth his Master's will,*" I said, "*and doeth it not, shall be beaten with many stripes, and thus have I chastened you.*"

"Yeah, hogwash like that, what I mean. Divine guidance. Holy will. Messages from up above. Durndest slop ever I heard of. And what did it get you? *What,* Reverend?"

I made no reply, even though now I had begun to understand what he was trying to say. I stopped looking at him and thrust my head into my hands, hoping that he would not find it necessary to go on.

"Here's what it got you, Reverend, if you'll pardon the crudity. It got you a pissy-assed record of total futility, the likes of which are hard to equal. Threescore white people slain in random butchery, yet the white people still firmly holdin' the reins. Seventeen niggers hung, including you and old Hark there, nevermore to see the light of day. A dozen or more other nigger boys shipped out of an amiable way of life to Alabama, where you can bet your bottom dollar that in five years the whole pack of 'em will be dead of work and fever. I've seen them cotton plantations. I've seen them rice layouts too, Reverend—niggers up to their necks in shit from day clean to first dark, with a big black driver to whip 'em, and mosquitoes the size of buzzards. This is what you brung on them kids, Reverend, this is what Christianity brung on them boys. I reckon you didn't figure on that back then, did you?"

I was silent for a moment, considering his question, then I said: "No." For indeed, to be most truthful, I had not figured on it then.

"And what else did Christianity accomplish?" he said. "Here's what Christianity accomplished. Christianity accomplished the mob. The *mob*. It accomplished not only your senseless butchery, the extermination of all those involved in it, black and white, but the horror of lawless retaliation and reprisal—one hundred and thirty-one innocent niggers both slave and free cut down by the mob that roamed Southampton for a solid week, searching vengeance. I reckon you didn't figure on that neither back then, did you, Reverend?"

"No," I said quietly, "no, I didn't."

"And furthermore, you can bet your sweet ass that when the Legislature convenes in December they're goin' to pass laws that make the ones *extant* look like rules for a Sunday School picnic. They goin' to lock up the niggers in a black cellar and throw away the key." He paused, and I could sense him leaning close to me. "*Abolition*," he said in a voice like a whisper. "Reverend, single-handed you done more with your Christianity to assure the defeat of abolition than all the meddlin' and pryin' Quakers that ever set foot in Virginia put together. I reckon you didn't figure on that either?"

"No," I said, looking into his eyes, "if that be true. No."

His voice had risen to a mocking, insistent monotone. "*Christianity!* Rapine, plunder, butchery! Death and destruction! And misery and suffering for untold generations. That was the accomplishment of your Christianity, Reverend. That was the fruits of your mission. And that was the joyous message of your faith. Nineteen hundred years of Christian teaching plus a black preacher is all it takes— Is all it takes to prove that God is a God durned lie!"

He rose to his feet, moving briskly now, his voice softer as he spoke, pulling on his dingy gloves. "Beg pardon, Reverend. I've got to go. No offense. All in all you've been pretty fair and square with me. In spite of what I said, I reckon a man has to act according to his own lights, even when he's the victim of a delusion. Good night, Reverend. I'll look back in on you."

When he had gone Kitchen brought me a pan of cold pork and hoe cake and a cupful of water, and I sat there in the chill dusk, eating, watching the light fall and fade away against the gray sky to the west. Presently I heard Hark on the other side of the wall, laughing softly. "Dat man sho give you down de country, Nat. What dat man so sweat up about?"

But I didn't reply to Hark, rising instead and shuffling the length of the chain to the window.

Over Jerusalem hung a misty nightfall, over the brown and stagnant river and the woods beyond, where the water oak and cypress merged and faded one into the other, partaking like shadows of the somber wintry dusk. In the houses nearby, lamps and lanterns flickered on in yellow flame and far off there was a sound of clattering china and pots and pans and back doors slamming as people went about fixing supper. Way in the distance in some kitchen I could hear a Negro woman singing—a weary sound full of toil and drudgery yet the voice rich, strong, soaring: *I knows moonrise, I knows star-rise, lay dis body down* . . . Already the dusty fall of snow had disappeared; a rime of frost lay in its place, coating the earth with icy wet pinpricks of dew, criss-

crossed by the tracks of squirrels. In chilly promenade two
guards with muskets paced round the jail in greatcoats,
stamping their feet against the brittle ground. A gust of wind
swept through the cell, whistling. I shivered in a spasm of
cold and I closed my eyes, listening to the lament of the
woman far off, leaning up against the window ledge, half
dreaming in a half slumber of mad weariness and longing: *As
the heart panteth after the water brooks, so panteth my soul
after thee, O God. My soul thirsteth for God, for the living
God. Deep calleth unto deep at the noise of thy waterspouts:
all thy waves and thy billows are gone over me* . . .

For what seemed a long time I stood leaning near the
window, my eyes shut tight against the twilight. Maybe he is
right, I thought, maybe all was for nothing, maybe worse
than nothing, and all I've done was evil in the sight of God.
Maybe he is right and God is dead and gone, which is why I
can no longer reach him . . . I opened my eyes again, looking
out into the gloaming light, above the woods where wild
ducks skimmed southward against a sky as gray as smoke.
Yes, I thought, maybe all this is true, otherwise why should
God not heed me, why should he not answer? Still the
woman's rich sweet voice soared through the gathering dusk:
*I walks in de moonlight, walks in de starlight, to lay dis body
down* . . . Grieving, yet somehow unbending, steadfast, un-
afraid, the voice rose through the evening like memory, and a
gust of wind blew up from the river, dimming the song, rustling the trees, then died and became still. *I'll lay in de grave
and stretch out my arms* . . . Suddenly the voice ceased, and
all was quiet.

Then what I done was wrong, Lord? I said. *And if what I
done was wrong, is there no redemption?*

I raised my eyes upward but there was no answer, only
the gray impermeable sky and night falling fast over Jerusalem.

Part

II

OLD

TIMES PAST

Voices, Dreams, Recollections

Part

II

OLD
TIMES PAST

Voices, Dreams, Recollections

✦ ✦ ✦ ✦ ✦ ✦ ✦ ✦ ✦ ✦ ✦ ✦ ✦

ONCE WHEN I WAS A BOY OF TWELVE OR
thereabouts, and living with my mother in the big house at
Turner's Mill, I remember a fat white man who stopped one
night and had supper with my owner of that time, Samuel
Turner. This traveling man was a bluff, hearty soul with a
round red face, cruelly pockmarked, and a booming laugh. A
dealer in farm implements—ploughs and harrows, shares and
cultivators and the like—he traveled up and down the country with several huge wagons and a team of dray horses and a
couple of boys to help him, stopping for the night at this or
that farm or plantation, wherever he happened to be ped-
dling his wares. I no longer recall the man's name (if I ever
knew it) but I do remember the season, which was the beginning of spring. Indeed, it was only what this man said
about the weather and the season that caused me to remember him at all. For that evening in April, I was serving at the
supper table (I had just recently begun this chore; there
were two older Negroes in attendance, but it was my apprentice duty alone to replenish the glasses with cider or buttermilk, to pick up whatever fell to the floor, and to shoo away
the cat and the dogs) and I recollect his voice, very loud but
genial, as he orated to Marse Samuel and the family in the
alien accent of the North: "No, sir, Mr. Turner," he was saying, "they is no spring like it in this great land of ours. They is
nothing what approaches the full springtide when it hits Vir-

ginia. And, sir, they is good reason for this. I have traveled all up and down the seaboard, from the furtherest upper ranges of New England to the hottest part of Georgia, and I know whereof I speak. What makes the Virginia spring surpassing fine? Sir, it is simply this. It is simply that, whereas in more southern climes the temperature is always so humid that spring comes as no surprise, and whereas in more northerly climes the winter becomes so prolonged that they is no spring at all hardly, but runs smack into summer—why, in Virginia, sir, it is unique! It is ideal! Nature has conspired so that spring comes in a sudden warm rush! Alone in the Virginia latitude, sir, is spring like the embrace of a mother's arms!"

I remember this moment with the clarity of a great event which has taken place only seconds ago—the breath of spring still in my nostrils, the dusty evening light still vivid and golden, the air filled with voices and the gentle clash of china and silverware. As the traveling man ceases speaking, the clock in the far hallway lets fall six thudding cast-iron notes, which I hear through the soft yet precisely enunciated cadences of Samuel Turner's own voice: "You are perhaps too complimentary, sir, for spring will soon also bring us a plague of bugs. But the sentiment is well taken, for indeed so far Nature has been kind to us this year. Certainly, I have but rarely seen such ideal conditions for planting."

There is a pause as the sixth and final chime lingers for an instant with a somnolent hum, then dwindles away dully into infinity, while at this same instant I catch sight of myself in the ceiling-high mirror beyond the far sideboard: a skinny undersized pickaninny in a starched white jumper, the toes of one bare foot hooked behind the other leg as I stand wobbling and waiting, eyes rolling white with nervous vigilance. And my eyes return quickly to the table as my owner, for the traveling man's benefit, gestures with his fork in a fond, circular, spacious motion at the family surrounding him: his wife and his widowed sister-in-law, his two young daughters around nineteen or twenty, and his two nephews—grown men of twenty-five or more with rectangular, jut-jawed faces and identical thick necks looming above me, their skin creased and reddened with sun and weather. Samuel Turner's gesture embraces them all; swallowing a bite, he clears his throat elaborately, then continues with warm humor: "Of course, sir, my family here can hardly be expected to welcome such an active time of the year, after a winter of luxurious idleness." There is a sound of laughter, and cries of "Oh, Papa!" and I hear one of the young men call above the sudden clamor: "You slander your industrious nephews, Uncle Sam!" My eyes wander to the traveling man; his red, evilly cratered face is crinkled in jollity, and a trickle of gravy threads its way down the side of his chin. Miss Louisa, the eldest of the daughters, smiles in a vague and pretty way, and blushes, and she lets drop her napkin, which I instantly scurry to retrieve, replacing it upon her lap.

Now in the twilight the merriment slowly subsides, and the conversation proceeds in easy ruminative rhythms, the women silent, the men alone chatting garrulous and full-mouthed as I circle the table with the china pitcher of foaming cider, then return to my station between the two thick-necked nephews, resume my one-legged heron's stance and slowly turn my gaze out into the evening. Beyond the veranda the pasture slopes away green and undulating toward the pinewoods. On the coarse weedy grass a score of sheep munch placidly in the yellow light, trailed by a collie dog and a small, bowlegged Negro shepherdess. Past them, far down the slope where a log road separates the lawn and the looming forest, I can see an empty cart drawn by two flop-eared mules, making its last trip of the day from the storehouse to the mill. On the seat of the cart sits a Negro man, a yellow straw hat raked down upon his head. As I watch, I see that the man is trying to scratch his back, first his left arm snaking up from his waist, then his right arm arching down over his shoulder as the black fingers grope in vain for the source of some intolerable itch. Finally, as the mules plod steadily down the slope and the cart ponderously rocks and veers, the man stands up with a lurching motion and scrapes his back cowlike up and down against the sidepost of the cart.

For some reason, I find this wonderfully amusing and I suddenly am aware that I am giggling to myself, though not so loudly that the white people may notice. Long moments pass as I watch the cart drift rocking across the margin of the woods, the man seated again as cart and mules pass with a distant drumming of hooves and creaking axles over the little bridge then around the murky lower rim of the millpond, where two white swans glide stately and soundless, finally vanishing behind the forest-shadowed white shape of the sawmill with its dull and sluggish rasp of metal-tortured timber drifting up faintly through the dusk: *hrrush, hrrush.* Closer now, the yap of the collie dog starts me out of my daydream, and I turn back to the table and the bright tinkling collision of china and silver, the traveling man's voice broadly ingratiating as he speaks to Marse Samuel: ". . . a new line of sundries this year. Now for instance, I have some pure sea salt from the Eastern Shore of Maryland, for preserving and table use only, sir . . . They is nothing better in the market . . . And so you say they is ten people here, including the overseer and his family? And sixty-eight grown Negroes? Presuming it goes mostly for salt pork then, sir, I should say five sacks will do you nicely, a splendid bargain at thirty-one dollars twenty-five cents . . ."

Now again my mind begins to wander. My thoughts stray outdoors once more where the brilliant fuss of chattering birds intrudes in the fading day—blackbirds and robins, finches and squawking jays, and somewhere far off above the bottomlands the noise of some mean assembly of crows, their calls echoing venturesome and conniving and harsh. Again the scene outside captures my attention, so now slowly and with irresistible pleasure I turn to gaze at the coarse green slope with its slant of golden light and its nimble bustle of many wings, the flower bed only feet away ferny and damp with the odor of new-turned earth. The little black bow-legged shepherdess has vanished from the pasture, sheep and collie too, leaving behind a haze of dust to tremble in the evening light. Rising on fat whirlpools of air, this haze fills the sky like the finest sawdust. In the distance the mill still rasps with a steady husking noise above the monotonous roar of water from the sluiceway. Two huge dragonflies dart across the evening, wild and iridescent, a swift flash of trans-parency. *Springtime*. Worried that my excitement will show, I feel my limbs stretch and quiver with a lazy thrill. A sense of something quickening, a voluptuous stirring courses gently through my flesh. I hear the blood pulsing within me like some imagined wash of warm oceanic tides. In my mind I echo the traveling man's words—*Full springtide, spring, spring*, I find myself whispering to myself—and this awaken-ing brings to my lips the shadow of a grin. I feel half stunned, my eyes roll like marbles. I am filled with inexplicable happi-ness and a sense of tantalizing promise.

As the traveling man's voice drifts back into hearing, I turn again and feel the gaze of my mistress, Miss Nell, upon me, and I look up then and see her mouth forming the whis-pered word "cider." I grasp the heavy pitcher with two hands and again make my circuit of the table, filling the glasses of the women first, taking pains that not a drop is spilled. My care is meticulous. I hold my breath until the edge of the table swims dizzily before my eyes. Now finally I am at the elbow of the traveling man, who, as I serve him, ceases his talk of commerce long enough to look down at me and good-naturedly exclaim: "Well, I'll be durned if that crock ain't bigger than you are!" I am only half aware that he is address-ing these words to me, and I am unconcerned as I pour the cider, replace the glass, and continue my tour around the table. "Cute little nipper too," the traveling man adds in an offhand tone, but again I make no connection between myself and what is said until now, drawing near to Miss Nell, I hear her voice, gentle and indulgent as it descends from the rare white prodigous atmosphere above me: "And smart, you wouldn't believe! Spell something, Nat." And then to the traveling man: "Ask him something to spell."

Suddenly I am fastened to my tracks and I feel my heart beat wildly as I realize that I am the focus of all eyes. The pitcher in my hands is as heavy as a boulder. He beams down at me; the radish-red broad cheeks are all benevolence as the man pauses, reflects, then says: "Can you spell 'lady'?" But abruptly, before I can reply, I hear Samuel Turner interrupt, amused: "Oh *no*, something difficult!" And the traveling man scratches the side of his pitted face, still beaming: "Oh well," he says, "let's see, some kind of flower . . . 'Columbine.' Spell 'columbine.' " And I spell it, without effort and instantly but in a pounding fury of embarrassment, the pulse roaring in my ears as the letters tumble forth in a galloping rush: ". . . i-n-e, spells *columbine!*" And the laughter at the table that follows this, and a shrill echo from the walls, makes me realize in dismay that I am yelling at the top of my lungs.

"It is I am sure a kind of unorthodoxy, and considered thus by some," I hear my master say (I resume my station, still flustered and with a madly working heart), "but it is my conviction that the more religiously and intellectually enlightened a Negro is made, the better for himself, his master, and the commonweal. But one must begin at a tender age, and thus, sir, you see in Nat the promising beginnings of an experiment. Of course, it is late for this child, compared with white children, yet . . ." As I listen to him speak, not completely comprehending the words, my panic and embarrassment (which had been made up in equal parts of childish self-consciousness and terror at the thought that I might publicly fail) diminish, fade away, and in their place I feel stealing over me a serene flow of pride and accomplishment: after all, I may have been a loudmouth, but I did know the word, and I sensed in the sunny laughter a laurel, a tribute. All of a sudden the secret pleasure I take in my exploit is like a delectable itch within, and though my expression in the mirror is glum, abashed, and my pink lips are persimmon-sour, I can hear my insides stirring. I feel wildly alive. I shiver feverishly in the glory of self.

But I seem to be quickly forgotten, for now the traveling man is again talking of his wares: "It is the Carey plough, sir, of stout cast iron, and I calculate it will supplant all ploughs presently in the market. They has been a big demand for it in the Northern states . . ." Yet even as he talks and my thoughts wander astray again, the proud glow of achievement hangs on, and I am washed by a mood of contentment and snug belonging so precious that I could cry out for the joy of it. Nor does it go away. It is a joy that remains even as the pinewoods begin to crowd ragged trembling shadows into the deserted pasture, and a horn blows far off, long and lonesome-sounding, summoning the Negroes from the mill and the distant fields. As abruptly as some interrupted human grumble, the sawmill ceases its harsh rasp and husk, and for a moment the silence is like a loud noise in my ears. Now twilight deepens over the meadow, where bats no bigger than sparrows are flickering and darting in the dusk, and I can see through the evening shadows in the distance a line of Negro men trooping up from the mill toward the cabins, their faces black and barely visible but their voices rising and falling, wearily playful with intermittent cries of laughter as they move homeward with the languid, shuffling, shoulder-bent gait of a long day's toil. Snatches of their talk rise up indistinctly across the field, sounds of gentle, tired skylarking in the twilight: "*Hoo-dar*, Simon! . . . *Shee-it*, nigger! . . . Cotch you, fo' sho!" Quickly I turn away (could there have been a whiff of something desperate and ugly in that long file of

sweating, weary men which upsets my glowing childish
housebound spirit, disturbs the beatitude of that April
dusk?) and circle the table with my pitcher one last time
while the two other Negro house servants, Little Morning
and Prissy, clear away the dishes and light thick candles on
pewter candelabra that fill the darkening room with a
pumpkin-hued glow.

My master is talking now, his chair pushed back, the
thumbs of both hands hooked in the pockets of his vest. He is
in his early forties (to be precise, he will be forty-three at five-
thirty in the morning on the twelfth day of the coming June,
according to one or another of the old house servants, who
know more about the events in white people's lives than white
people do themselves) but he looks older—perhaps only to
me, however, since I hold him in such awe that I am forced
to regard him, physically as well as spiritually, in terms of the
same patriarchal and venerable grandeur that glows forth
from those Bible pictures of Moses on the mount, or an ancient Elijah exploding in bearded triumph at the transfigura-
tion of Christ. Even so, the wrinkles around his mouth are
early; he has worked hard, and this accounts for those lines
and for the cheek whiskers which end in small tufts whiter
than a cottontail's butt. "Ugly as a mushrat," my mother has
said of him, and perhaps this is true: the angular face is too
long and horselike, the nose too prominent and beaked, and,
as my mother also has observed, "Lawd didn't leave Marse
Sam a whole lot of jawbone." So much for my master's chin.
But his eyes are kindly, shrewd, luminous; there is still
strength in his face, tempered by a curious, abiding sweetness
that causes him ever to seem on the verge of a rueful smile.
At this time, my regard for him is very close to the feeling
one should bear only toward the Divinity.

"Let us adjourn to the veranda," he says to the traveling
man, pushing back his chair. "We usually retire more or less
promptly at eight, but tonight you and I will share a bottle of

port while we make out a requisition for my needs." His hand falls lightly on the shoulder of the traveling man, who is rising now. "I hope you will forgive me if it sounds presumptuous," he continues, "and it is a most unusual thing for me to say, but for a peddler who has the difficulties of so much travel, you sell an extremely reliable line of wares. And this, sir, as you must be aware, is of the greatest importance in a region like ours, removed so far from the centers of commerce. Since last year I have taken the opportunity of commending you to my friends." The traveling man shines with pleasure, wheezing a little as he bows to the women and the young men, then moves on toward the door. "Well, thank you, sir . . ." he begins, but my owner's voice interrupts, not rude, not even abrupt, but in continuation of his praise: "So that they shall be as satisfied as I have been in the past. And what did you say was your tomorrow's destination? Greensville County? Then you must stop by Robert Munson's place on the Meherrin River . . ."

The voices fade, and while I busy myself around the table, helping the old man Little Morning and the young woman Prissy clear the dishes, the rest of the family rises, slowly scattering in the last brief hours before bedtime: the two nephews to attend to a mare ready to foal, Miss Nell to take a poultice to a sick Negro child in the cabins, the three other women—all astir with gay anticipation as they bustle toward the parlor—to read aloud from something they call *Marmion*. Then these voices too fade away, and I am back in the kitchen again amid the clumping of crudely shod Negro feet and the sharp stench of a ham hock steaming on the stove, back with my tall, beautiful mother banging and grumbling in a swirl of greasy smoke—" 'Thaniel, you better get dat butter down in de cellar lak I told you!" she calls to me—back in my black Negro world . . .

But that evening in the early darkness while I lie awake on my straw bed, the word *columbine* is like a lullaby on my tongue. I caress the word, whispering it over and over again, letting each letter form its own shape, as if suspended magically above me in the night. I lie at the drowsy edge of sleep, listening to the sounds of evening, to the feathery fuss and clumsy stir of chickens in their shed, a far-off howling dog, and from the millpond a steady passionate shrilling of frogs numberless as stars. All around me the smell of manure is rank and strong like the earth itself. Presently I hear my mother's footsteps as she moves with a tired *slat-slat* of bare calloused feet from the kitchen, enters our tiny room, and lies down beside me in the dark. Almost at once she is fast asleep, breathing in a gentle rhythm, and I reach out and lightly touch the rough cotton shift above her ribs, to make certain that she is there. Then at last the spring night enfolds me as if with swamp and cedar and with drowsy remembrance, and dimly I hear a whippoorwill call through the dark, the word *columbine* still on my lips as I sink away into some strange dream filled with inchoate promise and a voiceless, hovering joy.

It was memories like this which stayed with me all through the few days left until my death. During the night just after the trial I came down with some kind of fever, and when I awoke the next morning my arms and legs were trembling with the cold, even though I was soaked in sweat and my head was afire and swollen with pain. The wind had risen and in the sunless morning light, pale as water, a blast of cold air howled through the open window, bringing with it a storm of gritty dust and pine needles and flying leaves. I started to call out to Kitchen, to ask him to fetch a blanket to stop up the window, but then I thought better of it, remained quiet: the white boy was still too scared of me even to answer. So again I lay back against the plank, shivering, and fell into a feverish doze when once more I was lying in the little boat, my spirit filled with a familiar yet mysterious peace as I drifted through the afternoon quiet of some wide and sunlit river toward the sea. In the distance I heard the ocean booming with the sound of mighty unseen breakers crashing on the shore. Far above me on its promontory stood the white temple, as ever serene and solitary and majestic, the sunlight bathing it as if with the glow of some great mystery as I moved on downriver past it, without fear, to the sandy cape and the tumultuous groaning sea . . . Then this vision glimmered out and I awoke, raging with fever, and I fell asleep again, only to awake sometime later in the day with the fever diminishing and my brow cold and dry and the remnant of something frail and unutterably sweet, like a bird call, lingering in my memory. Then not very long after this the fever commenced again and my mind was a wash and flow of nightmares, nightmares filled with unending moments of suffocation . . .

And so in this way, between waking and oblivion, with these reveries, voices, recollections, I passed the days and nights before the day of my execution . . .

My mother's mother was a girl of the Coromantee tribe from the Gold Coast, thirteen years old when she was brought in chains to Yorktown aboard a schooner sailing out of Newport, Rhode Island, and only a few months older when she was sold at auction beneath a huge live oak tree in the harborside town of Hampton, to Alpheus Turner, who was Samuel Turner's father. I never laid eyes on my grandmother —nor for that matter a Coromantee girl—but over the years I heard about her and her kind, and in my mind's eye it is easy to see her as she squats beneath the live oak tree so many years ago, swelled up with child, panting in a slow fright, lifting her face slightly at Alpheus Turner's approach to reveal a mouth full of filed teeth and raised tattoos like whorls of scattered birdshot on her cheeks, patterns blacker even than her tar-black skin. Who knows what she is thinking at

the moment Turner draws near? Although his face is illumined by a beneficent smile, to her it is a fiendish smirk,
and besides he is white, white as bone or skulls or deadwood,
whiter than those malevolent ancestral ghosts that prowl the
African night. And his voice is the voice of a ghoul. *"Gnah!"*
he roars as he touches her, feeling the soundness of her limbs.
"Fwagh!" He is saying only "Good!" and "Fine!" to the trader,
but in her terror she believes she is about to be eaten. The
poor thing nearly takes leave of her senses. She falls from her
perch on the block and her mind reels back in space and time
toward some childhood jungle memory of warm, enveloping
peace. As she lies asprawl, the dealer's line of talk is to her a
witch doctor's jabber of disconnected croaking sounds, having to do with ritual chops and stews. "They all take such
fright, Mr. Turner, never mind! A fine little heifer! Aye, look
at them fat tits! Look how they spring! I'll wager she pops a
ten-pound boy!"

But that same summer it was my mother who was born
(publicly begat upon the same slave ship by some unknown
black father) and it became well known around Turner's Mill
that when my young grandmother—who by this time had
been driven crazy by her baffling captivity—gave birth to my
mother, she was sent into a frenzy, and when presented with
the babe, tried to tear it to pieces.

I expect that if my grandmother had not died soon after
this, I would have later become a field or timber hand at the
Turner place, or maybe a mill hand, which was only a small
cut better. But on account of my grandmother I was lucky
and became a house nigger. My grandmother died within
days of my mother's birth, refusing to eat, falling into a
stupor until the moment of her last breath, when it was said
that the black skin turned to the gray of ashes, collapsing in
upon the inhabiting bones until the body of the child (for
that is what she was) seemed so fragile as to be almost

weightless, like a whitened, burnt-out stick of lightwood ready to crumble at the softest touch. For years there was a cedar headboard in the Negro graveyard, not far from the mill, with carved letters which read:

"TIG"
AET. 13
BORN AN
HEATHEN
DIED BAP-
TISED IN CHRIST
A.D. 1782
R.I.P.

That graveyard is in an abandoned corner of a meadow, hard by a scrubby grove of juniper trees and loblolly pine. A plain pole fence, dilapidated to begin with but long since fallen into splintery ruin, sets off the place from the rest of the field; many of the headboards have toppled over to rot and mingle with the loamy earth, while in the spring those that remain become half hidden in a jungle of wild coarse greenery—skunk cabbage and cinnamon fern and a prickly tangle of jimson weed. In the summer the underbrush grows so thickly that you can no longer see the mounds where the Negroes are laid to rest. Grasshoppers sail through the weeds with small scaly whickerings, and ever so often a blacksnake slithers among the green, and on August days the odor is ripe and rank and very close, like a hot handful of grass. "How come you all de time studyin' dat grabeyard, 'Thaniel?" my mother says. "Ain't no place fo' chillun to go studyin' 'bout." And it is true: most of the Negroes avoid the place, filled with superstitious dread, and this in some measure (the rest being lack of time; attention to the dead requires leisure) is the reason for the unsightly disrepair. But there is a left-over savage part of me that feels very close to my grand-mother, and for a couple of years I am drawn irresistibly back to the graveyard, and often I steal away from the big house during the hot break after midday dinner, as if seeking among all those toppled and crumbling wood markers with their roll call of sweetly docile and abbreviated names like so many perished spaniels—"Peak" and "Lulu" and "Yellow Jake"—some early lesson in mortality. How strange it is, after all, at age thirteen to ponder the last resting place of your own grandmother, dead at thirteen herself . . .

But the next spring it is all gone. A new graveyard will be laid out at the edge of the woods, but before that—because it is drained and level and easy to get at—even this tiny remnant of crop land is needed, to raise sweet potatoes. I am filled with wonderment at how quickly the graveyard vanishes. It takes less than half a morning—burnt off by a gang of black field hands with casks of turpentine and blazing pine fagots, the weatherworn cedar headboards consumed by flame, the dry underbrush crackling and hissing as the bugs spring up in a swarm and the field mice scuttle away, the cooling black char leveled down by mule team and harrow, so that nothing remains of "Tig," not the faintest trace nor any vestige of the rest—of the muscle, sleep, laughter, footsteps, grimy toil and singing and madness of all those black unremembered servitors whose shaken bones and dust, joining my grandmother's in the general clutter underground, are now made to complete the richness of the earth. Only when I hear a voice—the voice of a Negro man, an old field hand standing by amid the swirling smoke, slope-shouldered, loose-lipped, grinning with a mouthful of blue gums, gabbling in that thick gluey cornfield accent I have learned to despise: "Dem old dead peoples is sho gwine grow a nice passel of yams!"—only when I hear this voice do I begin to realize, for nearly the very first time, what the true value of black folk is, not just for white men but for niggers.

So because my mother was motherless, Alpheus Turner brought her up out of the cabins and into his own home, where she was reared by a succession of black aunts and grannies who taught her nigger-English and some respectable graces and where, when she grew old enough, she became a scullery maid and then a cook, and a good cook to boot. Her name was Lou-Ann, and she died when I was fifteen, of some kind of tumor. But I am ahead of myself. What matters here is that the same happenstance that caused my mother to be brought up in Alpheus Turner's house caused me in the course of events to become a house nigger, too. And that may or may not have been a fortunate circumstance, depending upon how you view what came to pass in Jerusalem so many years later.

"Quit *pesterin'* 'bout yo' daddy," says my mother. "What make you think *I* knows where he done run off to? What his name? I done tol' you dat twenty times. He name Nathaniel jes' like you! I done tol' you dat, now quit pesterin' 'bout yo' daddy! When he run off? When de las' time I seen him? Law me, chile, dat so long ago I ain't got no rec'lection. Les' see. Well, Marse Alpheus he died 'leven years ago, bless his name. And seem lak 'twarn't but a year after dat when me an' yo' daddy was cou'tin'. Now dere was some fine-lookin' man! Marse Alpheus done bought him in Petersburg fo' to work strippin' logs in de mill. But yo' daddy he too smart fo' dat kind of low nigger work. And he too good-lookin', too, wid dem flashin' bright eyes, and a smile—why, chile, yo' daddy had a smile dat would light up a barn! No, he too good fo' dat low kind of work, so Marse Alpheus he brung up yo' daddy to de big house and commenced him into buttlin'. Yes, he was de number-two butteler helpin' out Little Mornin' when first I knowed yo' daddy. Dat was de year before Marse Alpheus died. And me an' yo' daddy lived right here together dat time—a whole year it was—right in dis room . . .

"But quit *pesterin'* 'bout dat, I tells you, boy! How I know *where* he done run off to? I don' know nothin' 'tall 'bout dat mess. Why sho he was angered! Ain't no black man goin' run off less'n he's angered! Why? How I know? I don' know nothin' 'bout dat mess. Well, awright, den, if you really wants to know, 'twas on account of Marse Benjamin. Like I tol' you, when Marse Alpheus die 'twas Marse Benjamin come to own ev'ything on account of he was de oldest son. He five years older dan Marse Samuel so he gits to own ev'ything, I mean de house an' de mill an' de land an' de niggers an' ev'ything. Well, Marse Benjamin he a good massah jes' like Marse Alpheus, only he kind of young an' he don' know how to talk to de niggers like his daddy. I don' mean he nasty or wicked or nothin' like dat; no, he jes' don' know how to ack *easy* with nobody—I means white folks *an'* niggers. Anyways, one evenin' yo' daddy he buttlin' at de table an' he do somethin' dat Marse Benjamin think ain't quite right an' he *hollers* at yo' daddy. Well, yo' daddy he ain't used to havin' no one *holler* at him like dat, an' he turns aroun' still smilin', see—he always smilin', dat man—an' he mock Marse Benjamin right back. Marse Benjamin he done said somethin' like, 'Nathaniel, dis yere silver is filthy!' An' yo' daddy, he say: 'Yes, dis yere silver is filthy!' Only he *hollerin'* at Marse Benjamin back, smilin' jes' as pretty as you please. Well, Marse Benjamin he jes' fit to be tied, an' he gits up right dere in front of Miss Elizabeth an' Miss Nell an' Marse Samuel and all de chilluns—dey jes' young things den, 'bout yo' age—and what he does, he whops yo' daddy across de mouf with his hand. Dat's all he does. One time—he jus' whop him one time across de mouf an' den he sit down. I'se lookin' in at de door by dat time an' all de family's in an awful commotion at de table, Marse Samuel stewin' an' fussin' an' sayin' to Marse Benjamin, 'Lawd knows he was uppity but you didn' have to whop him like that!' an' all, an' de chilluns all a-cryin', leastwise de girls. 'Cause you see, Marse Alpheus he didn' like to smite no niggers anyways an' he never done it much, but whenever he done it he always took keer to do it way off in de woods out of sight of de white folks an' de black folks, too. So

de fambly dey ain't never seen a black man hit. But dat ain't
no nem'mine fo' yo' daddy. He jes' come on out of dere and he
march straight through de kitchen with dis yere smile still on
his face an' a little bitty strick of blood rollin' down his lip,
an' he jes' keep marchin' on back to de room where we stays
at—dis yere room right yere, chile!—an' he packs up some
food in a sack, an' dat night he done light out fo' good . . .

"Where he done went to? How I know 'bout dat? You
says on account of you'd like to find him! Lawd, chile, ain't
nobody goin' find dat black man after all dese many years.
What you say? Didn' he say nothin', nothin' at all? Why sho
he did, chile. An' ev'ytime I thinks of it my heart is near 'bout
broke in two. Said he couldn' stand to be hit in de face by
nobody. Not *nobody!* Oh yes, dat black man had pride,
awright, warn't many black mens aroun' like him! And lucky
too, why, he must had him a whole bag full of rabbit foots!
Ain't many niggers run off dat dey don' soon cotch someways.
But I don' know. Said he was goin' run off to Philadelphia,
Pennsylvania, and make him lots of money an' den come back
an' buy me an' you into freedom. But Lawd, chile! Philadelphia, Pennsylvania, dey say dat's a misery long ways off from
here an' I don' know where yo' daddy ever went."

Two hundred yards or so behind the room where my
mother and I stay, at the end of a path through the back
meadow, is the ten-hole privy shared by the house servants
and the mill hands living in the compound of cabins near the
big house. Sturdily built of oak and set above the steeply
sloping bank of a wooded ravine, the privy is divided by a
board partition; five holes are for women and small children,
the other five are for the men. Because the big house is isolated from mill and field, and because the affairs of house
servants transpire as if in a world apart, this privy is one of
the few places where my daily life intersects with the lives of
those Negroes who already I have come to think of as a lower

order of people—a ragtag mob, coarse, raucous, clownish, uncouth. For even now as a child I am contemptuous and aloof, filled with disdain for the black riffraff which dwells beyond the close perimeter of the big house—the faceless and nameless toilers who at daybreak vanish into the depths of the mill or into the fields beyond the woods, returning like shadows at sundown to occupy their cabins like so many chickens gone to weary roost. Most of my way of thinking is due to my mother. It is the plague of her life that amidst so many other comparative comforts she must still make that regular trek to the edge of the ravine and there mingle with the noisy rabble so beneath her. "Hit's a shame in dis world," she fusses to Prissy. "Us folks in de house is *quality!* And we ain't got no outhouse for our own selfs, hit's a cryin' shame! I'll vow dem cornfield niggers is de akshul *limit.* Ev'y one dem chillun dey lets pee on de seat, and don' none of 'em close down dem lids, so's it stinks like misery. Druther go to de privy settin' 'longside some ole sow dan one dem cornfield nigger womans! Us house folks is *quality!*"

Equally disdainful, I avoid the morning rush, training my bowels to obey a later call when I can enjoy some privacy. The earth around the entrance to the men's side (which I have used since I was five) is bare of vegetation, black hard clay worn glossy smooth by the trample of numberless bare or broganed feet, imprinted daily with a shifting pattern of booted heels and naked toes. Designed to prevent either malingering or seclusion—like the doors to all places frequented by Negroes—the privy door too is lockless, latchless, swinging outward easily on leather hinges to reveal the closet within drowned in shadows, almost completely dark save for slivers of light stealing in through the cracks between the timbers. I am used to the odor, which is ripe, pungent, immediate, smothering my nose and mouth like a warm green hand, the excremental stench partly stifled by quicklime, so that the smell is not so much repellent to me as endurable, faintly sweetish like stagnant swampwater. I raise one oval lid and seat myself on the pine plank above the hole. Between my thighs light floods up from the slope of the ravine and I look downward at the vast brown stain splashed with the white of quicklime. I sit here for long minutes, in the cool beatitude and calm of morning. Outside, somewhere in the woods, a mockingbird begins a chant which ripples and flows like rushing water, ceases, commences again, falls ineffable and pure through the tangle of grapevine and the honeysuckle and the tree-shadowed thickets of ivy and fern. Here within, amid the sun-splashed gloom, I relieve myself in pleasant unhurried spasms, contemplating a blackberry-sized spider weaving in one corner of the ceiling a thick web which shakes, stretches, trembles in milky agitation. Now through the walls of the privy, from the distant back porch of the big house, I hear my mother calling. " 'Thaniel!" she cries. "You, Nathaniel! Nathan-*yel!* You, boy! *Better come on here!*" I have dallied too long, she wants me near the kitchen to fetch water. "Nathaniel Turner! *You,* boy!" she cries. The mood of contentment dwindles away, the morning ritual nears its end. I reach out toward a tattered sack on the floor —a croker sack filled with corncobs . . .

All of a sudden a searing heat seizes me from underneath; my bare bottom and balls feel set on fire and I leap up from the seat with a howl, clutching at my scorched nether parts while smoke floats up through the hole in a greasy white billow. "Ow! *Ow!* Dag*gone!*" I shout, but it is mainly from surprise—surprise and mortification. For even as I cry out, the pain diminishes and I gaze back down through the hole, beholding the grinning light-brown face of a boy my age. He stands off at the edge of the mire below, grasping in one hand a blazing stick. With his other hand he is clutching his stomach in an agony of delight, and his laughter is high, loud, irrepressible. "Daggone you, Wash!" I yell. "Jest daggone yo' no-good black soul!" But my rage is in vain, and Wash keeps

laughing, doubled up amid the honeysuckle. It is the third
time in as many months that he has tricked me thus, and I
have no one but myself to blame for my humiliation.

THE LIFE AND DEATH
OF
MR. BADMAN

PRESENTED TO THE WORLD IN

A FAMILIAR DIALOGUE BETWEEN
MR. WISEMAN
&
MR. ATTENTIVE

❡ WISEMAN. Good morrow, my good neighbour,
Mr. Attentive; whither are you walking so early
this morning? Methinks you look as if you were
concerned about something more than ordinary.
Have you lost any of your cattle, or what is the
matter?

❡ ATTENTIVE. Good sir, good morrow to you. I
have not as yet lost aught, but yet you give a right
guess of me, for I am, as you say, concerned in
my heart, but it is because of the badness of the
times. And, Sir, you, as all our neighbours know,
are a very observing man, pray, therefore, what
do you think of them?

❡ WISE. Why, I think, as you say, to wit, that
they are bad times, and bad they will be, until
men are better; for they are bad men that make
bad times; if men, therefore, would mend, so
would the times. It is a folly to look for good
days so long as sin is so high, and those that
study its nourishment so many . . .

The life of a little nigger child is dull beyond recounting.
But during one summer month when I am nine or ten a cou-

ple of curious events happen to me, one causing me the bitterest anguish, the other premonitions of joy.

It is midmorning in August, hot and stifling, so airless that the dust-stained trees along the edge of the distant woods hang limp and still, and the grinding of the mill seems blurred, indistinct, as if borne sluggishly through heat waves trembling like water above the steaming earth. High in the blue heavens, buzzards by the score wheel and tilt and swoop in effortless flight over the bottomlands, and I lift my eyes from time to time to follow their somber course across the sky. I squat in the shadow of the little room projecting from the kitchen, where my mother and I live. From the kitchen comes the odor of collard greens cooking, the smell faintly bitter and pungent; midday dinner is far off, I feel my insides churning with hunger. Although I am not underfed (to be the child of the cook is to be, as my mother constantly points out, the "luckiest little nigger 'live") I seem nonetheless to exist at the edge of famine. On the sill of the kitchen window above me, a row of muskmelons, half a dozen pale globes, stand ripening in the shade, unattainable as gold. I consider them gravely and with a yearning that brings water to my eyes, knowing that even to touch one of them would fetch upon me calamity like the crack of doom. Once I stole a pot of clabber cheese, and the walloping my mother gave me left me sore as a carbuncle.

It is my duty to wait here near the door, to carry water and bring up things from the cellar, to run errands for my mother whenever she commands. My chores today are light, for it is a slack moment in the year when the corn crop has been laid by awaiting harvest and the mill works at half-time. During such a lull it has always been the custom of the brothers Turner, together with their wives and children, to make their annual trip to Richmond, leaving the place for a week or so in the hands of the overseer. Since with the family away my mother has only to cook for ourselves and the house servants—Prissy and Little Morning and Weaver and Pleasant—time hangs heavy for me, and the boredom is like a knife-edge at the back of my skull. It is not an unusual situation, because for a Negro child, denied the pleasures of schooling, there is generally nothing to do, nothing at all; reading no books, taught no real games, until twelve or so too small to work, black children exist in a monotony like that of yearling mules at pasture, absorbing the sun, feeding, putting on flesh, all unaware that soon they will be borne down for life with harness, chain, and traces.

My own condition is more than unusually solitary, since the Turner children with whom I might ordinarily be expected to play are a good deal older than I, and either help run the plantation or are off at school; at the same time, I feel myself set apart from the other Negro children, the children of the field hands and mill hands who are so scorned by my mother. Even Wash (who is the son of one of the two Negro drivers, Abraham—almost the only Turner slave with any responsibility at all) I have drawn away from as I have grown older, in spite of the fact that his circumstances put him a notch above the common cornfield type. At six or seven we played crude games together—climbed trees, hunted for caves in the dark ravine, swung on grapevines at the edge of the woods. Leaning over the brink of the ravine, we tried to see who could pee the farthest. Once we stood in a shadowed clearing near the swamp, and with skinny black arms outstretched, in self-inflicted torture, marveled as a swarm of fat mosquitoes engorged themselves on our blood, finally dropping to earth like tiny red grapes. We built a fort of mud and then smeared our naked bodies with the liquid clay; drying, it became encrusted, a dull calcimine, ghostly, and we howled in mad delight at our resemblance to white boys. Once we dared to steal ripe persimmons from the tree growing behind Wash's cabin, and were caught in the act by his mother—a light West Indian woman, part Creole, with black ringlets around her head like writhing wet serpents—and were thrashed with a sassafras switch until the welts stood up on our legs. Wash's sister had a doll that Abraham had made for her; fashioned of jute sacking, its head was an old split maple doorknob. Whether it was meant to be a white baby or a nigger child I could never tell, but I regarded it with wonder; aside from a cast-off cracked wooden top I had gotten at Christmas from one of the young Turners, it was the first toy I can remember. On gray winter days when rain streamed from the heavens, Wash and I crouched in the poultry shed, with pointed sticks tracing patterns upon the white damp crust of chickenshit. For a while it became my favorite kind of play. I drew rectangles, circles, squares, and I marveled at the way two triangles placed together in a certain way formed that mysterious star I had seen so often when (curiosity getting the better of me as I trailed my mother through Samuel Turner's library) I risked a glimpse of the pictures in a gigantic Bible:

I scratched this design over and over again on the lime-cool, bittersweet-smelling white floor of the chicken shed, a hundred interlocking stars engraved in the dust, quite heedless of Wash, who stirred and fidgeted and mumbled to himself, bored quickly, unable to draw anything but aimless lines.

But these were dumb little games, the brainless play of kittens. As I grow older now there steals over me the understanding that Wash has almost no words to speak at all. So near to the white people, I absorb their language daily. I am a tireless eavesdropper, and their talk and comment, even their style of laughter, vibrates endlessly in my imagination. Already my mother teases me for the way I parrot white folks' talk—teases me with pride. Wash is molded by different sounds—even now I am aware of this—nigger voices striving clumsily to grapple with a language never taught, never really learned, still alien and unknown. With such a poor crippled tongue, Wash's way of speaking comes to seem to me a hopeless garble, his mind a tangle of baby-thoughts; so gradually that I barely know it, this playmate floats away out of my consciousness, dwarfish and forgotten, as I settle deep into my own silent, ceaselessly vigilant, racking solitude.

I cannot as yet read *The Life and Death of Mr. Badman,* not even the title; my possession of it terrifies me, because I have stolen it, yet at the same instant the very idea of the book fevers me with such insupportable excitement that I can feel a loosening in my bowels. (Although I have come late to the joys of reading and still cannot properly "read," I have known the crude shapes of simple words ever since I was six, when Samuel Turner, a methodical, tidy, and organized master, and long impatient with baking alum turning into white flour and cinnamon being confused with nutmeg, and vice versa, set about labeling every chest and jar and canister and keg and bag in the huge cellar beneath the kitchen where my mother dispatched me hourly every day. It seemed not to matter to him that upon the Negroes—none of whom could read—these hieroglyphs in red paint would have no effect at all: still Little Morning would be forced to dip a probing brown finger in the keg plainly marked MOLASSES, and even so there would be lapses, with salt served to sweeten the breakfast tea. Nonetheless, the system satisfied Samuel Turner's sense of order, and although at that time he was unaware of my existence, the neat plain letters outlined by the glow of an oil lamp in the chill vault served as my first and only primer. It was a great leap from MINT and CITRON and SALTPETRE and BACON to *The Life and Death of Mr. Badman,* but there exists both a frustration and a surfeit

when one's entire literature is the hundred labels in a dim
cellar, and my desire to possess the book overwhelmed my
fear. Even so, it had been a dismal moment. In Samuel
Turner's library, where my mother had gone to fetch a new
silver ladle for the kitchen, the books had been locked up
behind wire, row after row of lustrous leather-swaddled
volumes imprisoned as in a cage. On the morning I accompanied her there, I lingered long enough to be captured by
the sight of two volumes, almost exactly alike in size and
shape, lying together on a table. Opening one of them, seeing
that it was aswarm with words, I was seized with the old
queasy excitement in my guts, and fright clashed with greedy
desire. My yearning won out, however, so that later that day
I crept back to the library and took the book, covering it with
a flour sack and leaving behind its companion—something
which I later learned was called *Grace Abounding*. Just as I
had expected, and to my wild anxiety, the fact that the book
was missing was gossiped throughout the house. Yet I was
not alarmed as I might have been, since I think I must have
instinctively reasoned that although white people will rightly
suspect a nigger of taking almost anything that is not nailed
down, they would certainly not suspect him of taking a
book.)

This morning, squatting in the shadow of the kitchen, I
think longingly of *The Life and Death of Mr. Badman,* wondering if I can summon the courage to remove it from its
hiding place and try to read it without being found out. Finally I get up and sidle toward the place where it is hidden. I
have stored the book underneath the house—part of which is
elevated above the ground—in a dark shelflike recess formed
by one of the great oak sills. There spiders stir in the gloom
and in the dim light hundreds of flying ants swarm in a pale
flutter of brownish transparent wings. Protected by its flour
sack, *The Life and Death of Mr. Badman* reposes in the dark.
I creep forward on my knees a yard or so, reach up and

remove the sack, then inch back toward the edge of the house where a splash of sunshine falls on the damp bare earth. Here I turn about and sit down with my legs crossed. I open the book and sunlight floods the white page, hurting my eyes. It. is cool here, with a ferny smell of dampness, and mosquitoes moon about my ears as I begin my laborious journey through a wild strange country where words of enraging size, black and incomprehensible, blossom like poisonous flowers. My lips move silently, I trace sentences with a quivering finger. Thick words with mysterious syllables, lugubrious and fathomless, obstruct my way like great logs and boulders; small words are no better, obdurate as hickory nuts. I press on in despair, searching for the key, hunting for the soft and sweetly familiar, SUGAR, GINGER, CAPSICUM, CLOVES.

Suddenly I hear footsteps stamping up the dirt path from the cabins and I draw back underneath the house, hidden again, watching. It is the black driver, Abraham. A stout, muscular Negro, very dark, he is dressed in the green denim shirt which is the badge of his authority; he hurries along up the path, sweating in the fierce morning heat, a set, stern, indignant look frozen on his face as his brogaged feet tramp the ground inches from where I lay in hiding and then clatter up the back steps into the kitchen. Moments pass and I am aware of nothing. Soon I steal out toward the patch of sunlight again, preparing myself to read, when now I hear voices from up above, in the alcove between the kitchen and the pantry. Abraham is talking to my mother and his tone is agitated, tense, severe.

"You better *had*," he is saying, "you better jes' *had*, Lou-Ann. Dat man he mean as pizen! I knows. You better light on out ob here!"

"*Shoot*," I hear my mother say, "dat man ain't no trouble. He gib me a bad time an' I smack him one wid dis yere kettle—"

"But you ain't seed him dis time!" Abraham breaks in. "He

worse'n I ever seed! An' ain't no fambly folks aroun' to say ary
word! I jes' tellin' you, Lou-Ann, dat's all I got to say!"

"*Shoot*, he ain't goin' gib Lou-Ann no bad time. Leastwise
not today . . ."

I hear them move from the alcove, the footsteps shuffling
on the timbers above my head, their voices becoming indistinct. Presently they are silent and then I hear the door slam
open and Abraham's heavy tread as he thunders down the
back stoop and past me once more, his feet sending up small
puffs of dust, half trotting now in the direction of the mill.

The mystery, and my perplexity, last only a moment. As
soon as Abraham has vanished around the corner of the stable, I sidle out on my behind again to the edge of the house,
throwing open the book. The morning is still once more.
While I bend my head down to study the open page, my
mother begins to sweep in the kitchen above. I hear the
steady *whisk-whisk* of the straw broom on the floor, then the
sound of her voice, so faint that I can barely make it out, as
she commences a lonesome song.

> "Bow low, Mary, bow low, Martha,
> For Jesus come and lock de do',
> An' carry de keys away . . ."

The song lulls and distracts me, draws me away for a
moment from the maddening printed lines. I listen to her
sing, and my head falls slowly against a cedar post of the
house while I gaze away drowsily at the buildings and shops
and stables stretching westward to the swamp, the Negro
cabins below them somnolent in the morning heat, and high
above all the buzzards in patient and unceasing soar and
swoop and meditation, a noiseless quivering tilt of black
wings over some dying thing fallen in the far-off woods, hapless and struggling. Nearby, two Negroes with a wagonless
mule team shamble up from the woods toward the mill. I
hear their laughter and the jingle of a harness, and they pass

out of sight. Once again I smell the collard greens steaming;
hunger swells inside me, then hopelessly dies. *"Bow low,
Mary, bow low, Martha,"* my mother sings, rich now, and far,
and I let my eyelids close together, and soon I seem to be in a
kitchen—is it this one I know so well?—at Christmas, and I
hear the voice of some white mistress (Miss Elizabeth? Miss
Nell?) calling out *Christmas gift!* in a cheery voice, and I
drink the sweet eggnog descending to me from above in short
greedy gulps, which does nothing to assuage my hunger.
Then Christmas fades away and I am in a honeysuckle glade,
filled with the bumbling hum of bees. Wash is with me, and
together we watch a horde of Negroes laboring with hoes in a
steaming field of young corn. Like animals, glistening with
sweat, brown backs shining mirror-bright beneath the blazing sun, they ply their hoes in unison, *chop-chopping* beneath
the eyes of a black driver. The sight of their dumb toil fills me
with a sickening dread. Huge and brawny, the driver looks
like Abraham, even though he is not Abraham, and now he
spies Wash and me and, turning about, comes toward us.
Gwine git me two little nigger boys, he says, smiling, *Gwine
git me two little boys to chop de corn.* Terror sweeps through
me. Voiceless, in mad flight, I plunge through the honeysuckle, treading air as if across empty space back through a
sunlit morning toward the refuge of the kitchen looming
near, where now a sudden low hubbub of voices interrupts
my fright, waking me with a different fright. My eyes fly
open and I crouch forward beneath the house, alert, listening, heart pounding.

"Gwan outa here!" my mother cries. "Gwan away! I ain't
havin' no truck with you!" Her voice is shrill, angry, but
edged with fear, and I can no longer understand the words as
she moves to another part of the room above. Now I hear
another voice, this one a man's deep grumble, thick and
somehow familiar, but speaking words I am unable to make
out as I scramble to my feet at the edge of the house and

stand there listening. Again my mother says something, insistent, still touched with fear, but her voice is blotted out by the man's grumble, louder now, almost a roar. Suddenly my mother's voice is like a moan, a single long plaintive wail across the morning silence, making my scalp tingle. In panic, wishing to rush away but at the same time drawn as if by irresistible power to my mother's side, I run around the corner of the house and up the back stoop, throwing open the kitchen door. "There, God damn, ye'll have a taste of me big greasy," says a voice in the shadows, and though I am blinded by the sudden darkness, seeing only two blurred shapes wrestling together near the pantry, I now know who the voice belongs to. It is the white man named McBride—since winter the overseer of the fields—a yeasty-faced, moody Irishman with a shock of oily black hair and a bad limp, also a drunkard who has whipped Negroes despite the Turner brothers' rules to the contrary. My mother is still moaning, and I can hear McBride's stringy breathing, loud and labored like that of a hound dog after a run.

Blinking, my eyes take in the scene, and I am aware at once of two things: of the fruity odor of apple brandy from a bottle shattered into splinters on the kitchen floor and of the broken neck of this bottle glinting in a shaft of sunlight, clutched in McBride's hand and flourished like a dagger at my mother's neck. She is on her back upon a table in the pantry, supporting the full weight of the overseer, who with his other hand fumbles and fights with her clothes and his own. I stand rooted at the door, unable to move. The jagged neck of the bottle clatters to the floor, shattering in a powder like greenish snow. All at once a kind of shudder passes through my mother's body, and the moan is a different moan, tinged with urgency, and I do not know whether the sound I hear now is the merest whisper of a giggle ("Uh-huh, awright," she seems to murmur) for McBride's voice, thick and excited, obliterates her own—"There now, me beauty, ye'll have *earrings*," the words an awful sigh—and he makes a quick convulsive motion, while her brown long legs go up swiftly to embrace his waist, the two of them now joined and moving in that same strange and brutal rhythm I have witnessed with Wash through the cracks of half a dozen cabins and which in the madness of complete innocence I had thought was the pastime, or habit, or obsession, or something, of niggers alone.

I fly from the house, headed for nowhere; my only notion is to keep running. Around the stable I scamper, past the weaver's shed, past the smokehouse and the blacksmith shop, where two ancient black codgers idling in the shade gaze at me in slow wonder. On around the barn I run, faster and faster, across the edge of the apple orchard and along the other side of the house through a shimmering white spider web that clings to my face in damp feathery strands. A stone punctures my bare toe in a tiny starburst of pain, but nothing hinders my flight; I am bound for the ends of the earth. A hedgerow blocks my way; I plunge through it, alighting upon a stretch of sunblasted brown lawn above which tiny butter-flies flutter in a swarm of bleached wings like the petals of daisies, swooping up now to escape me. With pinwheeling legs, flailing arms, I hurdle a new ditch and commence rushing down the ailanthus-shaded lane leading to the country road when now, abruptly, my pace slackens, I begin a slow dogtrot which in turn becomes a walk, feet scuffing along. Finally I stop in my tracks, staring at the forest rising up like an impenetrable green wall beyond the fields. There is no place to go.

For long moments I stand in the shade beneath the ailanthus trees, panting, waiting. It is hot and still. Far off, the mill rumbles in a dull undertone, so faint I can barely hear it. Insects stir and fidget among the weeds, their swift random industry like a constant stitching noise amid the heat. I stand and wait for a long time, unable to go farther, unable to move. Then at last I turn and slowly retrace my steps up the lane and across the lawn in front of the house—taking care that Little Morning, pushing a sluggish rag mop on the veranda, will not see me—and now cautiously I part the brittle sticks and branches of the parched hedge, slipping sideways through it, and then dawdle across the lot to the kitchen.

As I come back to my hiding place beneath the house, the door of the kitchen smacks open with a clatter and McBride appears on the rear stoop, blinking in the sunlight, running a hand through his black disheveled hair. He does not see me as I creep back under the house, watching. He blinks steadily, and with his other hand he adjusts one gallus on his shoulder, then runs his fingers over his mouth—a curious, tentative motion almost of discovery, as if touching his lips for the first time. Then a slow and lazy smile steals over his face and he lurches down the steps, missing the last one or not fully connecting with it, so that the heel of his boot makes a sudden popping noise against the timber while at the same instant he sprawls forward, regains his balance and stands erect, wobbling slightly, muttering *God blast!* Yet he is still smiling, and now I can see that he has caught sight of Abraham, who just at this moment is rounding the corner of the stable.

"Abe!" he shouts. "*You*, Abe!"

"Yassuh!" I hear the voice call back.

"They's ten hands pickin' worms down in the bottom cornfield!"

"Yas, Mistah Mac!"

"Well, you fetch they black asses out of there, hear me!"

"Yas, Mistah Mac! Ah do dat!"

"Hit's too hot even for niggers!"

"Yassuh!" Abraham turns and hustles down the slope, his green shirt plastered black with sweat against his shoulders. Then he is gone and it is McBride alone who seems to fill the entire space within my sight, prodigious even as he stands weaving, grinning to himself in the blighted, sun-baked yard, prodigious and all-powerful, yet mysterious in his terrible authority, filling me with dread. The appearance of his round, heavy face, uplifted to the sun in dreamy pleasure, sickens me inside, and I feel a sense of my weakness, my smallness, my defenselessness, my *niggerness* invading me like a wind to the marrow of my bones.

"God blast!" he says finally, with baffling glee, and lets out a soft happy cry, totters a bit, and fetches his booted foot up against the remains of a decayed bucket, which flies off in splinters across the yard. In dismay, a great old hen squawks, flees toward the shed, and a cloud of snuff-brown barnyard manure floats aloft like the finest powder, amid tiny pinfeathers bursting everywhere. "God blast!" McBride says again, in a kind of low shout, and he is off and away, limping, in the direction of his own house down the slope. *God blast!*

Like something shriveled, I draw up within myself underneath the kitchen, the book shut now as I clutch it to my chest. The smell of cooking greens is still warm and pungent on the air. Presently I hear my mother's feet on the floor above, the broom whisking against the boards, her voice again, gentle, lonesome, unperturbed and serene as before.

"For Jesus come and lock de do'
An' carry de keys away . . ."

On another morning later that same month, the rain comes down in great whistling cataracts, whipped into spray by a westerly wind and accompanied by cracklings of lightning and thunder. Fearful for the book's safety, I rescue it from its precarious shelf beneath the house and steal up the kitchen steps, taking refuge in the pantry behind a barrel of cider. Outside the storm rages but there is enough light to see by, and I crouch in the apple-sweet damp with the book thrown open upon my knees. The minutes pass, my legs grow numb beneath me. The book with its ant-swarm of words is like an enemy, malevolent, wearisome, incomprehensible. I draw taut, crucified on a rack of boredom, yet I know I am in the presence of a treasure; lacking the key to unlock it, I possess that treasure nonetheless, and so with grubby fingers and gritty eyes I persevere . . .

All at once, very close to me, there is a noise like a thunderclap and I give a jump, fearful that the house has been hit by lightning. But now as I look up I see that it is only the great cedar door to the pantry which has been thrown violently open, flooding the room with a yellowish chill light; at the entry stands the tall, stoop-shouldered, threatening shape of Little Morning, his bloodshot eyes in a leathery old mean wrinkled face gazing down at me with fierce indignation and rebuke. "Dar, boy!" he says in a hoarse whisper. "Dar! I done foun' you out at last! *You* de one dat *stole* dat book, lak I figured all de time!" (How could I have known then what I realized much later: that with suspicion founded upon the simplest envy, he had been spying on me for days? That this creaking old man, simple-headed and unlettered and in the true state of nigger ignorance for a lifetime, had been sent into a fit of intolerable jealousy upon his realization that a ten-year-old black boy was going through the motions of learning to read. For that was the uncomplicated fact of the matter, doubtless dating from the time when, correcting him, watching him haul up from the cellar a keg of MOLASSES instead of the keg of OIL he had been ordered to fetch, I had answered his haughty *How you know?* with a superior *Be-cause it say so,* leaving him flabbergasted, spiteful, and hurt.)

Before I can reply or even move, Little Morning has my ear pinched between his thumb and forefinger, and in this way hoists me to my feet, propelling me out of the pantry and into the kitchen, pulling me forward and with an insistent pinch and tug stretching the skin of my skull as he stalks down the hallway. In helpless tow, I flounder after him, the book clutched against my chest. The tail of Little Morning's frock coat flaps in my face; the old man utters hoarse indignant breaths, *huffanapuff huffanapuff,* mingled with threats chilling, dire: "Marse Samuel gwine fix *you,* boy! Marse Samuel gwine send yo' thievin' black soul to Georgia!" Fiercely he yanks at my ear, but the pain seems nothing, obliterated by terror so vast that the blood rushes down in red sheets before my eyes. I half swallow my tongue and I hear my voice, strangled, going *aaaagh, aaaagh, aaaagh.* On we press down the dark hallway, past ceiling-high windows streaming with rain, lit by lightning flashes; I regard the heavens with twisted neck and eyes upside down. "I *knowed* you was de rascally little debbil dat stole it!" Little Morning whispers. "I knowed it all de time!"

We burst into the great hall of the house, a part of the mansion I have never seen before. I glimpse a chandelier blazing with candles, walls paneled in glossy pine, a stairway winding dizzily upward. Yet my impression of these things is brief, fleeting; filled with horror, I realize that the lofty room is crowded with white people, almost the entire family— Marse Samuel and Miss Nell and two daughters, Miss Elizabeth, one of Marse Benjamin's sons, and now Marse Benjamin himself, clad in a glistening wet rain cape as he plunges through the front door in a spray of water and a gust of cold wind. Lightning crackles outside and I hear his voice above the drumming of the rain. "Weather for the ducks!" he shouts. "But, Lord, it smells like money! The pond's spilling over!" There is a moment's silence and the door slams shut, then I hear another voice: "What have we got, Little Morning?" The old man lets go of my ear.

"Dat book," he says. "Dat book dat was stole! Dis yere de robbah dat done it!"

Nearly swooning with fright, I clutch the book to my chest, unable to control my voice and the sobs welling up *aaaagh aaaagh* from deep inside. I would weep, but my anguish is in a realm beyond tears. I yearn for the floor to open and swallow me. Never have I been this *close* to white people, and their nearness is so oppressive and fearful that I think I am going to vomit.

"Well, bless my boots," I hear a voice say.

"I just don't believe it," says another, a woman's.

"Whose little darky is that?" asks still another voice.

"Dis yere Nathaniel," says Little Morning. His tone is still heavy with anger and indignation. "He belong to Lou-Ann in de kitchen. He de culprick. He de one dat snitch de volume." He wrests the book from my grasp, regarding it with scholarly lifted eyebrows. "Dis de volume dat was took. Hit says so right here. *De Life and de Death of Mr. Badman* by John Bunyam. Hit de selfsame volume, Marse Sam, sho as my name's Little Mornin'." Even in the midst of my fright I am aware that Little Morning—the old humbug—has memorized the title by ear and is fooling no one with this display of literacy. "I knowed it war de same book when I cotched him readin' it in de pantry."

"*Reading?*" The voice is that of Marse Samuel, wondering, quite incredulous. I look up now, slowly. The white faces, viewed for the first time so closely—especially those of the females, only lightly touched by sun and weather—have the sheen and consistency of sour dough or the soft underbellies of mushrooms; their blue eyes glint boldly, startling as ice, and I regard each yawning pore, each freckle, with the awe of total discovery. "Reading?" Marse Samuel says now, with amusement in his voice. "*Come* now, Little Morning!"

"Well, natchel he warn't exackly readin'," the old man adds contemptuously. "He jes' lookin' at de pitchers, dat's all. Hit was on account of de pitchers dat he took de book anyways—"

"But there are no pictures, are there, Nell? It was your volume, after all—"

Could it have been, as I sometimes thought years later, that at that moment I sensed a fatal juncture, realized with some child's wise instinct that unless instantly I asserted my small nigger self I would be forever cast back into anonymity and oblivion? And so could it have been that right then—desperate, lying, risking all—I mastered my terror and suddenly turned on Little Morning, howling: " 'Tain't so! 'Tain't so! I can *so* read the book!"?

Whatever the case, I remember a voice, Samuel Turner's, his wonder and amazement fled, saying in sudden quiet, judicious, tolerant tones, silencing the family's laughter: *"No, no,* just wait, maybe he *can,* let us see!" And as the storm grumbles far off to the east, diminishing, the only sound now rain dripping from the eaves and a distant angry chattering of wet bluejays in the ailanthus trees, I find myself seated by the window. I have begun to cry, aware of white hovering faces like ghostly giant blobs above me, and whispering voices. I struggle briefly, pawing through the pages, but it is beyond all hope: I cannot manage a single word. I feel that I am going to suffocate on the sobs mounting upward in my chest. My distress is so great that Marse Samuel's words are miles beyond comprehension—a muffled echo I can only dredge up from memory years later—when I hear him cry out: "You see, Ben, it is true, as I've told you! They will try! They *will* try! And we shall teach him then! Hurrah!"

The most futile thing a man can do is to ponder the alternatives, to stew and fret over the life that might have been lived if circumstances had not pointed his future in a certain direction. Nonetheless, it is a failing which, when ill luck befalls us, most of us succumb to; and during the dark years of my twenties, after I had passed out of Samuel Turner's life and he and I were shut of each other forever, I spent a great deal of idle and useless time wondering what may have befallen my lot had I not been so unfortunate as to have become the beneficiary (or perhaps the victim) of my owner's zeal to tamper with a nigger's destiny. Suppose in the first place I had lived out my life at Turner's Mill. Suppose then I had been considerably less avid in my thirst for knowledge, so that it would not have occurred to me to steal that book. Or suppose, even more simply, that Samuel Turner—however decent and just an owner he might have remained anyway— had been less affected with that feverish and idealistic conviction that slaves were capable of intellectual enlightenment and enrichment of the spirit and had not, in his passion to prove this to himself and to all who would bear witness, fastened upon *me* as an "experiment." (No, I understand that I am not being quite fair, for surely when I recollect the man with all the honesty I can muster I know that we were joined by strong ties of emotion; yet still the unhappy fact remains: despite warmth and friendship, despite a kind of *love*, I began as surely an experiment as a lesson in pig-breeding or the broadcasting of a new type of manure.)

Well, under these circumstances I would doubtless have become an ordinary run-of-the-mill house nigger, mildly efficient at some stupid task like wringing chickens' necks or smoking hams or polishing silver, a malingerer wherever possible yet withal too jealous of my security to risk real censure or trouble and thus cautious in my tiny thefts, circumspect in the secrecy of my afternoon naps, furtive in my anxious lecheries with the plump yellow-skinned cleaning maids upstairs in the dark attic, growing ever more servile and unctuous as I became older, always the crafty flatterer on the lookout for some bonus of flannel or stew beef or tobacco, yet behind my stately paunch and fancy bib and waistcoat developing, as I advanced into old age, a kind of purse-lipped dignity, known as Uncle Nat, well loved and adoring in return, a palsied stroker of the silken pates of little white grandchildren, rheumatic, illiterate, and filled with sleepiness, half yearning for that lonely death which at long last would lead me to rest in some tumbledown graveyard tangled with chokeberry and jimson weed. It would not have been, to be sure, much of an existence, but how can I honestly say that I might not have been happier?

For the Preacher was right: *He that increaseth knowledge increaseth sorrow.* And Samuel Turner (whom I shall call Marse Samuel from now on, for that is how he was known to me) could not have realized, in his innocence and decency, in his awesome goodness and softness of heart, what sorrow he was guilty of creating by feeding me that half-loaf of learning: far more bearable no loaf at all.

Well, no matter now. Suffice it to say that I was taken into the family's bosom, so to speak, falling under the protective wing not only of Marse Samuel but of Miss Nell, who together with her older daughter Louisa had spent the quiet winter mornings of several years—"riding their hobby," I remember they called it—drilling me in the alphabet and teaching me to add and subtract and, not the least fascinating, exposing me to the serpentine mysteries of the Episcopal catechism. How they drilled me! How Miss Nell kept after me! I never forgot these glossy-haired seraphs with their soft tutorial murmurs, and do not blame me too much when I say—I shall try not to allude to it again—that there was at least one moment during the earthquake twenty years later when I lingered on the memory of those sweet faces with a very special and savage intensity.

"No, no, Nat, not *sucklings and babes—babes and sucklings!*"

"Yessum. *Out of the mouths of babes and sucklings hast thou ordained strength because of thine enemies, that thou mightest still the enemy and the avenger.*"

"Yes, that's just right, Nat. Now then, verses three and four. Slowly, slow-*ly!* And careful now!"

"*When I consider thy heavens, the work of thy fingers, the moon and the stars, which thou hast ordained.* And— And— I forgets."

"*Forget,* Nat, not forgets. No darky talk! Now— *What is man—*

"Yessum. *What is man that thou art mindful of him? and the son of man, that thou visiteth him?* Well, uh— And, *For thou hast made him a little lower than the angels and hast crowned him with glory and honor!*"

"Wonderful, Nat! Oh, wonderful, wonderful! Oh, Sam, there you are! You should just *hear* Nat coming along! Come here, Sam, sit beside us for a moment and listen, sit here by the fire! Listen to our little darky recite out from the Bible! He can speak it from memory as well as the Reverend Eppes! Isn't that so, Nat, you smart little tar baby, you?"

"Yessum."

But suppose again that it had been Marse Samuel who had died, instead of Brother Benjamin. What then would have happened to that smart little tar baby?

Maybe you will be able to form your own judgment from some things I overheard on the veranda one sultry, airless summer evening after supper, when the two brothers were entertaining a pair of traveling Episcopal clergymen—"the Bishop's visitants," they called themselves—one of them named Dr. Ballard, a big-nosed, long-jawed bespectacled man of middle years garbed entirely in black from the tip of his wide-brimmed parson's hat to his flowing cloak and gaiters buttoned up along his skinny shanks, blinking through square crystal glasses and emitting delicate coughs behind long white fingers as thin and pale as flower stalks; the other minister dressed like him in funereal black but many years younger, in his twenties and bespectacled also, with a round, smooth, plump, prissy face which at first glimpse had caused me to think of him as Dr. Ballard's daughter or maybe his wife. Not as yet advanced to the dining room, I labored in the kitchen as Little Morning's vassal, and it was my duty at the moment to fetch water from the cistern and to keep the

smudge pot going: positioned upwind in the sluggish air, it
sent out small black-oily clouds of smoke, a screen against
mosquitoes. Across the meadow, fireflies flickered in the dusk,
and I recall from within the house the sound of a piano, the
voice of Miss Elizabeth, Benjamin's wife, breathless, sweet, in
quavering, plaintive song:

> "Would you gain the tender creature,
> Softly, gently, kindly treat her . . ."

Though usually the sedulous snoop, I had paid no attention to the conversation, fascinated instead by Benjamin,
wondering if this would be one of those evenings when he fell
out of his chair. As Marse Samuel and the ministers chatted, I
watched Benjamin stir in the chair, heard the wickerwork
crackling beneath his weight as he let out a sigh despairing
and long, raising his brandy glass on high. While Little
Morning came forward to serve him he sighed again and the
sound was aimless, distracted, dwindling off into a little *uh-
uh-uh* like the tail end of a yawn. I think I recall Dr. Ballard
glancing at him uneasily, then turning back to Marse Samuel.
And the *uh-uh-uh* sound again, not loud, still pitched between yawn and sigh, glass half filled with sirupy apple
brandy extended negligently in midair, the other hand
clutching the decanter. I watched his cheeks begin to flush,
blooming tomato-pink in the twilight, and I said to myself:
Yes, I think again tonight he might fall right on out of that
chair.

But even as I watched him I heard him suddenly exclaim:
"Ha!" Then he paused and said: "Ha! Ha! Jesus bloody
Christ! Come out and say it!" And then I realized that despite
his yawns and rude noises, he was listening to Dr. Ballard
and so then I too turned and gazed at the minister, who was
explaining: "—and so the Bishop is marking time, as he says.
We are at the crossroads—that is the Bishop's own expression
—we are at the crossroads, marking time, awaiting some

providential wind to guide us in the right direction. The Bishop is so gifted in his choice of expressions. At any rate, he is aware that the Church all too soon must make some decision. Meanwhile, as his visitants, we are able to send him reassuring news as to the condition of the slaves on at least *one* plantation." He paused, with the bleak and wintry suggestion of a smile.

"It will be so reassuring for the Bishop," said the younger minister. "He will be interested, too, in knowing your general views."

"General views?" Marse Samuel inquired.

"General views on the institution itself," Dr. Ballard explained. "He is greatly concerned to know the general views held by—how shall we say it?—the more *prosperous* landowners of the diocese."

For a long moment Marse Samuel was silent, his face drawn and reflective as he sucked at a long clay pipe. It was becoming dark. A mild gust of wind, feather-light upon my own brow, sent an oily curl of smoke across the veranda. In the distant swamp, frogs sang and throbbed in a wild, passionate monotone. Little Morning approached Dr. Ballard with a silver tray balanced on the tips of black fingers. "Is you gwine have some mo' port wine, mastah?" I heard him ask.

Still Marse Samuel remained silent, then finally he said in a slow and measured voice: "Doctor, I will be as direct with you as I can. I have long and do still steadfastly believe that slavery is the great cause of all the chief evils of our land. It is a cancer eating at our bowels, the source of all our misery, individual, political, and economic. It is the greatest curse a supposedly free and enlightened society has been saddled with in modern times, or any other time. I am not, as you may have perceived, the most religious of men, yet I am not without faith and I pray nightly for the miracle, for the divine guidance which will somehow show us the way out of this terrible condition. It is evil to keep these people in bondage, yet they cannot be freed. They must be educated! To free these people without education and with the prejudice that presently exists against them would be a ghastly crime."

Dr. Ballard did not immediately answer, but when he did his voice was detached and indistinct. "How interesting," he murmured.

"Fascinating," said the other minister, sounding even more far away.

Suddenly Benjamin lurched erect from his chair and walked to the far edge of the veranda. There in the shadows, unfastening himself, he commenced to piss into a rosebush. I could hear the noise of a lordly stream of water, urgent, uninterrupted, a plashing cascade upon leaf and thorn and vine, and now Benjamin's voice above the spatter: "Oh, my beloved brother! Oh, my brother's bleeding heart! What a trial, what a tribulation to dwell with such a saint, who would try to alter the mechanism of history! A *saint* he is, reverend visitants! You are in the presence of a living, breathing saint! Yas!"

Dr. Ballard blushed, murmuring something I could not understand. Watching from behind the smudge pot, I was suddenly tickled and I had to smother my amusement behind my hand. For the minister, in a desperate fidget, was obviously unaccustomed to conversing with anyone who was in the process of taking a piss, which Benjamin did without a flicker of a thought and in the most public way whenever he drank in the company of men. Yet now Dr. Ballard, though agitated, had to pay even more deference to Benjamin than he did to Marse Samuel, for distant and apart as Benjamin may have been this evening he was still the older brother and the plantation's titled owner. I watched joyfully as the minister's lips became puckered and bloodless, bespectacled eyes gazing in wild discomfort at Benjamin's back. Suddenly the

torrent ceased and Benjamin wheeled about, languidly lacing
up his fly. Weaving a little, he crossed the porch, drawing
near Marse Samuel and letting his hand fall upon the back of
his brother's neck; as he did so, Marse Samuel glanced up at
him with a sour-sweet look, rueful, glum, yet touched with
quiet affection. Although they were so dissimilar as to seem
born of different families, even the most unobservant house
servant was aware of the strong bond between them. They
had quarreled many times in the past in their fraternal and
peaceable way, seeming oblivious of all eavesdropping (or
more likely they did not care) and many a black servant
gliding around the dinner table had divined enough of their
talk to know where each brother stood, philosophically, at
least about his body if not his soul.

"My brother is as sentimental as an old she-hound, Doctor," Benjamin said in an amiable voice. "He believes the
slaves are capable of all kinds of improvement. That you can
take a bunch of darkies and turn them into shopowners and
sea captains and opera impresarios and army generals and
Christ knows what all. I say differently. I do not believe in
beating a darky. I do not believe, either, in beating a dog or a
horse. If you wish my belief to take back to the Bishop, you
can tell him that my belief is that a darky is an animal with
the brain of a human child and his only value is the work you
can get out of him by intimidation, cajolery, and threat."

"I see," Dr. Ballard murmured, "yes, I see what you
mean." The minister was paying Benjamin close attention,
with a squint-eyed look yet still very deferential. "Yes, I do
see clearly what you mean."

"Like my sentimental and most gentle-hearted brother,"
Benjamin continued, "I am against the institution of slavery
too. I wish to Jesus it had never come to these shores. If there
was some kind of steam engine you could invent to plant corn
or cut timber, another to pull suckers, another fine machine

to set out in the field and chop tobacco, still another big
grand machine to come chugging through the house, lighting
the lamps and setting the rooms in order—"

There was an attentive burst of laughter from the two
ministers, the younger one tittering behind his fingers while
Dr. Ballard made small chuckles and Benjamin himself continued, appreciatively grinning, with one hand resting
friendly and familiar on his brother's shoulder. Still the sour-
sweet expression lingered on Marse Samuel's face and the
faintest outline of a sheepish little smile. "Or a machine, I
fancy," Benjamin went on, "that when the mistress of the
household prepared herself for an afternoon's outing, would
harness up the mare and bring Old Dolly and the gig around
to the front entrance, and then with its strange mechanism
set the lady down on one seat and itself on another and prod
Old Dolly into a happy canter through the woods and
fields— Invent a machine like that, I vow, invent a machine
like that, furthermore, that won't eat you out of house and
home, that won't lie and cheat and thieve you blind, that is
efficient instead of being a paragon of blockheadedness and
sheer stupidity, that you can lock away at dark in its shed like
a pumping engine or a spinning jenny without fear that this
machine is going to get up in the dead of night and make off
with a prize goose or your fattest Guinea shoat and that when
this machine is worn out and beyond its usefulness, you can
discard it and buy another instead of being cursed with a no-
account old body that conscience dictates you've still got to
supply with shoes and molasses and a peck of corn a week
until the age of ninety-five— Hey! Invent a machine like
any of these, gentlemen, and I will say a happy adieu to
slavery the moment I can lay my hands on the likes of such a
mechanism!" He paused for a moment, taking a swallow from
his tumbler, then he said: "Needless to say, I do not see in the
near future the possibility of such a machine eventuating."

There was a brief spell of silence among the company. Dr.

Ballard continued to chuckle faintly. Miss Elizabeth had ceased singing, and now in the deep shadows of evening I could hear only the whine of mosquitoes at bay beyond the cloud of dark smoke, and nearby the soft insistent cooing of a mourning dove, a dull fretful sigh—*weehoo-hoo-hoo*—like a sleepy child in pain. Dr. Ballard crossed his legs abruptly, then said: "Well, from the general tenor of your remarks, Mr. Turner, I presume—well, how shall I say it?—I presume that you feel that the institution of slavery is—well, something we must *accept*. Would that be a proper interpretation of your remarks?" When Benjamin failed to reply immediately, still gazing down with a crooked bemused smile at Marse Samuel, the minister went on: "And would it also be accurate to discern in what you have just said a conviction that perhaps the Negro lags so far behind the rest of us—I mean, the white race—in *moral* development that, well, for his own welfare it might be best that he—well, be kept in a kind of benevolent subjection? I mean, is it not possible that slavery is perhaps—how shall we say?—the most *satisfactory* form of existence for such a people?" He paused, then said: "*Cursed be Canaan. A servant of servants shall he be unto his brethren.* Genesis, ninth chapter, twenty-fifth verse. Certainly the Bishop is not completely disinclined to take this viewpoint. I myself—"

But he hesitated, falling silent then, and the whole veranda was quiet, disturbed only by the creaking of chairs. As if his mind for a moment had wandered far away, Benjamin stood there and made no reply, gazing gently down at Marse Samuel, who sat very still in the gathering dark, calmly chewing on his pipe but with a woebegone expression, strained and pinched. He made a movement with his lips, thought better of it, said nothing.

Then Benjamin looked up and said: "You take a little slave like that one there—" And it was an instant before I realized he was speaking of me. He made a gesture toward me with his hand, turning about, and as he did so the others turned too and suddenly I could feel their eyes upon me in the fading light. *Nigger, Negro, darky,* yes—but I had never heard myself called a *slave* before. I remember moving uneasily beneath their silent, contemplative gaze and I felt awkward and naked, stripped down to bare black flesh, and a wicked chill like cold water filled the hollow of my gut as the thought crashed in upon me: *Yes, I am a slave.*

"You take a little slave like that one there," Benjamin went on, "my brother here thinks he can take a little slave like that and *educate* him, teach him writing and arithmetic and drawing and so on, expose him to the masterpieces of Walter Scott, pour on the Bible study, and in general raise him up with all the amenities of learning. Gentlemen, I ask you, in all seriousness, ain't that a *whangdoodle* of a notion?"

"Yaanh-s," said Dr. Ballard. The "yes" was a thin whickering sound high in the nose, vaguely distant and amused, *yaanh-s.*

"Although, gentlemen, I do not doubt that given my brother's belief in colonization and emancipation and his faith in education and God knows what all, given his passion to prove that a darky has the native gifts granted to the average college professor, he could take a little slave like that one there and teach him the alphabet and his sums and the outlines of geography and right before your eyes you'd think his case was proved. But, gentlemen, let me tell you, my brother does not know darkies like I do. Either that or his saintly belief in reform prevents him from seeing the truth. For, gentlemen, I know better, I know darkies better. I'll swear to you that if you show me a little darky whom you've taught to read the complete works of Julius Caesar forward and backward in the original Latin tongue, I will show you a darky who is *still* an animal with the brain of a human child that will never get wise nor learn honesty nor acquire any human ethics though that darky live to a ripe old age. A darky, gentlemen, is basically as unteachable as a chicken, and that is the simple fact of the matter." He halted, then slowly yawned: "Ah, time for bed!"

The ministers and Marse Samuel rose, murmurously chatting, but now as night fell and the bright globe of a full moon rose radiant above the distant woods, I felt Little Morning squeeze me hard on the flesh of my arm, a signal, and I ceased listening to anyone talk, turning to help the old man carry bottles and glasses from the veranda, dousing the smudge pot with sprinkled water, busying myself with a mop against the planks of the pine floor. The chill in my bones would not leave nor was I able for a long time to banish from my mind the thought which hung there as if written on a banner: *I am a slave.* After some minutes, returning from the pantry, I saw that Benjamin had disappeared, and then I spied Marse Samuel lingering alone at the edge of the veranda. He leaned with one hand propped against the railing and his eyes seemed to follow the two ministers as they made their slow way, black against a blacker black, into the shadows of the night. "God watch over your dreams, Mr. Turner!" the younger one called in a tone girlish and clear.

"And your dreams too," Marse Samuel replied, but his voice was the thinnest murmur and they could not have heard it. Then he was gone from the veranda and I stood suddenly afraid, listening to Little Morning all agrumble, in gloomy discussion with himself as he limped stiffly among the chairs. A fragrance of tobacco smoke still hung sweetly on the hot still air. For a moment the two ministers, groping their way across the lawn toward the wing of the house, were illumined in a shaft of moonlight, then they vanished for good among the shadows, while the moon itself, rising behind a black frieze of sycamore trees thick with summer leaves, was suddenly obscured, pitching house and lawn into smothering darkness. *Well, I am a slave,* I thought, and I shivered in the windless, sultry night which seemed—just for an instant—to surround me cold and treacherous and, more somberly, beyond the hope of ending, as if its long ticking course through the hours might lead only to a deeper darkness, without waking, without green glimmerings of dawn or the sound of cockcrow.

Only a few months after this Benjamin died, way out in the swamp, crushed beneath a gigantic bald cypress just as he was engaged in brandy-befuddled remonstrance with two black timber hands. The Negroes later claimed that they had tried to warn of the great tree toppling at their master's back, but their gesticulations and whispers had been ignored, and they themselves had skipped lightly away as the monster crashed down upon poor drunken Benjamin. Certainly from the rate at which Benjamin had begun to stow away liquor, the story seemed true enough. Among the Negroes for years after there were dark hints, barely spoken, of foul play—but for myself I doubted it. Slaves have put up with far meaner owners than Benjamin.

Anyway, whatever final constraints Marse Samuel may have felt about continuing my education were removed by his brother's passing. Beyond doubt Benjamin would never have been a cruel master, a nigger-breaker. But if Benjamin's death brought no rejoicing among the Negroes, it would not be accurate either to say that any were plunged into mourning. Even the dumbest slave shelling corn down in the most rundown and ramshackle cabin had gotten wind of at least the general drift of Marse Samuel's charitable notions, and they all knew they had passed into more promising hands; so on the day of Benjamin's funeral, as the scores of humble darkies gathered with sorrowing downcast looks behind the big house and the more musically inclined lifted their voices in tender lament—

> "O my massah's gone! massah's gone!
> My massah's gone to heaven, my Lord!
> I can't stay behind!"

—the insincerity of their simple words was as plain as the difference between gold and brass . . .

And so during all those boyhood years when the horn blew at the first crack of dawn, when Abraham stood at the edge of the stable in the still-starlit dark trumpeting in sad hoarse notes the awakening call which brought firelight flickering at the doors of the cabins down the slope—that horn did not blow for me. I alone could stir and turn and sleep another hour, until the full light of sunup roused me to my kitchen chores long after the other Negroes had vanished to mill and woods and fields. Not for my soft pink palms— accustomed to the touch of silver and crystal, of pewter and glossy oiled oak—was the grimy feel of the hoe handle and the sickle and the ax. Not for me was the summer heat of the blacksmith shop or the steaming, gnat-mad fields of corn or the bone-cracking labor of the woods, rump deep in decaying slime, or the racket and toil of the mill where the weight of grain and timber ruptured the gut and twisted shoulders and spine into a stooped attitude of toil as immutable as statues carved in black marble. And although Marse Samuel—certainly a bountiful master by any standard—could never be accused of starving his Negroes, it was nonetheless not the field-hand diet of hog and hominy to which my palate became accustomed, but finer fare, lean ham and game and pastry—leftovers to be sure, but I rarely knew what it was like not to partake of the same food that the Turners themselves enjoyed.

As for work itself, it would be a stretch of the truth to say that my days were idle; indeed, the memory of my youth at Turner's Mill is one of a constant hustling about the house from dawn until dusk. But honestly recollected, my tasks were light, far from the sweat and stink of the field. I cleaned, I washed, I scrubbed; I polished doorknobs and built fires and learned to set a meticulous table. The hand-me-down clothes I received were baggy, but they didn't scratch. Off and on for another year or two I continued with my lessons under the tutelage of Miss Nell, a patient, wispy creature who because of some private inner crisis had intensified her already fervid religious bent, now abandoning not only Walter Scott but even John Bunyan and all such secular work in favor of the Bible, especially the Prophets and the Psalms and the Book of Job, which we continued to read together beneath a great tulip poplar, my young black woolly head brushing her silken bonnet. Do not consider me impertinent when I say that years later, immersed in the project which is the reason for this account, I breathed a silent word of gratitude to this gentle and motherly lady, from whose lips I first heard those great lines from Isaiah: *Therefore will I number you to the sword, and ye shall all bow down to the slaughter, because when I called ye did not answer . . .*

It seems to me now, as a matter of fact, that it was Miss Nell who inadvertently conveyed to me the knowledge of my own very special standing within the family, during a spell of illness a year or so before my mother died and which I reckon to have been in the autumn when I had just turned fourteen. I did not know then nor was I ever told the name of my affliction, but it could not have been anything but grave, for I passed dark streams of blood from my bladder and for days and nights I was racked by an aching fever which sent my mind off into crazed visions and nightmares through which daylight and dark, waking and sleeping were hopelessly jumbled together and my surroundings became as unreal to me as if I had been transported into another land. Dimly I recall being moved from the corn-shuck bed I had shared for so long with my mother to some other room in the house, where I lay upon an enormous bedstead with linen sheets amid the hushed sound of whispers and tiptoeing footsteps. There in my delirium I was attended to every moment; my head was gently lifted, I drank water from a tumbler held to my lips by soft white hands. These same pale hands reappeared constantly, hovering over my eyes as in a dream to cool my burning brow with strips of flannel dipped in cool water.

After a week I slowly began to recover, and the week following this I returned to my mother's room, quite infirm at first
but after a while ready to resume my daily chores. Yet I was
never able to forget how in the midst of my sickness—during
a single moment of clarity which came over me before I fell
back into a fevered nightmare—I heard Miss Nell's tearful
voice, her whispered words beyond the strange door of the
strange room: "Oh Lord, Sam, our little Nat! Poor little Nat!
We must pray, Sam, pray, pray! He mustn't be allowed to
die!"

I became in short a pet, the darling, the little black jewel
of Turner's Mill. Pampered, fondled, nudged, pinched, I was
the household's spoiled child, a grinning elf in a starched
jumper who gazed at himself in mirrors, witlessly preoccupied with his own ability to charm. That a white child would
not have been so sweetly indulged—that my very blackness
was central to the privileges I was given and the familiarity I
was allowed—never occurred to me, and doubtless I would
not have understood even if I had been told. Small wonder
then that from the snug, secure dominion of my ignorance
and self-satisfaction I began more and more to regard the
Negroes of the mill and field as creatures beneath contempt,
so devoid of the attributes I had come to connect with the
sheltered and respectable life that they were worth not even
my derision. Let some wretched cornfield hand, sweating and
stinking, his bare foot gashed by a mishandled hoe, make the
blunder of appearing at the edge of the veranda, with a
piteous wail asking that I get old massah to please fetch him
some kind of "portice" for his wound, and I would direct him
to the proper rear door in a voice edged with icy scorn. Or
should any black children from the cabins invade, no matter
how guilelessly, the precincts of the big house and its rolling
lawn, I would be at them with a flourished broomstick and
shrill cries of abuse—safe however behind the kitchen door.
Such was the vainglory of a black boy who may have been
alone among his race in bondage to have actually read

pages from Sir Walter Scott and who knew the product of nine multiplied by nine, the name of the President of the United States, the existence of the continent of Asia, the capital of the state of New Jersey, and could spell words like Deuteronomy, Revelation, Nehemiah, Chesapeake, Southampton, and Shenandoah.

It must have been during the spring of my sixteenth year that Marse Samuel took me aside on the lawn after one midday dinner and announced a rather surprising change in the routine of my life. Despite the sense I had of belonging and of a closeness to the family, I was not of course really of the family and there were intimacies I was denied; days and weeks might go by without Marse Samuel paying any note of me, especially during the long busy seasons of planting and harvest, and thus those special moments when I was the object of his attention I can recall with the greatest clearness and intensity. On this particular afternoon he spoke of my work in the house, commending me on my alertness and industry and on the good reports brought to him by Miss Nell and the young mistresses regarding the nimble way I applied myself not only to my lessons but to my daily chores.

Now, all this was laudable, he said, and the duteous way I attended to my work was something in which I myself should take pride. The fact remained, however, that I owned too much ability and intelligence to labor for long as a house servant—a career which could not help but stunt and diminish the capacities he felt I had for development and lead me early into a barren dead end. Did I not honestly think that such a way of life was suitable only for rickety old codgers like Little Morning or ancient mammies with bandannas and rheumy eyes and with a bulge of snuff in their wrinkled cheeks? Certainly a boy who had learned as much as I had could not contemplate such a fruitless lifetime with anything but despondency and dread.

For a moment I was unable to answer. I do not believe

that I had ever thought of the future; it is not in the mood of a Negro, once aware of the irrecoverable fact of his bondage, to dwell on the future at all, and even I in my state of relative good fortune must have simply assumed without thought that the days and years which stretched out before me would present only the familiar repetitious and interminable clutter of dirty dishes, chimney ashes, muddy boots, tarnished door-knobs, chamber pots, mops and brooms. That something *different* might befall my lot had never occurred to me. I do not know what I was about to reply when he slapped me gently on the shoulder, exlaiming in an eager, hearty voice: "I have grander plans for this young darky."

Grand plans indeed. The beginning of an apprentice-ship in carpentry, which, as it turned out for long years, was of as little use to me or anyone as so much rotting sawdust clogging a millwheel. But I could not have known that then. I flung myself into this new fresh field of learning with all the delight and anticipation and hungry high spirits of a white boy setting off for the College of William & Mary and an education in the mysteries of law. Marse Samuel had, for one thing, just recently acquired the services of a master carpen-ter, a German from Washington called Goat (it occurred to me long afterward that this could not have been the proper spelling, that it must have been something like Godt, but no one ever told me otherwise and in my recollection the man remains forever Goat), and it was these hands into which my owner delivered me for further instruction. For two years under the guidance of Goat I learned the carpenter's trade in the dusty shop down the slope between the big house and the cabins. I had become fairly good-sized for my age, and was strongly muscled and capable with my hands; all this combined with the fact that I had more than the rudiments of an education, and could measure and calculate nearly as well as any grown white man, made me an able student of the craft and I quickly learned to handle the saw and the adze and the plane and could set a row of joists parallel and straight beneath the laths of a new corncrib roof almost as skillfully as Goat himself. Goat was a large beefy man slow of movement and of words. Outside of carpentering, he seemed content to live by himself and to raise chickens. He had a crown of wispy hair and a shaggy beard the color of cinnamon and he supplied emphasis to his slow, cluttered, growling speech with choppy motions of knobbed and beefy hands. We were able to say little enough to each other, yet somehow he taught me carpentry well and I always felt grateful to him.

One thing about the carpenter's shop has always lingered in my mind and I should tell it, even though it concerns a matter I would hesitate to dwell on had I not resolved to make this account as truthful as possible. Like most boys of sixteen or thereabouts I had begun to feel severely the pressures of my new manhood, yet I was in an unusual position compared to the other Negro boys, who found an easy outlet for their hunger with the available and willing little black girls whom they took during some quick stolen instant at the edge of a cornfield or amid the cool concealing grass of a stand of sorghum down at the edge of the woods. Isolated as I was from the cabins and such activity, I grew up in almost total ignorance of these fleshly pleasures, and whatever further knowledge I might have gained was confounded by the fear (and this was a fear I must confess I was unable to shake totally free of even in later life) that adventures in this sphere were unholy and obnoxious in the sight of the Lord. Nonetheless, I was a vigorous and healthy boy, and try as I might to fight down temptation I could not resist accepting the opportunity to excite myself whenever the force of my desire became overwhelming. For some reason at that time it seemed plausible to believe that the Lord would not chastise me too harshly so long as I was moderate in taking my pleasure, and thus I limited these solitary moments to once a week—usually Saturdays, close enough to the Sabbath so as to make my penitent prayers on that day all the more forceful and devout.

I would go to a small, low-ceilinged storage shed that was connected to the carpenter's shop by a door which I could lock with a peg and thong. It was always a nameless white girl between whose legs I envisioned myself—a young girl with golden curls. The shed smelled strongly of freshly hewn timber and there was a resinous odor of loblolly pine, pungent and sharp enough to sear the nostrils; and often in later times, walking through noontime heat past a stand of pine trees, that same spicy and redolent odor of cut timber would arouse my senses and I would feel a sudden surge and stiffening at my groin as I thought of the carpenter's shop and as the memory began achingly to return, mingling tenderness and desire, of my vision of the golden-haired girl with her lips half open and whispering, and my young self so many years before crouched panting in the pine-smelling sweetness.

I suspect that it was a kind of loneliness, together with the fact that I had an amount of leisure not granted to many other slaves, which helped cause me at this time so zealously to precipitate myself into a study of the Bible, where I acquired—even at that early age—such a reverence and a sense of majesty in the presence of the Psalms and in the teachings of the great Prophets that I resolved that no matter where my destiny took me, no matter what humdrum tasks befell my lot in later years, I would become first and foremost a preacher of the Word. At Christmas time one year Miss Nell made me a gift of a Bible—one of several left at Turner's Mill by an itinerant messenger of the Bible Society in Richmond. "Heed this good book, Nathaniel," she said in her soft and distant voice, "and happiness shall attend you wherever you go." I will never forget my excitement as she pressed the brown leather-covered Bible into my hands. Surely at that moment I must have been (though all unaware) the only black boy in Virginia who possessed a book.

My joy was so great that I became dizzy, and I began to tremble and sweat, though windy drafts swept through the house and the day was bitterly cold. I was overtaken by such a bewildering emotion that I could not even thank the good lady, but merely turned and went to my little room, where I sat on the corn-shuck tick in the slanting icicle light of Christmas afternoon, quite unable to lift the cover and look at the pages. I recall the scent of cedar logs burning in the kitchen beyond the wall behind me, and the kitchen warmth stealing through the cracks of the timbers at my back. I recall too the echo of the spinet piano dimly tinkling far off in the great hall of the house and the sound of white people's voices lifted in song—*Joy to the world! the Lord is come*—while with the Bible still clutched unopened in my hands I gazed through a warped and crinkled isinglass windowpane to the sere wind-swept slope outside: there a mob of Negroes from the cabins was trooping toward the house. Muffled up against the cold in the coarse and shapeless yet decent winter garments Marse Samuel provided for them, they straggled along in a single line, men, women, pickaninnies, prepared to receive *their* gifts—a beanbag or a hunk of rock candy for the children, a yard of calico for the women, a plug of tobacco or a cheap jackknife for the men. They were a disheveled, ragged lot, and as they clumped past on the frozen ground near the window I could hear the babble of their voices, filled with Christmas anticipation, laughter high and heedless, and loutish nigger cheer. The sight of them suddenly touched me with a loathing so intense that it was akin to disgust, belly-sickness, and I turned my eyes away, throwing open the Bible at last to a passage whose meaning was lost on me then entirely but which I never forgot and now in the light of all that has since come to pass shimmers in my memory like a trans-figuration: *I will ransom them from the power of the grave; I*

will redeem them from death: O death, I will be thy plagues;
O grave, I will be thy destruction . . .

Except for Marse Samuel and Miss Nell (and that single
fleeting recollection of Brother Benjamin), there is little
enough I seem to be able to remember about the Turner
family. Miss Elizabeth—Benjamin's widow—remains but a
shadow in my mind; a bony, weepy-looking, raw-elbowed
woman, she sang hopefully in a quavering voice and whenever I try to conjure her up in memory it is mainly the voice
that lingers—disembodied, pining, frail as a reed, a fluty
desiccated Anglo-Saxon whine. She was tuberculous, and
since her ailment required her to be often on the coast near
Norfolk, where it was thought by the doctors that the damp
salt air was curative, I saw her infrequently and then only
from afar.

Benjamin's two sons had both studied something called
Progressive Agronomy at the College of William & Mary, and
soon after his father's death the older son, Willoughby, removed himself and his bride to a smaller dwelling at the
lower, thickly wooded edge of the plantation; from this
house, called the New Retreat, he supervised as his father
had before him the logging and timber-cutting operations of
the Turner enterprise, and so him too I rarely encountered or
had any dealings with.

The other agronomist, Lewis, who was a bachelor—ruddy-
faced and stocky and about thirty—shared with his uncle in
the management of the plantation and in effect had become
the general overseer upon the abrupt departure of the
inebriate McBride, whom Marse Samuel eventually fired for
his lecherous ways. (I have no idea whether Marse Samuel
ever learned of the Irishman's encounter with my mother although I'm fairly certain that the man, perhaps daunted by
her basic unwillingness, never dared to approach her again.
Whatever, it is testimony I believe to Marse Samuel's toler-

ance and patience—and is perhaps too a measure of something touchingly ingenuous in his nature—that he not only put up with McBride's drunkenness long beyond the point when another gentleman planter would have sent him packing, but became aware of his proclivity to Negro women a full two years after everyone else on the place had noted the marvel of at least three little slaves born with a palish cast, light curly hair, and a long fat Irish lip.) Lewis was an easygoing master (though I do not believe overly bright; he made errors in his speech which I in my young black wisdom secretly sneered at), and he tended to follow his uncle's guidance in most practical matters including the handling of Negroes, and in his treatment of those who came within his purview was more or less fair and good-humored, which is all that any slave could ask. When he was not at work he seemed to be most of the time out in the woods on horseback or shooting birds in the meadows, and thus stayed pretty much apart from the Negroes and such private affairs as they might be said (with a stretch of the imagination) to have.

Of the Turners, then, there remains only to speak of Marse Samuel's two daughters, Miss Louisa and Miss Emmeline. The older girl, Miss Louisa, aided her mother in my earliest instruction, as I have already recounted; and the swift, assured way in which I learned to read and spell and do my sums gives me reason to believe that she was an excellent teacher. But our relationship in the end was so shortlived that it is hard for me to summon up an image of her. When I was around fourteen she got married to a young land speculator from Kentucky and moved away with him forever, leaving my tutelage completely in the hands of my protectress, her Scripture-beset mother.

Miss Emmeline was the last, the youngest. At the time I am speaking of she was twenty-five, perhaps a little more, and I worshiped her—from a great distance, of course—with the chaste, evangelical passion that could only be nurtured in

the innocent heart of a boy like myself, reared in surroundings where women (at least white ladies) seemed to float like
bubbles in an immaculate effulgence of purity and perfection. With her lustrous rich auburn hair parted at the center
and her dark intelligent eyes and the sweet gravity of her
mouth which lent to her face such an air of noble calm, she
would have been a great beauty even in a society far removed
from this backwater, where work and isolation and the
weather tended quickly to harshen a white mistress's charms.
Perhaps city life had had something to do with this, since
after attending the female seminary nearby in Lawrenceville
she had gone north to Baltimore, and there she had spent several years in the home of a maternal aunt. During that time
she had fallen victim (or so it was rumored—and so it was
bruited about the kitchen by Prissy or Little Morning or one
of the house servants, all of them by training chronic snoops)
of an unhappy love affair—so grievous that it had threatened
a physical decline—and thus Marse Samuel had summoned
her home, where she now helped Miss Nell in the management of the household. Eventually it seemed that her spirits
were restored, and she fell without strain into the routine of
a young plantation mistress, attending to the ill and the feeble in the cabins, laying up preserves and making fruit cakes,
and in the spring and summer taking care of the cultivation
of a large vegetable garden not far from the carpenter's shop.

The vegetable garden was her particular devotion; she
planted by herself all the seeds and seedlings, and for hours
on end, her head sheltered by an enormous straw hat, she
would labor side by side with the two small Negro girls who
were her assistants, plucking weeds beneath the hot summer
sun. Working in the carpenter's shop, I would often raise my
eyes and watch her secretly, bewitched, suddenly short of
breath, yearning with a kind of raw hunger for that moment
which I knew was about to arrive, and did—that moment
when, pausing to look upward at the sky, she let her fair and

slender fingers pass lightly over her damp brow, all the while
remaining motionless upon her knees, the eyes gently reflective, her teeth glinting through lightly parted lips, a vein
throbbing at her temple while she offered me quite unawares
the rare glimpse, face to face, of her pure, proud, astonishing
smooth-skinned beauty.

Yet my passion for her was virginal, miserably and obscurely connected with my own religious strivings. I believed
in purity and goodness, and there was something about her
total beauty—a sadness, but a restless and lonely independence of manner, a proud serenity about the way in which she
moved—which was pure and good in itself, like the disembodied, transparent beauty of an imagined angel. In later life,
of course, I learned that such an infatuation for a beautiful
white mistress on the part of a black boy was not at all uncommon, despite the possibility of danger, but at the time my
adoration of her seemed to me eerie, unique, and almost
insupportable, as if I had been afflicted at the roots of my
soul by some divine sickness. I do not believe that during this
year-long period of my worship she spoke ten words to me
and I dared say nothing to her except to breathe once or
twice a queasy "Yessum" or "No'm" to some casual question.
Since I no longer worked in the house our paths crossed seldom, and I only asked the Lord that I be allowed sight of her
once or twice a day. Naturally she had been aware for a
number of years of my unusual standing as a privileged
young servant, but her mind was on anything but a nigger
boy and although her manner toward me was not unkindly
she seemed only faintly conscious of the fact that I lived and
breathed. Once from the veranda she called me to help her
hang a flower pot; in my jangled fumbling and confusion I
nearly allowed the pot to fall, and when, standing at my side,
she caught my bare arm amid a shower of earth and cried in
a sharp voice, "Nat! Silly goose!" the sound of my name on

her lips was as cooling as a benediction and the contact with her white fingers was like the touch of fire.

Then one night in late summer about a year after Miss Emmeline's return to the plantation from Baltimore, there was a party at Turner's Mill—and this in itself was an event worthy of note. Social affairs at the plantation were rare (at least within the memory of my time at the big house), not only because of the remoteness of the place but because of the perilous conditions of transportation—deep fords, fallen trees, and washed-out roads making intercourse between the various Tidewater estates in each case a major venture, not to be considered lightly or to be undertaken in an impetuous mood. Once in a great while, however—every two years or so, usually in the late summer when the crops were laid by— Marse Samuel would decide to have what he called, humorously, an "assemblage," and a score of people would come from miles around, planters and their families from the James and Chickahominy rivers and from down in North Carolina, people with names like Carter and Harrison and Byrd and Clark and Bonner arriving in elegant coaches and accompanied by a hustling, noisy entourage of black nursemaids and body servants. They would stay for four or five days, sometimes as long as a week, and daily there would be fox hunts with the hounds of Major Vaughan, whose plantation was not far away, and turkey shoots and contests in horsemanship, pistol matches and picnics and a great deal of contented, somnolent, easy palaver among the ladies on the veranda, and at least two fancy balls in the great hall, bedecked for each evening's merriment in yards of pink and blue bunting.

It became my duty on these occasions (after I had reached the age of sixteen or thereabouts) to act in the capacity of "chief usher," a title which Marse Samuel bestowed upon me and which involved my supervision of all the

Negro help outside of the kitchen. (It is possibly a measure of Marse Samuel's confidence in me that he entrusted me with this position, as young as I happened to be; doubtless on the other hand I simply *was* quicker and smarter than all the rest.) Caparisoned for a week in purple velvet knee-length pantaloons, a red silk jacket with buckles of shiny brass, and a white goat's-hair wig which culminated behind in a saucy queue, I must have presented an exotic sight to the Carters and the Byrds, but I reveled in my role and took great pleasure in bustling about and lording it over the other black boys —most of them enlisted from the fields, dumb callow kids all thumbs and knobby knees and popping eyes—even though each day I was kept feverishly busy from dawn to dusk. It was I who greeted the carriages and coaches and helped the ladies dismount, I too who rode herd on Lucas and Todd and Pete and Tim, making certain that they polished each night each gentleman's boots, that they cleaned up the litter on the lawn, that they hurried about ceaselessly, fetching ice from the ice cellar, retrieving a lady's lost fan, tethering horses, untethering them, doing this, undoing that. I was the first to arise long before dawn (to help Little Morning prepare daily a stirrup cup of whiskey for the fox hunt was one of my most important chores) and nearly always the last to retire, and the fact that I was up and about at a truly unearthly hour was the only reason that caused me one morning, between ball and hunt, to nearly stumble over Miss Emmeline and someone else in the moonless and murky dark.

It was not the loud whisper of her voice that shocked me so much—though I instantly distinguished it—but the Lord's name in her mouth, uttered in a frenzy, the first time in my life I had heard blasphemy on a woman's tongue. And so astonished was I by the words that as I stood there rooted in the dark it did not just then occur to me to consider the event which occasioned them, and I thought she was in some great and nameless peril: "Oh mercy . . . oh God . . . oh Jesus . . .

wait! . . . oh Jesus . . . now wait! . . . quick . . . put it back . . . now then . . . slowly . . . oh Jesus Christ . . . slowly! . . . wait!"

A man's soft groan from the lawn behind the hedge now made me aware of the other presence, and I remained half paralyzed, fascinated yet suddenly sick nearly unto death at the sound of the Saviour's name spoken thus, as if He had been stripped shamelessly naked by the hot urgency of her lips. "Wait, wait!" she again implored, and a gentle sigh came from the man's throat, and once more she continued her rhythmic whispering: "Oh mercy . . . mercy . . . wait now, slowly! . . . oh Jesus . . . oh Christ . . . oh Christ . . . oh yes, *now!* . . . Oh mercy . . . mercy . . . mercy . . ."

Abruptly then, in a prolonged and dwindling little sob, the voice died and all was silent, and I could hear nothing but the piping of frogs in the millpond and a dull thumping of horses against the stable stalls and the sound of my own heart racing madly, so loud that I thought surely it must be heard above the soughing of a night wind in the sycamore trees. I stood there unable to move, my spirit a shambles from chagrin and shock and fear. And I recall thinking wretchedly: This is what comes of being a nigger. It ain't fair. If I wasn't a nigger I wouldn't find out about things I don't want to find out about. It ain't fair.

Then after a long silence I heard the man's voice, impassioned, tremulous: "Oh my love Em, my love, my love, *Em* my love!"

But there was no reply from Miss Emmeline and time crept by slowly and painfully like something crippled and old, causing my mouth to go dry and a numbness, premonitory with the clammy touch of death, to spread a tingling chill through my legs and thighs. At last I heard her voice again, placid now, composed, but edged with contempt and bitterness. "Finally you've accomplished what you've been after for ages. I hope you're satisfied."

"Oh Em, my love, my *love*," he whispered. "Let me—"

"Stay away from me!" she said, her voice rising now in the darkness. "Stay away from me, do you hear! If you touch me, if you say another word to me I'll tell Papa! I'll tell Papa and he'll *shoot* you for *ravishing* your own cousin."

"But oh my darling Em!" he protested. "You *consented* to—Oh *Em*, my love, my dear—"

"Just stay away from me!" she repeated, and again she fell silent and there was no sound for a long while until suddenly I heard her burst out in words touched with raw and abandoned despair: "Oh God, how I hate you. Oh God, how I hate this place. Oh God, how I hate life. Oh *God*, how I hate God!"

"Oh don't, Em!" he whispered in a frantic voice. "My love, my love, my love!"

"This God damned *horrible* place. I would even go back to Maryland and become a whore again, and allow the only man I ever loved to sell my body on the streets of Baltimore. Get your God damned hands *off* me and don't speak another *word* to me again! If you do I'll tell Papa! Now leave me, leave me, leave me, *leave me alone!*"

I have spoken elsewhere in this narrative, and more than once, of a Negro's ubiquity and the learning he acquires, so often unbeknownst to white people, of the innermost secrets of their hearts. That evening was one such time, but it seemed to me, too, as I watched Miss Emmeline rise from the grass and in a rustle of taffeta disappear into the blue shadows of the house and then saw her cousin Lewis rise also and slouch off miserably through the night, that no matter how much covert knowledge a Negro possessed there were questions always left unanswered and a mystery, and that therefore he should not feel himself too wise or all-knowing. Certainly this was true in regard to Miss Emmeline, who, all the while I pondered her after that evening, became ever more wrapped in a dark and secret cloak. She did not speak another word to Lewis nor, so far as I was able to observe, did he dare speak to her; her threat, her admonition triumphed, and some months later the poor man left Turner's Mill entirely, going down to Louisiana to try to set himself up in sugar or cotton.

As for what I heard and saw that night, please do not consider my account simply—well, *mischievous*—for in truth such an episode had the effect of altering my entire vision of white women. For now the glow of saintliness which had surrounded Miss Emmeline in my mind dimmed, flickered out, disappeared; it was as if she suddenly stood disrobed and the fascination she held for me was of a different order, just as my hopeless and unending frustration was of a different kind though no less severe. For a while I was still maddened by her. I still worshiped her beauty from a distance but I could not help but be shaken to my guts by the words of blasphemy I had heard her utter, which now inflamed my thoughts, and like pinpoints of fire, pricked and agitated my very dreams. In my fantasies she began to replace the innocent, imaginary girl with the golden curls as the object of my craving, and on those Saturdays when I stole into my private place in the carpenter's shop to release my pent-up desires, it was Miss Emmeline whose bare white full round hips and belly responded wildly to all my lust and who, sobbing "mercy, mercy, mercy" against my ear, allowed me to partake of the wicked and godless yet unutterable joys of defilement.

One day in October just after I became eighteen—a day recollected with that mysterious clarity of all days upon which transpire the greatest of events—I discovered the actual outlines of that future which Marse Samuel had envisioned for me all these weeks and months and years.

It was a Saturday, one of those dusty, ocherous autumnal days whose vivid weather never again seems so sweet and inviting after that youthful time of discovery: wood smoke and maple leaves blazing in the trees, an odor of apples everywhere like a winy haze, squirrels scampering for chinquapins at the edge of the woods, a constant stridor of crickets among the withering grass, and over all a ripe sunny heat edged with feathery gusts of wind smelling of charred oak and winter. That morning I had as usual risen early and gone to the shop, where I busied myself in loading some short two-by-fours on a barrow. Marse Samuel had only a few days before made his seasonal inspection of the field hands' cabins, finding several of them in a state of sorry dilapidation. This day Goat and I would set up the two-by-fours as underpinning for a couple of new floors; afflicted by the summer's seepage and rot, many of the old timbers had dissolved into a kind of crumbling splintery sawdust, the cabins themselves then exposed to the raw damp earth and infested by field mice, roaches, ants, beetles, and worms. Although I had grown very fond of my apprenticeship as a carpenter and took pride in my growing mastery of the craft, I despised with a passion that part of my job which required me to work on repairs to the cabins. For one thing alone (and this in spite of all Marse Samuel's efforts to teach a fundamental cleanliness) there was the odor—the stink of sweat and grease and piss and nigger offal, of rancid pork and crotch and armpit and black toil and straw ticks stained with babies' vomit—an abyssal odor of human defeat revolting and irredeemable. "*Ai*, yi, yi," Goat would whisper to the air in his German rattle, "dese people is not animals even," and lifting a post or beam would make a convulsive face and spit on the floor. At such moments despite myself, the blood-shame, the disgrace I felt at being a nigger also, was as sharp as a sword through my guts.

But that bright morning, appearing at the shop door with a cheery smile, Marse Samuel rescued me before I had even gotten well along on my task. "Throw a saddle on Judy, Nat," he said, "we're off to Jerusalem." Behind the look of humor on his face there was something secretive, conspiratorial, and he lowered his voice to say: "Come November third, Miss Nell and I will have been married for a quarter of a century. I must needs celebrate this anniversary with an appropriate gift." He plucked me by the sleeve of my shirt, drawing me outside the shop. "Come now, let's saddle Judy and Tom. I need company to share this splendid day. But you mustn't breathe a word about the gift, Nat!" He looked about him right and left, as if fearful of being overheard, then said in a whisper: "Someone sent news from over at the Vaughans' place that a jeweler from Richmond will be passing today through town."

I was of course wonderfully pleased—not alone because I was freed of an ugly job but because I liked riding so much and always stole a ride on the rare occasions I was given the opportunity, and also because Jerusalem itself was an exciting place for me; although it was no more than fifteen miles away, I had been there only once several years before and then the little village touched me with wonder despite the solemnity of our mission. That time too I had gone with Marse Samuel, but in a wagon, to help pick out a headstone for my mother's grave. No cedar headboard for her, no weed-filled corner of some field splashed with tatterdemalion wild-flowers. My mother, alone among all the Negroes at Turner's Mill, had been laid honorably to rest in the family plot among white folks (scant yards away, indeed, from the un-sentimental Benjamin, now spinning in his coffin) with a marble headstone not one inch smaller nor a shade less white than theirs. I am no longer oppressed by the fact (as I was for so many years after I had grown to manhood and was able to reflect long and hard on these matters) that the name on that headstone was not a nigger woman's forlorn though honest "Lou-Ann" but the captured, possessed, owned "Lou-Ann Turner."

We rode out the long front lane over a carpet of fallen

leaves. At the entrance to the lane half a dozen field hands supervised by Abraham were clearing a drainage canal which rimmed a part of the land; Marse Samuel greeted them with a loud halloo, and they in turn stood erect and grinned in a servile show of doffed hats and loose-limbed droll shufflings, shouting back: "Mawnin', massah!" and "Fare 'ee well, Marse Sam!" I eyed them with aloof, privileged disdain. Their calls echoed behind us even as we set out through the woods by way of a leaf-strewn sunken wagon track leading toward the log road which would take us to Jerusalem. It was a gusty, brilliant morning alive with tossing branches and swirling eddies of leaves beneath us. Marse Samuel's horse, a glittering black Irish hunter, quickly set the pace and took the lead and for half an hour or so we rode without speaking through the forest until finally, slackening his gait, Marse Samuel let me draw abreast and then I heard him say: "I hear that you are quite a young craftsman." I found no way to answer these words which were both so pleasing and discomfiting, and I kept quiet, risking only a swift glance at Marse Samuel and catching his eye then shifting my gaze a bit. I saw a pleasant twinkly look on his face, a kind of half-smile as if he were on the verge of divulging a secret. He sat upon a horse with great style and presence; his flowing hair had become a silvery gray in the past few years, and more lines creased and webbed his face, adding to his dignity; for an instant I imagined I was riding in the company of a great Biblical hero— Joshua perhaps, or Gideon before the extermination of the Midianites. I could say nothing as usual; my awe of him was so great that there were moments when I could no more reply to him than if someone had sewn up my lips.

"Mr. Goat told me that you planed down and finished twenty sills and chimney girts as smooth and as clean as could be, mortice and tenons and all and not one bad joint nor a single timber to throw away in the lot! Fine work, my excellent young carpenter! What I expect I shall have to do—"

Was he on the edge then of telling me what he had to say later? Perhaps. But I do not really know, for at that instant Marse Samuel's horse suddenly reared in a panic and the mare too heaved up beneath me, neighing with alarm, and across the wagon trace three deer bolted in high bounds from a thicket, a buck and two does dappled in the leafy morning light; they flew past us in floating shapes wild-eyed and silent until one after another they struck the blanket of leaves on the far side of the road and vanished into the woods with a clamorous diminishing storm of thudding hooves and snapping branches. *"Hoo, Tom!"* Marse Samuel shouted, reining in his horse, calming him, and I too tightened in the mare, and for a moment we stood there in the checkered flickering light, gazing at the place where the white tails of the deer had melted into the woods, listening as the sound of the plunging feet vanished far off among the trees. But it had given us both a start. "A yard farther and they'd have been on top of us, Nat!" Marse Samuel called with an uneasy laugh, and he swung Tom around and galloped ahead, saying no more until a few minutes later when the wagon trace ended, merging with the log road which led to Jerusalem. *"Then shall the lame man leap as a hart,"* he said, glancing back at me, *"and the tongue of the dumb sing: for in the wilderness* —How does it go, Nat?"

"For in the wilderness shall waters break out, and streams in the desert," I answered. *"And the parched ground shall become a pool, and the thirsty land springs of water: in the habitation of dragons, where each lay, shall be grass with reeds and rushes."*

"Yes, yes," he replied. We had drawn to a stop near the end of the trace, beneath a grove of gnarled and ancient apple trees once part of a large cultivated grove but now turned back to the underbrush and the wildwood. Fallen from the branches apples by the bushel lay in disordered piles and rows in a shallow ditch at the edge of the trace; scattered ranks of the red and yellowish fruit were faintly rotting with a cidery odor. Even as we stood there others fell, *plop-plopping* on the ground. Gnats swarmed over all, barely visible, and the two horses bent down their necks and began to munch at the apples with succulent crunching sounds. "Yes, yes," Marse Samuel said, "I had forgotten. I had forgotten." He smiled suddenly, adding: "By God's grace I can afford to forget the Bible with *you* to rely on. *For in the wilderness shall waters break out and streams in the desert—* Lord Almighty, would that it were really so!" He looked about him for a moment, searching the distances with a hand shielding his eyes from the bright sun. "Lord Almighty!" he said again. "What a desolate prospect hereabouts!"

I looked about me too but could see nothing out of the ordinary: apple trees, road, fields, distant woodland—all seemed to be in place.

He turned and regarded me soberly. "Those deer now, Nat. Take those deer for example. Used to be you never saw any deer on this trace, up in this quarter. Too many people around that kept them down. Fifteen, sixteen years ago when you were but a small tadpole the woods would be resounding with gunfire in November, December when old John Coleman and his boys would be laying up venison. They kept the deer population down to a proper size. Let his darkies hunt, too. Had a big driver named Friday who was one of the best deer shots in all of Southampton. But it's all gone now. When the deer come back it means poor times. It means the people have gone." He looked around again, the expression on his face still earnest, worried, thoughtful. "This grove here," he murmured, "John Coleman's too. Taken care of, those trees gave the sweetest Jonathans ever you might ask for. Now look at them, all gone to pieces, fit only for the worms. God, what a pity! What a waste and a shame!"

He said little else for a while as we rode at a slow canter toward Jerusalem. Something seemed to have taken possession of his thoughts and he remained buried within himself, lost in some troubled reverie which contrasted suddenly and puzzlingly with his happy mood of the early morning but which of course I could not presume to intrude upon. We rode in silence for an hour or a little more, the log road lying straight and level as a roofbeam before us, the woods at either side like a whispery wall, wind-thrashed and afire with leaves. Here, unlike the tamed land around Turner's Mill, it seemed a true wilderness, for the copper and gold landscape was astir with wilderness life: partridge sprang up beyond the edge of the road, and from the forest's windswept roof fat grouse exploded, booming as they sought the sky. Squirrels and cottontails crisscrossed the road all along the way. Once a red fox considered us from his perch on the trunk of a fallen oak; seated panting, grinning, his tongue lolled out between rows of small wicked teeth.

Yet even as we rode along I was made aware—because of what Marse Samuel had said—of the strange bleak tracts of land which at intervals broke up the forest, patches of scrubby bramble-choked earth which had once been tobacco fields but now lay in fallow ruin. Scrub oak and pine saplings poked up through these meadows; the earth was raw and weedy and great stretches of chalky, storm-runneled earth upon which nothing could grow blotched the landscape like open wounds. Here and there a forlorn last growth of stripped tobacco stalks stuck up through the briers in stiff withered spines. As we rode past one of these fields I could see on the far horizon the remnant of a great old farmhouse with its roof caved in; the tumbledown outbuildings surrounding it, rotting and abandoned like the ruined offspring of something itself long dead, made the distant view even more sinister, and I turned away from it, beginning to share Marse Samuel's pensive mood without knowing exactly why, and rode silently along behind him as the woods closed in again on either side around us.

There was little movement on the road, and such of it as

there was seemed to be coming toward us, away from Jerusalem: two peddlers' wagons, several farmers in gigs and buggies—all of whom Marse Samuel hailed, being hailed warmly in return with elaborate, deferential greetings—and a half-blind old free Negro woman named Lucy, a ragpicker well known in the region, quite drunk and crazed and astride a spavined motheaten mule, who when Marse Samuel pressed a few pennies into her bleached palm, cackled in a voice which followed us for half a mile: "Bress yo' soul, Marse Samuel, you Jesus hisself! Yes, you des Jesus hisself . . . Jesus hisself . . . *Jesus hisself!*"

In the outline of a vast arrowhead, flashing and wavering, a flock of geese raced south high in the pure blue above; a gust of wind caught Marse Samuel's cloak, blowing it about his head, and as he reached up to recover it he said: "How old are you now, Nat? Eighteen, am I correct?"

"Yes sir, Marse Samuel, I turned eighteen first day of this month."

"Mr. Goat has splendid things to tell me about you," he went on. "It's really most remarkable the progress you've made." He turned to look at me with the suggestion of a smile. "You're quite an unusual darky, I suppose you know."

"Yes sir, Marse Samuel, I reckon I am." I do not recall replying with immodesty; that I was in many ways both exceptional and fortunate was a fact of which I had long been well aware.

"You have by no means acquired what is known as a liberal education," he said. "That was not my intention nor within my powers, even though I am sure that young people of your race will get that kind of learning someday. But you seem to be equipped now with the best part of an elementary schooling. You can read and write, and you can count. You have the most amazing knowledge of the Good Book of anyone within my ken, and that includes several white ministers I know. You will doubtless take on much more learning as you go forward, so long as books are within your reach. In addition to all this you have gained command of a craft, and are exceedingly skillful at everything which has been taught you. You are the walking proof of what I have tried so hard and usually so vainly to persuade white gentlemen, including my late beloved brother, namely, that young darkies like yourself *can* overcome the natural handicaps of their race and at least acquire such schooling as will allow them to enter into pursuits other than the lowest menial animal labor. Do you understand what I am getting at, Nat?"

"Yes sir, Marse Samuel," I said, "I understand fine."

"In three years you will be twenty-one, you will have attained your manhood. Until then I wish to see you function on a new basis at the Mill. Commencing tomorrow, you will work only half a day at the shop under Mr. Goat's direction. During the rest of the time you will act as assistant driver on the plantation, working together with Abraham in controlling the affairs of the fields and the mill itself but answerable only to me. During some of that time this fall I will be seeking your assistance in putting my library in order, it is in sorry need of straightening out. That last shipment from the factor in London contained over one hundred volumes in agronomy and horticulture alone, not to speak of the rest of my books and those of my father's which stand in need of arrangement. Do you think you can help me in all this?"

"I will certainly try, Marse Samuel, I will most surely do my best."

"There may be some items which will be a bit of a trick for you as yet, but you will learn in the process and I think all in all we shall manage handsomely." He had reined in his horse, and I stopped too; now we stood abreast at the edge of the road and Marse Samuel clutched the pommel of his saddle in a gloved hand, watching me gravely. The road was empty of travelers here, desolate, traversed by small whirlwinds of brown leaves and gritty dust. Flat fields of briers rolled away to the rim of the horizon, a wasteland of dying thorns; somewhere far off a wildfire in the woods burned unchecked and its fragrance, sharp with cedar, floated around us in a powdery sweet haze.

"Now, I have long debated in my mind and heart," he went on slowly, "whether to tell you of this other decision, for fear that it would hinder you in some way or cause you to occupy your head with fanciful notions when you should be attending to your work."

I could not think what it was he was preparing to tell me but there was something in the tone of his voice that put me on the alert, anticipating, and in a wild and sudden fantasy I thought: Maybe he's going to say that if I do everything right he'll give me old Judy; he let Abraham have a horse only two years ago . . .

"When I was up in Richmond this last August, I saw Mr. Bushrod Pemberton, who has taken a great interest in the news I have had to convey to him in regard to you—"

A vision of the mare disappeared, and I was thinking instead: What has Richmond got to do with me? And Mr. Bushrod Pemberton? What does either of them got to do with anything in the world?

"Mr. Pemberton is one of the wealthiest gentlemen in Richmond. He is an architect and a builder of houses and he is in great need of skilled hands right now. Besides being a man of cultivation and learning, Mr. Pemberton shares most of the ideas I myself possess about the use of labor. In his business in Richmond he employs many accomplished free Negroes and slaves as carpenters, bricklayers, tinsmiths, and other artisans. What I propose to do, Nat, is simply this. If all goes well with you during the next three years—and I have no reason to doubt that anything will go awry—"

He's going to hire me out, I thought, he's going to hire me out to Mr. Pemberton, that's what he's going to do. I began to feel a creeping fear, thinking: So he trained me all these years just so he could hire me out in Richmond to Mr. Bushrod Pemberton—

"—Then I shall send you to Mr. Pemberton, under whose employ you will work as a carpenter for the following four years. Mr. Pemberton lives in a beautiful old home in the shadow of St. John's Church. I have seen the quarters where he sleeps his servants; they are in a quiet alleyway behind the house and I can tell you, Nat, that never a darky could wish for a nicer place to live. Another thing, Mr. Pemberton is engaged in building a block of fine row houses in the center of town, and I expect you will fit in perfectly on the job from the very beginning. You will pay me half of the wages you earn from him—"

So it is all as simple as that. He's getting rid of me. And so what all this means is that I will have to go away from Turner's Mill. It ain't fair. It ain't fair.

"—retaining the other half for yourself in savings for the future. Thereupon, at Mr. Pemberton's good report of your labor—and again I have no doubt that this might be anything but exemplary—I shall draw up the papers for your emancipation. You will then at the age of twenty-five be a free man."

He paused and gave my shoulder a soft nudge with his gloved fist, adding: "I shall only stipulate that you return to Turner's Mill for a visit every blue moon or two—with whichever young darky girl you have taken for a wife!"

Suddenly I realized that he was trembling with emotion. He ceased talking and blew his nose with a loud honk. Baffled, helpless, I opened my mouth but my lips parted on a fragile wisp of air, unable to speak a word, and just at that moment he turned aside brusquely and tapped his horse into a quick trot, calling back: "Come on, Nat, time's flying! We must get to Jerusalem before that jeweler has sold out all his pearls!"

A free man. Never in a nigger boy's head was there such wild sudden confusion. For as surely as the fact of bondage itself, the prospect of freedom may generate ideas that are immediately obsessed and half crazy, so I think I am being quite exact in saying that my first reaction to this awesome magnanimity was one of ingratitude, panic, and self-concern. And the reasons were as simple and as natural as a heartbeat. Because such was my attachment to Turner's Mill—the house and the woods and the serene and familiar landscape which had composed my entire memory and the fact of my *becoming* and had fashioned me into what I was—that the idea of leaving it filled me with a homesickness so keen that it was like a bereavement. To part from a man like Marse Samuel, whom I regarded with as much devotion as it was possible to contain, was loss enough; it seemed almost insupportable to say good-bye to a sunny and generous household which, black though I was, had cherished me as a child and despite all—despite the unrelenting fact of my niggerness, the eternal subservience of my manner and the leftovers I ate even now and my cramped servant's room and the occasional low chores I was still compelled to do, and the near-drowned yet lingering and miserable recollection of my mother in a drunken overseer's arms—had been my benign and peaceable universe for eighteen years. To be shut away from this was more than I thought I could bear.

"But I don't want to go to any Richmond!" I heard myself howling at Marse Samuel, galloping after him now. "I don't want to work for any Mr. Pemberton! *Naw* sir!" I cried. "Unh-*unh*, I want to stay right here!" (Thinking now of my mother's words long ago, and still another fear: *Druther be a low cornfield nigger or dead than a free nigger. Dey sets a nigger free and only thing dat po' soul gits to eat is what's left over of de garbage after de skunks an' dogs has et . . .*) "Naw!" I yelled. "Unh-*unh!*"

But all I could hear was Marse Samuel shouting not to me but to his horse, now plunging ahead through flying and pinwheeling billows of autumn leaves: "Hey, Tom! Old Nat won't feel that way for . . . long . . . will . . . he . . . boy!"

And of course he was right. For many months afterward I worried off and on about my future in Richmond. But my worst fears began to melt away even that morning as we approached Jerusalem, when like some blessed warmth there slowly crept over me an understanding of this gift of my own salvation, which only one in God knew how many thousands of Negroes could hope ever to receive, and was beyond all prizing. I would have, after all, several years before I'd be leaving Turner's Mill. As for the rest, to be a free man in a fine city working at a trade he cherished was not a fate to be despised; many a poor outcast white man had inherited far less, and therefore I should give thanks unto the Lord. I did so that day in Jerusalem, while waiting for Marse Samuel in the shadow of a stable wall, taking my Bible from the saddle-bag and praying alone on my knees while carts clattered by and the sound of a blacksmith's hammer rang out like the clang of a cymbal: O *God, thou art my God; early will I seek thee . . . because thy lovingkindness is better than life, my lips shall praise thee . . .*

Yet that afternoon on the way back to Turner's Mill, just as my joy and exultancy grew and I listened to Marse Samuel describe the kind of good work that would be in store for me in Richmond (he too was in radiant spirits, he had bought Miss Nell a resplendent gold and enamel French brooch and was glowing with pride), we encountered on the road a sight so troubling that it was like a shape of darkness passing across the bright October sun, and it looms over my memory of this day as persistently as the recollection of some exhausted moment toward the year's end when one looks out and finds that all is hushed and that night has begun to fall, and there steals over the tongue the first flat dead taste of winter.

The slave coffle had halted at the side of the road, not far below the clearing where the wagon trace began. Had we

started out ten minutes later it would have been on its way
again, we should not have seen it. I began to count, and I saw
that there were about forty Negro men and boys skimpily clad
in ragged cotton shirts and trousers; they were linked to each
other by chains that girdled their waists and each was man-
acled with double cuffs of iron which now lay loose in
their laps or on the ground. I had never seen Negroes in
chains before. None of them spoke as we passed, and their
silence was oppressive, abject, hurtful, and chilling. They sat
or squatted in a line straggling through the fiery mounds of
fallen leaves at the wayside; some were chomping on handfuls of corn pone in a listless fashion, some dozed against
each other, one gangling big fellow rose as we approached
and wall-eyed and expressionless began to piss into the ditch,
a small boy of eight or nine lay weeping desperately and
hopelessly against a fat middle-aged shiny liver-colored man
gone sound asleep where he sat. Still no one spoke, and as we
moved on I heard only a faint chinking sound of their chains
and now the single lugubrious plunking of a jew's-harp, very
slow, tuneless, and with a weird leaden monotony, like someone pounding in senseless rhythm on a crowbar. The three
drovers were youngish sort of sun-reddened men, fair-haired
and mustached, and all wore muddy boots; one of them carried a leather bullwhip and it was he who tipped his wide
straw hat to Marse Samuel as we came up to them and
stopped. The chains chinked faintly in the ditch, the jew's-
harp went *bunk-bunk-bunk-bunk.*

"Where are you bound?" Marse Samuel said. He had lost
all trace of his gaiety now, and his voice sounded disturbed
and strained.

"Dublin, in Georgia, sir," was the reply.

"And where do you hail from?" he asked.

"Up in Surry County, near Bacon's Castle, sir. They done
broke up the Ryder plantation and these here is Ryder's niggers, sir. Georgia bound, we is."

"When did you leave Surry?" Marse Samuel said.

"Morning of the day afore yesterday," the drover said. "We'd be a heap further along excepting we took a wrong turning after dark somewheres up in Sussex and got ourselves proper lost for a bit." He grinned suddenly, exposing teeth so black with tobacco stain that they seemed almost lost in the hollow of his mouth. "It ain't always easy to find the way down here, sir. In Jerusalem we got many misdirections. Are we headed the right way for Carolina and the routes south, sir?"

But Marse Samuel failed to respond to the question then, exclaiming in a voice touched with disbelief: "The Ryder plantation too! And these are the Ryder Negroes. Lord God, things must be getting bad up there when—" But abruptly he broke off and said in reply: "Yes, you should arrive at Hicks' Ford after nightfall. Then I believe there is an overland trace which will take you across the line to Gaston, thence down to Raleigh by the regular route. When do you expect to reach your destination in Georgia?"

"Well, sir," the drover replied, still beaming, "I has taken many a gang of niggers from Virginia down to Georgia though never from Surry before on account of the trading gentleman I works for is Mr. Gordon Davenport, who has bought most of his niggers up on t'other side of the James in counties like King William and New Kent. The niggers from up there is mostly old stock Lower Guinea niggers with short leg shanks and poor constitutionals and seeing as how you can't walk niggers like that for more'n twenty miles a day you'd be lucky sometimes to make Savannah River inside of six weeks. And has to lash the mortal shit out'n 'em all the way." He paused and spat into the leaves. "But see, sir," he continued patiently to explain, "I happens to know that these Southside niggers from Surry and Isle of Wight and Prince George is most all of them late stock true Upper Guineamen with long shanks and healthy constitutionals, by and large, and you can get twenty-five even thirty miles a day out of 'em easy, even the bitches and young'uns, and hardly ever have to lay on none of 'em a stroke of the whip. Which is all fine with me. So I reckon that except for floods and such like we will fetch Dublin the second week in November."

"And so the Ryder place is finished too!" Marse Samuel said after a long pause. "I knew it was failing but—so soon! The last grand old place in Surry; it is hard to believe!"

" 'Tain't hard to believe, sir," the drover said. "Land up there has got so miserable poor you can't make a gift of it. Ain't nothing but the acorns to eat in Surry, sir. They says a bluejay flyin' over has to tote his own food—" One of the other drovers began to chuckle and snort.

As he spoke, my mare who was disposed to sidle at times sidestepped her way a few yards down the line away from the drovers, tossing her mane and drawing to a nervous stop near the place where the jew's-harp was dully strumming. *Bunk-bunk.* Suddenly the noise ceased and the mare jerked about and I could hear the chinking of the chains along the ditch and the child's heartbroken wail as he sobbed without ceasing against the plump liver-colored grayhead who now blinked awake and cast rheum-filled dreamy eyes down at the little boy, murmuring: "Das awright." He stroked the child on his kinky brown head and said again: "Das awright." And then he began to repeat the phrase gently, over and over, as if they were the only words he knew: "Das awright . . . das awright . . ."

Without warning a gust of wind came up, and a moment's shadow crossed the face of the day, and the frost-tinged shuddering breeze ran down the line of Negroes, shoveling the leaves up around their decrepit lumpish shoes, flicking the edges of their cotton sleeves and the cuffs of their gray tattered trousers. I felt myself give a shiver, then as quickly as it had come the shadow vanished, the day brightened warmly like a blossom, and at that moment I heard at my elbow a voice soft and slick as satin: "Isn't you gwine give Raymond a nice sweet potato, honey chile?"

I ignored the voice, still listening to Marse Samuel, who was saying: "I presume they are separating Negro families in Surry then, otherwise you'd have a number of women in this coffle."

" 'Deed I couldn't say, sir," the drover replied. "Mr. Davenport jest hires me to drive 'em."

"Pretty please, honey chile," the voice below persisted, "isn't you got a nice sweet potato for ole Raymond? Us is jes' sick of apples. And pone. Sour apples from de road an' pone. Us is jes' sick of dat mess. Come on, honey, isn't you got a nice sweet potato fo' Raymond? Or a tiny ole piece of bacon?"

I looked down and saw a freckled ginger-colored Negro, squat and muscular, with thick lips and a sparse reddish head. Thirty-five or perhaps forty, he had the blood in him somewhere of an Irish overseer or the scion of a James River manor or a traveling Pennsylvania tinker; from the way he sat with a certain shabby yet subtle prestige—maybe it was the manner in which the two boys chained on either side had cozied up against him, or the impudence of the jew's-harp clutched in one thick clumsy hand—I could tell that deference was paid and due him: there was a Raymond on every plantation. It was surely owing to his white blood that Raymond achieved his eminence but also to some native bankerish wit and sagacity which, however forlornly crippled, made him store up a meager authority and was ever a beacon for all the others. What caused an eclipse of the moon? Raymond knew. *Hit caused by a gret mystery cloud flyin' up out'n de swamp.* Was there a way to cure rheumatism? Ast old Ray. *Make you a portice of turkentine wid red earthworms and de juice of a red onion, dat's de onliest way.* Having a little trouble with your old woman at night? *Git you de cotton dat she's thowed away when she got her monthlies and wear it*

sewed up inside yo' pants, dat'll start a woman humpin'.
When would the niggers be free? *In 1842, I seed it in a
dream, niggers led by a wooden-legged white man from up in
Paris, France.* And so the talk goes round among the niggers:
*Ast ole Ray. Raymond he know near 'bout ev'ything in de
whole wide world.* Won't it be bad times down in Georgia?
*Naw, dat's rich peopleses' country, dat's why us is goin' dar.
Niggers down in Georgia eats fried eggs three times a day . . .*

"What yo' name, sweet?" he whispered up at me.

"Nat," I said. "Nat Turner."

"Where you live at, honey chile?"

"Live at Turner's Mill," I said, "down-county." So little
called for were the words I uttered next that I have wondered
since why the Lord did not wrench out my tongue. "My
mastah's goin' to set me free in Richmond."

"Well, ain't dat jes' de nicest thing," said Raymond.

"God's truth," I replied.

"Come on, sugah," he importuned in his glossy voice,
"don' a rich nigger boy like you got a bite to eat for ole
Raymond? My, dat's a pretty bag on dat saddle. I bets dey's
all kinds of nice things to eat in dat bag. Come on, sugah,
give ole Raymond a bite to eat."

"Dey's on'y a Bible in dat bag!" I said impatiently, though
full-lapsed into a field nigger's tongue. I gave the mare a slap
behind the ears, checking her crabwise gait, and brought her
about toward Marse Samuel. Late afternoon had begun to
settle down upon us as we stood there, it had grown cold.
Light from the descending sun fell amid the October leaves
and through wood smoke and haze lay streaming upon a tangled desolation of weeds and brambles, so furiously luminous
that it seemed a field ready to explode into fire. Drawing near
Marse Samuel I heard the jew's-harp again, *bunk-bunk-bunk.*

"Come, we must be on our way," he said to me, wheeling
about, and we turned together then; for some reason I hesitated and stopped entirely, gazing back, and he said again:

"Quickly! *Quickly!* We must be on our way!"

Now moving again down the long line of Negroes, I was
aware that the jew's-harp had stopped playing; we came by
the place where Raymond sat in his chains and I heard him
call to me as we trotted past—the voice sweet and slow, high-
pitched, not unkind, as ever knowing and prophetic and profound: "Yo' shit stink too, sugah. Yo' ass black jes' like mine,
honey chile."

At along about this time in my life—it must have been
the following spring—I came to know a Negro boy named
Willis. Save for Wash and my mother and house servants like
Little Morning, Willis was the first Negro I was ever close to.
Two or three years younger than I, the son of a woman who
had done much of the weaving at the Mill and who had died
that winter of some lung complaint, he had caught Marse
Samuel's eye as a suitable replacement for me in the carpenter's shop, now that my duties called for me to work in the
shop only half a day. As soon as I saw him at work, learning
how to plane and hammer under the tutelage of Goat, I could
understand why Marse Samuel had chosen him to be my
successor, for unlike most Negro boys—who become clumsy
and ruined for anything but the sloppiest jobs after four or
five years of bent-over toil chopping and hoeing in the cornfields, and in whose hands a hammer only turned into a
weapon to fracture their own shins—Willis was skillful and
neat, a quick learner, and he gained Goat's favor and approval
almost as quickly as I had done. He could not read or write a
word, of course, but he had a sunny, generous, obliging nature and was full of laughter; despite my early suspicion of
him—a hangover from my lifelong contempt of all black
people who dwelt down the slope—I found something irresistible about his gaiety and his innocent, open disposition
and we became fast friends. Considering my habitual scorn,
I do not know why this happened: perhaps it was as if I had

found a brother. He loved to sing as he worked, helping me
brace a timber, the voice a soft little rhythmical chatter:

"Gonna milk my cow, gonna catch her by de tail,
Gonna milk her in de coffee pot, po' it in de pail."

He was a slim, beautiful boy with fine-boned features,
very gentle and wistful in repose, and the light glistened like
oil on his smooth black skin. His only faith, like most of the
Negroes', was in omens and conjurs: with the long hairs from
the cock of a bull that had died of the bloat he had tied up
three fuzzy patches on his head, to ward off ghosts; the fangs
of a water moccasin he wore on a string around his neck, a
charm against fever. His talk was childish and guileless and
obscene. I was very fond of him; feeling thus, I was troubled
for his soul and longed to bring him out of ignorance and
superstition and into the truth of Christian belief.

It was not easy at first—leading this simple, unformed,
and childlike spirit to an understanding of the way and an
acceptance of the light—but I can recall several things working in my favor. There was his intelligence for one thing, as I
have said: unlike so many of the other black boys, half
drowned from birth in a kind of murky mindlessness in which
there appeared not the faintest reflection of a world beyond
the cabin and the field and the encompassing woods, Willis
was like some eager, fluttering young bird who might soar
away if only one were able to uncage him. Perhaps growing
up near the big house had something to do with this, only
briefly had he known the drudgery of the fields. But there
was also the mere fact of his nature, which was—different.
He had come into life blessed with an unencumbered, happy
spirit, bright and open to learning; everything about him was
lively, dancing, gay, free of that stupid and brutish inertia of
children born to the plow and the hoe.

More than all this, however, was the sway I kept over him
by virtue of what I had simply become. I possessed an un-

usual position and authority, especially for a Negro who was so young, and I was certainly fully conscious of the respect and even awe in which I was held by all the black people at the Mill now that it had become known that I was second only to Abraham in control. (Being too young, too dumb, too prideful at the time, I could not have realized—as I sat astride Judy in some noisy timber lot thronged with toiling Negroes, aloof, disdainful, intoning from a requisition in a voice ostentatiously educated and loud—how much sour resentment boiled behind those awed, respectful glances.) Owning such power and advantaging myself of Willis's innocence and the trust he had in me, I was able eventually to bring him into an awareness of God's great handiwork and the wonder of His presence abiding in all the firmament. Do not think ill of me when I confess that it was during these hours with Willis in that spring of my eighteenth year, praying with him in the stillness of a noontime meadow, exhorting him to belief as I clutched my Bible with one hand and with the other pressed long and hard on the smooth heft of his shoulder until I could feel him shudder and sigh in response to my whispered supplications—"Oh Lord, receive this poor boy Willis, receive him into Thy almighty care, receive him into belief, yes, Lord, yes, yes, he believes," and Willis's voice in a gentle fluting echo, "Das right, Lawd, Willis he believes" —do not think ill of me, I say, when I confess that then for the first time like a yellow burst of sunlight which steals out from behind a cloud and floods the day, there swept over me the mysterious sense of my own hidden yet implacable and onrushing power.

That spring I remember we went fishing together on Saturdays and Sundays. A muddy creek wound through the swamp beyond the millpond. The walnut-brown water was thick with bream and catfish and we sat long morning hours in a swarm of gnats on the slippery clay bank, angling with pine poles we made in the shop, our hooks fashioned from bent nails upon which we skewered crickets and earthworms. Far off the mill groaned, a muffled watery rushing and mumbling. The light here was diaphanous, the air warm and drowsy, astir with darting buggy shapes and the chattering of birds. One day, his finger pricked by a hook or the sharp spine of a fish, Willis cried out—"fuckin' Jesus!" he yelled— and so swiftly that I hardly knew what I was doing I rapped him sharply across the lips, drawing a tiny runnel of blood. "A filthy mouth is an abomination unto the Lord!" I said. His face wore a broken, hurt look and he reached up to lightly finger the place where I had struck him. His round eyes were soft and childlike, trusting, and suddenly I felt a pang of guilt and pain at my anger, and a rush of pity swept through me, mingled with a hungry tenderness that stirred me in a way I have never known. Willis said nothing, his eyes were brimming with tears; I saw the moccasin fangs dangling at his neck, bone-white and startling against his shiny bare black chest. I reached up to wipe away the blood from his lips, pulling him near with the feel of his shoulders slippery beneath my hand, and then we somehow fell on each other, very close, soft and comfortable in a sprawl like babies; beneath my exploring fingers his hot skin throbbed and pulsed like the throat of a pigeon, and I heard him sigh in a faraway voice, and then for a long moment as if set free into another land we did with our hands together what, before, I had done alone. Never had I known that human flesh could be so sweet.

Minutes afterward I heard Willis murmur: "Man, I sho liked dat. Want to do it agin?"

For a time I couldn't bring myself to look at him, averting my eyes, keeping my gaze up toward the sun through leaves atremble like a forest of green fluttering moths. Finally I said: *"The soul of Jonathan was knit with the soul of David, and Jonathan loved him as his own soul."*

Time passed and Willis said nothing, then I heard him

fidget on the ground next to me, and he said, chuckling: "You know what jizzom puts me in mind of, Nat? Hit look jes' lak buttermilk. Look dere."

My skin still tingled with pleasure, a tired gentle luxurious feeling which at the same time I felt to be a danger and a warning. I recall a catbird high in the water oak above, swinging like a rag amid the branches, jabbering and screeching; gnats whirred madly in the air around my ears, beneath my skull the clay bank was as cold as a sliver of ice. *They kissed one another, and wept one with another,* I thought, *until David exceeded. And he rose and departed. And Jonathan went into the city . . .*

"Come on," I said, rising. He pulled his pants up and I led him to the edge of the creek.

"Lord," I said in a loud voice, "witness these two sinners who have sinned and have been unclean in Thy sight and stand in need to be baptized."

"Das right, Lawd," I heard Willis say.

In the warmth of the spring air I suddenly felt the presence of the Lord very close, compassionate, all-redeeming, all-understanding, as if His great mercy dwelt everywhere around us like the leaves and the brown water and the chattering birds. Real yet unreal, He seemed about to reveal Himself, as fresh and invisible as a breath of wind upon the cheek. It was almost as if God hovered in the shimmering waves of heat above the trees, His tongue and His almighty voice trembling at the edge of speech, ready to make known His actual presence to me as I stood penitent and prayerful with Willis ankle-deep in the muddy waters. Through and beyond the distant roaring of the mill I thought I heard a murmuration and another roaring far up in the heavens, as if from the throats of archangels. Was the Lord going to speak to me? I waited faint with longing, clutching Willis tightly by the arm, but no words came from above—only the sudden presence of God poised to shower Himself down like summer rain, and the wild and many-voiced, distant, seraphic roaring. "Lord," I cried, "Thy servant Paul has said: *And now why tarriest thou? arise and be baptized, and wash away thy sins, calling on the name of the Lord.* That's what he said, Lord, that's what he said! You know that, Lord!"

"Amen!" Willis said. Beneath my fingers I could feel him begin to stir and shudder and another "Amen!" came from him in a gasp. "Das right, Lawd!"

Again I waited for God's voice. For an instant indeed I thought He spoke but it was only the rushing of the wind high in the treetops. My heart pounded wildly and I recall thinking then: Maybe not now. Maybe He don't want to speak now, but at another time. A thrill of joy coursed through me as I thought: He's just testing me now. He's just seeing if I can baptize. He's going to save His voice for another time. That's all right, Lord.

I turned to Willis, tugging at his arm, and together we went out into water waist-high where I could feel the mud squirm warm between my toes. Off near the other bank a little water snake scurried along like a whip on the surface of the creek, in frantic S-shaped ripples disappeared upstream; I took it as a good omen.

"*For by one Spirit are we all baptized into one body,*" I said, "*whether we be Jews or Gentiles, whether we be bond or free, and have been all made to drink into one Spirit . . .*"

"Amen," said Willis. I grasped the back of his head and shoved him under, pressed him down beneath the foaming murky waters. It was the instant of my first baptism, and the swift brief exaltation I felt brought a sudden flood of tears to my eyes. After a second or two I brought him up in a cloud of bubbles, and as he stood there dripping and puffing like a kettle but with a smile as sweet as beatitude itself on his shining face, I addressed myself to the blue firmament.

"Lord, I am a sinner," I called, "let me be saved by these redeeming waters. Let me henceforth be dedicated to Thy

service. Let me be a preacher of Thy holy word. In Jesus'
name, amen."

And then I baptized myself.

Walking back to the Mill that afternoon we passed down
a lane of dogwood, white and pink in wanton lovely splashes,
and a mockingbird seemed to follow us through the woods,
making a liquid chanting sound among the wild green leaves.
Willis kept up a steady excited chatter all the way—we had
caught half a dozen bream—but I paid little heed to him,
being lost in thought. For one thing, I knew that I must
consecrate myself to the Lord's service from this point on, as
I had promised Him, avoiding at all costs such pleasures of
the flesh as I had experienced that morning. If I could be
shaken to my very feet by this unsought-for encounter with a
boy, think what it might be, I reflected, think what an obsta-
cle would be set in my path toward spiritual perfection if I
should ever have any commerce with a *woman!* Difficult as it
might become, I must bend every effort toward purity of
mind and body so as to unloose my thoughts in the direction
of theological studies and Christian preaching.

As for Willis—well, I realized now that loving him so
much, loving him as a brother, I should do everything within
my power to assure his own progress in the way of the Lord.
I must first try to teach him to read and write—I figured he
was still not too old for learning; that accomplished, maybe it
was not beyond the bounds of possibility that Marse Samuel
might be persuaded that Willis, too, was fit for freedom and
could be set loose in the outer world—Richmond perhaps!
—with a grand job and a house and family. It would be hard
to describe how much it pleased me to think of Willis free
like myself in the city, the two of us dedicated to spreading
God's word among the black people and to honest work in
the employ of the white.

The thought filled me with such hope and joy that I
stopped on the path beneath the dogwood trees and there in

the clear spring air knelt with Willis in thanksgiving and blessed him in the Lord's name, replacing before I arose again his moccasin fangs with a tiny white cross I had carved from the shinbone of an ox.

Whenever in later times I recollected that day and thought of my first eighteen years, it seemed to me that all that long while it was as if I had been mounting a winding and pleasant slope toward the distant hills of the Lord, and that that day was a kind of promontory on the way. Not knowing the future, I had expected to pause at this lofty place and then go on, proceeding upward by gentle stages to the remote, free, glorious peaks where lay the satisfaction and fulfillment of my destiny. Yet as I say, whenever I reflected upon that eighteenth year of mine and that day and the events which quickly followed, it was plain to me that this promontory had been not a restful way station but an ending: beyond that place there was no gentle, continuing climb toward the great hills but a sudden astonishing abyss into which I was hurled like a willow leaf by the howling winds.

One long weekend late that spring there was to be a Baptist camp meeting just outside of Jerusalem. A well-known revivalist named Deacon Jones would be the leader, coming all the way down from Petersburg, and Baptists for miles around were expected to meet there—hundreds and hundreds of planters and farmers and their families from a dozen counties, some traveling from as far away as the coast of North Carolina. Tents would be pitched, for four days and nights there would be singing and praying and feasting from wild turkey and barbecue. There would be a laying-on of hands and organ and banjo music, and general salvation for all lucky enough to attend. Some of the slaveowners, I knew, would bring what Negroes they owned and these privileged souls too might partake of the spirit of the revival, and would be welcome just like the white people to approach the holy bench, even though few of *them* would get a taste of the turkey or the barbecue. When I learned of the camp meeting I became greatly excited, and I asked Marse Samuel if I might be permitted to go for the Saturday gathering, taking several of the servants in one of the wagons. I intended to include Willis and Little Morning, who had gotten religion many years before and who, ailing now and feeble and with a pitiful wandering mind, might be going to his last revival. Although Marse Samuel was an Episcopalian he had long ago put churchgoing out of his head; yet he did not scorn the Bible and often sought ways that his Negroes might be led into religious instruction—I myself of course being the chief example. Thus when I asked him if I might go on this Saturday expedition he readily gave his permission and said that he would write out a pass for the group, warning me only that I should return before nightfall and that I must keep an eye on the other Negroes, who might fall into the hands of the wise and knowing darkies from some James or Blackwater River plantation; these were smart darkies who had been exposed to white rivermen and traders and thus to vice, and they would literally swindle our innocent backwoods Negroes out of their trousers or their shoes.

Ever since the day I baptized Willis, I had begun to teach him to count and also to read, using my Bible as a primer and spelling out the words on the back wall of the shed next to the carpenter's shop, with a cattail dipped in lampblack as a kind of brush to write the letters. It pleased me to see how quickly he responded to my instruction; if I persevered, and took advantage of every opportunity, I was sure that it would not be long before he knew the alphabet and would be able to see the connection between the letters and the words in such a simple line as the third verse of the entire Bible, which of course goes: *And God said, Let there be light: and there was light.* Willis too was excited at the prospect of going to the camp meeting. Although I myself had never been to such a revival, I knew from tales told long ago by my mother and Little Morning just what sort of colorful bustle and activity might be expected, and thus I was able to tell Willis all about it and infect him with my own anticipation. On the afternoon before the day of the camp meeting I borrowed two juicy pullets from Goat's brood, promising to pay him back in extra work, and I made up a large and festive meal for us Negroes who were going—fried chicken, a rare treat, and a couple of loaves of shortening bread I was able to wheedle out of Abraham's wife, who had become cook at the big house—and I put the chicken and bread in a small pine box together with a jug of sweet cider, placing all in the carpenter's shed where it would be safe from pilfering black hands, and then went to bed at a very early hour since we would be leaving for Jerusalem long before dawn the next morning.

At along about midnight I was awakened by a soft whisper and, suspended like clinking bells above my face, the tinkling of a lantern in whose sudden yellow glow the eyes of a little Negro girl were as round as eggshells. It was one of Wash's younger sisters—another of Abraham's numberless children —and she mumbled that I must come down to the cabin right away, her daddy had sent her, her daddy was miserable sick. I dressed and followed the girl down the slope through the moonlit, frog-filled, balmy night and there in the cabin found Abraham as the girl had said, feverish and in bed, coughing and hacking away, his broad black chest glistening with streams of sweat in the glare of the lamp.

" 'Tain't nothin', Nat," he said weakly. "Hit jes' de misery I gits ev'ry springtime. I gwine be awright come next week." After a pause he went on: "But nem'mine dat. Marse Samuel done told me I gots to take dem four boys up to whar de trace begins at two in the mawnin'. What time hit now?"

"I just heard the clock ring twelve," I said. "What boys you talking about, Abe?"

"Marse Samuel done hired out four boys to chop tobacco fo' two weeks over to de Vaughans' place. Vaughan's got a wagon dat's gwine meet our wagon up whar de trace commences. I uz supposed to carry dem boys up dere but now I got dis misery, so you got to carry 'em, Nat. Dat's at two o'clock, so git on now an' let dis po' sick man rest his bones. I gwine be awright."

"But I'm goin' to the camp meeting, Abe," I started to protest, "all this time I figured on the camp meeting—"

"You kin *still* go to de camp meetin', boy." he insisted, "you jes' ain't gwine git a whole lot of sleepin', dat's all. Now git on, Nat, and carry dem boys on up dere in de wagon. Dey waitin' right now behin' de stable. Here, you got to take dis yere paper."

Of course Abraham was right about the camp meeting: I might still make it to the beginning of the trace and back, pick up Willis and Little Morning and the others and be off to Jerusalem just as I had planned—provided only that I was willing to do without sleep, a minor burden. What I had not counted on, however, was that among those four Negro boys I must take to meet the Vaughans' wagon, among those sleepy black faces upturned to the moonlight in the hushed luminous space of ground behind the stable's lowering wall, was that of Willis himself, and my heart gave a sickening heave as I caught sight of him and as there came over me a chill, clammy sense of betrayal.

"But he said you could go to the camp meeting!" I fumed while I harnessed up the two mules, shortening their traces amid the manure-sweet stable gloom. Willis padded drowsily about barefooted in the darkness, helping me, saying not a word. "*Daggone*, Willis!" I whispered urgently. "He didn't mention *nothin'* at all about bein' hired out to Major Vaughan. *Nothin'!* Now daggone it, you goin' to be over at the Vaughans' for two weeks choppin' tobacco and maybe it'll be a whole 'nother year before you get to go to a camp meetin'." I was nearly frantic with disappointment, and the radiant globe of pleasure and anticipation in which I had buoyantly dwelt for so long cracked and fell away from me like shattered glass as I yanked the mules out onto the moon-drenched lawn and, wildly impatient, urged the boys up into the wagon. "Daggone it," I said, "I fixed fried chicken and there's *cider* too! C'mon, nigger boys, move yo' butts!" The three other boys scampered up over the tailgate; young field hands of fifteen or sixteen, they giggled nervously as they clambered into the wagon; all three of them wore rabbits' feet attached to a leather bracelet on the left ankle—that year a plantation fashion; one boy was able to disgorge at will large bullfrog belches and this he began to do without ceasing, bringing forth from the other boys squeals of child-ish laughter. Willis climbed onto the seat beside me. "Git up, mules!" I said angrily. It was the first time I had ever felt even the trace of disillusionment with Marse Samuel and this strange new feeling itself added to my distress. "Daggone Marse Samuel anyway!" I said to Willis as we set forth down the lane. "If he was going to hire you out to the Vaughans for two weeks, how come he didn't tell me and you first so we wouldn't get all prepared about goin' to the camp meeting?"

In a little while my chagrin and anger drained away, fad-ing off into that mood of resignation to which most Negroes become accustomed sooner or later, no matter what the oc-casion. After all, there were worse blows, I figured as we rocked along slowly through the moon-white woods; suppose Willis could not go to *this* camp meeting, did it really mat-ter? Certainly there would come along other revivals I could take him to, and his failure to attend this one would make but a tiny gap in his spiritual education. I looked at him tenderly as the moon spread a pale light over his features; nodding next to me, he was half asleep, his delicate lips apart and his eyelids fluttering in a fight against slumber. I aroused him with a nudge and a question: "What's two and three?"

"Five," he said after a pause, rubbing his eyes.

"And three and four?"

"Seven." He began to say something else, hesitated, then went on: "Nat, how come you figures Marse Samuel done hired *me* out? I'se a 'prentice carpenter."

"I don't know," I said truthfully, "I reckon they need extra hands over there. But that's all right. Marse Samuel only hires out to good people, I know that, and the Vaughans are quality folk, treat you well. Anyway, listen, it ain't but for two weeks, no time at all. Then you'll be back and we'll have more teaching. What's three and eight?"

"Fo'teen," he said, yawning hugely.

Behind us in the cart the three boys had gone to sleep, sprawled against each other lifeless and limp in the moonlight. The night was clamorous with frogs and katydids, warm, fragrant with cedar, clear like day, the moon powdering the trees in light as starkly white as the dust of bone. The lop-eared mules, plodding along with a crushed rasping sound against the dewy weeds, found their way ahead as if they knew the road by heart, and I let the reins go slack in my hand, drowsing too, and fitfully slept until the end of the trace, roused only once and then dimly by the high wail of a bobcat miles off in the swamp, its distant scream echoing through some perplexed strange dream like the sound of claws scraped in anguish across the bare face of the heavens.

Presently I felt Willis stir on the seat and sensed the other boys moving about behind me; then I woke with a start and realized that the mules had stopped. Here in the moonlight at the end of the trace I saw the log road stretching east and west through the weeds and now against the trees the outline of the Vaughans' wagon, huge and canvas-covered and motionless, the floppy white roof making it look like the picture of a sailing ship, foundered now upon the edge of the forest.

The figures of two white men disengaged themselves from the shadows of the wagon, and one of them—a portly gentleman with a plump aging face beneath a shiny wide-brimmed planter's hat—approached as we sat there, and said to me in a not-disagreeable voice: "You Abraham?"

"Nawsuh," I said. "I'se Nat. I'se de numbah-two driver. Abraham he done took sick, yassuh, 'deed he took real sick." Nigger gabble.

He drew closer to the wagon and all of a sudden a tinkling musical sound and a jaunty little tune interrupted the silence, sending a spooky chill up my back, and then I saw that the man had taken from his vest a silver watch and had opened it, and that it was from this watch that the music was coming, in miraculous plinkety notes, as if he held a tiny spinet piano and tiny pianist—I thought of one of the beribboned Turner ladies—imprisoned in his hand. My wonderstruck eyes must have betrayed me, for the man said then: "Quite a little timepiece, no? A triumph of the watchmaker's art. That, my boy, is Loodwig van Beethoven." He snapped the watch shut, strangling the music in mid-passage. "And you are no more than ten minutes late and deserve praise for your promptitude. Look alive, boy!" He tossed up at me a plug of chewing tobacco, which I caught in midair. "Now then, Abe—or what's your name—you have four young hands for the Vaughans here, right? And a paper for me to sign which you will take back to your master." He turned aside from me for an instant and called in a breezy, amiable voice toward the back of the wagon: "All right, boys! Up now into the other wagon! Hop to, lads! We've nearly to Greensville County to go tonight." Willis and the other boys scrambled down off their perch and moved somnolently toward the Vaughans' great white wagon across the road. "Sleepyheads, I see!" he said with a chuckle. "Well, you'll find the Major's wagon a cozy enough place for a snooze. Hop to now, me young bucks! Hurry up and we'll be on our way!"

"Good-bye, Nat," Willis said, starting across the road.

I made a silent, parting wave to Willis and watched as the man spread the paper which Abraham had given me against the footboard beneath my legs and scratched something across it with a stubby quill, humming to himself in a breathy, hoarse voice the same tune he had just let loose from his watch. *"Todd,"* he whispered, *"Jim, Shadrach, Willis . . .* There, boy," he added finally, "You take that receipt back to your master, and mind that you don't lose your way. Go home straight away, do you hear me? Good night, laddie."

"Good night, massah," I said. I watched him cross the log road and mount the wagon with slow and corpulent difficulty, seating himself next to the other white man, a shaggy blur in the moonlight, who tapped all four mules into an ambling start, then gave the hindmost mule a sharp and savage stroke with his whip, causing the wagon to sway out of the ditch, groaning as it picked up a ponderous sluggish speed and continued to totter and sway in a precarious lopsided angle above the log road and with a great noise like the collision of countless barrels gained a final momentum, the uproar diminishing as the white shape passed westward through the moon's relentless glare and out of sight.

The Vaughans' ain't west, I thought. The Vaughans' place is east.

I sat there without moving. One of my mules stamped wearily, setting the traces to jingling. Around me in the woods the sound of frogs was deafening, shrilling in a ceaseless insensate choir like wind through a million reeds. Almost imperceptibly the moon sank slowly behind a thicket of cypress trees, and the log road was shadowed in a tangle of bent silhouetted limbs and branches, black as human arms. From the south a gentle breeze sprang up and I heard a whispering and a stirring across the leafy roof of the forest.

"Lord?" I said aloud.

Still I listened to the soft and sibilant rustling among the moonlit treetops, and I held my breath as if waiting for the sound of some immanent, hovering voice.

"Lord?" I called again. But as I sat listening the wind died, and along with it the whispering and rustling, the unspoken voice, and the night once again was enveloped in a shrilling of frogs, the ripe hot chirruping of katydids among the trees.

I must have waited there for an hour or more. Then slowly I started back—with an emptiness such as I had never felt before—knowing that I did not have to read the paper in my hand to make me sure of what I already knew, thinking miserably, fiercely: Willis. And those boys! Gone, Lord. Plain gone for good! Listen, Lord. Not hired out, not Vaughan's, not anything but that man with the watch who was nothing but a nigger trader. Simple as that, yes, Lord! Not hired out but Jesus Christ Almighty sold . . . Sold, Lord, sold!

And he was saying: "One might think I was a blockhead not to know why you've been moping around for so long and regarding me so accusingly. But though I will take the blame for poor management of an already bungled transaction, I will have to still steadfastly defend myself from any charge of insensibility. For is that not what you find me guilty of?"

"I don't understand what that word means," I said. "The charge of—something."

"The charge of insensibility. The charge that I somehow blithely allowed you to arrange to take the boy to a camp meeting while fully aware that he was to be sold before you ever got to Jerusalem. Which brings me to another matter that I should mention in passing. And that is the camp meeting itself. I was in Jerusalem that Friday, which as you may remember was the first day of the revival. I believe I counted no more than twenty-four of the faithful, not including several stray cats and dogs, at the meeting grounds. They packed up and left the next day, and had you gone there with your wagonload of wild-eyed apostles you would have been greeted by a deserted field of grass. Which only goes to show that this benighted countryside cannot sustain a religious revival any more than it can feed itself. So I mention in passing that I saved you from a bad disappointment. But as for the lad in question, I must only repeat that I had no more idea that you were taking *him* to that camp meeting than I had knowledge that the two of you were what you describe as inseparable friends. Lacking eyes in the back of my head, or a seventh sense, I can scarcely be asked to mark the relationship between every human being among the eighty or so of all colors that exist on this property. And I think it was a great Frenchman, Voltaire, who said that the beginning of wisdom is the moment when one understands how little concerned with one's own life are other men, they who are so desperately preoccupied with their own. I knew *nothing* about you and that boy, nothing at all."

I remained silent, wetting my lips with my tongue and feeling desolate and miserable, gazing at the library floor.

"I have told you more than once now that had you come to me the next day and stated your case—had you made yourself immediately clear instead of for two weeks casting me these looks of *canine* reproach—I should have taken steps to get the boy back, buy him back even though that might mean money and travel to an extent quite out of the ordinary. But I must try to convince you that surely by now he has passed through the Petersburg market—though even of the place I cannot be really certain, it may be that he was taken to a sale in Carolina—whatever, that he has been passed on into some buyer's hands and must now be on the way to Georgia or Alabama, though one can hope that a kindly providence has seen fit that he somehow remain in Virginia. This, however, I sincerely doubt. The fact remains that he would now seem to be all but irrecoverable. I am in no way blaming you for lacking the presence of mind to come to me earlier when I may have been able to do something about it. I am only asking you now to try to understand the impossibility of my position. Do you see what I mean?"

"Yes," I said after a moment. "Yes, I do but—"

"Yes, *but* again," he interrupted, "you are still eaten up about that one thing that will not let you alone. Even though you say you told him of your own surprise, you are devoured by the terrible idea that the boy for the rest of his life will think that you were a party to, an accomplice in, his disposal. Am I correct in this? Isn't that what you said you are unable to shake from your mind?"

"Yes," I replied, "that's right."

"Then what can I say? Say that I too am sorry? I've said that over and over to you before. Perhaps he will think that, perhaps not. Possibly it would be better for your peace of mind if you envisioned him thinking charitably of you—if indeed it occurs to him to think of you as being involved in his disposition at all—envisioned him thinking of you only as an unwitting and ignorant dupe in the whole transaction, which you were. But if he thinks otherwise, I can only repeat again and for the last time that I am sorry. There is nothing else that I can say. Understand again: I had no idea that Abraham would fall ill and that you would become the—the instrument by which those boys were delivered into—into other hands." He halted then and looked at me, lapsing into silence.

"But—" I began slowly, "but I—"

"But what?"

"All right," I went on, "I see pretty well, I guess, about Willis, you didn't know about him and I. How I was teaching him and all. But this other thing I don't understand. I mean, going out at night like that and thinking they was going to be hired out at the Vaughans'." I paused. "I mean, everyone was going to know what really happened anyway, by and by. Or not by and by. Soon."

He looked away from me and when he spoke at last his

voice was faint and faraway; suddenly I realized how weary he seemed, how gaunt were his cheeks and how red-rimmed and vacant were his eyes. "I will be truthful with you. I was quite simply troubled—afraid. I got confused, lost my bearings. Only twice do I recall darkies ever being sold away from here—both times by my father, both of the darkies, I'm afraid, crazy people who were a threat to the community. Furthermore and aside from that, there has never until now been any need. So I had never sold off hands before, and as I have readily admitted, it was a bungled transaction. I had not wanted the word to get around, I was afraid of the trouble and unrest that would ensue once the darkies knew that some of the people were being sold. So in my confusion I conceived the idea of disposing of the first four under the cover of night and in the guise of a fortnight's hire to Major Vaughan. I thought that somehow the shock would be less this way, that it would be easier for the place to become accustomed to their absence. Worst of all, I conspired with a trader. It was folly to expect anything to come of this method. It was devious and cowardly. The duplicity! The masquerade! I should have done it in broad daylight with all the plantation as gaping onlookers to a plain and simple sale, with money changing hands in full view. Of the entire proceedings the only redeeming feature may be that at least I tried to make certain that my first sale would involve no separation of families. It was unfortunate for you, perhaps imponderably unfortunate for your young friend, that my resolve to pick only boys who were old enough to make the break, boys who additionally had already been orphaned and who thus had no family ties to sever—well, it was unfortunate that *he* was one of four who answered to that description." He halted again, remaining silent, then said in a faint voice: "I'm sorry. God, how sorry I am, that Willie . . ."

"*Willis*," I said. "And so you just had to sell them. There just wasn't any other way."

His back was to me now, he stood facing the great high

window open to the spring garden, and his voice, dim enough at the outset, was barely audible and I had to strain to hear it, as if it belonged to someone so infirm and depleted, or so lacking in spirit or hope, that whether the words could be understood was at last a matter of indifference. He went on as if he hadn't heard me.

"Well, soon all of them will be gone—everything—not just the land now utterly consumed by that terrible weed, not just the wagons and the pigs and the oxen and the mules but the men too, the white men and the women and the black boys—the Willies and the Jims and the Shadrachs and the Todds—all gone south, leaving Virginia to the thorn bushes and the dandelions. And all this we see here will be gone too, and the mill wheel will crumble away and the wind will whistle at night through these deserted halls. Mark my word. It is coming soon."

He paused, then said: "Yes, I had to sell those boys because I needed the money. Because anything non-human I had to sell was unsellable. Because those boys were worth over a thousand dollars and only through their sale could I begin to make the slightest inroad upon those debts I have accumulated for seven years—seven years during which I have lied to myself night and day in an effort to believe that what I saw around me was an illusion, that this mutilated and broken Tidewater would survive in spite of itself, that no matter how wrecked and eaten up the soil, no matter how many men and chattel began to move south to Georgia and Alabama, Turner's Mill would forever be here grinding out timber and meal. But now it is timber and meal for ghosts." He ceased speaking for a moment, then again the weary voice resumed: "What should I have done instead? Set them free? What a ghastly joke! No, they had to be sold, and the rest of them will be sold too, and soon Turner's Mill will stand a dead hulk like the others on the landscape, and somewhere in the far South people may remember it but it will be remembered as if it were the fragment of a dream."

For a long time now he fell silent and then finally he said (or I *think* he spoke my name, I was straining so hard to hear), "*Nat* . . ." And when he spoke again, his voice was the barest murmur as if whispering from the far bank of a stream against a rising wind. "I sold them out of the desperation to hang on pointlessly a few years longer." He made an abrupt gesture with his lifted arm, and it seemed that he passed his hand in a quick angry motion across his eyes. "Surely mankind has yet to be born. *Surely* this is true! For only something blind and uncomprehending could exist in such a mean conjunction with its own flesh, its own kind. How else account for such faltering, clumsy, hateful cruelty? Even the possums and the skunks know better! Even the weasels and the meadow mice have a natural regard for their own blood and kin. Only the insects are low enough to do the low things that people do—like those ants that swarm on poplars in the summertime, greedily husbanding little green aphids for the honeydew they secrete. Yes, it could be that mankind has yet to be born. Ah, what bitter tears God must weep at the sight of the things that men do to other men!" He broke off then and I saw him shake his head convulsively, his voice a sudden cry: "In the name of money! *Money!*"

He became silent and I stood waiting for him to continue, but he said nothing, turned with his back toward me in the dusk. Afar and high above I heard Miss Nell call out: "Sam! *Samuel!* Is there anything wrong?" Yet again for a long while he made no sign, no motion, so at last I moved quietly toward the door and left the room.

Three years after this episode (and a galloping swift three years they seemed to me)—a month before my twenty-first birthday and at just about the time I had originally been destined to start my life anew in Richmond—I was removed from Marse Samuel's purview and passed into the temporary

custody of, or fell under the protection of, or was rented out
to, or was borrowed by, a Baptist preacher named the Reverend Alexander Eppes, pastor to an impoverished flock of
farmers and small tradesmen living in a district called Shiloh
about ten miles to the north of Turner's Mill. For a long time
I was never quite clear as to the relationship between me and
the Reverend Eppes. Yet, one thing is certain, and this is
that I was not "sold," in the unadorned, mercenary sense of
the word. The other Negroes at Turner's Mill might be sold—
and sold they were, with depressing regularity—but the notion that *I* could be disposed of in this way was, up to and
including the moment when I passed into the hands of the
Reverend Eppes, quite inconceivable. Thus for the next three
years, aware though I might have been of the uncertainty of
the future that lay before me, I never thought once that
Marse Samuel would not still ensure my freedom in Richmond as he had so eagerly promised—and I kept up this
sunny optimism and complacency even as I watched Turner's
Mill and all of its land and its people and its chattel and its
livestock disintegrate before my eyes like one of those river
islands at flood time which slowly crumbles away at the
edges, toppling all of its drenched and huddled ragtag occu-
pants, coons and rabbits and blacksnakes and foxes, into the
merciless brown waters.

The Negroes—because they were by far the most valuable of the property, because at anywhere between four hundred and six hundred dollars apiece they represented the only
safe, solid capital which Marse Samuel could liquidate in
order to meet his creditors' incessant demands (the creditors
too were packing up and leaving the Tidewater, hence an
urgency in their claims)—the Negroes began to be sent off at
a steady rate, in twos and threes or singly, a family here,
another there, though often months might go by without a
sale. All at once would appear a man in a gig, a gentleman
with white side whiskers and a thick gold watch chain,

stamping the mud from his mirror-bright boots. In the library
I would serve biscuits and port from a silver tray, listening to
Marse Samuel's voice wan and weary in the summer dusk:
"It is the traders who are an abomination, sir, the traders!
That they will generally pay more means nothing to me.
They are unscrupulous, sir, and would think nothing of separating a mother from her only child. That is why, helpless as
I am in this dreadful situation, I can at least insist upon
dealing with a gentleman . . . Yes, with one bad exception, so
far all my sales have been with gentlemen like yourself . . .
You are from the York County Fitzhughs, you say? Then you
must be a cousin of Thaddeus Fitzhugh, a classmate of mine
at William & Mary . . . Yes, the last lot of people I sold was to
a gentleman heading west to the Boonslick country, I believe, in Missouri; I sold him a family of five . . . A most
humane and learned gentleman from Nottoway he was . . .
You are favored by the gods, sir as you must know, to have a
mill situated near a city like Richmond, free of the burden,
the curse of land . . . I do not know, sir, it is clear that time is
drawing short for me here. Perhaps I shall go to Kentucky or
Missouri too, though I have heard of interesting prospects in
Alabama . . . Come now, I will show you George and Peter,
the best mill hands I have left, you may be sure that they are
uncommonly likely Negroes . . . Only a few of my darkies will
have been fortunate enough to remain in Virginia . . ."

So George and Peter would go, or Sam and Andrew, or
Lucy and her two young boys, packed off in a wagon which I
myself would often drive to deliver them in Jerusalem, and
always I was haunted and perplexed by the docile equanimity and good cheer with which these simple black people,
irrevocably uprooted, would set out to encounter a strange
and unknown destiny. Although they might cast backward
what appeared to be the faintest glimmer of a wistful glance,
this final parting from a place which had been their entire
universe for years caused them no more regret than did the

future cast over them worry or foreboding: Missouri and
Georgia were as far away as the stars, or as near as the next
plantation, it was all the same to them, and with despair I
marked how seldom they seemed to bother even bidding
farewell to their friends. Only the rupture of some family tie
I felt could grieve them, and such calamities did not happen
here. Twittering and giggling, they mounted the wagon poised
to carry them to an impossible fate at the uttermost ends of
the earth, and they could speak only of an aching knee, the
potency of a hairball from a mule's stomach as a charm
against witches, the proper way to train a dog to tree a possum, and mumble incessantly about eating. Slumbrous in
broad daylight, they would flop asleep against the side
boards of the wagon, pink lips wet and apart, nodding off into
oblivion even before they had been taken beyond the gate,
even before they were carried past the bounds of that land
which had composed the entire smell and substance and
geography of their lives and whose fields and meadows and
shimmering woodland now dwindled away behind them, unseen and unremarked, forever. They cared nothing about
where they came from or where they were going, and so
snored loudly or, abruptly waking, skylarked about, laughing
and slapping each other, and trying to clutch at the passing
overhead leaves. Like animals they relinquished the past
with as much dumb composure as they accepted the present,
and were unaware of any future at all. Such creatures de-
served to be sold, I thought bitterly, and I was torn between
detestation for them and regret that it was too late for me to
save them through the power of the Word.

And so at last an alien quietude and stillness settled over
the plantation, a hush so profound that it was in itself like the
echo or reverberation of a faint remembered sound upon the
ear. Finally it was not alone the Negroes who were disposed
of but all the rest—the mules and the horses and the pigs, the
wagons and the farming implements and the tools, saws and

spinning wheels and anvils and house furniture, buggies and
buggy whips and spades and scythes and hoes and hammers,
all and anything movable or unhingeable and detachable and
worth more than half a dollar. And the absence of these
things left a silence astonishing and complete. The great mill
wheel, its last revolution accomplished, lay idle on its oaken
shaft bedecked with dried mattings of greenish pond weed
and grass, motionless now, the deep-throated steady grumble
and roar as much a memory as those other diurnal sounds,
far more faint yet persistent, that had echoed in all weathers
season after season from dawn till dusk: the *chink-chinking*
of hoes in the distant cornfields, sheep bleating on the lawn
and a Negro's sudden rich laughter, an anvil banging in the
blacksmith's shop, a snatch of song from one of the remotest
cabins, the faint crashing in the woods of a felled tree, a
stirring within the big house, a fidget and a buzz, a soft musical murmuration. Slowly these sounds diminished, faded,
became still altogether, and the fields and rutted roadways
lay as starkly deserted as a place ravaged by the plague:
weeds and brambles invaded the cornfields and the meadows;
sills, frames, and doors fell apart in the empty outbuildings.
At night, where once glowing hearths lit each cabin down the
slope, now all lay in suffocating dark like the departure of the
campfires of some army on the plains of Israel.

As I have already said, Marse Samuel soon found that it
was not possible for me to be delivered to that Mr. Pemberton in Richmond on my twenty-first birthday as he had
hoped. Through the solemn moments of one evening after
supper he explained to me how the depression which afflicted
the Tidewater had washed over the city too, and how the
market for such clever labor as I might provide had severely
diminished—indeed was "busted," as the saying goes. Thus
my master was faced with a troublesome dilemma. He could
not on the one hand simply set me free without a period of
"seasoning" in the hands of a responsible person: all too many

young Negroes, given their freedom without sponsorship, without some protection, had found themselves one morning beaten senseless, their papers stolen, bumping about in a daze as the wagon wheels rumbling underneath their cracked skulls bore them south to the fields of cotton. At the same time to take me with him to Alabama (that is where, almost at the last moment, he decided to try the remnants of his luck) would altogether defeat his plans for me, since opportunities for the rich life of a free Negro craftsman were almost non-existent down in those townless river-bottom swamps and stews. So finally Marse Samuel had decided upon a provisional course, entrusting my body to the good Christian shepherd of whom I have spoken, the Reverend Eppes—this devoted and pious gentleman who could be expected to complete the documents in regard to my freedom as soon as the times got better up in Richmond (as they surely would) and who as recompense for his compassion and his overseeing of my destiny would receive the fruits of my labor for a while, *gratis*.

And so there came a September morning, hot and throbbing with the sound of locusts, when Marse Samuel bade me farewell for all time.

"I told him we were leaving this morning," he said to me, "so the Reverend Eppes should be here to fetch you sometime around noon, maybe before. As I have told you before, Nat, you need have nothing to worry about. Although a Baptist, the Reverend Eppes is a gentleman of great probity and kindliness and will treat you in exactly the manner I would wish. You will find him a man of simplicity, and of modest resources, but he will be good to you. I shall be in touch with him by post from Alabama, and I shall be in touch with my own representatives in Richmond. And thus after a year or so, no more, the Reverend Eppes will arrange for your apprenticeship in Richmond and your eventual emancipation in just the same way I would have done had I been here. It is all written up in the agreement we made in Jerusalem and its legality is unquestioned. More important, though, Nat, is the trust I have in the Reverend Eppes. He will provide for all your needs, physical and spiritual. He is truly a gentleman of humanity and honor."

We stood in the shade of a great sycamore tree; the day was sultry, breathless, the air close and damp like a warm mouth-enveloping hand. The four wagons with which Marse Samuel would make the long trip were ready, waiting, the mules stamping and stirring in their traces. The rest of the family—the older nephew and his wife, Miss Emmeline, Benjamin's widow, Miss Nell—had gone away already; they had stopped down in Raleigh with cousins or (in the case of the older ladies) had begun a sojourn in Petersburg, from whence Marse Samuel would summon them once all was safely established on Alabama soil. Of the Negroes, only Prissy and Little Morning and Abraham and his family were left; house Negroes, they had memories of happy times, and they wept loudly, the mourning lot crammed into one wagon. In tears I had said good-bye to them all, kissing Prissy and clasping Abraham in a warm mute embrace and, at last, taking Little Morning's cold old-leathery feeble hand and pressing it to my lips; hair white as frost now, palsied and totally gone in the head, he lay propped sightless and uncomprehending at the rear of the wagon, heading south at his life's withered and weary end from the only home he had ever known. The mules stirred and stamped in their traces. Try as I might, I seemed unable to stifle my grief.

"You mustn't take on so, Nat," Marse Samuel said, "it is not like a death, it is like a new life for all of us. We shall always be in touch by the post. And you—" He paused for an instant, and I knew that he too was moved. "And you—*you,* Nat—think of the freedom that you will have, after all! Keep that in mind always and the sorrow of this parting will fade in your memory. The *future* is all that matters in our lives."

Again he ceased speaking and then, as if struggling to choke back his own feelings, began to say all sorts of commonplace things in a forced voice touched with false cheeriness: "Come now, Nat, chin high! . . . The receiver of the land, Judge Bowers in Jerusalem, is sending around a man who will remain here as the custodian and he might even be here today . . . Meanwhile, Prissy has left noontime dinner for you in the kitchen . . . Chin high, Nat, chin high always and good-bye! . . . Good-bye! . . . Good-bye!"

He embraced me awkwardly, swiftly. I felt his whiskers against my cheek, and heard Abraham's bullwhip crack far ahead like a musket. Then he turned about and was gone, and the wagons were gone, and it is the last I ever saw of him.

I stood in the lane until the final echo of the wheels vanished rattling in the distance. My desolation was complete. As sundered from my root and branch as a falling leaf fluttering on eddies of air, I was adrift between that which was past and those things yet to come. Great boiling clouds hung on the far horizon. For a long moment I felt myself like Jonah cast into the deep, in the midst of the seas, with floods compassing me about and all God's billows and waves passing over me.

And now I began to look forward to the coming of the Reverend Eppes, but it took an almighty long time for him to fetch me. All morning I sat on the steps of the bare veranda, stripped of its furniture, waiting for the clergyman to arrive, awaiting the sound of hoofbeats, the rattle of some conveyance coming up the lane. It was hot and muggy and a moist haze with a hint of storm about it blurred the greenish sky; by late morning the sun burned down through murky waves of heat, so oppressive that even the locusts became still and the birds retreated, silent, to the leafy blue sanctuary of the woods. For two or three hours I read from my Bible, commit-

ting several Psalms to memory. (My Bible was the only possession I had to take away from Turner's Mill save for these
things: a single change of denim pants, two cotton shirts, an
extra pair of what are elegantly known as nigger brogans,
some little bone crosses I had carved, a needle and some
thread, a pewter cup left to me by my mother, and a ten-
dollar gold piece which Marse Samuel had given me the day
before. It was a matter of custom that the person into whose
hands I was delivered would supply the rest of my needs.
The gold piece I had sewn into the belt band of my pants,
and I kept everything wrapped in a large blue bandanna.) It
seemed appropriate to the moment, suspended as I was between two existences, troubled by abandonment and loss,
heartsick at the void I felt upon the departure of all the
dearest and best friends I had ever known, yet at the same
time obscurely excited by the promise of a new world, liberty, the fruition of all those dreams I had entertained in the
recent past of myself a freedman jauntily striding toward
church or job down some Richmond boulevard—it seemed
appropriate to this mingled mood, as I say, that I study a
Psalm in which sorrow and exaltation were joined, and I recollect that it was Psalm 90 that I put to memory that morning, the one beginning, *Lord, thou hast been our dwelling
place in all generations*, and which contains the verse that
goes: *A thousand years in thy sight are but as yesterday
when it is past, and as a watch in the night* . . .

Noon came and went, the coppery sun sank toward the
afternoon: still no Reverend Eppes, and I was hungry. I remembered then (having in my absorption forgotten) the
meal waiting for me, and so with my sack thrown over my
shoulder I walked back through the bare, deserted halls to
the kitchen. There on a shelf over the great brick hearth was
the last meal ever to be served here to a Turner: four pieces
of fried chicken, half a loaf of shortening bread, sweet cider
in a cracked mug—decent big-house food, proper for a fare-

well repast, thoughtfully covered by a worn clean flour sack as a screen against flies. That I recall with great clarity such small details may have something to do with the overall sense of ominousness, the spidery disquietude and perplexity which, like the shadows of vines creeping up a stone wall in descending sunlight, began to finger my spine as I sat on the window sill in the empty kitchen eating that chicken and bread. The stillness of the plantation was at this instant almost complete, so oppressive and strange that I suddenly thought, jittery with a vague terror, that I had been stricken by deafness. I ceased eating for a moment, both ears cocked and straining, waiting for some sound outside—a bird call, the plashing of a duck on the millpond, a whisper of wind in the forest—to convince me that I could hear, but I heard nothing, nothing at all, and my panic swelled until just then the startling noise of my own bare callused foot scuffing roughly on the pine floor reassured me: I chided myself for my silliness and continued eating, and was further soothed by a fly's insensate deafening mutter as it settled on the topmost edge of my ear.

But the feeling of an ominous hush and solitude would not leave me alone, would not fade away, clung to me like some enveloping garment which, try as I might, I could not ease from my shoulders. I tossed the chicken bones down into the weed-choked flower bed below the kitchen window, and wrapping the remains of the bread carefully in my sack along with the broken mug—I thought it would become of use somehow—ventured out into the great hall of the house. Dismantled of everything that could be moved—of crystal chandeliers and grandfather's clock, carpets and piano and sideboard and chairs—the cavernous room echoed with a tomblike roar to my sudden sneeze. The reverberation smashed from wall to wall with the sound of waterfalls, cataracts, then became silent. Only a lofty mirror, webbed with minute cracklings and bluish with age, embedded immovably

between two upright columns against the wall, remained as
sure proof of past habitation; its blurred and liquid depths
reflected the far side of the hall, and there four immaculate
rectangles marked the vanished portraits of Turner forebears;
two stern gentlemen in white wigs and cocked hats, two
serene ladies with modest bosoms bedecked in ribbons and
flounces of pink satin, they had been nameless to me yet over
the years as familiar as kin: their absence was suddenly
shocking, like swift multiple deaths.

I went back out on the veranda, again waiting for the
sound of hooves and wheels, and again there was only silence. Even then I had begun to feel that I was alone, abandoned, forgotten, and that no one was going to come and
fetch me; the sensation caused me fear and foreboding but
part of the emotion was not unpleasant, and way down inside
I felt my bowels stirring with a mysterious, queasy, voluptuous thrill. I had never felt this way before and tried to put it
out of my mind, laying my sack down on the veranda steps
and strolling to the small promontory at the side of the house,
where in almost one glance it was possible to survey the entire prospect of abandoned dwellings, decaying shops and
sheds and ruined land—an empire devastated by the hordes
of Gideon. The heat had become wicked, unrelenting, pouring down from a smudged, greasy sky in which the sun pul-
sated like a faint pink coal through the haze. As far as my eye
could reach, the cabins lay in weatherworn rows to the vast
bottom cornfield, now a majestic jungle of weeds, sunflowers,
and impenetrable green bramble. The sense of excitement,
gut-deep, warm, squirmy, returned irresistibly as I watched
the scene, as my eyes lingered on the ranks of empty cabins
then returned to regard the shops close by, the outhouses and
stables and sheds, and the big house looming near, unpeopled
and silent in the terrible heat.

Only a dripping of water through the cracked millpond
dam disturbed the silence now—only a steady unhurried

dripping and nearby the flickering hum of grasshoppers in the weeds. I tried to force back the sharp and growing excitement but even as I did so I felt my pulse pounding and the sweat flowing beneath my arms in streams. There was no wind, the trees in the surrounding woods were quiet; yet because of this very stillness they seemed a solid mass stretching out on all sides of me in perfect circumference to the last boundaries of the world, an all-pervading triumphant mass of greenery. Nothing but this still and ruined plantation existed; it was the very heart of the universe and I was the master not alone of its being at the present instant but of all its past and hence all its memories. Solitary and sovereign as I gazed down upon this wrecked backwater of time, I suddenly felt myself its possessor; in a twinkling I became white—white as clabber cheese, white, stark white, white as a marble Episcopalian. I turned about and moved to the very crest of the slope, hard by the circular drive where carriages had come and gone and ladies in crinoline and taffeta had lightly and laughingly dismounted upon carpeted footboards, their petticoats spilling on the air like snow as I steadied their outstretched arms. Now, looking down at the shops and barns and cabins and distant fields, I was no longer the grinning black boy in velvet pantaloons; for a fleeting moment instead I owned all, and so exercised the privilege of ownership by unlacing my fly and pissing loudly on the same worn stone where dainty tiptoeing feet had gained the veranda steps a short three years before. What a strange, demented ecstasy! How white I was! What wicked joy!

But my blackness immediately returned, the fantasy dissolved, and I was again overtaken by wrenching loneliness and a pang of guilt. The Reverend Eppes did not appear, though I strained my ears for the sound of his approach on the road. I went back to my Bible once more, reading and committing to memory one of my favorite passages—the story of Samuel and the ark of the covenant—while afternoon lengthened and light dimmed on the veranda and thunder grumbled and heaved faintly on the smoky horizon.

As it grew dark I knew that the Reverend Eppes would not arrive that day. I got hungry again and had a twitch of sharp discomfort when I realized that there was no more to eat. Then I remembered the shortening bread in my sack, and when night fell, I ate the rest of the loaf, washing it down with water from the cistern behind the kitchen. Inside the house it was as black as the swamp on a moonless night, clammy and stifling, and I stumbled aimlessly about while clouds of mosquitoes whined about my ears. My little bedroom had been stripped bare like all the rest, and there was no use sleeping there, so I lay down on the floor in the great hall near the front door with my sack as a pillow beneath my head.

Then along about what must have been eleven o'clock a storm descended on the plantation, scaring me out of wits and sleep; titanic lightning bolts illumined the dark, in flashes of eerie green outlined the deserted mill and the millpond, where steely rain swept the surface of the water in windy sheets and torrents. Cracklings of thunder rent the heavens, and a single shaft of lightning suddenly broke in two a huge old magnolia nearby in the woods, toppling half the behemoth to earth with a squealing and a groaning like a stricken madman. The night filled me with terror, I had never known such a storm, never in my life; it seemed a special storm ordained by God, and I hid my head between my sack and the bare planks of the floor, wishing that I had never been born. At last the storm slackened, dwindled away with a soft dripping noise and I raised my head up, recollecting the flood: *The fountains also of the deep and the windows of heaven were stopped, and the rain from heaven was restrained* . . . I whispered thanks to the Lord in a prayer, and finally went off to sleep, listening to the wet sound of an owl, blown in by the storm, as it stirred and shivered somewhere high on a ledge of the hall above me, fussing *hoot*-oo, *hoot*-oo, *hoot*-oo.

Then I heard a voice—"Git on up, boy"—and I awoke in a dazzle of morning light to see and feel the toe of a black boot prodding me awake—not a gentle prod, either, but an insistent sharp boring-in between my ribs which caused me to gasp and rise instantly onto my elbows, gulping morning air as if I had been half drowned.

"You Nat?" I heard the man say. Even as he spoke I knew it was the Reverend Eppes. He was clad from head to toe in clerical black; motheaten black preacher's leggings he wore too, level with my eyes now, and I saw that several buttons were missing and for some reason the gaiters exuded, or seemed to exude, a sour, worn, unclean smell. My eyes traveled up the length of his long black-clad shanks and his seedy black mohair frock coat and lingered for the barest instant on the face, which had a skinny, big-nosed, pentecostal, Christ-devoured, wintry look of laughterless misery about it; bespectacled with oval wire-framed glasses, belonging to a man of about sixty, redly wattled in the neck like a turkey gobbler's, bitter of countenance and opaque of eye, it was a face graven with poverty, sanctimony, and despair, and both my heart and my belly suddenly shriveled within me. If nothing else, I knew I had had my last piece of white bread for some time to come.

"You Nat?" he said again, more insistent now. It was a barren and suspicious voice, nasal, full of cold November winds, and something in it warned me that with this clergyman it would not do to display any educated airs. I scrambled to my feet and retrieved my sack from the floor and said: "Yas, massah, das right. I'se Nat."

"Git on in that buggy down 'ere," he ordered.

The buggy was at the veranda steps, drawn by the most pathetic sway-backed old spotted mare I had ever seen. I clambered up onto the worn seat and waited there in the sunlight for half an hour or more, watching the sad old nag switch her tail against a hide covered with sores upon which flies supped greedily and listening to the muffled commotion made by the Reverend Eppes as he stamped about in the far recesses of the house. Finally he returned and climbed up on the seat beside me, bearing with him two huge iron pothooks (I had thought it impossible that the house could yield anything else to a scavenger) which he had managed to yank with his great raw-knuckled fists out of the solid oak of a kitchen wall. "*Gee*-yup, Beauty," he said to the horse, and before I knew it we had gone down the lane beneath the trees shrill with locusts, and Turner's Mill, abandoned to the beetles and the meadow mice and the owls, was out of my life forever.

We must have traveled several miles up the wagon trace before the Reverend Eppes spoke again. During this part of the journey, the sorrow and the sense of dislocation and loss I had felt—the ache of desperate homesickness which had tormented me ever since I had been left alone the day before —was obscured by the pure fact of hunger in my stomach, and I thought longingly of yesterday's chicken, and felt my insides painfully rumbling, all the while hoping that if the Reverend Eppes opened his lips to utter a thought it would be a thought concerning the question of food. But this was not to be.

"How old you be, boy?" he said.

"I'se twenty, massah," I replied, "twenty-one come de first day October." It is good for a Negro, when trying to ingratiate himself with a strange white man, to convey an impression of earnest simplicity and this may often be achieved by adding to such a reply as mine some phrase like "Das de truth," or "Das right." I think that I must have tacked on then a sweet and open "Das de truth," and by so doing made the mistake of arousing in the Reverend Eppes a further consciousness of my youth, my innocence.

"You ever git any of them little nigger girls in the bushes?" he said. A funky stale smell seemed to pour from his threadbare clothes, an odor of grease and soil and deep poverty; I wanted to avert my nose but dared not. There was something about the man that filled me with an uneasiness verging on dread. Dismayed by his question, I felt myself honestly unable to answer and tried to let myself off the dilemma in typical nigger fashion by a slow soft giggle and a great mouthful of inarticulate syllables. "Aa! Eeh— Haw!"

"Mr. Turner done told me you religious-minded," he said.

"Yassuh," I replied, hoping that religion would work to my advantage somehow.

"So you religious-minded," he went on. He had a dry barren voice, monotonously reedy and harsh, like the crepitation of a cricket in the weeds. It seemed impossible that such a voice could ever exhort people to anything. "And if you religious-minded, then you shorely know, boy, what King Solomon son of David said about women, 'specially whores. He said a whore is a deep ditch, and a strange woman is a narrow pit. She also lieth in wait as for a prey, and increaseth the transgressors among men. That right, boy?"

"Yassuh," I said.

"He said by means of a whorish woman a man is brought to a piece of bread, and the adulteress will hunt for the precious life. That right, boy? He said keep thee from the evil woman, from the flattery of the tongue of a strange woman. Lust not after her beauty in thine heart, neither let her take thee with her eyelids. You *know* that's right, boy."

"Das right," I replied, "yassuh, I 'spect das right." We had not looked at each other; I sensed rather his wintry and eaten face next to mine, gazing despairingly straight ahead, and I smelled the sour, yeasty odor seeping from his clothes; my mouth went as dry as sand.

"But a young man," he said, "now that's a different idea. A

young man is beauty and sweetness. He said eat thou *honey,* because it is good, and the honeycomb which is sweet to thy taste. Eat thou *honey.* That right, boy? He said the glory of young men is their strength and the beauty of old men is the gray head. He said when thou liest down thou shalt not be afraid, yea, thou shalt lie down. Yes, boy? Hope deferred maketh the heart sick but when the *desire* cometh, it is a tree of life. The true root and the tree of life, praise God."

"Yassuh," I sighed wretchedly.

We rode for a long time in silence. We had taken a side turning off the trace and passed now through country I had never seen before. It was poor, eroded land with weed-choked red-clay fields bare of habitation. Scraggly pine groves stretched across the landscape, and high in the blue above us turkey buzzards swooped and wheeled, touching me with gloom and with visions of bleached skeletons, decayed flesh, and slow suffering deaths. A smoky haze hung over the land, and crows cried dismally from afar. It was as if all the people had suddenly vanished from the earth.

"Tell me something, boy," he said finally, the reedy voice suddenly strained, hesitant yet fraught with some terrible decision. "I hear tell a nigger boy's got an unusual big pecker on him. That right, boy?"

I became feeble with anxiety and could make no reply. The buggy had stopped and we rested in the shade of a spindly old oak, half dead in a shroud of leaves prematurely yellowing and withering, the great hulk of its trunk smothered in the green fecund moist embrace of honeysuckle and Virginia creeper. Dizzy with apprehension, I kept my eyes fixed toward my feet. A fragrance of honeysuckle mingled with the presence now of the Reverend Eppes; he was sweating in streams, and I could see the sweat as it drained from beneath his black shiny cuff and onto the back of the great ungainly sun-blistered hand which now tensely clutched his knee.

"You know what I hear tell, boy?" he went on, placing the same tight and tormented hand on the fleshy part of my upper leg. His voice trembled, his old ugly red fingers trembled, and I too felt myself trembling inwardly as I made a silent, urgent plea to the heavens: *Lord? Are you there, Lord?* A cloud passed over the day then, and a sudden breath of coolness came, borne as if on the air freshening in the treetops; now with a leafy tremor the coolness fled, light blossomed blindingly, and the stench of the Reverend Eppes once more was sour and close. "I hear tell your average nigger boy's got a member on him inch or so longer'n ordinary. That right, boy?"

I remained as silent as the space within a tomb, feeling the quivering fingers on my thigh. When I made no reply, he fell somberly quiet, then after a long moment he squeezed down remorselessly on my flesh and whispered: "You goin' to mind me, boy?"

But this time when I failed to answer, he removed his hand from my leg and we started off anew, squeaking dustily along northward through the sullen and woebegone countryside. Perhaps half an hour passed before he spoke again, and his dry ageless cricket's voice was filled with despair and hatred and love and misery and retribution as he said: "You *better* mind me! You jest *better* mind me, that's all, you hear!"

Time grows brief in this chronicle of my early years. My residence with the Reverend Eppes was short-lived. There remains need to tell only of the way in which the Reverend Eppes's stewardship of my fortunes led me not toward that freedom I had for so long anticipated as a natural consequence of the transfer of my person into his custody, but toward something entirely and surprisingly different.

It had been Marse Samuel's intention, I believe, that I labor only for a short while in the service of the minister.

However, it turned out that I worked there for less time than Marse Samuel must even have imagined. As you have doubtless seen, one of Marse Samuel's characteristics was a fetching ingenuousness and faith in human nature; being a poor judge of people anyway, it was especially unfortunate that abstaining as he did from formal religious observance, he should still retain a traditional respect for and trust in the goodness of the clergy. This trust was a central mistake. I think that in handing me over to the Reverend Eppes he envisioned a charming, benign, and mutually satisfying relationship between an adorable old bachelor preacher and his black acolyte—already "religious-minded" and learned in the Scripture—the two of us dwelling in perfect Christian concord as I celebrated with honest labor the spiritual harvest that his age and wisdom might shower upon me. What a splendid vision. What tender dreams of charity one hopes blessed my late master's slumber amid the balmy Alabama night!

Well, old Eppes ceased trying to ravish me (and this is one of the few tolerable aspects of my stay) fairly early on, so that by the time autumn arrived I was free at least of that worry, which for a spell had been a burdensome one. There had been a few days after my arrival at Shiloh when he had ambushed me in the sagging, pestilential two-hole outhouse which served both his own pitiful dwelling and the church; there, cosseting me loudly again with proverbs and other suasions from Holy Writ, he tried to break me down by the same route he had traveled on the day of our first encounter, his big old beak leaking the dew of frustration onto his upper lip and his voice a paradigm of anguish as he clutched at me amid the swarming flies. But one day he made a great and defeated shudder, and with wormwood in his mouth, abandoned the quest, to my relief and puzzlement. Only much later, when I grew older and considerably more reflective, did it occur to me that his desire for me, intense as it was, must have been at war with and was finally exceeded by his desire for my domination. Had he reached his lesser goal, had I submitted to his malodorous gropings, he would have gained a pet but lost a slave; it is not easy totally to master someone you've buggered behind the woodpile, and if I had become the compliant vessel of his cravings he might have found it much harder to run me until my legs felt like stumps.

Which is what he did—eighteen and twenty hours a day, seven days a week, *especially,* I should add, on Sunday —and for the first time in my life I began to sense the world, the *true* world, in which a Negro moves and breathes. It was like being plunged into freezing water. Further, I soon realized that my predicament was made even more onerous by the fact that I was the only slave in Shiloh, a grim and pious little crossroads community of some thirty-five souls. Small farmers for the most part, scratching for life itself in arid patches of corn and sweet potatoes, these were the leftovers and castoffs from the same cataclysmic depression which had sent the more prosperous of their fellow citizens, like Marse Samuel, to the far South: failed overseers, one-armed tinkers, bankrupt country storekeepers, reformed drunks, God-maddened paralytics, they were a bleak and undone brotherhood of true believers with scarcely a dollar to divide among them and only the hope of the soul's rescue through total immersion to preserve them and their goiterous women and pale, straw-haired, worm-infested children from absolute disintegration.

As the only two-legged chattel in Shiloh, then, it befell my lot not only to do the chores for the Reverend Eppes—to chop kindling and haul spring water and feed Beauty, the sway-backed mare, and shell corn and slop the three pigs and build the morning fires, acting both as a sort of grotesque valet to the preacher in the shack he called a parsonage and as a sexton at the rickety church—but to be of service to the rest of the congregation as well. As I deviously learned, the good pastor had never been in possession of a Negro before (that I must have become, however briefly, the answer to a lifelong prayer is a fact which often touched me in later years), and in the first flush of enthusiasm over the bonanza that I represented, he obviously had a deep Christian urge to share me equally with the members of his flock. Thus all that fall and winter—one of the most frigid years within living memory—I found how swiftly the body loses its sap and the soul its optimism through having one's energies split three dozen ways. It seemed to me that I had been plunged into a hallucination in which I had parted from all familiar existence and was suddenly transformed into a different living creature altogether—half-man, half-mule, exhausted and without speech, given over to dumb and reasonless toil from the hours before dawn until the dead of night. In the tiny three-room parsonage I slept in what was called the kitchen, on a straw tick covered with rags near the back door. Bitter winds moaned through all the cracks in the house; even stoked to the limit the fireplace gave scant warmth; when banked at night it gave no heat whatever, and as I lay shivering on the floor in the dim light I could see ice congealing on the surface of the preacher's chamber pot. He snored cavernously all night long, throbbing like a mill wheel through my restless dreams. Sometimes he would give a great strangled noise and wake up chattering disconnected words from the gospel. "I also *am* of Christ!" he howled once, and another night I saw his white nightshirted shape lurch upright as he wailed: "*Lewdness*, O ye Jews!" Even in the unbelievable cold the house was fetid and rank like a chicken pen in summer.

Lord, what a time! How I yearned for the days and months to pass and for the winter to end; how I waited for the moment to come when I would be delivered from this pesthole, to Richmond and into freedom. But it became an endless and wicked season, with no relief in sight. Thrice monthly the post coach came through from the South, but the mail it dropped off was scanty anyway, and there was never a letter from Marse Samuel—certainly not a word for me nor (at least so far as I was able to tell) any message to the Reverend Eppes. And so I labored through icy months, sustained by the gloomy comfort of Ecclesiastes, whose words I managed to put to memory in the few moments wrested each day from sleep and work. It was good to realize, as I hauled away the contents of the privy in a leaky bucket, that all is vanity; the great Preacher succored me through hours of ceaseless toil.

In the mornings I sweated for the Reverend Eppes, chopping wood, toting water, sweeping, whitewashing the outer timbers of the house and the church—an unending task not made easier by the fact that the whitewash often froze on the brush. After midday dinner (we bowed our heads together in blessing and then ate in silence in the kitchen, he on the single chair, I crouched on my haunches on the floor, devouring a meal that was unvaryingly terrible—fatback and corn pone drenched in molasses—but at least abundant: in that fearsome weather my protector could not afford to have his labor source lose power through meager victualing) there would come a rattling of wagon wheels outside on the frozen rutted ground, and a cry: "It's me, George Dunn, Parson! I've got the nigger this afternoon!" And off I would go to the Dunn place three miles away at the edge of the pinewoods, there to work for another six hours felling trees, burning brush, emptying privies, shelling corn or performing any of a dozen low and muscle-wrenching chores it might strike a doomed, chilblained red-necked Baptist farmer needed doing. Other days I often walked to my afternoon's labor, trudging two miles or more along some snow-covered woodland path, to arrive finally with freezing toes at a shack or cabin in a clearing and hear a woman's voice from the front stoop: "*Leander!* The nigger's here!" I began to feel myself loutishly half existing, my identity fading, as a Percheron must feel if it feels, never more so than those times when after hours of frostbite and sweat on the roof of a barn, I was compelled to carry back to the Reverend Eppes the actual rental for my labor—a silver dollar rarely, most often a cramped, brain-tormented:

> Rev. Eppes I. O. U.
> $0.50 U.S.
> Use of nigro 5 hours
> Ashpenaz Groover. 12 Jan.

on a scrap of coarse brown paper, or a crock of pickled okra, a pound of goat cheese wrapped in a flannel rag, or a jar of candied sweet potatoes—delicacies, moreover, I never got to taste. No one beat me, and I was rarely even scolded. Generally speaking, I was accorded the cheerful respect due any superbly efficient mechanism.

My despair and loneliness grew until the existence I led seemed a nightmare from which I was frantically trying to arouse myself; the burden of my daily wretchedness felt an actual weight, heavy and immovable, bearing down like a yoke upon my shoulders. For the first time in my life I considered the extremity of running away (following honorably in my father's barefooted path), but I was dissuaded from such a course not alone by the two hundred miles of trackless and freezing wilderness which lay between myself and Pennsylvania, but by the fear, of course, that in so doing I would simply forfeit the very liberty I had been assured was soon to be mine. Yet all remained the same. With a fingernail purchase on freedom, I found myself laboring like an ox. Every ten days the mail coach came up from the South, and departed, leaving no advice from Marse Samuel. Despair and gloom pressed down upon me like merciless hands. Each morning I awoke praying that on *this* day I would be taken to Richmond, there to be delivered into the hands of that civilized and enlightened master whose only concern was eventually to obtain my freedom. The moment never arrived. I squatted silently with the Reverend Eppes in the draughty kitchen, choking down my corn pone and molasses. Overhead, day after sullen day, the sun was a wafer of light barely visible, wanly tracing the hours across a creepy black sky dreamed by Jeremiah.

I cannot calculate what my value was in cheese and okra but I made a mental accounting of the hard cash I brought in, and figured that between October and the middle of February I earned for the Reverend Eppes a total of $35.75.

About the services in the ramshackle church (keeping four stoves fueled all afternoon and evening with hickory logs made Sunday one of my most arduous days) it is best to remain for the most part quiet, drawing over these mysteries —as Sir Walter Scott might say—a prudent veil. For although I myself in later years acquired great power in preaching and exhortation, and found myself deeply stirred by the way in which people took flame from the Word and became exalted by it, sometimes losing possession of all their senses; and although through total abandonment it is often possible to obtain a close communion with the Spirit—nonetheless these white people at Shiloh were a scandal, whooping and shouting and bubbling at the mouth as the Reverend Eppes raked them through hellfire in his dry cracked voice, and amid the sweat and steam, falling into a kind of ultimate frenzy, stripping to their underdrawers, male and female, and riding each other bareback up and down the aisles. It seemed to me Babylonian, a mockery, and I was always glad when the Sunday night service was over and I could clean up the mess they made and go to bed.

Once at dusk, coming back from a weary afternoon's work at a farm deep in the pinewoods, I paused for a short while in the middle of a clearing. Heavy snow lay over the floor of the woods and in the trees, and there was not a sound anywhere. Darkness was pressing on fast, and I knew that if I did not get back to the parsonage before nightfall I would surely lose the way and just as surely freeze to death in the forest. Yet for some reason I was not frightened by the notion; it seemed a friendly and peaceable idea, to fall asleep amid the snow and the pines and never wake up—delivered into the bosom of eternity, forever safe from mean and dishonorable toil. It was a blasphemous, faithless vision but somehow I thought God might understand. And for a long moment I loitered there in the cold, silent clearing, watching the gray twilight descend, half yearning for the night to overtake me and enfold me close within its benign, chill, indifferent arms.

But then I recalled the new life which awaited me in Richmond and the grand future I would have as a free man, and a sudden panic seized me. I began to run through the snow, faster and faster, and reached the parsonage just before the last light faded from the sky.

On February 21, 1822, in the village of Sussex Courthouse, Virginia, the Reverend Eppes sold me into bondage for $460. I'm certain that this sum is true because I watched Evans or Blanding—I do not know which one—of Evans & Blanding, Incorporated, auctioneers, pay that amount in twenty-dollar bills as we stood in the anteroom of the nigger pen that the traders had set up in a crumbling brick tobacco warehouse on the outskirts of the village. The date, too, I know to be exact because it was outlined in flagrant red upon a big corporate wall calendar, not ten feet from where we stood, along with the inscription in ragged journeyman printer's type:

$ $ $
PLAY SAFE WITH "E. & B."
SPOT CASH PAID FOR
LIKELY NEGROES
$ $ $

The fifteen-mile trip by buggy up across the county line from Shiloh, the sale itself—everything had taken less than half a day. It had all happened before I could even think about it. And I stood there in the windy barnlike building, clutching my sack and watching the old preacher convey me into a trader's hands.

I recall crying out: "But you can't do this! You and Marse Samuel had a written agreement. You was to take me to *Richmond!* He *told* me so!"

But the Reverend Eppes said not a word, counting bills, each golden second climbing from penury to riches, his spectacles frosting up as with wettened forefinger and eagerly moving lips he verified his booty.

"You *can't!*" I shouted. "I've got a *trade,* too! I'm a carpenter!"

"Somebody hush the nigger up!" I heard a voice say nearby.

"That nigger boy, gentlemen," the preacher explained, "is a little tetched in the head about that one item. But he jest bully where it matters. He jest a *bully* worker. Got right smart strength for one so slender, and a good mind on him—can actual spell out some words, and has a God-fearin' spirit. Reckon he might be a likely stud, too. Mercy, ain't this been a winter?" Then without further comment he turned and on a frosty blast of air was gone.

I cannot make sense out of most of the rest of that day. I do recollect, however, that in the evening, as I lay slumped in the crowded, noisy pen with fifty strange Negroes, I experienced a kind of disbelief which verged close upon madness, then a sense of betrayal, then fury such as I had never known before, then finally, to my dismay, hatred so bitter that I grew dizzy and thought I might get sick on the floor. Nor was it hatred for the Reverend Eppes—who was really nothing but a simple old fool—but for Marse Samuel, and the rage rose and rose in my breast until I earnestly wished him dead, and in my mind's eye I saw him strangled by my own hands.

Then from that moment on (until the occasion of beginning this account of my life) I banished Marse Samuel from my mind as one banishes the memory of any disgraced and downfallen prince, and I refused to give him ten seconds' thought ever again.

One night soon after this there was a thaw and it started to rain. Torrents of water came down, lashed by a bitter west wind. Later the temperature began to fall and the rain turned to sleet, so that by the next morning all of the countryside was sheathed in a glistening, crystalline coverlet of ice, as if dipped in molten glass. Finally the sleet stopped, but the sky remained leaden and overcast, and the ice-encrusted woods seemed to merge without definition into the glassy and brittle underbrush of the fields, casting no shadow. That day, after I had been sold at auction to Mr. Thomas Moore, we rode back south out of Sussex Courthouse in a wagon drawn by two oxen, and the wheels squealed and crackled against the white troughs of ice in the rutted road and the iron-shod hooves of the oxen crunched cumbersomely on the hard frozen earth.

Moore and his cousin, another farmer whose first name was Wallace, sat hunched up on the seat behind the oxen, and I leaned up to the rear of them on the wagon's open tailboard with my feet dangling over the edge. It was fearsomely cold and as we creaked along I shivered, although the frayed woollen overcoat which was the single legacy of my stay at the Reverend Eppes's gave me a certain protection against the wind. Yet it was not the weather which now concerned me, but an irreparable and still, to me, inconceivable violation of my all too meager property. For less than an hour before, after having bought me, Moore had found and grabbed the ten-dollar gold piece I had so carefully sewn up inside my extra pair of pants. Like some avid little weevil or roach he had homed as if by the sheerest primitive instinct upon my few possessions and within seconds had extracted the gold piece from the belt band, ripping the seam, his round small pockmarked rustic's face puckered with sly relentless triumph—"I figgered a nigger once't lived at Turner's Mill ud steal him some loot," he muttered to his cousin—as he bit down on the coin then thrust it into the pocket of his jeans.

All my life I had never owned so much as a tin spoon, and the gold piece had been the only real treasure I had ever possessed; that I had kept it so briefly and had parted with it so quickly was something I could barely comprehend. I had wanted to save it against the time when I might start a church in Richmond, now it was gone. Coming as it did after three days' and nights' wait in the nigger pen—my limbs poorly warmed and even more poorly nourished on cold cornmeal mush—and joined with the quick disposal of my body to Mr. Thomas Moore, this final act of piracy left me numb and beyond outrage, and I sat stiff, bolt upright on the tailboard of the wagon, clutching my sack tight against my lap with one hand and with the other holding the Bible pressed against my chest. I felt a dull ache around the edge of my jaw and wondered in a distant way at the reason for it, then recollected that it had been caused by Moore's begrimed and knobby fingers when he had thrust them into my mouth to ascertain the soundness of my teeth.

I listened vaguely to the conversation between Moore and his cousin Wallace, the words coming as if from yards and yards away, from the treetops or across the margin of a remote and snow-covered field.

"They was this hoor I knowed in Norfolk, on Main Street, name Dora," the cousin was saying, "she would do it three ways if'n you'd pay a dollar-fifty—fifty cents each way and take all afternoon." He began to snort and chuckle, his voice thickening. "Second time you shoot, hit jest like a covey of quail flyin' straight out yo' ass—"

"Sho," Moore put in, chuckling too, "sho, I knowed this other hoor who done it three ways, name of Dolly—"

I put their godless talk out of my mind and stared at the glassy and desolate woods, silent now save for the remote noise, every so often, of a branch cracking beneath the weight of ice or the patterning faint sound of a hare as it scampered through the frozen meadows. I shivered suddenly and felt my teeth clicking together in the fierce cold. We had approached a fork in the road, and as I turned my head slightly I glimpsed a wooden signpost sparkling beneath transparent ice and two crude painted signs, one pointing to the southwest:

N. Carolina via Hick's Ford

The other to the southeast:

Southampton County Line 12 mi.

All of a sudden the wagon stopped and I heard Moore say: "Hit's the right-handed fork to Southampton, ain't it, Wallace? I recollect that's what Pappy said to take when we come back out of Sussex. Ain't that what he said, Wallace?"

Wallace was silent for a moment, then he murmured in a puzzled voice: "Goddam me, I can't recollect *what* he said." He paused again, finally adding more confidently: "If'n we hadn't come up here by way of that trace through the marsh, I'd know for sure, but now hit *do* seem to me he said take the right-handed fork comin' back. Yah, I could swear he said the right-handed fork. The left-handed fork'll end you up in Carolina. Gimme 'nother suck on that jug."

"Yah," said Moore, "that's what he said now, I know for sure, the right-handed fork. That sho is what Pappy said."

A whip cracked on the cold air, the hooves of the oxen resumed their crunching on the rutted road, and as we took the right fork southwest toward Carolina, I thought: Trouble is, since neither of them ignorant scoundrels can read we're likely to get into worse problems if I don't set them straight right away, right now. We'll sure end up lost twenty miles south of here. Anyway, I might get warm sooner.

I turned around and said: "Stop the wagon."

Moore's head swiveled about to face me, the wicked little eyes bloodshot, bulging, incredulous. I could smell an odor of brandy the length of the wagon. "What did you say, boy?" he murmured.

"Stop the wagon," I repeated, "this way goes to Carolina."

The wagon stopped, wheels sliding and squealing against the ice. Then the cousin turned about, incredulous too, silent, staring, licking his pink peeling lips amid a scraggle of reddish beard.

"How you know this way goes to Carolina?" Moore said. "Jest how do *you* know?"

"The sign said so," I replied quietly. "I can read."

. Moore and his cousin glanced at each other, then back at me.

"You can read?" said Moore.

"Yes," I said, "I can read."

Again they exchanged quick suspicious glances, and the cousin turned to me, glaring, and said: "Try him, Tom. Try him with the writin' on that shovel."

Moore held up a shovel which had lain clotted with earth below them at the front of the wagon. Along its ashwood shaft ran an inscription burnt large and deep with a branding instrument.

"Read them words there, boy," said Moore.

"It says, 'Shelton Tool Works, Petersburg, Virginia,'" I replied.

The shovel clattered back onto the floor of the wagon, and as I once more turned around I saw the white woods roll before my eyes in a slow blurred procession of glittering ice-crowned trees while the wagon itself wheeled about in a clumsy half-circle then moved briefly north to the signpost, pivoted, and resumed its ponderous journey southeast now, toward Southampton. An emptiness clutched my stomach as I realized suddenly how hungry I was, after three days on cornmeal mush. Never had I known such hunger before, never in my life, and I was astonished at the urgency of its pain, the desperation of its clamorous appeal deep within my guts.

Moore and his cousin brooded quietly for a long while, then at last I heard Wallace say: "Onliest nigger I ever knowed about could read was a free nigger up in Isle of Wight. Had him a little shoe-cobblin' business in Smithfield and wrote out letters and such for some of the white folks. When he died they cut open his head and looked at his brain and it had wrinkles in it just like a white man's. And you know, they was a story 'bout how some of the niggers got holt of a part of that brain and actual *et* some of it, hopin' they'd git smart too."

"Hit don't do no good for a nigger to git learning," Moore said somberly, "hit don't do no good in any way whichever. Like Pappy says, a nigger with a busy head is idle with the hoe. That's what Pappy says."

"A nigger with learning bound to git uppity," Wallace agreed.

"Hit don't do no good in any way whichever."

"I'm hungry," I said.

Like the hunger, I had never felt a whip before, and the pain of it when it came, coiling around the side of my neck like a firesnake, blossomed throughout the hollow of my skull in an explosion of light. I gasped and the pain lingered, penetrating to the inside of my throat, and I gasped again, feeling that the pain might throttle me to death. Only at that moment, seconds later, did the noise of the whip impress itself on my mind—oddly quiet, a sedate whickering like a sickle slicing through air—and only then did I raise my hand to touch the place where the rawhide had cut my flesh, sensing on my fingertips a warm sticky flow of blood.

"When I gits ready to feed I'll tell ye, hear me?" said Moore. "And say *master!*"

I was unable to speak, and now again the whip struck, in the same place, blinding me, sending me afloat outside myself on a reddish cloud of pain.

"Say *master!*" Moore roared.

"Mastah!" I cried in terror. "Mastah! Mastah! *Mastah!*"

"That's better," said Moore. "Now shut up."

Once in the last days before my trial, when I was pondering my own death and was filled with a sense of the absence of God, I remember Mr. Thomas Gray asking me what had been the various things in time past that God had spoken to me. And although I was trying to be truthful I had been unable to answer him exactly, for it was the most difficult kind of question and had to do with a mysterious communion which was almost impossible to explain clearly. I told him that God had spoken to me many times and had surely guided my destiny but that He had never *really* given me any complicated messages or lengthy commands; rather He had spoken to me two words, and always these words alone, beginning on that day in the back of Moore's wagon, and that it was through these words that I was strengthened and that I made my judgments, absorbing from them a secret wisdom which allowed me to set forth purposefully to do what I conceived as His will, in whatever mission, whether that of bloodshed or baptism or preaching or charity. Yet just as they were words of resolution they were words also of solace. And as I told Gray, God had a way of concealing Himself from men in strange forms—in His pillar of cloud and His pillar of fire, and sometimes even hiding Himself from our sight altogether so that long periods on earth would pass during which men might feel that He had abandoned them for good. Yet all through the later years of my life I knew that despite His hiding Himself for a while from me, He was never far off and that more often than not whenever I called He would answer —as He did for the first time on that cold day: "I abide."

I wiped the blood from my neck and crouched down shivering into my overcoat. I listened to the wheels crunching and bumping along the rutted road, uneven here and littered with fallen icy branches, so that the wagon yawed and heaved and pitched me back and forth in a soft rhythm against the boards. Moore and his cousin were silent. A cold winter wind breathed suddenly across the roof of the woods.

"Lord," I whispered, raising my eyes. "Lord?"

Then high at the top of the icy forest I heard a tremendous cracking and breaking sound, and that voice booming in the trees:

I abide.

I clutched my Bible against my heart and leaned against the boards as the wagon, heaving and rocking like a rudderless ship amid a sea of frozen glass, bore me southward again into the dead of winter.

Part

III

STUDY WAR

AN EXQUISITELY SHARPENED HATRED FOR the white man is of course an emotion not difficult for Negroes to harbor. Yet if truth be known, this hatred does not abound in every Negro's soul; it relies upon too many mysterious and hidden patterns of life and chance to flourish luxuriantly everywhere. Real hatred of the sort of which I speak—hatred so pure and obdurate that no sympathy, no human warmth, no flicker of compassion can make the faintest nick or scratch upon the stony surface of its being— is not common to all Negroes. Like a flower of granite with cruel leaves it grows, when it grows at all, as if from fragile seed cast upon uncertain ground. Many conditions are required for the full fruition of this hatred, for its ripe and malevolent growth, yet none of these is as important as that at one time or another the Negro live to some degree of intimacy with the white man. That he know the object of his hatred, and that he become knowledgeable about the white man's wiles, his duplicity, his greediness, and his ultimate depravity.

For without knowing the white man at close hand, without having submitted to his wanton and arrogant kindnesses, without having smelled the smell of his bedsheets and his dirty underdrawers and the inside of his privy, and felt the casual yet insolent touch of his women's fingers upon his own black arm, without seeing him at sport and at ease and at his hypocrite's worship and at his drunken vileness and at his lustful and adulterous couplings in the hayfield—without having known all these cozy and familial truths, I say, a Negro can only *pretend* hatred. Such hatred is an abstraction and a delusion. For example. A poor field Negro may once in a while be struck by the whip of an overseer riding on a tall white horse, that same Negro may be forced onto short rations for a month and feel his stomach rumble daily in the tight cramps of near-starvation, again this Negro might someday be thrown into a cart and sold like a mule at auction in pouring rain; yet if this selfsame Negro—surrounded from childhood by a sea of black folk, hoeing and scraping in the fields from dawn to dusk year in and year out and knowing no white man other than that overseer whose presence is a mean distant voice and a lash and whose face is a nameless and changing white blob against the sky—finds himself trying to hate white men, he will come to understand that he is hating imperfectly, without that calm and intelligent and unrepenting purity of hatred which I have already described and which is so necessary in order to murder. Such a Negro, unacquainted with white men and their smell and their blanched and bloodless actuality and their evil, will perhaps hate but with a hatred which is all sullenness and impotent resentment, like the helpless, resigned fury one feels toward indifferent Nature throughout long days of relentless heat or after periods of unceasing rain.

During the four or five years approaching 1831, when it had become first my obsession and then my acceptance of a divine mission to kill all the white people in Southampton, and as far beyond as destiny might take me, it was this matter of hatred—of discovering those Negroes in whom hatred was already ablaze, of cultivating hatred in the few remaining and vulnerable, of testing and probing, warily discarding those in whom pure hatred could not be nurtured and whom therefore I could not trust—that became one of my primary concerns. Meanwhile, before telling of my years at Moore's and of the circumstances leading up to the great events of 1831, I should like to dwell on this mysterious quality of hatred which it is possible for a Negro to cherish for white people, and to describe one of the moments in my own experience when I felt this hatred at its most deranging and passionate.

This must have been in the summer of 1825, when I had been Moore's property for a little over three years—a time of great inner confusion and turmoil for me since I was "on the fence," so to speak, toying with the notion of slaughter and already touched with the premonition of a great mission, yet still fearful and laden with anxiety and unwilling to formulate any definite plans or to ready myself for a firm course of action.

On this day of which I am speaking, Moore and I had driven a double wagonload of firewood into Jerusalem from the farm, and after we had unloaded our deliveries (a considerable portion of Moore's income derived from supplying wood for private homes, also the courthouse and the jail) my owner had gone off to buy some things elsewhere, as was his custom on Saturdays, leaving me to while away several hours by myself. I had become at that time deeply involved in reading the Prophets—mainly Ezekiel, Daniel, Isaiah, and Jeremiah, whose relevance to my own self and future I had only commenced to divine. It was my habit therefore not to waste time with the other Negroes who stood about chattering idly or wrestling in the dust of the field behind the market or quarreling over some black girl of the town one of them might manage to lure behind a shed. (Often this would lead to group fornication, but through the Lord's grace I was never tempted.) Instead I would take my Bible to a sunny corner of the wooden gallery at the front of the market and there, some feet apart from the hubbub and the confusion, I would squat for hours with my back against the wall, immersed in the great prophetic teachings.

It was on this pleasant morning that I found myself distracted by a white woman who emerged from a corner of the gallery and suddenly paused, one hand held up against her forehead as if to shield her eyes from the dazzling sunlight. She was an extremely beautiful woman of about forty, stately and slender, dressed in blue-green silk the color of a brandy bottle, with whorls of faint pink in it which swirled and vanished and reappeared even as she stood there, stirring a little, a look of perplexity on the pale oval of her face. She carried a frilly parasol and a richly brocaded purse, and as she paused at the edge of the gallery, frowning, I suddenly knew that such lustrous finery and such delicate and unusual beauty could only mean that this was the woman whose arrival in town had caused a storm of rumor—gossip of course not unremarked by the Negroes, and in this case gossip of such a nature as to evoke only a kind of awed respect. The recently acquired fiancée of Major Thomas Ridley—one of the wealthiest landowners in Southampton, still rich enough to hold onto fifteen Negroes—the woman was from the North, resident of a place called New Haven, and it was bruited that the fortune to which she was heir was in itself of a size that would dwarf the riches of all the estates in Southampton put together. Her extraordinary beauty, her clothes, her strangeness: all of these were of such rarity that it is not remarkable that on that bright morning her appearance among the grubby mob of Negroes caused a reverential hush, sudden and complete.

I watched her step down from the gallery and onto the dusty road, the brass tip of her parasol making an agitated *tat-tat* while she gazed about again, as if searching for direction. And just at this moment her glance fell upon a Negro who was idling nearby directly below me. I knew this Negro, at least by repute, which was doleful indeed. He was a free Negro named Arnold—one of a handful of the free in Jerusalem—a gaunt grizzle-polled old simpleton black as pitch and with an aimless slew-footed gait, the result of some kind of paralysis. Years before he had been set at liberty through the will of his owner, a rich up-county widow, an Episcopal churchwoman shattered by guilt and pining for eternal bliss. I suppose one might praise this high-minded gesture, yet one must add that it was grimly misguided because Arnold was a troubling case. Rather than becoming an embodiment of the sweet fruits of freedom, he exemplified by his very being an all but insoluble difficulty.

For what could freedom mean to Arnold? Unschooled, unskilled, clumsy by nature, childlike and credulous, his spirit numbed by the forty years or more he had spent as a chattel, he had doubtless found life affliction enough while dwelling in a state of bondage. Now having been set free through the grace and piety of his late mistress (who had left him a hundred dollars—which he had squandered in brandy during his first free year—but who had not thought to teach him a trade), the oafish old fellow dwelt upon life's furthest rim, more insignificant and wretched than he had ever been in slavery, a squatter in an unspeakably filthy lean-to shack on the outskirts of town, hiring himself out as a part-time field hand but existing mainly as a ragpicker or an emptier of privies or in the worst of times as a simple beggar, the bleached palm of his black hand extended for a penny or a worn British farthing and his lips working in a witless "Thank-ee, massah" to those townsmen no longer his masters in fact but in spirit masters more tyrannical than ever before. Of course, a few of the townspeople took pity on Arnold and his brethren but most of them resented his freedom, not because he himself was any threat but because he was in truth a symbol—a symbol of something gone asunder in the institution yet even more importantly a walking reminder of freedom itself and of menacing words, rarely spoken aloud, like emancipation and manumission, and therefore they despised him in a way they could never despise a Negro held in subjection. As for the slaves, among their company he was hardly better off, for if they had no reason actually to despise him he was still the incarnation of freedom, and such freedom was, as any fool could see, a stinking apparition of hopelessness and degradation. Thus their impulse was to rag Arnold mercilessly and play cruel tricks on him and to treat him with humorous contempt.

Surely even the poor lepers of Galilee, and all the outcasts to whom Jesus ministered in those awful times, lived no worse than such a free Negro in Virginia during the years of which I think and speak.

The woman stepped close to Arnold, who immediately bent forward in a groveling fashion, plucking from his head as he did so an absurd black wool hat several sizes too large for him and half devoured by moths. And then she spoke, the voice clear, resonant, quite gracious and polite, in rapid yet pleasantly warm Northern tones: "I seem to have lost my bearings"—the accent now touched with vague anxiety— "Major Ridley told me that the courthouse was next to the market. But all I see is a stable on one side and a dram shop on the other. Could you direct me to the courthouse?"

"Yam," Arnold replied. His face was all nervous obsequiousness, eager, his mouth agape in a ridiculous grin. "Majah Riblees he lib dar, ap yonnah road ap yonnah." He made a elaborate gesture with his arm, pointing away from the courthouse, down the road leading out of Jerusalem to the west. "Yam, me tek 'ee dar, missy, me tek 'ee dar." I listened closely. It was blue-gum country-nigger talk at its thickest, nearly impenetrable, a stunted speech unbearably halting and cumbersome with a wet gulping sound of Africa in it. There were occasions when it was hard enough for some town Negroes to grasp everything in such speech; no wonder that the lady from the North stood dumbstruck, gazing at Arnold with the panicky eyes of one in sudden confrontation with a lunatic. She had understood absolutely nothing, while the Godforsaken Arnold, understanding only a fraction more, had battened upon the name Ridley and had conceived the notion that she wished to be directed to the Major's home. He kept on gabbling away, groveling, now lowering to the ground his wreck of a hat in a servile, swooping motion. "Yam, missy, me tek 'ee Majah Riblees!"

"But—but—" the woman began to stammer, "I don't seem to know what—" And she halted, her expression now full of chagrin, sorrow, something even more disturbing—perhaps it was horror, but it seemed even more to be akin to pity. At any rate, it was what then took place—and it had to do not alone with Arnold and the Northern lady but with the sudden upheaval in myself—that caused this encounter to be graven upon my brain as long as I was possessed of memory. For the woman said nothing more, simply stood there while her arm went limp and the parasol clattered to the road, then raised her clenched fists to her face as if she were striking herself— an angry, tormented gesture—and burst into tears. Her whole frame—backbone, shoulders, rib cage—all the bones which moments before had supported her so proudly seemed to collapse inward with a rush, and she became helpless and shrunken as she stood there in the road, fists pressed to her eyes, shaken by loud racking sobs. It was as if something long pent up within her had been loosed in a torrent. On the gallery of the market and in the street I could both see and sense a score of Negroes watching her, all of them silent now, puzzled, mouths agape as they regarded her with round wondering eyes.

I had risen in the meantime with my Bible clasped between my hands, and as I drew nearer to the edge of the gallery I was seized by a hot convulsive emotion that I had never known so powerfully before—it was like a roaring in my ears. For what I had seen on this white woman's face was pity—pity wrenched from the very depths of her soul—and the sight of that pity, the vision of that tender self so reduced by compassion to this helpless state of sobs and bloodless clenched knuckles and scalding tears, caused me an irresistible, flooding moment of desire. And it was, you see, pity alone that did this, not the woman herself apart from pity. For there is peril enough in the first hint of a black man's lust for a white woman, and since anyway I had striven for years to stifle all fleshly desire—feeling that it was the Lord's command—there had been little temptation for me to covet such a wild and hazardous prize: to fornicate with a white woman in the ordinary course of events is for most Negroes so remote a possibility, and so mortally dangerous, as to remain hardly even the stirring of a shadowy idea upon the margin of consciousness. But this was something I had never seen. It was as if, divesting herself of all composure and breaking down in this fashion—exposing a naked feeling in a way I had never seen a white woman do before—she had invited me to glimpse herself naked in the flesh, and I felt myself burning for her. Burning!

And even as I stood there trying to dominate and still this passion, which I knew to be abominable to the Lord, I sensed that my thoughts had already run galloping beyond control, and in a swift fantasy I saw myself down on the road beginning to possess her without tenderness, without gratitude for her pity but with abrupt, brutal, and rampaging fury, watching the compassion melt from her tear-stained face as I bore her to the earth, my black hands already tearing at the lustrous billowing silk as I drew the dress up around her waist, and forcing apart those soft white thighs, exposed the zone of fleecy brown hair into which I drove my black self with stiff merciless thrusts. The vision would not be mastered nor leave me alone. I stood at the edge of the gallery, looking down while the sweat began to stream from my brow and my heart beat with an urgent and oppressive drumming in my throat. Far off in the back of the market I could hear a banjo plinking and the clatter and jingling of a tambourine, and a surge of nigger laughter. Still the woman kept weeping into her hands, the smooth back of her neck exposed now, white as a water lily, and as silken-tender and vulnerable; yet still in my mind's eye I was mounted upon her in the dust of the road, hot as a coupling fox, my excitement gathering as I conceived not of any pleasure I might cause her or myself, but only the swift and violent immediacy of a pain of which I was complete overseer, repaying her pity by crushing my teeth against her mouth until the blood ran in rivulets upon her cheeks, displaying my gratitude for that feathery compassion not by murmured endearments but by clasping my hands from underneath ever more fiercely upon the firm flesh of squirming buttocks until drawn up full against my black groin she cried out in the wildest anguish while I shot off within her in warm outrageous spurts of defilement.

"I don't understand!" I heard the woman cry. "Oh God, I don't understand!" And then she raised her head from her hands, and at that instant it was as if my hot vision and her sudden seizure had simultaneously dissolved, vanished. She shook her head in a quick furious motion, paying no attention to Arnold, her pale and beautiful face tear-streaked yet no longer haggard with pity but quite proud, with a kind of buried exultancy, and angry; and as she said it again now—"Oh, no, I *just don't understand!*"—her voice was calm with a flat emphatic outrage and she reached down and retrieved her parasol from the road then turned and strode very briskly but with stately and composed steps up the street, the resplendent silk of her dress making a slippery swishing as she disappeared, erect and proud, past the corner of the market. I later learned that soon she left town and never came back. But now I watched her go, my body still hot and swollen and agitated, even though the power of the emotion and my raging heartbeat had begun to slacken as the woman had gained control of herself. Suddenly she was gone. I was left depleted, beaten, and with a choked sensation in my throat as if, trying to utter a single word at that moment, I would find myself bereft of speech.

Below me I saw Arnold shuffle away, mumbling to himself, nodding his head in woolly bewilderment. There was a buzz and yammer among the Negroes around the gallery, cackles of nervous uncomprehending laughter, and then the rhythms of the old Saturday morning market commotion started up again, and all was as it had been before. I stood there for an instant, watching the place in the road where I had taken the woman. It seemed so real in my imagination that I felt there should be some scuffed, trampled place in the dust, marking our struggle. Though the fever of my excitement had passed, I heard a Negro youth snicker nearby and I saw that he was eying me; then I realized that I was still in the virile state and that this showed through my trousers, and so in embarrassment I sidled away to the rear of the gallery, where I squatted down again in a patch of sunlight. For a long while I was unable to shake the memory of what had just happened and I felt a deep shame, closing my eyes and breathing a prayer to the Lord, supplicating His pardon for this terrible moment of lasciviousness. *Thine eyes shall behold strange women and thine heart shall utter perverse things . . . He which is filthy, let him be filthy still.*

I prayed for a bit with passionate contrition; it was a prayer from the soul and I felt that the Lord had understood and had granted me forgiveness for this lapse. Even so, the intensity of my passion troubled me greatly, and all the rest of the morning I searched my Bible, trying to discover some key to this powerful emotion and the reason for my thinking these savage thoughts when the woman broke down so pathetically, drowned in her sympathy. But the Bible offered me no answer, and I remember that later this day, when Moore fetched me from the market and we drove back to the farm in the wagon through waning summer fields growing yellowish and parched, I was filled with somber feelings that I was unable to banish, deeply troubled that it was not a white person's abuse or scorn or even indifference which could ignite in me this murderous hatred but his pity, maybe even his tenderest moment of charity.

My years with Mr. Thomas Moore lasted nearly a decade and seemed to me twice as long, filled as they were with sweaty and monotonous toil. Yet I must say that those same years were in certain ways the most fruitful I ever spent, since they offered many occasions for reflection and spiritual contemplation and presented opportunities in the field of evangelism such as I had never known even within the lenient world where I had spent my early life. I suppose the truth is simply that it was possible for benefits like these to accrue only to a Negro lucky enough to remain in the poor but relatively benign atmosphere of Virginia. For here in this worn-out country with its decrepit little farms there was still an ebb and flow of human sympathy—no matter how strained and imperfect—between slave and master, even an understanding (if sometimes prickly) intimacy; and in this climate a black man had not yet become the cipher he would become in the steaming fastnesses of the far South but could get off in the woods by himself or with a friend, scratch his balls and relax and roast a stolen chicken over an open fire and brood upon women and the joys of the belly or the possibility of getting hold of a jug of brandy, or pleasure himself with thoughts of any of the countless tolerable features of human existence.

To be sure, it was a way of life far from, let us say, Elysian but it was also not Alabama. Even the most childlike, ignorant, and benighted Negroes in Virginia had heard that name, and its lovely liquid syllables could arouse only a sickening chill; likewise they had all heard of Mississippi and Tennessee, Louisiana and Arkansas, and by way of scary tales shuddering up through the vast black grapevine which spread throughout the South, had learned to fear those names like death. Indeed, I must confess that I myself never was totally free of this dread even when my ownership by Moore seemed the most secure or when later, owned by Travis, I was safer still. Often during those years I reflected upon the mysterious providence of God which on that icy cold day of a February past had seen to it that I not be swallowed up into the ant-swarm and the faceless extinction of a nigger-crawling 10,000-acre plantation in the deepest South but that I be delivered instead into the dilapidated but homey surroundings which were the result of my sale to this pinched, puckerfaced little Southampton farmer named Moore.

As for Moore, never again did he lift a hand against me after that day when he struck me with his bullwhip. Not that he didn't still thoroughly detest me with a profound detestation that lasted, I'm certain, until the moment of his premature and unlamented death. He hated all Negroes with a blind, obsessive hatred which verged upon a kind of minor daily ecstasy, and I was certainly not exempt, especially in the light of my book-learning. Even so, he possessed a countrified shrewdness, the vestige of a native intuition which must have warned him that it could only work to his own disadvantage to mistreat or vent his generalized hatred upon the compliant, exemplary, honey-tempered piece of property I determined early to become. And such property I became— a paragon of rectitude, of alacrity, of lively industriousness, of sweet equanimity and uncomplaining obedience. Nor do I exaggerate all this, even though never a day went by when I was not conscious of the weird unnaturalness of this adopted role. For now as all the promise and hope I had ever known flickered out and died and as I sank into the smothering night of bondage, it seemed plain that I must patiently suffer the evil things in store for me, gaining time to meditate upon such possibilities as the remote future might offer and to consult the Scriptures for guidance as to an endurable way of life. Above all I realized that I must not take panic, lashing out in futile retaliation at this analphabetic, squinty-eyed new owner of mine, but instead, like one caught in swamp quicksand who stays each muscle to avoid sinking deeper in the mire, must steel myself to accept without blinking all indignities, all befoulment, all mean hurts forthcoming—at least for the present time. There are occasions, as I have pointed out, when in order to buy some advantage from a white man it is better not even to say "please" but to silently wrap oneself up in one's niggerness like the blackest of shrouds.

Certain Negroes, in exploiting their own particular niggerness, tell dumb jokes on themselves, learn to shuffle and scrape for their owners, wallowing in the dust at the slightest provocation, midriffs clutched in idiot laughter, or they master the rudiments of the banjo and the jew's-harp or endear themselves to all, white and black, through droll interminable tales about ha'nts and witches and conjurs and the cunning little creatures of the swamp and woods. Others, by virtue of some indwelling grittiness and strength, reverse this procedure entirely and in *their* niggerness are able to outdo many white people at presenting to the world a grotesque swagger, becoming a black driver who would rather flog a fellow Negro than eat Smithfield ham, or at the most tolerable limit becoming a tyrannical, fussy, disdainful old kitchen mammy or butler whose very security depends upon maintaining without stint—safely this side of insolence—an aspect of nasty and arrogant dominion. As for myself, I was a very special case and I decided upon humility, a soft voice, and houndlike obedience. Without these qualities, the fact that I could read and that I was also a student of the Bible might have become for Moore (he being both illiterate and a primitive atheist) an insufferable burden to his peace of mind. But since I was neither sullen nor impudent but comported myself with studied meekness, even a man so shaken with nigger-hatred as Moore could only treat me with passable decency and at the very worst advertise me to his neighbors as a kind of ludicrous freak.

"I done bought me a black gospeler," he would announce in those early days, "a nigger that done learnt the Bible near 'bout by heart. Recite us about Moses, boy." And I, confronting a circle of brandy-fragrant sun-scorched snaggle-mouthed anus-scratching farmers, would intone in a soft and placid voice a chapter or so from Numbers, which I did indeed know from memory, all the while returning with unfaltering pious glance their looks of mingled wonder, malevolence, suspicion, and shifty-eyed respect, all the while counseling myself to patience, patience, *patience* to the end. At such moments, though Moore's hatred for me glittered like a cold bead amid the drowned blue center of his better eye, I knew that somehow this patience would get me through. Indeed, after a while it tended to neutralize his hatred, so that he was eventually forced to treat me with a sort of grudging, grim, resigned good will.

So all through the long years of my twenties I was, in my outward aspects at least, the most pliant, unremarkable young slave anyone could ever imagine. My chores were toilsome and obnoxious and boring. But with forbearance on my part and through daily prayer they never became really intolerable, and I resolved to follow Moore's commands with all the amiability I could muster.

Moore's farm was a humble one, lying ten miles or so to the southeast of Jerusalem near the settlement of Cross Keys and abutting in part upon the property of Mr. Joseph Travis, whom, it may be recalled, I have mentioned earlier in this narrative and into whose ownership I ultimately passed after Moore's death. (The contiguity of Moore's and Travis's farm land was of course one of the fateful reasons for the marriage to Travis by Moore's widow, Miss Sarah, and also for my coming to know Hark, as will be seen.) Aside from a ramshackle and unwhitewashed raw-timbered farmhouse, Moore owned twenty acres in corn and cotton and truck crops and fifty more in the woodland which supplied such a generous part of his otherwise meager income. Since I was the only Negro Moore possessed (though from time to time he had to hire other Negroes to supplement my muscle power) and since it was a dirt farm in the dirtiest sense of the word, my carpenter skills were almost never needed—save for crude jobs like patching the pigpen or boarding up a shattered window—and I fell into that daily grind of nigger work which only short months before I had foolishly believed could not ever become my lot, not in a thousand lifetimes. As an efficient, smoothly operating, all-purpose chattel, then, I was engaged at Moore's in a score of jobs: plowing the wet fields behind a team of mules in the spring, chopping weeds in the cotton patch throughout half the summer, shelling corn, slopping the pigs, getting up hay for the stock, spreading manure, and when all this was done or during spells of gloomy weather, helping Miss Sarah in various scullery and scrubbing chores or at any number of other housemaidenly tasks around the farm.

Nor was there any such thing as "nothing to do," for looming like a bleak wall above and beyond all this work, no matter what the season, was the stand of pine and gum and poplar and oak which I had to help Moore cut down and drag by ox-team half a mile to the farmyard, there to be hacked up into firewood lengths and thrown upon the growing mountain of logs which regularly went to stoke the Jerusalem hearths and forges and stoves. Though one might not forever plow or hoe, there was always time to chop. Some days the broadax I used seemed an extension of my hands, a still-moving phantom part of me, and at night I went to sleep with its rhythmic pounding aquiver along the muscles of my back and arms. Never to my recollection was I driven beyond endurance—doubtless because I set a productive, industrious pace for myself the final gain of which my owner could hardly in good sense abuse by demanding more. Nonetheless, it was loathsome, unrewarding toil and I do not know how I would have survived those days and months and years without the ability to fall into meditation upon spiritual matters even when enduring the most onerous and gut-wrenching labor. This habit, which I had developed a long time before even as a boy, proved to be my salvation. It would be hard to describe the serenity I was able to attain—the rapt and mysterious quality of peace I knew—when amid the stinging flies and the chiggers and the fierce September heat, there in the depths of the woods, tugging at a log chain while Moore nattered and nagged in my ear and his cousin Wallace's ripe obscenities filled the air like small godless black bugs and I heard from afar, across the withering late summer meadows, the jingle of a cowbell like eternity piercing my heart with a sudden intolerable awareness of the eternity of the imprisoning years stretched out before me: it is hard to describe the serene mood which, even in the midst of this buzzing madness, would steal over me when as if in a benison of cool raindrops or rushing water I would suddenly sink away toward a dream of Isaiah and dwell on his words—*Ye shall not labour in vain, nor bring forth for trouble, for ye are the seed of the blessed of the Lord*—and for a long time, as in a trance, dream of myself safe in the new Jerusalem beyond all toil or heat or misery.

During most of those years I slept on a corn-shuck tick on the floor of a dark little cupboard off the kitchen, sharing the space with some emaciated mice and several bustling and friendly spiders for whom I trapped flies and lived with on the most genial terms. The food at Moore's may best be described as middling, depending upon the season, always far removed from the bounteous kitchen at Turner's Mill but a good cut above the animal rations served up by the Reverend

Eppes. For the greater part of the winter I subsisted largely off nigger food—half a peck of cornmeal and five pounds of fat salt bacon a week, and all the molasses I could gag down —and with these raw fixings I was expected to make my repast in the kitchen, morning and evening, after the white people had eaten. So from November to March the fare was pretty bad and my stomach growled without ceasing. That I managed to eat fairly well during other seasons was largely due to Miss Sarah, who, though not so gifted a cook as my mother or any who succeeded her at the Mill, was able to set a moderately decent table—especially during the long warm period when vegetables were abundant—and was liberal with the leftovers and the drippings from the frying pan.

Miss Sarah was a fat, silly, sweet woman with small intelligence but with an amplitude of good cheer that enabled her to disgorge without effort peals of jolly, senseless laughter. She could read and write with some strain and had a little inherited money (it had been her funds, I later divined, which allowed Moore to purchase me), and there was about her a plump unmean simplicity of nature that caused her, alone among the household, to treat me at times with what might pass, fleetingly, as genuine affection: this took the form of sneaking me an extra piece of lean meat or finding me a castoff blanket in the winter and once she actually knitted me a pair of socks, and I do not wish easily to malign her by declaring that the affection she bore toward me resembled the warm impulsive tenderness which might be lavished carelessly upon a dog. I even came to be fond of the woman in a distant way (but largely with attentive, houndlike awareness of her occasional favors) and I intend no sarcasm when I say that much later, when she became almost the very first victim of my retribution, I felt an honest wrench of regret at the sight of the blood gushing like a red sluiceway from her headless neck, and almost wished I had spared her such an ending.

Of the rest of Moore's household there is little enough to say. There was young Putnam, who has already been on view; he was six years old or so upon my arrival at the house, a whiny and foul-tempered child who inherited his father's hatred for my race and never within my hearing ever referred to me other than as "the nigger." Since even his father took eventually to calling me by my proper name, this habit of Putnam's required either great stupidity or self-conscious persistence, perhaps both, but in any case lasted right up until the time he was grown and had become Joseph Travis's stepson. Like his mother he was destined to have his head separated from his neck—quite a penalty to pay, it might be thought, for calling me "the nigger" so long a time but one which I did not honestly regret exacting. There were two other white people in residence: Moore's father, whom the family knew as "Pappy," and cousin Wallace. The old man, who had been born in England, was over a hundred years old, white-bearded, paralyzed, half deaf, blind, and incontinent in both bladder and bowel—a misfortune that became my misfortune too, since in the early days of my stay it fell my lot to clean up the mess he made, which was frequent and systematic. To my vast relief, on a quiet spring afternoon a year later, he produced a great and final evacuation in his chair, shuddered, and expired.

Wallace was practically a replica of Moore in body and spirit—a knobby-limbed benighted illiterate, filthy of tongue, blasphemous, maladroit even at such unskilled tasks as the ploughing and hoeing and wood-chopping which Moore extracted from him as recompense for board and keep. He treated me as Moore did, without any especial rancor but with watchful, guarded, unflagging resentment, and (since he is unimportant to this account) the less said about Wallace the better.

So my years at Moore's, particularly the early years, were far from happy ones but the opportunities I had for contemplation and prayer allowed them to become at least endurable. Most Saturdays I had several long free hours to myself in Jerusalem. In all weathers I found the chance to steal away from my cupboard and out in the woods and commune with the Spirit and read from the great prophetic teachings. Those first few years made up a time of waiting and uncertainty, yet I know that even then I had begun to sense the knowledge that I was to be involved in some grand mission, divinely ordained. The words of the Prophet Ezra were of consolation during that strange period; like him I felt that *now for a little space grace hath been shewn from the Lord my God, to give me a little reviving in my bondage.*

And soon I discovered a secluded place in the woods, a mossy knoll encircled by soughing pine trees and cathedral oaks no more than a short walk from the house, hard by a brook that sang and bubbled in the stillness. In this sanctuary I kept a weekly vigil from the very beginning, praying and reading, and after I became a little bit at ease at Moore's and my trips to the woods were more frequent I built a shelter out of pine boughs and used it as my secret tabernacle. Whenever work was slack and the opportunity arose I began occasionally to forsake eating altogether for as long as four or five days at a stretch, having been especially moved and troubled by those lines from Isaiah which go: *Is not this the fast that I have chosen? To loose the bonds of wickedness, to undo the heavy burdens, and to let the oppressed go free, and that ye break every yoke?* During these fasts I often grew dizzy and weak, but in the midst of such spells of deprivation a mood of glory stole over me and I was filled with a strange radiance and a languid, blissful peace. The crashing of deer far off in the woods became an apocalyptic booming in my ears, the bubbling stream was the River Jordan, and the very leaves of the trees seemed to tremble upon some whispering, secret, many-tongued revelation. At these times my heart soared, since I knew that if I continued praying and fasting, biding my days patiently in the Lord's service, I would sooner or later receive a sign and then the outlines of future events—events perhaps terrible and wrapped in danger— would be made plain.

Like mine, Hark's misfortune had been that he was only a small item among a man's total capital, and so he was instantly and easily disposable when the economy foundered. A Negro as fantastic as Hark could always command a lovely price. Like me, he too had been born and reared on a large plantation—his in Sussex County, which borders on Southampton to the north. This plantation had been liquidated at about the same year as Turner's Mill, and Hark had been bought by Joseph Travis, who at that time had not developed his wheel-making craft but was still engaged in farming. Hark's former owners, people or monsters named Barnett, proposed to develop a new plantation down in a section of Mississippi where field labor was at that moment abundant and female house labor scarce. And so they took Hark's mother and his two sisters with them and left Hark behind, the money gained from his sale financing the rather difficult and expensive overland trip to the delta. Poor Hark. He was devoted to his mother and his sisters—indeed, he had never spent a day in his life apart from them. Thus began one of a series of bereavements; seven or eight years later he was separated forever by Travis from his wife and his little son.

Hark was never (at least until I was able to bend him to my will) an obstreperous Negro, and for much of the time I knew him I lamented the fact that as with most young slaves brought up as field hands—ignorant, demoralized, cowed by overseers and black drivers, occasionally whipped—the plantation system had leached out of his great and noble body so much native courage, so much spirit and dignity, that he was left as humble as a spaniel in the face of the white man's presence and authority. Nonetheless, he contained deep within him the smoldering fire of independence; certainly through my exhortations I was later able to fan it into a terrible blaze. Certainly, too, that fire must have been burning when shortly after his sale to Travis—stunned, confused, heartsick, with no God to turn to—he decided to run away.

Hark once told me how it all happened. At the Barnett plantation, where life for the field Negroes had been harsh, the matter of running away was of continual interest and concern. All of this was talk, however, since even the stupidest and most foolhardy slave was likely to be intimidated by the prospect of stumbling across the hundreds of miles of wilderness which lay to the north, and knew also that even to attain the free states was no guarantee of refuge: many a Negro had been hustled back into slavery by covetous, sharp-eyed Northern white men. It was all rather hopeless but some had tried and a few had almost succeeded. One of the Barnett Negroes, a clever, older man named Hannibal, had vowed after a severe beating by the overseer to take no more. He "lit out" one spring night and after a month found himself not far from Washington, in the outskirts of the town of Alexandria, where he was taken prisoner by a suspicious citizen with a fowling piece who eventually returned Hannibal to the plantation and, presumably, collected the hundred-dollar reward. It was Hannibal (now a hero of sorts to many of the slaves, though to others a madman) whose advice Hark remembered when he himself became a runaway. Move in the night, sleep by day, follow the North Star, avoid main-traveled roads, avoid dogs. Hannibal's destination had been the Susquehanna River in Maryland. A Quaker missionary, a wandering, queer, distraught, wild-eyed white man (soon chased off the plantation) had once managed to impart this much information to Hannibal's group of berry pickers: after Baltimore follow close by the highway to the north, and at the Susquehanna crossing ask for the Quaker meeting house, where someone was stationed night and day to convey runaways the few miles upriver to Pennsylvania and freedom. This intelligence Hark memorized with care, particularly the all-important name of the river—rather a trick for a field hand's tongue—repeating it over and over in Hannibal's presence until he had it properly, just as he had been told: *Squash-honna, Squash-honna, Squash-honna.*

Hark had no way of knowing that Travis was at heart a more lenient master than Barnett had been. He understood only that he had been separated from all the family he had ever had and from the only home he had ever known. After a week at Travis's his misery and homesickness and his general sense of loss became insupportable. And so one summer night he decided to light out, heading for that Quaker church over two hundred miles away in Maryland which Hannibal had told him about months before. At first it was all very much a kind of lark since stealing away from Travis's was a simple matter: he had only to tiptoe out of the shed in which he was kept after Travis had gone to sleep and—with a flour sack containing some bacon and cornmeal, a jackknife, and flint for starting fires, all stolen, the entire parcel slung over his shoulder on a stick—make his way into the woods. It was easy as it could be. The woods were quiet. There he paused for an hour or so, waiting to see if by any chance Travis might discover his absence and raise an alarm, but no sound came from the house. He crept out along the edge of the trees, took to the road north, and sauntered along in high spirits beneath a golden moon. The weather was balmy, he made excellent time, and the only eventful moment of that first night came when a dog ran out from a farmhouse, furiously barking, and snapped at his heels. This proved Hannibal correct in his advice about dogs, and caused Hark to resolve that in the future he would give all dwellings wide berth, even if it meant losing hours by moving to the woods. He met no one on the road, and as the agreeable night passed he began to feel a tingling sense of jubilation: running away seemed to be no great undertaking after all. When dawn came he knew he had made good progress—though how far he had traveled he could not tell, lacking any notion of the size of a mile—and with the sound of roosters crowing in some distant barnyard he fell asleep on the ground in a stand of beech trees, well away from the road.

Just before noon he was aroused by the sound of dogs barking to the south, a quavering chorus of yelps and frantic howls which made him sit up in terror. Surely they were after him! His first impulse was to climb a tree but he quickly lost heart for this endeavor because of his fear of heights. Instead he crept into a blackberry thicket and peeked out at the road. Two slobbering bloodhounds followed by four men on horseback came out of the distance in a cloud of dust, the men's faces each set in a blue-eyed, grim, avenging look of outrage that made Hark certain that he was the object of their pursuit; he shivered in fright and hid his head amid the blackberries, but to his amazement and relief the baying and yelping diminished up the road, along with the fading clatter of hooves. After a bit all was still. Hark crouched in the blackberry patch until late afternoon. When dusk began to fall he built a fire, cooking over it a little bacon and some hoecake he made with water from a stream, and upon the onset of darkness, resumed his journey north.

His difficulties about finding the way began that night and plagued him all the long hours of his flight into freedom. By notches cut with his knife on a small stick each morning, he calculated (or it was calculated for him by someone who could count) the trip as having lasted six weeks. Hannibal had counseled two guides for the trip: the North Star and the great plank and log turnpike leading up through Petersburg, Richmond, Washington, and Baltimore. The names of these towns Hark too had memorized approximately and in sequence, since Hannibal had pointed out that each place would serve as a milestone of one's progress; also, in the event

that one got lost, such names would be useful in asking directions from some trustworthy-looking Negro along the route.
By remaining close to the turnpike—although taking care to
stay out of sight—one could use the road as a kind of unvary-
ing arrow pointing north and regard each successive town as
a marker of one's forward course on the journey toward the
free states. The trouble with this scheme, as Hark quickly
discovered, was that it made no provision for the numberless
side routes and forks which branched off the turnpike and
which could lead a confused stranger into all manner of
weird directions, especially on a dark night. The North Star
was supposed to compensate for this and Hark found it valuable, but on overcast evenings or in those patches of fog
which were so frequent along swampy ground, this celestial
beacon was of no more use to him than the crudely painted
direction signs he was unable to read. So the darkness en-
folded him in its embrace and he lost the road as a guide.
That second night, as for so many succeeding nights, he made
no progress at all but was forced to stay in the woods until
dawn, when he began to cautiously reconnoiter and found
the route—a log road in daytime busy with passing farm
wagons and carts and humming with danger.

   Hark had many adventures along the way. His bacon and
cornmeal ran out quickly but of all his problems food was the
least pressing. A runaway was forced to live off the land, and
Hark like most plantation Negroes was a resourceful thief.
Only rarely was he out of sight of some habitation or other
and these places yielded up an abundance of fruit and vegetables, ducks, geese, chickens—once even a pig. Two or three
times, skirting a farm or plantation, he imposed upon the
hospitality of friendly Negroes, whom he would hail at twilight from the trees and who would spirit him a piece of
bacon or some boiled collard greens or a pan full of grits. But
his great hulking prowling form made him conspicuous. He
was rightly fearful of having his presence known to anyone,

black or white, and so he soon began keeping strictly to himself. He even gave up requests for simple directions of the Negroes: they seemed to grow more ignorant as he progressed north and filled his ears with such an incoherent rigmarole of disaways and dataways that he turned from them in perplexity and disgust.

Hark's spirit took wing when at sunrise, a week or so after leaving Travis's, he found himself in the wooded outskirts of what, according to Hannibal's schedule, would be Petersburg. Having never seen a town of *any* size or description, he was flabbergasted by the number of houses and stores and the commotion and colorful stir of people, wagons, and carriages in the streets. To pass around the town without being seen was something of a problem but he managed it that night, after sleeping most of the day in a nearby pine grove. He had to swim a small river in the early darkness, paddling with one hand and holding his clothes and his sack in the other. But he moved without detection in a half-circle about the town and pushed on north somewhat regretfully, since he had been able to pluck from some back porch a gallon of buttermilk in a wooden cask and several excellent peach pies. That night in a wild rainstorm he got hopelessly lost and to his dismay discovered when morning came that he had been walking east toward the sunrise, to God knows where. It was bleak, barren pine country, almost unpopulated, filled with lonely prospects of eroded red earth. The log road, fallen into sawdust, petered out and led nowhere. But the next night Hark retraced his steps and soon had negotiated the short leg of his journey to Richmond—like Petersburg, a lively community with a cedarwood bridge leading to it over a river and abustle with more black and white people than he had ever imagined existed. Indeed, from his pinewoods view down on the town he saw so many Negroes moving in and out and across the bridge—some of these doubtless free, others on passes from nearby farms—that he was almost emboldened to mingle among them and see the city, taking a chance that he might not be challenged by a suspicious white man. Prudence won out, however, and he slept through the day. He swam across the river after nightfall and stole past the dark shuttered houses as he had at Petersburg, leaving Richmond like that other town poorer by a pie or two.

And so he made his way on north through the dark nights, sometimes losing the road so completely that he was forced to backtrack for several days until he regained the route. His shoes wore out and collapsed and for two nights he walked close to the road on bare feet. Finally one morning he entered the open door of a farmhouse while its people were in the fields and made off with a pair of patent leather boots so tight that he had to cut holes for the toes. Thus shod, he pushed through the gloomy woods toward Washington. It must have been August by now and the chiggers and sweat flies and the mosquitoes were out in full swarm. Some days on Hark's pine-needle bed were almost impossible for sleep. Thunderstorms rumbling out of the west drenched him and froze him and scared him half out of his wits. He lost sight of the North Star more times then he could count. Forks and turnings confused him. Moonless nights caused him to stray away from the road and lose himself in a bog or thicket where owls hooted and branches crackled and the water moccasins thrashed drowsily in brackish pools. On such nights Hark's misery and loneliness seemed more than he could bear. Twice he came close to being caught, the first occasion somewhere just south of Washington when, traversing the edge of a cornfield before nightfall, he nearly stepped on a white man who happened at that moment to be defecating in the bushes. Hark ran, the man pulled up his pants, yelled and gave chase, but Hark quickly outstripped him. That night, though, he heard dogs baying as if in pursuit and for one time in his life fought down his fear of high places and spent the hours perched on the limb of a big maple tree while the dogs howled and

moaned in the distance. His other close call came between
what must have been Washington and Baltimore, when he
was shocked out of his sleep underneath a hedge to find himself in the midst of a fox hunt. The great bodies of horses
hurtled over him as if in some nightmare and their hooves
spattered his face with wet stinging little buttons of earth.
Crouching on his elbows and knees to protect himself, Hark
thought the end had come when a red-jacketed horseman
reined in his mount and asked curtly what a strange nigger
was doing in such a dumb position—obtaining in reply the
statement that the nigger was praying—and believed it a
miracle when the man said nothing but merely galloped off in
the morning mists.

He had been told that Maryland was a slave state, but one
morning when he happened upon a town which could only
have been Baltimore he decided to risk exposure by creeping
out to the edge of the hayfield in which he had concealed
himself and calling in a furtive voice to a Negro man strolling
toward the city along the log road. *"Squash-honna,"* Hark said.
"Whichaway to de Squash-honna?" But the Negro, a yellow
loose-limbed field hand, only gazed back at Hark as if he
were crazy and continued up the road with quickening pace.
Undaunted, Hark resumed the journey with growing confidence that soon it would all be over. Perhaps there were five
more nights of walking when at last, early one morning, Hark
was aware that he was no longer in the woods. Here in the
gathering light the trees gave way to a grassy plain which
seemed to slope down, ever so gently, toward a stand of
cattails and marsh grass rustling in the morning breeze. The
wind tasted of salt, exciting Hark and making him press forward eagerly across the savanna-like plain. He strode boldly
through the marsh, ankle-deep in water and mud, and finally
with pounding heart attained a glistening beach unbelievably
pure and clean and thick with sand. Beyond lay the river, so
wide here that Hark could barely see across it, a majestic

expanse of blue water flecked with whitecaps blown up by a southerly wind. For long minutes he stood there marveling at the sight, watching the waves lapping at the driftwood on the shore. Fishnets hung from stakes in the water, and far out a boat with white sails bellying moved serenely toward the north—the first sailboat Hark had ever seen. In his patent leather boots, now split beyond recognition, he walked up the beach a short distance and presently he spied a skinny little Negro man sitting on the edge of a dilapidated rowboat drawn up against the shore. This close to freedom, Hark decided that he could at last hazard a direct inquiry, and so he approached the Negro confidently.

"Say, man," said Hark, remembering the question he was supposed to ask. "whar de Quakah meetin' house?"

The Negro gazed back at him through oval spectacles on wire rims—the only pair of glasses Hark had ever seen on a black man. He had a friendly little monkey's face with small-pox scars all over it and a crown of grizzled hair shining with pig grease. He said nothing for quite some time, then he declared: "My, you is some big nigger boy. How old is you, sonny?"

"I'se nineteen," Hark replied.

"You bond or free?"

"I'se bond," said Hark. "I done run off. Whar de Quakah meetin' house?"

The Negro's eyes remained twinkling and amiable behind his spectacles. Then he said again: "You is some *big* nigger boy. What yo' name, sonny?"

"I'se called Hark. Was Hark Barnett. Now Hark Travis."

"Well, Hark," the man said, rising from his perch on the rowboat, "you jes' wait right here and I'll go see about dat meetin' house. You jes' set right here," he went on, placing a brotherly hand on Hark's arm and urging him down to a seat on the edge of the rowboat. "You has had *some* kind of time but now it's all over with," he said in a kindly voice. "You jes' set right there while I go see about dat meetin' house. You jes' set right there and rest you'self and we'll take care of dat meeting' house." Then he hurried up the beach and disappeared behind a copse of small stunted trees.

Gratified and relieved to be at last so close to the end of his quest, Hark sat there on the rowboat for a long moment, contemplating the blue windy sweep of the river, more grand and awesome than anything he had ever seen in his life. Soon a lazy, pleasant drowsiness overtook him, and his eyelids became heavy, and he stretched out on the sand in the warm sun and went to sleep.

Then he heard a sudden voice and he awoke in terror to see a white man standing over him with a musket, hammer cocked, ready to shoot.

"One move and I'll blow your head off," said the white man. "Tie him up, Samson."

It was not so much that Samson, one of his own kind—the little Negro with the glasses—had betrayed him which grieved Hark in later times, although that was bad enough. It was that he had really journeyed to the ends of the earth to get nowhere. For within three days he was back with Travis (who had liberally stickered the countryside with posters); he had walked those six weeks in circles, in zigzags, in looping spirals, never once traveling more than forty miles from home. The simple truth of the matter is that Hark, born and raised in the plantation's abyssal and aching night, had no more comprehension of the vastness of the world than a baby in a cradle. There was no way for him to know about cities, he had never even seen a hamlet; and thus he may be excused for not perceiving that "Richmond" and "Washington" and "Baltimore" were in truth any of a dozen nondescript little villages of the Tidewater—Jerusalem, Drewrysville, Smithfield—and that the noble watercourse upon whose shore he stood with such trust and hope and joy was not "the Squash-honna" but that ancient mother-river of slavery, the James.

Since the practice was common in the region to hire out slaves from one farm to another, it was only natural that Hark's and my paths should cross not long following my sale to Moore and after Hark had been returned to Travis. Negroes were hired out for numerous jobs—plowing, chopping weeds, clearing land, helping to drain swamps or build fences, dozens of other chores—and if memory serves me right I first encountered Hark when he moved in to share my cupboard after Moore had borrowed him from Travis for a few weeks of wood-chopping. At any rate, we quickly became fast and even (when the pressures of our strange existence permitted) inseparable friends. At that time I had begun to retreat deeply into myself, into the vivid, swarming world of contemplation; a sense of dull revulsion bordering on an almost unbearable hatred for white people (I can only describe it as a kind of murky cloud which no longer allowed me to look directly at white faces but to perceive them sideways, as distant blurs, a muffling cloud of cotton which also prevented me from hearing any longer their voices save for the moments when I was given a command or was drawn to what they said by some distinct peculiarity of occasion or circumstance) had commenced to dominate my private mood, and since for a long stretch I was Moore's solitary Negro and had only white faces to consider, I found this situation gloomy and distracting. Hark's abrupt black presence helped to remedy this: his splendid good nature, his high spirits, his even-tempered and humorous acceptance of the absurd and, one might add, the terrifying—all of these things in Hark cheered me, easing my loneliness and causing me to feel that I had found a brother. Later of course, when I became Travis's property, Hark and I became as close as two good friends could ever be. But even before then, even when I was not working for

Travis or Hark for Moore, the proximity of the two farms
allowed us to go fishing together and to set up some traplines
for rabbits and muskrat and to take our ease in the deep
woods on a Sunday afternoon with a jug of sweet cider and a
chicken Hark had stolen, juicily broiled over a sassafras
fire.

Now late in 1825 what began as a simple dry spell developed into a searing drought that lasted far into the next year.
Winter brought neither rain nor snow, and so little moisture
fell during the springtime that the earth crumbled and turned
to dust beneath the blade of the plow. Many wells ran dry
that summer, forcing people to drink from muddy streams
reduced to trickling rivulets. By early August food had become a problem since the vegetables planted in the spring
yielded nothing or grew up in leafless stalks; and the cornfields, ordinarily green and luxuriant in rows higher than a
man, displayed hardly anything but withered little shoots
that were quickly eaten up by the rabbits. Most of the white
people had laid up cellar stores of potatoes and apples from
previous seasons, or had small quantities of pickled fruits, so
there was no risk of actual famine, at least imminently; besides, supplies of nigger food like salt pork and cornmeal still
existed in moderate amounts, and as a last resort a white man
could always partake of these victuals, allowing his palate to
experience what every slave had endured for a lifetime. But
the free Negroes of the region were not so lucky. Food for
them was bitterly scarce. They had no money to buy pork
and meal from the white people, who in any case, mildly
panicked, had hoarded such provisions for their slaves or
themselves, and the little gardens of sweet potatoes and kale
and cowpeas upon which they depended for sustenance year
after year brought forth nothing. By late summer the dark
rumor passed among the slaves that a number of the free
Negroes in the country were starving.

For some reason I date the events of 1831 from this summer, five years earlier to the very month. I say this because I had my first vision then, the first intimation of my bloody mission, and these were both somehow intricately bound up with the drought and the fires. For on account of the dryness, brushfires had burned unchecked all summer throughout the woods and the swamps and the abandoned fields of the ruined plantations. They were all distant fires—Moore's wood lot was not threatened—but the smell of their burning was constantly in the air. In the old days, when dwellings might have been in danger, white men with their slaves would have gone out and fought these fires with shovel and ax, setting backfires and creating long swaths of cleared land as defense against the encroaching flames. But now most of that remote land was in spindly second-growth timber and great tracts of bramble-choked red earth gone fallow and worthless, and thus the fires smoldered night and day, filling the air with a perpetual haze and the scorched bittersweet odor of burnt undergrowth and charred pine. At times, after a spell of feeble rain, this haze would disappear and the sunlight would become briefly clean, radiant; shortly thereafter the drought would set in again, interrupted by vagrant thunderstorms more wind and fury than rain, and the sawdust mist would begin its pungent domination of the air, causing the stars at night to lose their glitter and the sun to move day after day like a dulled round shimmering ember across the smoky sky. During that summer I commenced to be touched by a chill, a feeling of sickness, fright, an apprehension—as if these signs in the heavens might portend some great happening far more searing and deadly than the fires that were their earthly origin. In the woods I prayed often and searched ceaselessly in my Bible for some key, brooding long upon the Prophet Joel, who spoke of how *the sun and the moon shall be darkened and the stars shall withdraw their shining,* and whose spirit—like mine now, stirred, swept as if by hot winds, trembling upon discovery—was so constantly shaken with premonitions and auguries of a terrible war.

Then late that summer I had the opportunity to go on a five-day fast. Hark and I had together chopped several wagonloads of wood, because of the drought there was nothing to be done in the fields; and so Moore gave us five days of absence—a fairly common dispensation during August. Later we would cart the wood into Jerusalem. Having just stolen a plump little shoat from the Francis farm nearby, Hark declared that he would have nothing to do with fasting himself. But he said he was eager to accompany me to the woods and hoped that the odor of barbecued pork would not prove too much of a trial for my spirit or stomach. I assented to his company, adding only that he must let me have time for prayer and meditation, and to this he was cheerfully agreeable: he knew the fishing was good along the little stream I had discovered and he said that while I prayed he'd catch a mess of bass. Thus we passed the long hours—I secluded within my little thicket of trees, fasting and praying and reading from Isaiah while Hark splashed happily in the distance and warbled to himself or went off for hours in search of wild grapes and blackberries. One night as we lay beneath the smoky stars Hark spoke of his disappointment with God. "Hit do seem to me, Nat," he said in a measured voice, "dat de Lawd sho must be a white man. On'y a God dat was white could figger out how to make niggers so lonesome." He paused, then said: "On'y maybe he's a big black driver. An' if de Lawd is black he sho is de meanest black nigger bastid ever was born." I was too tired, too drained of strength, to try to answer.

On the morning of the fifth day I awoke feeling sickly and strange, with an aching emptiness at the pit of my belly and a giddiness swirling about in my brain. Never had a fast affected me with such weakness. It had grown wickedly hot. Smoke from the distant wildfires hung sulphurous in the air, so thick that the myriad shifting piney motes of it were

nearly visible like dust, all but obliterating the round unwink-
ing eye of a malign and yellow sun. Tree frogs in the oaks and
pines joined with great legions of cicadas to set up an ominous shrilling, and my eardrums throbbed at the demented
choir. I felt too exhausted to rise from my pine-needle bed
and so stayed there reading and praying as the hot morning
lengthened. When Hark came up from the creek I bade him
go back to the house since I wanted to remain alone. He was
reluctant to leave. He tried to force me to eat and said I
looked like a black ha'nt and clucked over me and fussed; but
he finally did go, looking morose and apprehensive. After he
had left I must have dropped off again into a deep slumber,
for when I awoke I had lost all sense of time: great oily
clouds of smoke coursed across the heavens and the sun had
disappeared as if behind a rack of flaxen haze, leaving me
with no notion of the hour of day. A languor like the onset
of death had begun to invade my bones, an uncontrollable
trembling seized my limbs; it was as if my spirit had slithered
out of my body, letting the flesh sink away like a crumpled
rag on the ground, all but lifeless, ready to be shivered,
flayed, blown apart by divine remorseless winds.

"Lord," I said aloud, "give me a sign. Give me the first
sign."

I rose to my feet with infinite difficulty and lassitude,
clutching at a tree trunk, but hoisted myself no more than a
foot or so from the ground when the sky began to whirl and
spots of fire like minute blossoms danced before my eyes.
Suddenly a calamitous roaring sound filled the heavens,
touching me with awe and fright, and I slid to the earth
again. As I did so, lifting my gaze upward, it was plain that a
vast rent appeared in the boiling clouds above the treetops. I
had become drenched in sweat and the droplets swarmed in
my eyes yet I was unable to turn away from the great fissure
yawning in the sky, seeming to throb now in rhythm to the
roaring noise overwhelming all, drowning out even the shrill-

ing forest din. Then swiftly in the very midst of the rent in the clouds I saw a black angel clothed in black armor with black wings outspread from east to west; gigantic, hovering, he spoke in a thunderous voice louder than anything I had ever heard: *"Fear God and give glory to Him for the hour of His judgment is come, and worship Him that made heaven and earth and the sea and the fountains of waters."* Then there appeared in the midst of the rent in the clouds another angel, also black, armored like the first, and his wings too compassed the heavens from east to west as he called out: *"If any man worship the beast and his image and receive his mark in his forehead, or in his hand, the same shall drink of the wine of the wrath of God, and he shall be tormented with fire and brimstone in the presence of the Lamb, and the smoke of their torment ascendeth up forever and ever."*

I started to cry out in terror, but at this moment the second black angel seemed to pour back into the clouds, faded, vanished, and in his place came still another angel—this angel white yet strangely faceless and resembling no living white being I had ever known. Silent, in glittering silver armor, he smote the remaining black angel with his sword, yet as in a dream I saw the sword noiselessly shatter and break in two; now the black angel raised his shield to face down his white foe, and the two spirits were locked in celestial battle high above the forest. The sun suddenly became dark and the blood ran in streams against the churning firmament. For a long time, or no time—what time?—the two angels struggled on high amid the blood-streaked billows and the noise of their battle mingled with the roaring sound within my senses like a hot wind until, half fainting, I felt as if I were about to be blown heavenward like a twig. Yet so quickly that it seemed but a heartbeat in space, the white angel was vanquished and his body was cast down through the outermost edges of the sky. Still I gazed upward where the black angel rode triumphant among the clouds, saying aloud now, and to me: *"Wherefore didst thou marvel? These shall make war with the Lamb and the Lamb shall overcome them, for he is Lord of lords and King of kings, and they that are with him are called, and chosen, and faithful. Such is your luck, such you are called to see, and let it come rough or smooth you must surely bear it."*

Instantly then the black angel was swallowed up into the empyrean and the great rent in the clouds melted at the edges and became one, leaving the sky murky and sulphurous as it had been before. An odor of burnt pine scorched and seared my nostrils, I felt surrounded by the flames of hell. I pitched forward on my hands and knees and vomited into the pine needles, vomiting without issue, retching in prolonged pained spasms that brought up only spittle and green strings of bile. Sparks as if from some satanic forge blew in endless windrows before my eyes, a million million pinpricks of catastrophic light.

"Lord," I whispered, "hast Thou truly called me to this?"

There was no answer, no answer at all save the answer in my brain: *This is the fast that I have chosen, to loose the bonds of wickedness, to undo the heavy burdens, to let the oppressed go free, and that ye break every yoke.*

I might not have interpreted such a vision as a mandate to destroy all the white people had there not taken place soon after this, and in quick order, a couple of ugly events which had the effect of further alienating me from white men and consolidating in me the hatred of which I have already spoken. My memory of these events begins shortly after I left the woods. I did not recover from my fast as readily as I had at other times. I was left feeling vacant and dizzy, with a continuing weakness which even ample portions from the leftovers of Hark's barbecued pig could not dispel; nor was I strengthened by a jar of preserved plums which he had stolen, and my lassitude hung on along with a feeling of somber melancholy, and I returned to Moore's the next morning with aches and agues running up and down my limbs and with the recollection of my terrible vision lurking at the back of my brain like some unshakable grief. Early as it was, the heat from the sun, trapped beneath a blanket of haze, had become almost intolerable. Even the cur dogs in Moore's barnyard sensed something gone wrong in the atmosphere; they snuffled and whimpered in their limitless misery, and the pigs lay snout-deep amid a stinking wallow, while the chickens squatted inert like swollen feather dusters in the steaming pen. Upon mounds of wet manure blowflies in multitudes greenly festered and buzzed. The farm smelled oppressively of slops and offal. A scene such as this, as I approached it, seemed timeless in its air of desolation; I thought of a hateful encampment of lepers in Judea. The lopsided weatherworn farmhouse stood baking in the sun, and when from within I heard a childish voice, Putnam's, call out, "Dad! The nigger's back from the woods!" I knew I was truly back.

I could hear Hark in the barn with the mules. The oxen that Moore once owned he had replaced with mules, partially because mules—unlike oxen and certainly horses—would sustain almost any punishment handed out by Negroes, a people not notably sweet-natured around domestic animals. (Once I overheard Marse Samuel lament to a gentleman visitor: "I do not know why my Negroes make such wretched husbandmen of horses and cattle." But *I* knew why: what else but a poor dumb beast could a Negro mistreat and by mistreating feel superior to?) Even Hark for all his tender spirit was brutal with farm stock, and as I came near the fence I heard his voice in the barn, loud and furious: "God dang yo' dumb mule asses! I gwine knock de livin' *mule shit* clean on out'n you!" He was harnessing a team of four to the wagons—two huge vehicles known as dray carts, linked together by a tongue—and this I knew meant I had returned just in time, for like Hark, I would be needed to ride into

Jerusalem and spend a sweaty two days delivering and un-
loading a small mountain of wood.

As we started out toward town—Moore and Wallace on
the seat together in the lead wagon, Hark and I behind
sprawled on the great pile of lightwood logs, the timber alive
with ants and pine-smelling in the heat—Moore essayed an
attempt at some humor involving me. "God durn if hit don't
rain soon, Wallace," he said, "I'm goin' to git the preacher
back there to bring me to religion and learn me to pray and
such all. God durn sweet corn in Sarah's lot, I done took a
look this mornin' and them ears ain't no bigger than a puppy
dog's peter. How 'bout it, preacher," he called back to me,
"how 'bout askin' the Lord to let loose a whole lot of water?
Lemme suck on some of that lightnin', Wallace." The cousin
handed him a jug and for a moment Moore fell silent. "How
'bout it, preacher," he said again, with a belch, "how 'bout
rattlin' off a special prayer and tell the Lord to unplug his
asshole and git the crops growin' down here."

Wallace guffawed and I replied in tones ingratiating,
ministerial—the accommodating comic nigger: "Yassuh,
Marse Tom, I sure will do that. I sure will offer up a nice
prayer for rain."

But although my voice was compliant and good-natured
it took all the self-restraint I had not to retort with something
raw and surly, dangerously more than insolent; a quick flash
of rage, blood-red, bloomed behind my eyes, and for an instant my hand tightened on a log and I measured the space
between it and the back of Moore's shaggy dirt-crusted red
neck, my arm tensed as if to knock the little white weevil
from his perch. Instantly then the rage vanished and I fell
back into my thoughts, not speaking to Hark, who presently
reached for a banjo he had made out of fence wire and some
pine strips and began to plunk out the lonesome strains of one
of the three tunes he knew—an old plantation song called
"Sweet Woman Gone." I still felt sick and shaken and a

weariness was in my bones. With the memory of my vision lingering in the recesses of my mind, it seemed that the visible world around me had changed, or was changing: the parched fields with their blighted vegetation and the wood lots on either side painted like the fields with dust, now utterly windless and still, drooping near death with yellowing leaves, and over all the cloud of smoke from remote fires burning unbridled beneath no man's eyes or dominion—all of these combined with my hangdog mood to make me feel that I had been transported to another place and time, and the bitter taste of dust on my lips caused me to wonder if this countryside might not in a strange manner resemble Israel in the days of Elias, and this barren road the way to some place like Jerusalem. I shut my eyes and drowsed against the logs while Hank softly sang and the words of "Sweet Woman Gone" invaded my dreaming, unutterably sorrowful and lonesome; then I sharply awoke to a low moaning sound from the side of the road and to the accents of my own troubled voice whispering in my brain: *But you are going to Jerusalem.*

My eyes opened upon a strange and disturbing sight. Back from the road stood a tumbledown house which in previous trips I had barely noticed: nothing more than a hovel constructed of rough pine logs, windowless, half caved in, it was the home of a destitute free Negro named Isham and his family. I knew very little about this Negro, indeed, had laid eyes on him only once—when Moore had hired him one morning and within short hours had sent him packing, the miserable Isham being possessed of some deep indwelling affliction (doubtless caused by a long-time insufficiency of food) that turned his frail limbs into quivering weak pipestems after no more than five minutes of labor with the broadax. He had a family of eight to support—a wife and children all under twelve—and in easier times he managed barely to survive through his pitiful efforts at work and by tending a little garden, the seeds and seedlings for which he obtained through the good will of nearby white men more charitable than my present owner. Now, however, in this time of perilous drought it was quickly apparent that Isham dwelt close to the brink, for around the shanty in its sun-baked clearing where once had grown corn and peas and collards and sweet potatoes all was withered and shrunken and the rows of vegetables lay blasted as if devoured by wild-fire. Three or four children—naked, the ribs and bones show-ing in whitish knobs beneath their skin—fidgeted spiritlessly around the crumbling doorstep. I heard the soft plaintive moaning sound at the roadside and gazed down and saw squatting there Isham's wife, bony and haggard, gently rock-ing in her arms the fleshless black little body of a child who appeared to be close to death.

I had only a glimpse of the child—a limp, shapeless tiny thing like a bundle of twigs. The mother cradled it close, with infinite and patient grief, pressing it next to her fallen breasts as if by that last and despairing gesture she might offer it a sustenance denied in life. She did not raise her eyes as we passed. Hark had ceased his tune and I looked at him as he too caught sight of the child; then I turned and glanced at Moore. He had briefly halted the team. His little puckered face had the sudden aspect of a man overcome by revulsion—revulsion and shame—and instantly turned away. In past time he had shown no charity to Isham at all; unlike one or two of the other white men in the vicinity—sorely beset themselves—who had nonetheless helped Isham by a little cornmeal, some preserves, or a pound of fatback, Moore had parted with nothing, turning Isham out after his brief stint of work without paying him the few cents which was his due, and it was plain now that the sight of the dying child had caused even his adamantine heart to be smitten by guilt.

Moore gave the lead mule a stroke with his whip, but just as he did so a gaunt Negro man appeared at the side of

the team and yanked at the traces, causing the wagon to stop
its lurching forward movement. This Negro I saw was none
other than Isham—a sharp-faced, brown, hawk-nosed man in
his forties with bald ringworm patches in his hair and with
eyes ravaged and lusterless, filmed over with aching hunger.
And immediately I sensed madness roving through his soul.
"*Ho*, white man!" he said to Moore in a garbled, crazy voice.
"You isn't give Isham ary bit to eat! Not ary bit! Now Isham
got a dead chile! You is a white fuckah! Das all you is, white
man! You is a sonabitchin' cuntlappin' fuckah! What you
gwine do 'bout some dead baby now, white fuckah?"

Both Moore and his cousin gazed down at Isham as if
dumbstruck. Never in their lives, I am sure, had they been
addressed in such a fashion by a Negro, bond or free, and the
words which assailed them like a bullwhip left them with
jaws hanging slack, breathless, as if they had found themselves in some sudden limbo between outrage and incredulity. Nor had I ever heard raw hatred like this on a Negro's
lips, and when I glanced at Hark, I saw that his eyes too were
bright with amazement.

"White man eat!" Isham said, still clinging to the traces.
"White man eat! Nigger baby she stahve! How come dat 'plies,
white fuckah? How come dat 'plies dat white man eat bacon,
eat peas, eat grits? How come dat 'plies like dat an' li'l nigger
baby ain't got ary bit? How come dat 'plies, white cuntlappin'
fuckah?" Trembling, the Negro sought to spit on Moore but
seemed disadvantaged by the intervening height and distance
and by the fact that he could bring up no spit; his mouth
made a frustrated smacking noise, and again he tried in vain,
smacking—a defeated effort awful to watch. "Whar de
twenny-fi' cents you owes me?" he shouted in his bafflement
and rage.

But now Moore did a curious thing. He did not do what a
few years of proximity to such an impassioned nigger-hater
made me think he would do: he did not strike Isham with his

whip nor shout something back nor clout him on the side of the head with his boot. What he did was to turn toadstool-white and in a near-frenzy give the lead mule a vicious, quick lash which started the wagon to rumbling swiftly forward, tearing the mules' harness from Isham's hands. And as he did this and as we moved ahead as fast as the wagon's ponderous bulk would allow, I realized that Isham's unbelievable words had at first thrust Moore into a strange new world of consciousness which lacked a name—so strange an emotion indeed that a long moment must have passed while voice called to voice across the squalid abysm inside his skull and finally named it: Terror. Furiously he lashed the beasts and the brindle wheel-mule gave a tormented *heehaw* that echoed back from the pines like crackbrained laughter.

I learned later that after the drought had broken within a few months, Isham and his family somehow survived their plight, having been restored from a state of famine to the mere chronic destitution that was their portion in life. But that is another matter. Now such an event along the road on this ominous morning, seen through the prism of my mind's already haunted vision, forced me to realize with an intensity I had never known before that, chattel or unchained, slave or free, people whose skins were black would never find true liberty—*never,* never so long as men like Moore dwelt on God's earth. Yet I had seen Moore's terror and his startled insect-twitch, a pockmarked white runt flayed into panic by a famished Negro so drained of life's juices that he lacked even the spittle to spit. This terror was from that instant memorialized in my brain as unshakably as there was engrafted upon my heart the hopeless and proud and unrelenting fury of Isham—he who as the wagon fled him through the haze shouted at Moore in an ever-dimming voice, *"Pig shit!* Someday nigger eat meat, white man eat pig shit!" and seemed in his receding gaunt contour as majestic as a foul-tongued John the Baptist howling in the wilderness.

O generation of vipers, who hath warned you to flee
from the wrath to come?

I think it may have been seen by now how greatly various
were the moral attributes of white men who possessed slaves,
how different each owner might be by way of severity or
benevolence. They ranged down from the saintly (Samuel
Turner) to the all right (Moore) to the barely tolerable
(Reverend Eppes) to a few who were unconditionally monstrous. Of these monsters none in his monsterhood was to my
knowledge so bloodthirsty as Nathaniel Francis. He was Miss
Sarah's older brother, and although in physical appearance
he resembled her slightly, the similarity ended there, for he
was as predisposed to cruelty as she was to a genuine, albeit
haphazard, kindness. A gross hairless man with a swinish
squint to his eyes, his farm lay several miles to the northeast
of Moore's. There on middling land of about seventy acres he
eked out a sparse living with the help of six field slaves—Will
and Sam (whom I have mentioned earlier in this narrative), a
loony lost young wretch, one of God's mistakes, named Dred,
and three even younger boys of about fifteen or sixteen.
There were also a couple of forlorn female house servants,
Charlotte and Easter, both of them in their late fifties and
thus too old to be the source of any romantic tumult among
the younger men.

Francis had no children of his own but was the guardian
of two nephews, little boys of seven or so, and he did have a
wife, Lavinia—a slab-faced brute of a person with a huge
goiter and, through the baggy men's work clothes she cus-
tomarily wore, the barely discernible outlines of a woman. A
winning couple. Perhaps in reaction to the wife or (it seems
more persuasive to believe) goaded by her after or before or
during whatever unimaginable scenes took place upon their
sagging bedstead, Francis achieved pleasure by getting
drunk at more or less regular intervals and beating his Ne-

groes ruthlessly with a flexible wooden cane wrapped in alligator hide. When I say "his Negroes," however, I should point out that this meant Will and Sam. I cannot tell why it was these two who became the victims of his savagery, unless it was only a matter of simple elimination—the three younger boys perhaps not possessing yet the stamina to take such killing abuse, the two women being likewise invulnerable on account of their advanced age.

As for poor Dred, his brains were all scrambled and he could barely speak. It may be that like a man stalking swamp bear who turns up only muskrat, Francis felt that young Dred was too lacking in distinction to be suitable prey for his ferocity. At any rate, he was able to invent for Dred other means of degradation. Dred was nineteen years old, so brainless that he was barely able to go to the privy without help. The condition of his poor addled head had been recognized by Francis only after he had bought him, sight unseen, from a trader with no more scruples than himself. Dred's very existence was the walking, living proof of a swindle, and enough to drive his owner to a frenzy. Now responsible for Dred, unable to sell him, and refraining from murder less because of legal restraints than because unprovoked murder of a slave bore a social odium hard for even Francis to abide, he revenged himself for the swindle not by such simple and crude extremes as whipping but by tormenting Dred with unspeakable tricks like causing him once (according to Sam, whom I had no reason to doubt) to copulate with a bitch dog before an assembly of local white trash.

Francis had bought Will and Sam at the Petersburg auction block when they were both around fifteen, and by the time I first encountered them—during periodic rentals to Moore or the idle hours we might spend together in Jerusalem on market day—they had endured their owner's thrashings for five or six years. Such abuse had caused both of them to run away more often than either of them could remember, and Francis's alligator-hide whip had left knobs like walnuts on their shoulders, backs, and arms. Francis might have been a moderately prosperous landowner had not his roaring need to inflict misery on his Negroes smothered that logic which must have tried to tell him that halfway decent treatment would keep the pair, however reluctantly, home and busy: as it was, each time Will or Sam, anguished past endurance, took to the woods Francis lost money just as surely as if he had dropped silver dollars down a well. For Will and Sam among the field Negroes he owned were the oldest, the strongest, and most capable. To fill the gap their absence made he was compelled to hire other Negroes at substantial prices he would not have been forced to pay had he restrained his imbecile cruelty.

Furthermore, many if not most of the other farmers in the area were aware of Francis's savage propensities. (This included Travis, his own brother-in-law, who never once allowed Hark near the Francis farm.) Even when they were not prompted by considerations solely humane (which I must confess some were) the landowners were understandably reluctant to let out any of their field hands to this ruffian who might send back to them a chattel worth five hundred dollars damaged beyond all repair. Thus whenever Sam or Will ran away, Francis was often unable to obtain replacement and he would be driven to an even greater pitch of rage. Setting off with a jug of brandy, his barbarous tublike shape jouncing and jostling astride a bay mare as he scoured the countryside, he would after several days find Sam or Will—or perhaps the fugitives would be returned to the farm by some local poor white eager for the customary reward—and once again they would be thrashed until they were bleeding and senseless and then left for a time locked in the barn until their stripes and welts began to grow scabs and they were ready for work. All in all it was a never-endingly ugly and

dispiriting situation. And easily the most sinister aspect of the
matter was what this treatment had done not so much to
their bodies but to their minds. Of the two Negroes, Sam was
the less affected. Which is to say that brutalized as he was,
wounded to the depths of his being, he managed to keep a
grasp on reality and—in spite of a wicked temper which
caused him to lash out mindlessly from time to time at other
slaves—presented more often the outward spirit of an ordinary young field hand, a frolicsome and happy-go-lucky air
that among certain Negroes, I have noticed, is a kind of necessary disguise for almost unendurable affliction. But Will
was altogether different. A livid stripe like a shiny eel ran
the length of his face from beneath his right eye to the tip
of his chin. Another blow, inflicted during the same beating,
had given his nose the appearance of a black mashed-in
spoon. He muttered to himself constantly, incoherently. The
torture that had been imposed upon him had made him hate
not just Francis, hate not just white men but all men, all
things, all creation—and because I myself dwelt within the
inchoate universe of that hatred I could not help but come to
fear him in a way I had never feared any man, black or
white, before . . .

The whole day after Moore's encounter on the road with
Isham we unloaded wood at various places in Jerusalem.
Moore had contracted to "store" at each house we visited and
at the courthouse and the jail. This meant no disorderly heap
of logs thrown in a hodgepodge behind the kitchen but rather
a tidy arrangement of cords which it was Hark's and my duty
to stack wherever Marse Jim or Marse Bob wished them
stacked. It was monotonous and gut-wrenching labor. This
strain, combined with the stifling heat of the town and my
continuing fatigue and dizziness, made me stumble often and
once I fell sprawling, only to be helped up by Hark, who
said: "You jes' take it easy, Nat, and let ole Hark do de work."
But I kept up a steady pace, retreating as was my custom into

a kind of daydream—a reverie in which the brute toil of the moment was softened and soothed by my mind's murmurous incantation: *Deliver me out of the mire, and let me not sink, let not the deep swallow me up, hear me O Lord, turn unto me according to the multitude of thy tender mercies* . . .

At noon Hark and I made our dinner in the shade of one of the wagons, eating cold hoppin' john—mashed cowpeas mixed with rice—and sat listlessly afterward cooling ourselves while Moore and Wallace went off to visit the town whore—a two-hundred-pound free mulatto woman named Josephine. The food revived me slightly but I still felt faint and weird, with the mystery and wonder of my vision in the woods lingering not in my mind alone but as if throughout my entire being, my soul, like the shadow of a cloud that has appeared out of nowhere to smudge the bright face of the day. I shivered, the mystery haunted me as if great fingers the size of pine boughs rested on my back, ever so lightly, and a mood of evil premonition stole over me as we went back to work. I could not shake the feeling off while we sweated through the waning afternoon. That night the languor and illness returned, I ached with fever, and as Hark and I lay asleep beneath one of the wagons, parked in a field smelling of sweet mustard and goldenrod, I had dreams of giant black angels striding amid a spindrift immensity of stars.

Then late in the forenoon of the next day after another hot morning's work, we made our delivery to the market—the last. It was a Saturday, market day, and as usual the gallery was thronged with Negroes from the country who were generally allowed a few idle hours to fritter away while their masters attended to business in the town. After we unloaded the last logs Moore and Wallace went off on some errand and Hark and I retired—he with his pine-strip banjo, I with my Bible—to a shady corner of the gallery where I could meditate on a certain passage in Job which had attracted my curi-

osity. Hark strummed softly, humming a tune. Quite a few
of the Negroes loitering about I had become acquainted with
by now, largely because of these market days. Daniel, Joe,
Jack, Henry, Cromwell, Marcus Aurelius, Nelson, half a
dozen more—they had arrived with their masters from all
over the county, had helped load or unload their owners'
produce, and now stood about with nothing to do but ogle
the passing bottoms or breasts of the Negro girls of the town,
jabbering the while loudly about poontang and pussy, goos-
ing each other and scuffling around in the dust. One or two
succeeded with the girls and stole off with them into a field of
alfalfa. Others played mumbletypeg with rusty stolen jack-
knives, or simply drowsed in the sunlight, waking now and
then to exchange their sorry belongings: a straw hat bartered
for a homemade jew's-harp, a lucky hairball from a cow's
belly for a bag of pilfered snuff. I looked at them briefly, then
returned to Job's racking, imponderable vision. But I found it
difficult to concentrate, for although I had recovered somewhat from my fever I could not dislodge the sensation that I
had somehow been utterly changed and now dwelt at a distance from myself, in a new world apart. It was noon and
Hark offered me a biscuit from a panful he had spirited out
of the kitchen of one of Moore's customers, but I had no
stomach for food. Even here in town the air was hazy, smelling of far-off fires.

Suddenly I became aware of a commotion—laughter and
shouts from a cluster of white men behind the blacksmith's
stable perhaps fifty yards away across the road. The bare
earthen plot at the rear of the stable was the Saturday gathering place for the poor whites of the county just as the market
gallery had become the social focus for the Negroes. These
white idlers were the rogues and dregs of the community:
penniless drunks and cripples, scroungers, handymen, ex-
overseers, vagabonds from North Carolina, harelipped roust-
abouts, squatters on pineland barrens, incorrigible loafers,

cretins, rapscallions, and dimwits of every description, they made my present owner by comparison appear to possess the wisdom and dignity of King Solomon. There by the stable each Saturday with straw hats and cheap denim overalls they gathered in a shiftless mob, cadging from each other quarter-plugs of chewing tobacco or snorts of rotgut brandy, palavering endlessly (like the Negroes) about pussy and cooze, scheming out ways to make a dishonest half-dollar, tormenting stray cats and dogs, and allowing the slaves from their market promontory a bracing glimpse of white men worse off—in certain important respects at least—than themselves. Now when I looked up to find the source of the disturbance among them I saw that they had assembled in a rough circle. In the midst of the circle, perched upon a horse, was the squat, hunched form of Nathaniel Francis, roaring drunk, his round face besotted with swollen pleasure as he gazed down at something taking place on the ground. I was only mildly curious, thinking at first that it was a white man's wrestling match or drunken fist fight: hardly a Saturday passed without one or the other. But through the baggy pants' legs of one of the bystanders I saw what appeared to be two Negroes moving about, engaged in doing what I could not tell. Cackles of glee went up from the crowd, wild hoots and cries. They seemed to be egging the Negroes on, and Francis drunk in the saddle caused the horse to stamp and prance at the space within the encircling mob, raising an umbrella of dust. Hark had risen to his feet to gawk and I told him that he had better go find out what was happening; he moved slowly off.

After a minute or so Hark came back to the gallery, and the sheepish half-smile on his face—I will never forget that expression, its mixed quality of humor and gentle bewilderment—filled me with a sad foreboding, as if I had known, sensed what he was going to say the instant before his mouth opened to say it.

"Ole Francis he puttin' on a show fo' dem white trash," he

proclaimed, loud enough for most all of the other Negroes to hear. "He drunker dan a scritch owl and he makin' dem two niggers Will and Sam fight each other. Don't neither of 'em want to fight but ev'y time one of 'em draw back an' *don't* whop de other, ole Francis he give dat nigger a stroke wid his whip. So dem niggers dey *got* to fight and Sam he done raised a bleedin' whelp on Will's face and Will I do believe he done broke off one of Sam's front teeth. Hit sho is some kind of cock fight."

At this, all the Negroes within hearing began to laugh—there was indeed something oddly comical about Hark's *way* of describing things—but at the same time my heart seemed to shrivel and die within me. This was *all*. All! Of the indignities and wrongs that a Negro might endure—blistering toil and deprivation, slights and slurs and insults, beatings, chains, exile from beloved kin—none seemed more loathsome, at that minute, than this: that he be pitted in brutal combat against his own kind for the obscene amusement of human beings of any description—but especially those so mean and reptilian in spirit, so worthless, so likewise despised in the scheme of things and saved from the final morass only by the hairline advantage of a lighter skin. Not since the day years before when I was first sold had I felt such rage, intolerable rage, rage that echoed a memory of Isham's fury as he howled at Moore, rage that was a culmination of all the raw buried anguish and frustration growing inside me since the faraway dusk of childhood, on a murmuring veranda, when I first understood that I was a slave and a slave forever. My heart, as I say, shrank inside me, died, disappeared, and rage like a newborn child exploded there to fill the void: it was at this instant that I knew beyond doubt or danger that—whatever the place, whatever the appointed time, whoever the gentle young girl now serenely plucking blossoms within a bower or the mistress knitting in the coolness of a country parlor or the innocent lad seated contemplating the cob-

webbed walls of an outhouse in a summery field—the whole
world of white flesh would someday founder and split apart
upon my retribution, would perish by my design and at my
hands. My stomach heaved and I restrained the urge to vomit
on the boards where I sat.

But now the commotion across the road dwindled, the
shouts fell away, and the circle of white men broke up as
they turned their attention to other pleasures. Aslant to one
side in the saddle, Francis rode off at a lurching pace down
the street, exhausted by his sport, smiling a smile of gratification and conquest. And at this moment I saw Will and Sam—
battered-looking, bruised, and dusty—cross the road together,
weaving toward the market. Will was muttering to himself as
he stroked a swollen jaw and Sam shivered while he walked,
trembling in pain, misery, and in the throes of grievous
shame and abasement—a short, wiry little mulatto neither
too old yet nor too calloused by suffering to be prevented
from sobbing bitterly like a child as he wiped the blood away
from a jagged cut across his lips. Still unperceiving of anything at all, still witlessly amused by Hark's account of the
fray, the Negroes on the gallery watched Sam and Will approach and kept laughing. It was then that I rose to face
them.

"My brothers!" I cried. "Stop yo' laughin' and listen to me!
Leave off from that laughin', brothers, and listen to a minister
of the Holy Word!" A hush fell over the Negroes and they
stirred restlessly, turned toward me, puzzlement and wonder
in their eyes. "Come closer!" I commanded them. "This here is
no time for laughin'! This is a time for weepin', for *lamentation!* For rage! You is *men,* brothers, *men* not beasts of the
field! You ain't no four-legged dogs! You is *men,* I say! Where
oh where, my brothers, is yo' pride?"

Slowly, one by one, the Negroes drew near, among them
Will and Sam, who climbed up from the road and stood gazing at me as they mopped their faces with gray slimy wads of

waste cotton. Still other shuffled closer—young men mostly, along with a few older slaves; they scratched themselves out of nervousness, some eyes darted furtively across the road. But all were silent now, and with a delicious chill I could feel the way in which they had responded to the fury in my words, like blades of sawgrass bending to a sudden wind. And I began to realize, far back in the remotest corner of my mind, that I had commenced the first sermon I had ever preached. They became still. Brooding, motionless, the Negroes gazed at me with watchful and reflective concern, some of them hardly drawing a breath. My language was theirs, I spoke it as if it were a second tongue. My rage had captured them utterly, and I felt a thrill of power course out from myself to wrap them round, binding us for this moment as one.

"My brothers," I said in a gentler tone, "many of you has been to church with yo' mastahs and mist'esses at the Whitehead church or up Shiloh way or down at Nebo or Mount Moriah. Most of you hasn't got no religion. That's awright. White man's religion don't teach nothin' to black folk except to obey ole mastah and live humble—walk light and talk small. That's awright. But them of you that recollects they Bible teachin' knows about Israel in Egypt an' the peoples that was kept in bondage. Them peoples was Jewish peoples an' they had names just like us black folk—like you right there, Nathan, an' you, Joe—Joe is a Jewish name—an' you there, Daniel. Them Jews was just like the black folk. They had to sweat they fool asses off fo' ole Pharaoh. That white man had them Jews haulin' wood an' pullin' rock and thrashin' corn an' makin' bricks until they was near 'bout dead an' didn't git ary penny for none of it neither, like ev'y livin' mothah's son of us, them Jews was in *bondage*. They didn't have enough to eat neither, just some miser'ble cornmeal with weevils in it an' sour milk an' a little fatback that done got so high it would turn a buzzard's stomach. Drought an' hunger run throughout the land, just like now. Oh, my brothers, that was a sad time in Egypt fo' them Jews! It was a time fo' weepin' an' lamentation, a time of toil an' hunger, a time of *pain!* Pharaoh he whupped them Jews until they had red whelps on 'em from head to toe an' ev'y night they went to bed cryin', 'Lord, Lord, when is you goin' to make that white man set us free?' "

There was a stirring among the Negroes and I heard a voice in the midst of them say, "Yes, yes," faint and plaintive, and still another voice: "Mm-huh, dat's *right!*" I stretched out an arm slowly, as if to embrace them, and some of the crowd moved nearer still.

"Look aroun' you, brothers," I said, "what does you see? What does you see in the air? What does you see blowin' in the air?" The Negroes turned their faces toward the town, raised their eyes skyward: there in amber translucent haze the smoke from the distant fires swam through the streets, touching the gallery, even as I spoke, with its acrid and apple-sweet taste of scorched timber, its faint smell of corruption.

"That there is the smoke of *pestilence,* brothers," I went on, "the smoke of pestilence an' death. The same smoke that hanged over the Jews in bondage down there in Egypt land. The same smoke of pestilence an' death that hanged over them Jews in Egypt hangs over all black folk, all men whose skin is black, yo' skin and mine. An' we got a tougher row to hoe even than them Jews. Joseph he was at least a man, not no four-legged dog. My brothers, laughter is good, laughter is bread and salt and buttermilk and a balm for pain. But they is a time for ev'ything. They is a time for weepin' too. A time for rage! And in bondage black folk like you an' me must weep in they rage. *Leave off* from such dumb laughter like just now!" I cried, my voice rising. "When a white man he lift a hand against one of us'ns we must not laugh but rage and weep! 'By the rivers of Babylon, there we sat down, yea, we wept when we remembered Zion!' That's right!" ("Mm-huh, dat's right!" came the voice again, joined by another.) " 'We hanged our harps upon the willows, for they that carried us away captive required of us a song. How shall we sing the Lord's song in a strange land?' *That's right!*" I said, the words bitter on my tongue. "White man make you sing an' dance, make you shuffle, do the buck-an'-wing, play 'Ole Zip Coon' on the banjo and the fiddle. 'They that carried us away captive required of us a song.' Yes! Leave off from that singin', leave off from that banjo, leave off from that buck-an'-wing! They is a time for ev'ything. This is no time fo' singin', fo' laughter. Look aroun' you, my brothers, look into each other's eyes! You jest seen a white man pit brother 'gainst brother! Ain't none of you no four-legged beasts what can be whupped an' hurt like some flea-bit cur dog. You is men! You is *men,* my dear brothers, look at yo'selves, look to yo' *pride!*"

As I spoke, I saw two older black men at the rear of the crowd mutter to each other and shake their heads. Glances of puzzlement and worry crossed their faces and they sidled off, disappeared. The others still listened, intent, brooding, nearly motionless. I heard a soft sigh and a gentle "Amen." I raised my arms to either side of me and extended my hands, palms outward, as if in benediction. I felt the sweat pouring from my face.

"In the visions of the night, brothers," I continued, "God spoke to Jacob an' He said, 'I am God, the God of thy father: fear not to go down into Egypt, for I will there make of thee a great nation.' An' Jacob went down into Egypt an' the peoples of Israel multiplied an' Moses was born. Moses he was born in the bulrushers an' he delivered the Jews out of Egypt an' into the Promised Land. Well, there they had a powerful lot of troubles too. But in the Promised Land them Jewish peoples they could stand up an' live like *men.* They become a great nation. No more fatback, no more pint of salt, no more peck of corn fo' them Jews; no more overseers, no more auction blocks; no more horn blow at sunrise fo' them mothahs' sons. They had chicken with pot likker an' spoonbread an' sweet cider to drink in the shade. They done got paid an honest dollar. Them Jews become *men*. But oh, my brothers, black folk ain't never goin' to be led from bondage without they has *pride!* Black folk ain't goin' to be free, they ain't goin' to have no spoonbread an' sweet cider less'n they studies to love they own *selves*. Only then will the first be last, and the last first. Black folk ain't never goin' to be no great nation until they studies to love they own black skin an' the beauty of that skin an' the beauty of them black hands that toils so hard and black feet that trods so weary on God's earth. And when white men in they hate an' wrath an' meanness fetches blood from that beautiful black skin then, oh *then*, my brothers, it is time not fo' laughing but fo' weeping an' rage an' lamentation! *Pride!*" I cried after a pause, and let my arms descend. "Pride, pride, *everlasting* pride, pride will make you free!"

I ceased speaking and gazed at the rapt black faces. Then I finished slowly and in a soft voice: "Arise, shine; for thy light is come, an' the glory of the Lord is risen upon thee. Amen."

The Negroes were silent. Far off in Jerusalem, through the hot afternoon, a church bell let fall a single chime, striking the half-hour. Then the Negroes one by one straggled away across the gallery, some with troubled looks, some stupid and uncomprehending, some fearful. Others drew toward me, radiant; and Henry, who was deaf, who had read my lips, came up close to me and silently clasped my arm. I heard Nelson say, "You done spoke de truth," and he too drew near, and I felt their warmth and their brotherhood and hope and knew then what Jesus must have known when upon the shores of Galilee he said: *"Follow me, and I will make you fishers of men."*

On another Saturday in Jerusalem, a month or so later, a curious thing happened which—although it bears only indirectly upon the great events I must soon describe—produced an important enough effect on me to compel its recounting. During the intervening weeks I had, on these Saturdays, formed a Bible class composed of seven or eight Negroes, including Daniel, Sam, Henry, and Nelson. Hark had returned to Travis, so he no longer accompanied me to town. I held this class in the shelter of a large maple tree behind the market. There, seated on the cool earth with the Negroes crouching or squatting in a ragged arc around me, I had the opportunity to bring some of these people into the presence of the Holy Word for the very first time in their lives. Few of them had the ability to become what one might call devout; none of them was disposed to really cease from foul language or to abstain from drinking whatever brandy could be filched from a white man's wagon. (Only Henry, owned by a pious master and walled up in his deafness, possessed what might be called a spiritual nature.) But as slaves who had had nothing to fill their heads save for old grannies' scare-stories about conjurs and ha'nts and omens, they responded eagerly to my description of the events in Genesis and Exodus—the tales of Joseph and his brothers and the passage of the Red Sea and Moses smiting the rock in Horeb—and each Saturday morning I noted with pride and pleasure that they had begun to greet me with the looks of those for whom my arrival marked their most treasured hour. After the lesson, which might last until well past noon, I bade them all a friendly good-bye and then retired by myself to the shade beneath Moore's wagon where I would have my midday dinner of pone and bacon. Already I had resolved to adopt an air of aloofness and mystery, believing that such a distant pose would work to my advantage when the time came at last to reveal to my followers the great plans in the offing.

On this particular Saturday, I had just left the group

when a strange white man sidled up to me and tapped me lightly on the elbow of my shirt.

"Oh, preacher," said a tremulous voice, "a word with you, if'n you please."

The tone was gentle; save for Moore's sarcastic thrusts I had never heard myself called "preacher" before and I looked down, startled, to behold a slope-shouldered little man who became known to me as Ethelred T. Brantley.

"I heerd you preach to the niggers t'other Sattidy," he murmured to me with a furtive, urgent sound. The voice was touched with desperation. "Oh, you preaches so good," he said. "What kin I do to be saved?"

Ethelred T. Brantley was a round womanish man of about fifty, with soft plump white cheeks upon which tiny sores and pustules congregated like berries amid a downy fringe of red hair. Dressed in a ragged gray denim jacket and pants, he stirred sluggishly on wide hips and his pale dirty little fingers fluttered as he talked. Now he pressed me to go with him behind the market; his eyes darted nervously, as if he were fearful that we might be seen together. There amid the weeds he told me about himself in a burst of words, his squeaky, piteous voice seeming at any moment about to crack and to dissolve into sobs. At present without regular employ or money, he had until the year before been third assistant overseer on a failing plantation down in Beaufort County, in Carolina. After having lost his position he had come back to Jerusalem to live in a shack with his elderly sister, who supported him on a pittance and who was dying of consumption. He did odd jobs but was in no way to do much. He had a bad cough himself; asthma, consumption too? Brantley didn't know. He hoped it was asthma. He might not die of asthma. The eruptions on his cheeks wouldn't go away, he'd had them since he was a boy. He was tormented by some kind of ailment in his guts that caused him to go to the privy a dozen times a day, frequently in his pants. He had been sent to jail once in Carolina. Now he was afraid again. Because— He had taken a woman—*No!* He hesitated, his eyes anxious behind flickering eyelids, a pink flush rising beneath the pustuled skin. That was wrong. No, he—He had done something *bad,* yesterday, with a boy. The son of a local magistrate. He had paid the boy a dime. The boy had told. He thought the boy had told. He wasn't sure. He was afraid. "*Oh Lord God,*" he exclaimed. He broke wind with a plaintive hiss and for an instant his exhalations filled my nostrils like air from a swamp bottom.

"I has always keered for niggers, tucken good keer of niggers," said Brantley. "I has never beat a nigger in my life. You preaches so good. I done heerd you. I'm so afeared. I'm so miser'ble. Oh, how can I be saved?"

"By baptism in the Spirit," I replied sharply.

"If'n I could read," he said, "maybe I'd know 'bout religion like you does. But I cain't read nor write neither, not ary word. Oh, I'm so miser'ble! I jest wants to *die.* But I'm skeered of dyin'. Kin all men have pride? Kin *all* men be redeemed?"

"Yes," I said, "all men can have pride. And all men can be redeemed—by baptism in the Spirit." Then in a rush it occurred to me that this might be some kind of white man's trap, a joke, a ruse. "But when you overheard me preach—" I paused. "When you heard me preach that day I was saying things that wasn't for white men's ears." A sudden apprehension overtook me, and I started to turn away from him. "I was preaching for black folk," I said in a harsh voice.

"Oh no, preacher," he implored me, plucking at my sleeve, "I needs he'p so bad, please."

"Why don't you go to your own church?" I retorted. "Why don't you go to the white man's church?"

He hesitated, then finally he said: "I cain't. I mean, I used to go at Nebo. That's where my sister worships at. On'y Reverend Entwistle, the preacher there, he—" Halting, he seemed unable to go on.

"He what?" I said.

"Oh, he done throwed me out," he blurted in a choked voice. "He said I was—" Again he paused, and with a sigh, cast his eyes toward the ground. "He said—"

"He said *what?*" I demanded.

"He said they will be no sotomite of the sons of Isr'el in the house of the Lord. He tole me the Bible said so. That's what he done said, I 'members ever' word of it. He said I was a sotomite. So I cain't go to Nebo. I cain't go nowheres." He looked up at me in anguish, tears swimming in his eyes. "Oh, preacher, *how* can I be redeemed?"

I was suddenly swept by pity and disgust, and I have wondered since why I said to him what I did but have failed to come up with a sure answer. It may be only that Brantley at that moment seemed as wretched and forsaken as the lowest Negro; white though he might be, he was as deserving of the Lord's grace as were others deserving of His wrath, and to fail Brantley would be to fail my own obligation as minister of His word. Besides, it gave me pleasure to know that by showing Brantley the way to salvation I had fulfilled a duty that a white preacher had shirked. Anyway—

"Then listen," I told him. "Fast for eight days until next Sunday. You must eat nothing except that once every two days you can have as much corn pone as you can fill the palm of one hand. Then next Sunday I will baptize you in the Spirit and you will be redeemed."

"Oh Lord have mercy, preacher!" Brantley cried, all asnuffle. "You done saved my life! I'm so happy!" He tried to clutch my hand and kiss it but I drew away, squirming.

"Fast, as I say," I repeated, "and meet me at Mr. Thomas Moore's next Sunday. We will be baptized together in the Spirit."

The following day was a Sunday, when it was customary for Negroes to be let off for most of the time between late morning and dusk. Early that afternoon I walked the four miles up the road and presented myself at the front door of

Mrs. Catherine Whitehead's. Set back from the road several
hundred yards, the house was a comfortable, rambling place
made of smooth-planed clapboard (unlike Moore's, put together with rough-hewn timbers), freshly whitewashed, shuttered, surrounded by a pleasant lawn of clover humming with
bees. A dusty field of budding cotton stretched to the far
woods. In the front yard reposed a gilt and cherrywood English brougham; it was drawn by a thoroughbred filly, plump,
beautifully currycombed, that now stood feeding placidly in
the deep grass and broke the hot afternoon silence with her
champing sound. Zinnias bloomed in neat red boxes on the
front porch, I smelled a warm odor of roses from a trellis.
Mrs. Whitehead was a gentlewoman, a lady of some wealth.
There was nothing fancy about the place but it was far better
than Moore's; I knew that she even owned books. Not since
my days at Turner's Mill had I brushed close to white people
of means, and as I stood on the porch, awaiting some response to my knock, I was made hurtfully aware of my descent in life and suddenly suspected that I reeked of mule
dung. Idly I wondered how in the midst of this drought a
place could retain such green grace, such color and lushness;
then I spied in the field a windmill—which brought up water
from a well—the only one for miles and a marvel to all who
beheld it. Its weathered blades made a faint sad clack
and flutter across the afternoon quiet.

My knock at the door was answered by Margaret Whitehead; it was our first encounter, and one that should retain
momentous syllables, intonations, recollected cadences,
glances, hues, harmonies, curvatures, refractions of late
summer light. But I remember only a dim pretty pale girl's
face—she must have been thirteen or so—and a gentle voice
that replied, "Why yes, he's here," unsurprised as if my skin
had been alabaster-white, when I said: "Please, young missy,
may I have a word with yo' brother the preacher?"

When Richard Whitehead appeared he had the crumbs of

midday dessert still on his lips; he lost no time in directing me around to the rear door. There I waited fifteen minutes before he came back again—a slender youngish man, rather frail, with a prim hostile mouth and the same petrified eyeballs I had seen once years before in a Turner library sketchbook, amid the hell-ravaged face of John Calvin. His voice was reedy, thin, touched with all of the Sabbath's hushed and purple melancholy. I realized I should not have come. Queasy, I was stricken with the old familiar nigger fear, and could not help but avert my glance.

"What is it that you want?" he demanded.

I hesitated for a moment—Out with it quick, I thought—then I said: "Please, mastah, I'm a minister of the gospel. I wonders if after all the folks is gone next Sunday I couldn't baptize a white gentleman down in yo' church."

A startled look came over his face, then faded. "Who are you?" he said.

"I'm Nat Turner," I replied. "My mastah's Mr. Thomas Moore, down by Flag Marsh."

"Yes, I've heard of you," he said shortly. "What is it you want again?"

Once more I made my request. He regarded me with unblinking eyes, then he said: "What you are asking is ludicrous. How can a darky claim to be an ordained minister of the gospel? Pray tell me where you acquired your background in divinity. Washington College? William & Mary? Hampden-Sydney? What you are asking—"

"I don't have to be ordained, mastah," I put in. "In God's sight I am a preacher of His Word."

He pursed his lips and I could tell that his incredulity was being slowly converted into anger. "I've never heard of such tomfoolery from a darky in my life," he exclaimed. "What are you up to, anyway? What sort of white gentleman do you propose to baptize in church?"

"Mr. Ethelred T. Brantley," I said.

"Brantley!" At the name he seemed to go ashen with outrage. "A *gentleman!* I know of that scum! Jailed in Carolina
for an abominable, unnatural crime against nature! He has
been turned out of one congregation in this county, and now
he would pollute the sacred altar of a Methodist temple
through seeking baptism by the likes of you! What did he pay
you to solicit me for such blasphemy?"

"Brantley is a poor man," I said. "He hasn't got ten cents.
And he is very sick. And lost. Doesn't the Bible say that the
Son of man is come to save that which was lost?"

"Get out of here!" Richard Whitehead cried, his voice
shrill now. I hopped sideways as he aimed a kick at me
through the door. "Get your devilish black self off of this
property, and don't come back! And tell that Brantley I
have better things to do than be made a fool of by a degenerate and by an uppity nigger! Your master will hear of this, I
promise *you-u-u!*"

His reedy voice trailed me as I departed by the way I
came, a hysteric wail upon which my imagination played
while I walked—the sound changing from that of a young
woman to something else, a trapped rabbit, a bird, and finally
to the scream a man emits at that last instant before the club
descends and obliterates together prim mouth and scream.

That week I decided that Brantley and I would be baptized in Persons' millpond, which lay on an abandoned plantation a few miles from Moore's. I sent this word to Brantley
by a Negro going into Jerusalem, and late in the afternoon on
the following Sunday he met me near the pond, where I was
waiting with Hark, Sam, and Nelson. Although obviously
weak from his fast, Brantley looked somehow healthier: a
pink glow of anticipation suffused his face, and he confided to
me that his bowels, for the first time in years, were notably
under control. "Oh, I'm so happy!" he whispered as the five of
us walked down the wooded lane toward the millpond.
Rumor of the baptism had, however, spread throughout the

county, and when we arrived a mob of forty or fifty poor
white people—including some pie-faced females in sunbonnets—rimmed the far banks, waiting for the show. When we
reached the water's edge they began to hoot and jeer at us
but kept their distance. Brantley shivered with excitement.
"Oh Lordy," he whispered over and over again, "I'm goin' to
be saved!" While my followers looked on from the near bank
I waded out with Brantley, fully clothed, to a place in the
pond where the water was chest-deep. There I recited the
passage from Ezekiel about the resurrection of the dry bones:
"*I will lay sinews upon you, and will bring up flesh upon you,
and cover you with skin, and put breath in you, and ye shall
live, and ye shall know that I am the Lord . . .*"

I pushed Brantley down. He slid under like a wet sack of
beans; after he came up, spluttering and choking, his face
took on a look of bliss such as I have rarely seen on any man,
of any shade.

"I baptize you," I said, "in the name of the Father, and of
the Son, and of the Holy Spirit."

"Oh Lord God Almighty!" Brantley cried. "Saved at last!"

Something struck the back of my head. The white
people on the bank had begun to pelt us with stones and
sticks from fallen trees. A thick chunk of wood bounced off
Brantley's neck but he did not flinch, aware of nothing but
the glory.

"Oh Lord God!" he gasped. "I'm truly saved! Hallelujah!"

Another stone hit me. I immersed myself with a prayer,
then rose. Beyond the white faces blooming dimly on the far
bank, heat lightning whooshed up in faint green sheets. Dusk
had come down like the shadow of a great wing. I felt a sharp
premonition of my own death.

"Brantley," I said as we struggled back through the water
toward my followers on the bank, "Brantley, I advise you to
leave the county soon, because the white people are going to
be destroyed."

But I'm sure that Brantley heard nothing. "Lordy, Lordy!" he shouted. "Saved at last!"

Toward the latter part of the decade, as I approached my thirtieth year, it was apparent that a measure of prosperity had come back to the region. Not wealth, by any means. Not luxury, not abundance, but a respectable atmosphere of security accompanied by the feeling that no longer were people threatened with starvation. For one thing, the long drought wore itself out, and periods of steady rain allowed the land to be restored to a state of modest fertility. For another, the log turnpike leading up to Petersburg and Richmond had been recently improved, and so opened up a market for the bonanza which, as if by remarkable oversight, the local gentry had failed to realize was stored up in their own backyards. This was the estimable brandy distilled from apples growing so plentifully throughout the county. For if the soil of Southampton was utterly wrecked for tobacco and could produce cotton in quantities adequate only for subsistence, a cornucopia of apples ripened on every hand—wild and in cultivated orchards, in bramble-choked groves on dead plantations, by the wayside of each land and road. They grew in all sizes and colors and varieties, and what had once lain in wormy, decaying heaps on the ground were now dumped by the wagonload into the stills which had become each farmer's most valued asset. There converted into high-quality applejack, the metamorphosed fruit was shipped in barrels to Jerusalem, where groaning carts drawn by mules and oxen hauled it off north to Petersburg and Richmond—hustling, optimistic, pleasure-seeking communities filled with citizens possessed of fat pocketbooks and serious thirsts. Considerable revenue was thus returned to the county, so although it was plain that Southampton would never wax as rich as Nineveh, the region had become, as I say, fairly prosperous, and it was in the midst of this prosperity that I gradually laid my plans for annihilation and escape.

One of the results upon me of this burgeoning affluence was that the professional skill I had gained at Turner's Mill—and which for so long had lain aslumber amid Moore's dismal enterprises—became quite an attractive matter to some of the neighboring landowners, especially those already a notch or two higher on the economic ladder. Prosperity fosters expansion, expansion breeds construction—barns, stills, stables, fences, sheds. Once I had detected the brisk new activity going on around me, it did not take me long to begin to energetically promote my talents as a carpenter. I suddenly found myself in great demand. Moore for his part could not have been happier—as hired-out property I became his chief source of income—and only I could have been happier than he, since I was now pretty well shut of his woodpile and his slop buckets and his cotton patch. Life for a time was provisionally tolerable. In my new routine I helped convert Travis's barn to a wheel shop (this only a year or so before Moore died and I became Travis's chattel through the matrimonial arrangement mentioned already); lent my hand to the construction of at least three barns and two stills in the vicinity of Cross Keys; designed and built for Major Ridley near Jerusalem an ingenious arrangement for his privy consisting of wooden sluiceways that led from a dammed creek, the pent-up water of which, at the yank of a chain, merrily whisked the product of one's visit into another stream down below—a triumph of plumbing that earned for me inordinate hurrahs from the Major and a serviceable second-hand pair of cordovan boots; participated in the building of a new armory in Jerusalem for the Southampton militia (by the purest chance allowing me knowledge of entry to the place—front, back, and side—and to the general location of each gun rack and ammunition store); and spent more days than I can recollect hired out to Mrs. Catherine Whitehead, who, in spite of her son Richard's continual resentment of my ministerial pretensions, valued my gifts so highly that she was willing to pay Moore, and later Travis, a premium for my services. She had

me design a barn for her prize oxen—which I also helped
erect—a stable, and a privy-flusher fed by water from her
windmill and based on the same principles as the celebrated
mechanism I had put together for Major Ridley. Often too I
filled in there as coachman and butler. Mrs. Whitehead was
an austere woman, very cool and withdrawn, and she minced
few words in dealing with her pet architect. She was, however, completely fair and honest, and brooked no mistreat-
ment of her Negroes. Several times she patted my arm and
risked a wan, faraway smile, connoting praise. At last I felt as
neutral toward her as I might feel toward a soon-to-be exca-
vated stump.

Yet all through this time I lived as if straddling two
worlds of the mind and spirit—a part of me dwelling in the
humdrum sphere of daily events and things, of hammer and
saw and plane and adze, responding "Yassuh!" with as much
cheer as I could muster to some white master's jibe or sally or
observation, playing always the good nigger a little touched
in the head with religion but, you know, by dad, a durned
black *wizard* with nails and timber; the other part of me
haunted still without ceasing by that forest vision, which as it
receded into the past became not less meaningful but swelled
in portent from day to day. This part of me fasted and prayed
and beseeched the Lord earnestly for revelation, guidance, a
further sign. I was in an agony of waiting. I knew that God
had told me *what* I must do, yet I had no means of deciding
how to accomplish my bloody mission, nor where, nor when.

Then one morning in the late winter of 1829, not through
a vision but by a spell of inspiration so beatifically simple
that I knew that the Lord must have ordained it, I determined on the *how* and the *where*—so that only the *when*
remained.

That day in Mrs. Whitehead's library, while ostensibly
engaged in repairing a table, I happened upon a surveyor's
map of Southampton County and the region lying eastward. I

had plenty of time to study the map and several hours later
found the occasion to sit down and begin to make a tracing,
using a large sheet of clear parchment and Mrs. Whitehead's
best quill pen—the latter borrowed, the first stolen. The map
made plain to me what had previously been in my mind only
hopeful speculation: a break for freedom, in terms of geography alone, was perfectly feasible. Given the propitious resolution of all the other factors involved, such a break for freedom should meet with every success. It would not be easy. I
knew I must consecrate every shred of my intelligence and
passion to the fulfillment of these events I was so manifestly
called to by God and by destiny.

This afternoon I locked myself in the library. Although
Richard was out riding among his parishioners, Mrs. Whitehead was home. Danger. That I might be surprised behind
fastened doors and the fact of the ensuing scene ("*What* were
you doing locked in there like that?" " 'Deed, Miss Caty, that
ole lock he jest snap shut all by hisself"—her dark suspicion
then, doubts, creepy surmise) were chances I was forced to
take. As the map took shape beneath my fingers, the details of
my grand scheme began to come miraculously clear. I could
hardly wait to get off by myself and write it all down.

In a fever, I finished the map and replaced the original in
the book where I had found it, then folded the tracing so that
it fitted flat against my stomach underneath my shirt and belt
band. At last I knelt on the carpet by the window for a while,
praying, giving thanks to God for this revelation; finally I
arose and unlocked the door and left.

I was crossing the yard toward the groom's quarters in the
stable (a tolerably comfortable room, with fireplace and straw
tick, that I usually occupied during my stays at the White-
heads') when I heard Miss Caty call me from the side porch.
It was the lackluster hazy oppressive weather between winter
and spring—damp, leafless, with a raw chill in the air. She
stood huddled in her shawl, a gaunt once-pretty white, white

female, middle-aged, shivering a little, regarding me with her widow's somber dispirited eyes. Her hair was parted at the middle and fell toward her shoulders in graying ringlets. I was still excited by the map and by my plans, and was vexed at the sight of the woman, who I felt had no right to intrude on my thoughts at such a crucial time. "Yessum?" I said.

"Did you fix the table as I told you?" she asked.

"Yessum."

"It was Captain Whitehead's favorite table. He used to write on it. It kept collapsing no matter how many times I'd try to get it fixed. Are you sure it won't break again? I should be able to get a fancy price for it."

"Yessum."

"How did you fix it?"

"I put three dowels in it made of oak. Whoever fixed it before used plain old bone glue and some thin wire, so no wonder it broke. Nice walnut table like that, you have to use strong dowels. It won't break no more, I can promise you that, Miss Caty."

She was by no manner the worst of white people, yet for some reason—perhaps only this interruption of my thoughts —my hatred for her *now* was like a sharp rock in the pit of my stomach. I could barely return her gaze and wondered if somehow she might not be able to detect my hatred, which had begun to pop out on my brow in little pinpoint blisters of sweat.

"Did you get around to the chair yet?" she said.

"No'm," I replied, "I spent all my time on that table."

"Well then, tomorrow instead of working with Jack and Andrew on those stall doors you can put the legs back on that chair. Jack is sick anyway. That darky has been sick half the winter." Annoyance passed over her face, her lips drew thin. "Also tomorrow—"

"Miss Caty," I put in, "tomorrow I'm supposed to go back to Mr. Moore's. It's the end of my hire."

"The end of your hire?" she exclaimed. "Why, it *couldn't* be! I hired you until the eighteenth."

"Yessum," I replied, "and today's that date—the eighteenth."

"Why, I—" Perplexed, she began to say something, then halted, her voice a sigh. "Oh *yes,* I reckon you're right. It *is* the eighteenth. And you—" Again she paused and then after several moments said: "I wish you didn't have to go back. You're the handiest young darky anywhere around. I suppose there's someone waiting to get you next, as usual."

"Yessum," I said, "Marse Tom told me Major Ridley's fencing in a lot of grass for his new stock and has got me for a fortnight to build fences. Before full spring comes." I had begun to find it difficult to keep the hatred from quivering in my voice. Why did she have to trespass on my thoughts like this?

"Well," she sighed, "I certainly wish I could have you for my very own. I've offered Mr. Tom Moore a lot of money to buy you but I expect he knows a gold mine when he sees it. It is hard enough to get darkies to work, and I don't mind saying that you turn out an honest day's work like no darky I've ever come across."

"I do my best, Miss Caty," I replied. "Paul said every man shall receive his own reward according to his own labor, for we are laborers together with God. I do believe that."

"Pshaw!" she exclaimed. "Don't blandish me with Scripture. Though indeed I'm sure you're right. I wish I hadn't mistaken the date," she went on. "I wanted that chair fixed and I had so hoped you would take the carriage tomorrow afternoon and fetch little Miss Peg from Jerusalem. It's her vacation. She's coming by stage from the Seminary in Lawrenceville. I so hoped you would be here to fetch her. I cannot trust any of the other darkies with those two horses."

"Yessum," I said, "I'm sorry."

"But I shall have you back before long, you may be sure of

that.' She essayed one of her distant, pallid smiles. "I expect you eat considerably better here than you do at Mr. Moore's, don't you?"

"Yessum," I said, speaking the truth.

"Or even at Major Ridley's, I'll vow."

"Yessum," I said again, "that's right."

"Oh, I wish I hadn't mistaken that date. Are you sure today is the eighteenth?"

"Yessum, on that calendar in your library."

"You're the only darky I would ever trust to drive Miss Margaret or Miss Harriet or Miss Gwen or any of the grand-children anywhere. I shudder to think of Hubbard or Andrew or Jack driving and that carriage going helter-skelter with all my children up and down the countryside." She paused for an instant, regarding me closely; I shifted my gaze. Then she went on: "Mr. Tom Moore's so stubborn in not selling you to me. Wouldn't you agree?"

I felt I had to compose some kind of answer. "Well, Miss Caty," I said, "Marse Tom makes a bit more money hiring me out, I reckon. In the long run."

"Well, I expect that he will eventually have to bow to the inevitable and sell you to a person with money and position, if not me then somebody else. You're too bright a darky to live down in that quagmire, as respectable as your owner may be. How old are you, Nat? About twenty-five?"

"I'm twenty-eight, Miss Caty," I said.

"Then at your age you should think of yourself as lucky. Consider the young darkies who lack your ability and can do almost nothing except push a hoe or a broom, hardly even that. I expect you will go far. I mean, for instance, you are actually able to comprehend all I am saying to you. Even if you aren't sold to someone like me, you will be hired out to people like me who value you enough to feed you well and clothe you warmly and take care of you. Certainly you have no reason to fear that you will ever be sold south, even now when there is a humming market in darkies for Alabama and Mississippi, and there are so many extra mouths to feed—"

As she spoke I saw two of her Negroes, Andrew and Tom, struggling across the field with a burden of sawhorses between them, the crude oaken timbers piled up on top of each other painfully cumbersome and heavy, all askew now and ready to fall to earth. *Ah!* They fell as I watched, tumbling down with a lumpish clatter. Then slowly the blessed nincompoops rearranged the sawhorses into a stack again, hoisted them up and continued their hunched, lead-footed pilgrimage across the field, two raggedy silhouettes against a frieze of pinewoods and wintry sky, bound as if for nowhere on to the uttermost limits of the earth—black faceless paradigms of an absurd and immemorial futility. I gave a quick shiver in the chill and thought: Why do men live at all? Why do men wrassle so with air, with nothing? For the briefest instant I was overcome by a terrible anguish.

Richard Whitehead, mounted on a sluggish fat white gelding, came riding into the distant barnyard and flapped an arm, the high-pitched drawl sacerdotal, sweet: "Evenin', Muvva!"

"Hay-o, Boysie!" she called in return. Her gaze lingered on him, then she cast her eyes back at me and said: "Do you know, I've offered Mr. Tom Moore a thousand dollars for you? *One thousand dollars.*"

Strange that, after a fashion, the woman's manner toward me had been ingratiating, even queerly tender, with a faint tongue-lick of unctuousness, benevolent, in a roundabout way downright maternal. Nuzzling around my black ass. In my heart of hearts I bore her no ill will. Yet she had never once removed herself from the realm of ledgers, accounts, tallies, receipts, balance sheets, purse strings, profits, pelf—as if the being to whom she was talking and around whom she had spun such a cocoon of fantasy had not been a creature with lips and fingernails and eyebrows and tonsils but some miraculous wheelbarrow. I gazed at the complacent oblong of her face, white as tallow. Suddenly I thought of the document beneath my shirt and again the hatred swept over me. I was seized with awe, and a realization: *Truly, that white flesh will soon be dead.*

"I hope you are aware of how much money one thousand dollars is," she was saying. "One does not pay that type of money for something one does not really value, or treasure. You are aware of that, Nat, aren't you?"

"Yessum," I said.

"No," she said after a pause, "I expect you will go far, for a darky."

No. 1. Early objective Mrs. C. Whitehead's. A gift from God. This house taken will mark end 1st phase of campaign. Whitehead gun room next to library. Trophies of Mrs. W.'s dead husband. 15 muskets, rifles & fowling pieces, 6 flintlock pistols, also 4 swords, 2 cutlasses, 4 small dirks, plenty powder & lead.

Once house taken & inhabitants destroyed these weapons sh'd even up balance. If attack be launched at midnight at Cross Keys (Moore's? Travis's?) then Mrs. W.'s sh'd be reached next day by noon. Houses in between w'l yield up little in way of guns etc. but must be taken & inhabitants destroyed. Before alarm can be sounded. Weapons taken here sh'd allow successful drive gen'ly N.E. to Jerusalem by noon 2d day. Also of course Mrs. W.'s 8 Morgans in stable plus 2 carriage horses. If time destroy oxen & other livestock.

Sh'd fire all houses after inhabitants killed? Expect answer No. W'ld be useful but fire & smoke w'ld only raise earliest alarm. All must be slain though. All.

No. 2. After Mrs. W. penultimate objective Jerusalem. The armory. Old negro Tim handyman there said 2 mos. ago over 100 muskets & rifles, 800 lb. powder, unknown amt. of ball shot in canvas bags but sufficient. Also 4 small bore cannon to be loaded on wagons. Good maybe for defense later w. ball & scatter shot loads.

Armory has many saws axes hardware etc. Useful later.

Also militia stable has 10 horses incl. 6 black Barbs from Albemarle perfect for sending fast vanguard east from Jeru. Entry into Armory not hard since side doors padlocked but loose fitting. Once guards killed simple to force entry by crowbars betw. door & uprights inside. Town will be devastated by fire. Therefore I shalt set my face toward the siege of Jerusalem & mine arm shall be uncovered & I shall prophesy against it.

No. 3. "Dismal swamp" ultimate objective. Joshua much better equip. than I w'ld not set forth on mission of total destruction w. out place to withdraw. Futile to attack as Joshua did fr. examp. Lachish & Eglon & 5 combined Kings unless safe place to retreat to as the camp at Gilgal. Therefore—

"Dismal swamp." It lays but 35 mi. E. by S.E. fr. Jeru. 2 days march & less than that from Jeru. if vanguard supplied w. horses. Road fr. Jeru. to pt. nearest swamp is good by map & this confirm'd by negroes I've talked to whove been that way to Suffolk and Norfolk. One (but only) possible main barrier is ford across Blackwater riv. betw. So. Hampton & Isle of Wight counties but in Aug. this sh'd be shallow. Find out if ferry there.

Will Lord give me the sign in Aug.? What yr?

"Dismal swamp" grand retreat for my force. Still trackless. Had no idea so huge. On map 30-35 mi. long N-S & 20 mi. at widest. In unknown territory defense has all advantage. Remember lecture to Marse Samuel by that Col. Persons or Parsons abt. 1812 war in marshes nr. Washington. Once in swamp my force w. supplies guns ammu., etc. c'ld withstand enemy search & attack indefinitely. Other negroes in Va. & N.C. maybe even S.C. will join us. ? ?

Negroes in Jeru. whove been there hunting w. masters—

Long Jim fr. examp. owned by Dr. Massenberg all say Swamp fantastic. Also Charlie & Edward on bear hunt with Col. Boyce. Talk to Edward again. Fair amt. of high dry ground tho. mainly low swampy land & savanna. Many fresh water springs & unbelievable profusion of game, deer, bear, boar hogs, turkey, mallards, geese, squirrel, hare, coon etc. Fish by millions. Trout, bass, bream, catfish, eels. Some land c'ld be cultivated for vegtbls. Of course endless supply of timber for shelter, revetments, etc. "Dismal swamp" not many miles from Atlantic. Maybe at last I'll see the ocean!

Many snakes, espec. water moccasin. Don't mention this to Hark!!!

No. 4. Total surprise essential & therefore must not reveal plans to followers until last possible moment. Trust the Lord will give me the sign for Aug.

No. 5. Problem of recruitment. Who will follow? Recall item in So'side Reporter recent telling how blacks in So. Hampton outnumber whites by 6-4 ratio which surprised me thinking it was the other way around. This all to the good.

No. 6. Unending patience & trust in God.

No. 7. Wait patiently for His last sign.

No. 8. Must sternly prevent violation of females. We shall not do to their women what they have done to ours. Also w'ld take up precious time.

No. 9. Slay all. No hostages, no impediments, nothing to encumber. All. The only possible way.

No. 10. Let Thy hand be upon the man of Thy right hand, upon the Son of man whom Thou madest strong for Thyself. Turn us again, O Lord God of hosts, cause Thy face to shine, and we shall be saved. Amen.

When O Lord?

The number of my followers—they who came from the original Bible class I held behind the market in Jerusalem—now had grown roughly a score. Many of the Negroes cared

little or nothing for learning and paid scant interest to what I
had to say: these quickly dropped away and joined the noisy
mob on the gallery. But others remained, and when I say
"followers" I mean those Negroes (including three or four of
the free) who had evidenced their faith in me and their at-
traction to me whether by devoted attention to the stories I
told them—stories drawn from Biblical history or from the
knowledge of world events I had gained at Turner's Mill—or
by their popeyed and thirsty eagerness to learn a little simple
geography (few of them even knew that they lived in a place
called Virginia; most thought the earth was as flat as a shin-
gle), or to apprehend the nature of the heavens (some figured the stars so near that they could be brought down by a
load of buckshot), or to listen to me as I told them about
Napoleon Bonaparte, whose exploits, bruited endlessly by the
elder Turners and their guests, had been part of my daily
education as a boy and who now was transformed by me,
with the utmost guile, into a seven-foot black prodigy and the
scourge of all white creation. Lord, how I strove to drive the
idea of a nigger Napoleon into their ignorant minds! Naturally, I wished to implant there too a sense of black militancy
and I was gratified to see how through my clever guidance
they were able finally to identify with this murderous con-
queror. Like Joshua and David (turned also into Negro
heroes by my artful tongue) he bestrode the wreckage of the
white man's world like an angel of the apocalypse. I described him as an African risen to sweep up and annihilate
the white tribes of the North. However childishly, they came
to believe in this dark demigod; their eyes glittered while I
told of his conquests, and it seemed to me I saw deep in those
same eyes the sparks of a newborn courage—hints, auguries
of a passion for blood that needed only my final prick of
animation to explode into fury. I forbore, however, trying to
teach these more simple and benighted of my followers to
read or to count. In their twenties or thirties, most of them,

they were too old for such frills; besides, what good would it do in the end? Nor of course did I yet intimate by the vaguest sign or word the true nature of my great plans. It was enough now, as the time grew short, that they stand in awe of me and warm to the light I knew I shed of ineluctable wisdom and power.

My "inmost four," as I called them to myself—those in whom I placed my greatest trust and who when the moment came would be the generals of my force—were Hark, Nelson, Henry, and Sam. Two of them, Nelson and Henry, were the oldest among my followers and I valued not only the experience their years had brought them but the cleverness and ability both would have possessed at any age. I sensed that they profoundly respected my superior intelligence and my powers to lead and to enthrall but they were not cowed by me as were so many of the others. Thus since neither of them was tongue-tied in my presence, there flourished a free and easy intercourse between us, and I was wise enough occasionally to pause and listen, profiting from their counsel. Now in his fifties, Nelson was impassive, slow-moving, grave-spoken, dirty-mouthed, wise, hate-ridden, and as solid as a slab of seasoned oak. I felt I could trust him to carry out without hesitation any command. So too for Henry, who, despite or perhaps because of his deafness, seemed to be craftily alert to his surroundings like no Negro I had ever known. He was about forty, square, squat, black as a tar pit. Some of the other Negroes swore that Henry could sniff bacon cooking at five miles, was able to track the scent of a possum like a hound, could point with his big toe to a plot of earth and disclose an underground cache of fish-bait earthworms swarming like maggots. Almost alone of all my followers he possessed a religious ardor, infusing light and fantasy through the gravestone silence of his inner world. His lips moved and fluttered in echo to my own, his better ear cocked, bright eyes rapt upon me as I recounted some tale of battle in old Israel: of my entire band of Negroes, save for Hark, I felt that Henry paid me the most constant devotion. Yet there was one consideration even greater than either ability or experience which made me cherish Nelson and Henry and caused me to repose in them my final trust. And this was that both of them (like Sam, the youngest of the inmost four, my desperate little half-berserk yellow runaway—liveliest, pluckiest, certainly the most venturesome and resourceful of all my disciples) were capable, in their own long-nourished hatred and rage, of slicing the liver out of a white man with as little qualm or conscience as if they were gutting a rabbit or a pig.

Ask the average Negro if he is prepared to kill a white man, and if he says yes, you may be sure that he is indulging in the sheerest brag. This was not the case with my inmost four, each of whom had specific grounds to nurture an unswerving hatred. Bondage had driven Nelson close to madness. Out of simple bad luck he had been sold a cruel number of times—over a half a dozen; his children were scattered to the winds; now in middle age having ended up the property of a vicious, stupid woodcutter who had once struck him in the face (but whom he had struck back) was an affliction Nelson could no longer suffer, and in the ache of his yawning desperation he waited upon me to ordain any course of action. Henry's rage was different, resigned, more patient, calmer—if rage can be restrained by a calmness—but no less indomitable; his rage blossomed in the muffled near-dead world of his hearing. Deafened as a little boy by a blow on the skull from a drunken overseer, he had since heard only thumps and rustlings, and the memory of that long-ago event daily stoked his placid fury. Each dimly perceived birdcall or unheard voice or child's mute laugh or the vacuum of soundlessness at the edge of a roaring brook memorialized that unspeakable and unavenged moment thirty years before: the instant he spilled a white man's blood, I felt, Henry would leap like a swallow straight up into the realm of hearing.

Sam's hatred was the least complicated of all: like some imprisoned animal aware only that the hulking shadow which falls from time to time across its cage is a being that brings nothing but senseless torment, Sam wished simply to eliminate Nathaniel Francis from the domain of his own existence. Uncaged, he would go straight for the throat of his tormentor and kill him, and devour all men that resembled him thereafter. As for Hark and *his* hatred, there was the fact, of course, that his wife and child had been sold south, and this I used as an instrument to break down his docility and his resistance, to undermine his childish fear of white people and his cowardly awe of their mere presence. It was not easy to make of Hark a potential killer, to generate true hatred in that large-hearted breast. Without causing him, as I did, to brood on the sale of his wife and child, I might have failed. But of all the Negroes, Hark was the most surely and firmly under my domination.

We congregated together often, the five of us, mainly on the free Sunday afternoons we were given throughout most of the year. Sam, Henry, and Nelson all lived within four or five miles from Moore's, so it was easy for us to gather at my hidden mossy knoll in the woods. Over the years my sanctuary had undergone great changes. What had once been a rough pine-bough shelter had now become, through the addition of scrap lumber and pine-gum caulking that I managed to borrow or extort from my various employers, a cozy tabernacle—a commodious and weatherproof refuge complete with little windows made of glass stolen from Travis by Hark, a smoothly planed plank floor, and even a rust-flaked, disintegrating but workable cast-iron stove that Nelson had carried off from a house one Sunday when its owner was at church. A barbecue pit in the shallow ravine nearby completed the hideaway; with Hark as our provider we gloried in (or at least the others did, since I preferred to remain generally abstemious) a plenitude of illicit pigs. Early on during these long afternoons as we talked among ourselves, I would always manage to steer the conversation with great craft and subtlety to the problem of a mass escape. I had fixed the Dismal Swamp already in my mind; it seemed to me even then, even before I had the map in hand, a perfect stronghold for a small band of resolute, woods-canny Negroes: though large (just how vast it really was I could not then know), trackless, forbidding, as wild as the dawn of creation, it was still profusely supplied with game and fish and springs of sweet water—all in all hospitable enough a place for a group of adventurous, hardy runaways to live there indefinitely, swallowed up in its green luxuriant fastness beyond the pursuit of white men. Biding their time in the wilderness, until at last their escape was forgotten, these fugitives might then abandon the swamp and make their way the short distance up to Norfolk, where it would be possible to hide, singly or together, on board one of the many great merchant ships bound for the North. A heady scheme, beyond doubt, swarming with problems, perils, uncertainties. But I knew that by the grace of God this escape could be achieved.

So that is how it all began. My little inner group of followers were excited about such a plan when first I outlined it to them. Bedeviled, torn apart by hatred, sick unto death of bondage, they would have cast their lot with the most evil ha'nt or phantom of the woods to be shut forever of the white man's world. They had nothing more to lose. They were passionately eager to set out with me any night, any day. "When?" said their eyes as I told them of my conception. "*When*, man?" Nelson asked bluntly, and I saw Runaway Sam's eyes glitter with the wildest agitation as he muttered: "Shit! C'mon, le's *go*." But I was able to calm them all and—counseling infinite cunning, slowness, and patience—quickly put their excited hopes to rest. "I've got to receive the last sign," I explained to them. "They's plenty time," I added.

"*Plenty time.*" And this was a phrase I found myself repeating over and over during the following months.

For what they did not know was that behind all my talk of simple flight was a grander design involving the necessity of death, cataclysm, annihilation. They could not know of my vision nor that a true escape into freedom must include not a handful of Negroes but many, and that the blood of white men must flow on the soil of Southampton. They could not know then, because my lips were sealed. But the Lord was about to remove that seal, and they would soon know—of that I was certain.

(Fragment of a memory.) It is the late spring of the next year after that gray winter day when I discovered the map. The library again. Early evening. June. Once more I have been hired out to Mrs. Whitehead, who has set me to installing new pine bookshelves against the remaining bare library wall. This is a job I enjoy—cutting the mortices and tenons and joining them, then boring straight through both pieces of wood with a cross-handled auger in order to pin them together with nails. Rising, shelf succeeds shelf. I work steadily through the twilight, laboring at a casual, rhythmic, unhurried pace. The weather is balmy, the air outside pollen-hazy, filled with the chattering of birds. That pungent smell of wood shavings which I love surrounds me as if in a piney sawdust mist, invisible and sweet. For some reason my plans for the future, which usually occupy my mind during such work, are far from my thoughts. With pleasure I think of the barbecue planned for the following Sunday in the woods. My four close disciples will be there, and in addition to them, three more Negroes whom Nelson and Sam have recruited to my scheme of flight to the Dismal Swamp. Nelson feels that they will make great converts. One of these, an older man named Joe, has told me that he wants to be baptized and I look forward to the rites with satisfaction. (It is rare enough that I encounter a Negro with spiritual aspirations, much less one who might also become, potentially, a murderer.) As I brood congenially on these matters, the auger suddenly slips from my grasp and the sharp point embeds itself in the fleshy under part of my left thumb. I give a gasp of pain. Almost immediately when I remove the point of the drill I see that the damage is slight. The pain too is not severe but I seem to be bleeding copiously. It has happened before. Unconcerned, I commence to bind up my hand with a cotton rag I carry in my tool box.

Now even as I bandage myself, I hear a voice from the hallway—Mrs. Whitehead's: "But I shan't let you go on that hayride, darling, without your cloak!" The tone is gently solicitous. "It's not full summer yet, dear, and nights can still get cold. Who's carrying you to the party?"

"Tommy Barrow," calls Miss Margaret, close by me in the hallway. "Oh, I've *got* to find that poem! I'll prove it to her yet. Where did you say the book would be, Mother?"

"On the far shelf, darling!" comes the reply. "Right next to the little whatnot near the window."

Margaret bursts into the library. Most of the time she is away at school, I have seen her only half a dozen times before. Concerned as I am with swathing my wound I am nonetheless unable to keep from staring at her erect, graceful, seventeen-year-old back. Nor is it the glossy tumbling mass of chestnut-brown hair that captures my attention, nor the freckled young shoulders, nor the slim waist pinched tight by the first corset it has ever been my necessity to see; it is the fact that she wears no skirt at all, only the white frilly ankle-length pantalettes that the unworn skirt is destined to conceal and which, had I not been a Negro and therefore presumably unstirred by such a revealing sight, she would never be so immodest to flaunt thus beneath my nose. Garbed to the ankles, she is nowhere near naked, yet the white pants make her seem wantonly unclothed. I am filled with abrupt confusion, hot panic seizes me: Do I keep looking or do I avert my eyes? I avert my eyes—not, however, before trying to avoid, unsuccessfully, a glimpse of the dim shadowed cleft between the round promontories where fabric clings tightly to her firm young bottom.

"I just know the word is *endurance*," she says aloud, as if to her mother again, or to space. "I'll prove it to her yet!" She has seized a book from the shelf and now, turning about to face me where I still half squat on the floor, thumbs in a flurry through the pages. She whispers to herself, inaudibly.

"*What*, dear?" Mrs. Whitehead asks from afar.

But now Margaret ignores her mother's call. A flush of triumph comes to her face and her voice is a little squeal. "*Endurance!* I knew that was the word. Not *forbearance* at all! I told Anne Eliza Vaughan twenty times if I told her once what the right word was, but she wouldn't *believe* me. Now I shall *prove* it."

"What, dear?" cries the mother's voice again. "I can't hear you!"

"*I told*—" Margaret begins to shout but then breaks off, giving a little shiver of annoyance. "Oh, nothing," she says to the empty air, and with perfect naturalness and poise continues—in her exuberant conquest—to talk to the only available listener: me. "Listen!" she says. "Now just listen!

> "The reason firm, the temperate will,
> *Endurance*, foresight, strength, and skill.
> A perfect Woman, nobly planned,
> To warn, to comfort, and command;
> And yet a spirit still, and bright
> With something of angelic light.

"Wordsworth!" she says to me. "*There*, I've won a dime from Anne Eliza Vaughan! I told the silly girl it was *endurance* not *forbearance* but she wouldn't believe me. And I shall win another dime!"

I look up in a quick furtive glance from the ragged bandage I am pressing against my hand, catch sight of the pantalettes again, turn my eyes away. I sweat. A vein pulses at my temple. I feel split upon a sudden and savage rage. How could she with this thoughtlessness and innocence provoke me so? Godless white bitch.

"Oh, Nat, maybe you can tell me the other. And we'll share the dime! Yes, we'll share it!" she exclaims. "Mother says you know so much about the Bible, maybe you can answer. I've bet Anne Eliza that the line that goes something about 'our vines have tender grapes' is from the Bible and she said it was from *Romeo and Juliet*. Now, tell me, Nat, isn't it from the Bible? Just *isn't* it?"

I shrink from looking up and continue to gaze at my right hand clasped tightly upon the other. The rage within me fades away. Controlling my voice I say finally, after a long hesitation: "You right, young missy. That part's from Solomon's Song. It goes: *Take us the foxes, the little foxes that spoil the vines: for our vines have tender grapes. My beloved is mine and I am his: he feedeth among the lilies.* That's the way it goes. So you win a dime, missy."

"Oh, *Nat!*" she cries suddenly. "Your *hand!* It's *bleeding!*"

"It ain't anything, missy," I reply. "It's just a little bitty cut. Some blood, that don't mean anything."

Now I sense (see? feel?) the white pantalettes as she moves close to the place where I am crouched, and reaching down with a swift but gentle motion of her fingers, takes hold of my unwounded right hand. That soothing many-fingered delicacy—it is like scalding water and with a quick jerk I pull my hand away. "It ain't anything!" I protest. "It ain't anything, missy, I *promise* you!"

She withdraws her hand and stands motionless beside me. I listen to her breathing. Then after a pause I hear her murmur softly: "Well, all right, Nat, but you must not fail to take care of it. And thank you about the Bible. I'll be sure to give you five pennies as soon as I get them from Anne Eliza Vaughan."

"Yes, missy," I say.

"Do take care of that hand, too. *Do*."

"Yes, missy."

"Or I won't give you the five pennies, mind you that!"

"What *are* you up to, little Miss Peg?" I hear the mother call. "It's seven already. They'll be here! You'll be late for the hayride! Hurry!"

"I'm coming, Mother!" she cries. "Bye-bye, Nat!" Gaily. Then she flits away and I watch the pantalettes receding, the firm young flesh beneath nearly visible in a pink nimbus behind teasing cotton, a translucent concealing infuriating veil. The fragrance of lavender hovers, fades, is gone. I stay crouched there on the floor in the balmy pine-smelling dusk. Outside birds cheep and chirrup, mad with spring. Through my wrists the blood rushes like a millrace. Again the rage returns and I cannot tell why my heart is pounding so nor why my hatred for Margaret is, if anything, deeper than my hatred for her mother.

"*God damn her soul*," I whisper—not an oath but a supplication. "*God damn her soul*," I say again, hating her even more than seconds before, or maybe less—thinking of those ruffled white pantalettes—not knowing which, less or more.

While yanking a borning calf from its mother's womb Moore suffered a bizarre and fatal accident: the cord parted abruptly, sending my owner in a sprawl backward until his head fetched up against a post and cracked open like a melon. Naturally he was good and drunk when the catastrophe happened. He lingered for half a day before he expired— a mortal leave-taking that plunged me into several seconds' grief from which I emerged feeling the greatest consternation. Few things are so ominous to a Negro as a death in the family to which he belongs, especially the death of a pater-

familias. Too often simple mad warfare breaks loose among
the covetous heirs all pouncing down upon the property, and
on will-reading day many a piece of property has found himself chained to a wagon bound for, say, Arkansas, sold off to
some rice or cotton demesne by a relative who kept him perhaps as long as a short afternoon before handing him over to
a nigger-hustler lurking like a buzzard close by. I myself was
overpowered by this dark fear for a while; it went hand in
hand with the intolerable notion that being sold would prevent me from fulfilling the great mission the Lord had ordained, and a few weeks passed during which my worry and
gloom were almost intolerable. However, it was not long before Joseph Travis came a-courting Miss Sarah and promptly
won her hand. Thus such property as I embodied, having
been assigned and devised to Moore's heirs (or heir, in this
case the snot-nosed Putnam), was transferred through marriage to Travis. The unkempt household in which I had lived
for nine years now dissolved, decamping to those more pleasant acres nearby, where—joining Hark in the cozy little alcove behind the wheel shop—I dwelt during that crucial and
climactic time whose quality I tried to convey early on in this
history.

These final two years or so (it may be recalled my telling) were all in all the most free and comfortable I had spent
since I left Turner's Mill. I do not mean to say that I found
myself at total leisure. Travis certainly gave me enough to do
around the wheel shop and he kept me occupied at chores
which, happily, exercised my ingenuity rather than my back.
I had of course worked for Travis several times in the past, so
I sensed the high value he placed upon my gifts as a craftsman. At risk of gross immodesty, I must say that I was fairly
well convinced that my presence in Miss Sarah's dowry
helped cause Travis to woo her in the first place. I rigged up
all sorts of artful contrivances for Travis's shop—a pole saw
that could be worked with a wooden foot treadle, a new bel-

lows for his forge, and a cluster of beautiful ashwood tool racks which Travis prized beyond anything in the shop and elicited from his otherwise laconic lips the most dazzling sort of praise. Thus supplied with a resident genius, my new owner, unlike Moore, was in no great sweat to hire out my body, and save for a few occasions that Mrs. Whitehead prevailed upon him to rent me to her (or, once or twice, when stumps needed pulling, to trade me for a yoke of her phenomenal oxen) I remained calmly in servitude with Travis, counting the days. Yet inside I was burning. Burning! Does it seem a hopeless paradox that the less toilsome became the circumstances of my life the more I ached to escape it? That the more tolerable and human white people became in their dealings with me the keener was my passion to destroy them?

Joseph Travis was at bottom a decent and sympathetic man; this I am compelled to admit despite the reservations I harbored about him during the many periods in the immediate past when he had hired me from Moore. Travis was not a native of Southampton. For reasons unknown, reversing the usual pattern of migration from east to west, he had come to the county from the wild slopes of the Blue Ridge Mountains. A craggy, hollow-cheeked, sandy-haired loner, he had the stormy look and mood of the wilderness about him, and the insanity of solitary months and years often flickered across his face; he appeared to me then a cranky, unpredictable, snarling, intolerant creature, venting his frustration on Negroes with rotten food, hard labor, and somber, savage jibes. Hark's life with Travis had been, in those early days, anything but pleasant. Then too, during that time, he had committed the unpardonable: he had sold Hark's wife Tiny and their little boy south, preferring to endure Hark's reproachful glances and sullen grief than to be faced with two extra mouths which it might have been a strain but hardly a killing sacrifice to feed. Maybe it was his mountain heritage, his lack of experience with Tidewater ways, that caused him to do something that no truly respectable slaveowner would do. It had become plain to me that white men reared outside the tradition of slavery often made the most callous taskmasters —what hordes of corrupt and ruthless overseers hailed from Connecticut and New Jersey! Who knows too but whether Travis's harsh morality did not tell him that since Hark and his woman had merely "jumped over the broomstick," since their "marriage" had no sanction under the law, he was bound by no rule of ethics when it came to selling "wife" and offspring—by this grim reasoning a little black bastard. It was a rationalization used without shame countless times before. At any rate, out of whatever cause—thoughtlessness, stupidity, ignorance, God only knew—Travis had done it and that was that.

Yet as I've said, the man had changed now in the most remarkable way. Prosperity had restored him to the craft he had learned as a boy. In the fullness of middle age he blossomed—or let us say he became unshriveled. He was genial, even generous in his behavior with me, insisting that Hark and I have comfortable accommodations in our bachelor quarters next to the shop, making certain that we ate well from the leavings of the house, permitting no abuse (at least physical) from the rest of the household, and in general comporting himself like every slave's ideal master. Although at first I was puzzled, I did not have to ponder long the mystery of this man's renascence. After years as a childless widower and a scrabbling dirt farmer he was now—at fifty-five and in the prime of life—anointed with good fortune: well married to a fat lady who laughed a lot and jollied his days, vigorously prospering at a skilled trade, father of a newborn son and heir, and owner of the smartest nigger in Southampton County.

I have described at length my encounter with Jeremiah Cobb in the late autumn of the year preceding the commencement of this account. This was the day that Hark was run up a tree by Putnam and Miss Maria Pope. It was several months after that strange afternoon, in the waning winter of the fateful year 1831, that I received the final mandate I had so long been hoping for, and began to elaborate upon and implement the plans I had drawn up during those cloistered moments at Mrs. Whitehead's. It all came about in the following manner . . .

The winter had been unseasonably mild, with an almost complete absence of snow and ice, and as a result Travis's shop had been exceptionally busy. The balmy climate allowed the shop to expand out of doors. Day after day not only the shop but the entire plot of bare earth surrounding it had been abustle with activity as Travis together with Hark and myself and the two apprentices, Putnam and the Westbrook boy, scampered about through the smoke and the steam, heating the great metal tires over the forge and firing the hoops until they turned a dull red and sledging the hoops onto the wheels with twenty-pound hammers. It was a noisy, boisterous scene, what with the hissing of the steam as we doused the hot wheels, and the clang of the hammers, and Hark's shouts, and the racket of tortured wood as it snapped and creaked beneath the suddenly cooled, contracting cast-iron tires. Decent, healthy, amiable work it was too—a far piece from the grime and sweat of the field—and if it had not been for Putnam's peevish yammerings and the constant taunts he threw Hark's way I might have actually celebrated such labor, since there was something deeply satisfying about this craft and the way in which straight lengths of nondescript rough wood and strips of crude black iron were transformed into symmetrically spoked, perfectly circular, sumptuously shellacked and polished wheels. The days were long but I relished the half-hour breaks we took morning and afternoon, when Miss Sarah would bring us from the house a plate of biscuits and mugs of sweet cider with a stick of cinnamon; such a pause in labor made the work itself more rewarding, and caused Travis to seem even more acceptable in my eyes.

With a residue of orders from all over the county (and from as far away as Suffolk and the lowland region of Carolina), Travis found it hard to keep up with the demand. Just before he acquired me he had bought a newly patented machine, hand-cranked, which could bend iron in a cold state and eliminated the old process of hammering out hot metal. This machine had merely created the need for another—a sawing contraption which might quickly reduce the growing stockpile of oak and black-gum timbers to manageable lengths—and so late in December, just after Christmas, Travis gave me some rough plans and set me to work on my most ambitious piece of carpentry to date: an enormous "apprentice mill," complete with ripsaw and treadmill designed to utilize either large Negro or middle-sized mule. It was a challenging assignment and I set to upon it with zeal, isolating myself in a high-roofed shed next to the shop, where (with the sometime help of Hark and the boy Moses) I painstakingly worked out the architecture of the complicated mechanism, carving one by one the gears and the gear-boxes, adding such clever wrinkles as a counterweight system to minimize jamming of the saw, and in all respects carrying through the project with a smooth professionalism that gratified me more than anything I could remember. Since I anticipated that I would be finished with the machine toward the end of February, I asked Travis if I might not please have several days off when I was done. I did not linger on it in so many words, but I wanted to go out into the woods to my sanctuary, there to fast and pray for a while—during these last days at work on the mill I had felt the spirit of the Lord hovering very close.

Anyway, I went. I told my owner that I wished to set up a new trapline; the old route had worn out its lure, the rabbits were getting wary. Travis agreed; my rabbits helped augment his income, and he could scarcely refuse. Besides, as I say, there lurked in his heart a basic albeit leaden decency and he knew I had earned the leave. One afternoon late in February, after spreading on a final coat of varnish, I finished the last work on the machine. I knelt and gave thanks to God for the skill of my hands, as I always did when I completed such difficult work, and then without further ado retreated into the woods, carrying with me only my Bible, my well-worn map, and some lucifer matches with which to start a fire.

The full eclipse of the sun began in the midafternoon of the following Saturday, three days after I set out for the woods. I had been fasting ever since the first day, seated next to the fire in my tabernacle, where I immersed myself in the Bible and prayed, taking no sustenance at all except for a little water from the stream and chewing on sassafras roots only to still the cramps that racked my stomach. Usually fasting was a method by which I helped quench all fleshly longings. Whether this time it was the pressure of the work I had just completed, I do not know, but during those first days I seemed beset by devils and monsters. I walked out and sat down amid the pines, trying vainly to rid myself of coarse hot desires. Visions of the flesh of women tempted me, inflaming my passions in a way I had rarely known before. Lust stormed my senses like a sick fever. I thought of a Negro girl I had seen often in the streets of Jerusalem—a plump doxy, every nigger boy's Saturday piece, a light-skinned kitchen maid with a rhythmic bottom and round saucy eyes. Heavy-breasted, full-bellied, she stood naked before me in my mind's eye, thrusting at me her glossy brown midriff with its softly rounding belly-bulge and its nest of black hair. Try as I might I could not banish her, keep her away; my Bible availed me nothing. *Does you want a l'il bit ob honeycomb, sweet pussy bee?* she crooned to me with those words she had wheedled others, and as she ground her hips in my face, with delicate brown fingers stroking the pink lips of her sex, my own stiffened. In hot fancy my arms went out to encircle her slick haunch and ripe behind, my mouth was buried in her wet crotch, and godless mad words struggled on my tongue: *Lap. Lick. Suck.* "Oh, my Lord!" I said aloud, and rose to my feet, but even so the desire would not vanish, would not fade. Sweating, I kissed and embraced the cold scaly trunk of a pine tree. "What can it be *like?*" I called again, as if to the heavens. The rage I had at that moment to penetrate a woman's flesh—a young white woman now, some slippery-tongued brown-headed missy with a sugar-sweet incandescent belly who as I entered her cried out with pain and joy and enveloped me convulsively with milky-white legs and arms—was like a sudden racking spasm or an illness so shattering to the senses that it imposed wonder, and disbelief. I thirsted to plunge myself into the earth, into a tree, a deer, a bear, a bird, a boy, a stump, a stone, to shoot milky warm spurts of myself into the cold and lonely blue heart of the sky. "Lord help me," I said aloud once more, "what can it be *like?*" The seed left me then, squirting in warm drops along my fingers; my eyelids slammed shut against the face of the day. I slumped shivering against the pine tree's unloving scaly breast. At last I opened my eyes, and the thought that lingered in mind was only half a prayer: Lord, after this mission is done I will have to get me a wife.

I slept the rest of the afternoon and through the night. The next day, which was Saturday, I awoke feeling groggy and weak. I drank some water and chewed on a sassafras root, and later dragged myself outside, where I sat reading, propped against a tree. It was while I was studying a few chapters from Jeremiah (for some reason, during a fast, I always savored Jeremiah, whose sour and mirthless temper was an appropriate companion for hunger) that I sensed a change in the atmosphere. The light paled, the stark shadows of the barren wintry trees grew hazy and dull, lost definition;

far off in the woods a flock of ragamuffin sparrows, late winter visitors, ceased their cheeping, became still in the false dusk. Around me the leafless gray trees, bleak as skeletons, were plunged into evening shade. I looked up then to see the sun wink slowly out as it devoured the black shape of the moon. There was no surprise in my heart, no fear, only revelation, a sense of final surrender, and I rose to my knees and shut my eyes in prayer, wood smoke sweet in my nostrils, half drowned in the cavelike sudden silence of the woods. For long minutes I knelt there in the somber unearthly hush; sightless, I felt the dark like a vapor around me, cold like the edge of zinc and touched with the graveyard's mossy damp. "*O Lord God to whom vengeance belongeth,*" I whispered, "*O God to whom vengeance belongeth, show thyself.*"

Lift up thyself, thou judge of the earth: render a reward to the proud . . .

In the distance, like a signal, I heard the noise of a gun, a single faint booming that echoed back and forth amid the hollows of the bare and wintry forest, dwindled, died, then fell quiet. Some solitary hunter: had he too seen the sun darken, fired in terror at the haloed black sphere floating in the heavens? Now when I opened my eyes the sun appeared to be disgorging the moon at the same grave and stately pace with which it had swallowed it up. Light moved softly back across the floor of the woods, daubing the carpet of fallen leaves with yellow bursts of sunshine. Warmth flooded over me, the sparrows in the trees resumed their clamor; the sun rode across the blue sky triumphant and serene. I was suddenly touched by a wild anticipation and excitement.

"Now, Lord," I said aloud, "the seal is removed from my lips."

That evening just before sunset Hark came up through the woods and paid me a visit, bringing me a pan of grits and bacon which I was still too agitated to eat. I could only insist that he go back and get in touch with Henry and Nelson and Sam, that he tell them that at noon the next day—a Sunday— they must all assemble here at my sanctuary. With some re- luctance because of his concern for my stomach ("Nat, you jes' gwine shribble up an' blow clean away," he said) he obeyed me. The following day Hark and the others came as I had ordered. I bade them sit around the fire next to me. Then after a session of prayer I turned to the subject at hand. I told them the seal had been removed from my lips and that I had received the last sign. I said that the Spirit had appeared to me in the form of the eclipse of the sun, which they them- selves had witnessed. The Spirit had informed me that the Serpent was loosened and Christ had laid down the yoke he had borne for the sins of men. I went on patiently to explain that the Spirit had commanded that I should take on the yoke and fight against the Serpent, for the time was fast approach- ing when "the first shall be last and the last shall be first."

Then as we sat there in the chill afternoon I unfolded to them my great plans. I made it clear that it was neither wise nor sufficient that our group of five (plus the score or so of Negroes I felt confident would join us) simply run off and get lost in the Dismal Swamp. In the first place, I pointed out, there was no possibility at all of a mob of twenty and more Negroes banding together and passing, even by night, thirty- five miles through two counties and part of another without being apprehended. Furthermore, even a smaller group would likely be doomed to failure. "Us five," I said, "we run off to the swamp together, those white men'll catch our asses before we get ten miles past Jerusalem. One or two niggers run off an' they send out the dogs. Three niggers run off an' they sent out the army." Also, how could even Negroes sur- vive long in the swamp without weapons and supplies? In addition, there was a seller's market in Negroes at the mo- ment, I explained; half a dozen traders were snooping around all over the county, and although I myself was doubtless safe

I could not say that I felt the same about the other slaves I knew— including those present—and feared that only a clock-tick and some owner's necessity or greed might separate any of them from Mississippi or Arkansas.

"Faithful followers, dear brothers," I said finally, "I believe they ain't none of you can live like this any longer. Therefore, they is only one thing to do . . ."

Here I stopped speaking altogether for a while, allowing these last words to enter their consciousness. Minutes passed and they said nothing, then Henry's voice broke the silence, his deaf man's bleat hoarse and cracked, a shock in the stillness: "Us gotta *kill* all dem white sonsabitches. Ain't dat what de Lawd done told you? Ain't dat right, Nat?"

It was as if by those words we were committed. *Us gotta kill* . . . I talked on, detailing my plans. I showed them the map; although they could not read it, they understood my projected route. Later I asked questions, and found that none of my followers shrank from the idea of killing; I made it plain that murder was an essential act for their own freedom and they welcomed this truth with the stolid acceptance of men who, as I have shown, had nothing on earth to lose. And so I spoke to them throughout the afternoon and into the early evening. In my excitement the weakness I had suffered from my long fast, the drowsiness and vertigo, all seemed to dissolve into the wintry air. I was gripped by a sense of exaltation, of mastery and of perfect assurance, that sent great cries and shouts of gladness throughout my being. I wondered if even Joshua or Gideon had felt such an ecstasy, or had heard that knowledge like a voice in the brain: "The first shall be last."

"An' de last shall be first," they replied. These lines became our password and our greeting, our benediction.

That evening after I dismissed my followers—swearing each to secrecy and silence as I sent them on their way back through the woods—I fell asleep by the fire and dreamed the most placid dreams I had dreamt in a lifetime. And when I awoke the next day and found a king snake, recently aroused from hibernation, sunning himself in my clearing, I blessed its presence in the Lord's name and saw it as a good omen.

Even so, there had begun to dwell in my mouth a sinister taste of death—a sweetish-sour and corrupt flavor that rose thickly up through the nostrils like tainted pork—which I had never experienced before and which I could not rid myself of; it persevered through all the great events of the following summer, and even to the very end of the upheaval. Moreover, I began to suffer from that strange illusion or dislocation of the mind that from then on I could not shake loose or avoid. In short, not always but often when I encountered a white person after that day—man, woman, or child—there was an instant when his living presence seemed to dissolve before my eyes and I envisioned him in some peculiar attitude of death. On the morning following my revelation to my followers, for example, when I came back out of the woods as I returned to Travis's, I was smitten by this hallucination to an intense degree. Now overtaken with weakness again from my fast, I headed east to the farm just before noon. As I walked unsteadily along the path which straggled out of the last clump of pine trees I saw that the place was a hive of activity and work. From the distance I could see the two boys, Putnam and young Joel Westbrook, carrying between them a sheaf of strip iron toward the wheel shop. Farther away, on the front porch of the house, Miss Sarah waddled about with a busy broom, sending up puffs of dust. Still farther off in the barnyard the angular, aproned form of Miss Maria Pope hunched along, strewing handfuls of corn amid a crowd of chickens. The big treadmill saw I had built stood outside the wheel shop; it drove across the field a singsong rasp of metal on wood, and a monotonous clatter. Below the treadmill Travis occupied himself with a hammer and chisel, while above him on the treadmill itself, looming naked to the

waist and enormous through a cloud of steam, Hark plodded
at a slant toward the sky, his great legs moving as if in some
ageless pilgrimage toward an ever-receding and unattainable
home.

As I approached the farm I saw that Travis, turning
about, had caught sight of me; he shouted something to me in
words that were lost on the wind, then pointed at the treadmill and threw me a welcoming, amiable wave with his hand.
He shouted again, and now I caught the words. "Durned
good job!" was what I heard; but I stopped then—stock-still
and with the taste of death sweet and yellow beneath my
tongue—seized for the first time by that hallucination. For
like the moment once in a far corner of childhood when at
Turner's Mill I had happened on a white child's book in
which the woodcut-shapes of small human beings were hidden among the trees, or in a grassy field, and I was teased by
the captions to know, "Where is Jacky?" or "Where is Jane?"
—now the distant people before me leaped out similarly from
their benign and peaceable scene and I discerned them instantly in the postures of death, prefigured in attitudes of
bloody immolation: the two boys sent sprawling with heads
bashed in, Miss Sarah disemboweled upon the quiet porch,
Miss Maria Pope hacked down amid her chickens, and Travis
himself impaled upon a pike, the ice of incomprehension
freezing his eyes even while he raised his arm, now, in beneficent greeting.

Only Hark endured as he strode ceaselessly upon his
treadmill—*Ah, Hark!*—high above the dead, paddling like a
glorious black swan toward the plains of heaven.

"Well yes, Nat," Hark told me once late that spring. "I
reckon I kin kill. I *kin* kill a white man, I knows dat now.
Like I done tol' you, I done had some hard times thinkin'
'bout killin' white folks when we start de ruction. I ain't neb-
ber killed nobody in all my bo'n days. Sometimes at night I

done woked up all asweat and atremble wid dese yere terrible dreams in my head, thinkin' 'bout how it gwine be when I got to kill dem white folks.

"But den I gits to thinkin' 'bout Tiny and Lucas an' Marse Joe sellin' dem off like dat, sellin' dem off widout no nem'mine fo' how *I* feels 'bout it, den I knows I kin kill. Hit like de Lawd *ax* me to kill, 'cause it plain long *sinful* to sell off a man's own fambly, like you say.

"Lawd, Nat, hit sho done cause me a powerful misery, de lonesomeness I done had in my heart after Tiny and Lucas was gone. Like Lucas now—I mean, you know hit kind of funny, de way I tried to figger out ways *not* to grieve over dat little boy. After dey took him away wid Tiny de lonesomeness got so bad I could hardly stan' it. An' so I begun to think 'bout all de *mean* things dat Lucas done. I begun to think 'bout all dem times dat he screeched an' hollered an' kep' me fum sleep an' de time he done got mad an' whopped me wid a hoe handle or dat time he th'owed a mess of grits right in Tiny's face. An' I'd think about all dese times an' I'd say to myse'f: 'Well, he was a mean young'un anyway, hit good to git shet of him.' An' dat ud make me feel better for mebbe a little bit. Den, Lawd, I'd think of de mean things I done to *him*, an' dat ud make me feel bad other way aroun'. But hard as I'd try I couldn't keep feelin' mad about dat little boy, an' by an' by I'd think about him a-chucklin' an' ridin' on my back an' us playin' together behin' the shed, an' de grief ud come back an' pretty soon I'd get so lonesome I could almost die . . .

"No, Nat, you right. Hit sinful to do dat to folks. So when you ax me kin I kill, I figgers I kin, easy 'nough. 'Thout Tiny an' Lucas I wouldn' like to hang roun' dis yere place any longer noways . . ."

That I chose Independence Day as the moment to strike was of course a piece of deliberate irony. It seemed clear to me that when our eruption was successful—with Jerusalem

seized and destroyed and our forces soon impregnably en-
camped in the Dismal Swamp—and when word of our triumph spread throughout Virginia and the upper southern
seaboard, becoming a signal for Negroes everywhere to join
us in rebellion, the fact that it had all arisen on the Fourth of
July would be an inspiration not alone to the more knowledgeable slaves of the region but to men in bondage in even
more remote parts of the South who might take flame from
my great cause and eventually rally to my side or promulgate
their own wild outbreaks. Yet the choice of that patriotic
extravagancy which I made in the spring also involved a very
practical consideration. For many years the Fourth of July
had been the largest, noisiest, and most popular of all general
celebrations in the country. The festivities had always been
held at the camp meeting grounds several miles from Jerusalem, and were attended by nearly every white person in the
region save for the feeble, the ailing, and those already too
drunk to travel. As has been seen, it was my purpose to
slaughter without hesitation each man, woman, and child
who lay in my path. Needless to say, however, I was sure that
the Lord wished me to take Jerusalem by the most expedient
means, and hence if I were able eventually to enter the town
by stealth and seize the armory when most of the people were
away at their jubilee, then so much the better—especially if,
in addition to the advantageous momentum such a thrust
would give me, it might result in naturally fewer casualties
among my men. Although Joshua's initial concept had been a
planned ambush—luring the people out—it was through a
somewhat similar maneuver of capturing an empty town that
he defeated the cities of Aī and Bethel—and this led after all
to the ultimate downfall of Gibeon and to the Children of
Israel's inheritance of the land of Canaan. Timing my assault
for the Fourth of July likewise seemed to me for a while to be
strategy inspired by the Lord.

But early in May my plans along such a line were dashed

to pieces. One Saturday while at the market in Jerusalem conferring with my inmost four disciples, I learned from Nelson that for the first time in local history it had been decided that the Independence Day to-do would be held not at the outlying meeting grounds but within the town itself. That of course made the prospect of attacking Jerusalem on July Fourth even more hazardous than it ordinarily might, and so in great consternation I abruptly canceled my plans. Now in a near-panic, unaccountably, I felt that the Lord was playing with me, taunting me, testing me, and shortly after that Saturday, I fell ill with a bloody flux and a racking fever that lasted nearly a week. During this interval I was wrenched with anxiety. In my despair I began to wonder if the Lord had really called me to such a great mission after all. Then I recovered from my seizure almost as quickly as I had been stricken. Pounds lighter but somehow feeling stronger, I rose from bed in my shed adjoining the wheel shop (where I had been nursed and fed, alternately, by Hark and the ever-ebullient Miss Sarah, soon to cease her existence) to learn of a new development that made me feel—in joyous relief mingled with shame at my faithlessness—that the Lord had not misused me; instead in His great wisdom He had caused me to wait for a grander day and the beginnings of an even more propitious design.

The news came to me one morning during the following month of June, when once again I had been hired out by Travis to Mrs. Whitehead. Or traded, I should say—traded for two months fair-and-square, as the phrase went, for a yoke of oxen that Travis sorely wanted to yank stumps on burnt-off land he intended to plant in apple trees. Mrs. Whitehead was in a sweat of pleasure as usual to have me back: she needed me both as coachman and as carpenter, having contemplated extensive additions to her barn. At any rate, it was while I was back at her homestead that I overheard a passing Baptist preacher inform his colleague, Richard

Whitehead, that a mammoth camp meeting had been planned for the brethren of his own sect late that summer down in Gates County, across the line in North Carolina. Hundreds if not thousands of Baptists from Southampton had already signified their joy to attend, the preacher—a wholesome-looking, ruddy-faced man—said to Richard, and added with a wink that he did not really mean to poach on Richard's territory by suggesting that Methodists too were more than welcome to come and shed their sins. We are all brothers in one faith, he asserted; the camping fee this year was only half a dollar a head—no charge for nigger servants and children under ten. Then he made a wan joke about Methodists and temperance. In recollecting Richard's answer, I seem to remember that he thanked his fellow pastor in tones characteristically bleak, chill, and dry, allowed as how he thought few Methodists would attend—being spiritually so well provided for here in their native parish—but went on to say that he would keep the event in mind and inquired desultorily about the time. When the other preacher replied, "From Friday the nineteenth of August until Tuesday, guess that's the twenty-third," I (who was holding the bridle of the preacher's horse) understood that the date of my great mission, emanating from those ecclesiastical lips, had just then been revealed to me as vividly as the fire of the Lord that showered down at the feet of Elijah. What an unforeseen bounty! Deprived of several hundred Baptist sinners—half of its population— Jerusalem should be child's play to capture and destroy. Silently I offered up a prayer of thanks. It was my very last sign.

There were left then a bare two months to complete the final preparations, although I was pleased that so much had been done since that day of the sun's eclipse. Primarily, I was gratified by the progress that had been made in the area of recruitment—a matter which, because of the extreme secrecy and confidence involved, I had thought would be formidably difficult but that had succeeded beyond my hopes. This was largely due to the skill, tact, and force of persuasion that both Sam and Nelson possessed to a high degree. (Henry gained one or two converts but his deafness made him less effective.) It was due also to the scientific manner in which I went about assembling my body of men. First I consulted the map where many months before I had outlined the direction of march toward Jerusalem. That route was not a direct assault upon the town by the most obvious approach—the seven-mile road from Cross Keys to the cedar bridge that provided entry into Jerusalem across the Nottoway River. Such a route, while arrow-straight and quite short, would leave us mercilessly exposed on either flank. I set down rather a plan of march in the shape of a slovenly, reclining "S," an enormous double loop nearly thirty-five miles in its total length which avoided the few main thoroughfares while at the same time took advantage of secluded lanes and cowpaths in its snakeline journey to the northeast across the countryside. Along the way, I calculated, our force would encounter over twenty plantations, farms, and homesteads—twenty-three to be exact—but all of these with scant exception were lands owned by the more affluent gentry of Southampton and so contained items of utmost importance to the success of our expedition: Negroes, horses, provisions, guns.

Mainly Negroes. Consulting the map and carefully listing the names of the owners of the properties which were due to be attacked, I made a meticulous inventory of the Negroes in each household—not too difficult a chore since on market day in Jerusalem, when from all of those places one or two Negroes at least came to town, it was a simple business for me or any one of my close followers to mingle among them and by asking innocent questions (and some not-so-innocent) to determine the composition of the slave brotherhood at each house. After this, a subtle whisper about runaways proved often to be an effective approach. Negroes who had run away were likely to have fiery spirits. Thus Nelson would sidle along toward a young Negro from Benjamin Blunt's estate, exchange a few words of pointless palaver, and offering the boy a bit of sorghum sugar or a chaw of tobacco, might ask in a sly voice: "You done got any peoples up at yo' place dat evah run off?" As often as not this would elicit a little head-scratching, followed by galloping eyeballs and the cautious disclosure that uh-huh, well, dey was a nigger boy run off not long ago. Name of Nathan. Was gone three weeks. Massah done cotched him though. And so the following Saturday, or the next, Nelson would cozy up to Nathan—a strapping brown buck with a glint mean and rebellious in his unhappy eyes—and draw him aside into the patch of weeds behind the market, where he would sound him out about his runaway nights and days, and lazily jaw along with him about freedom and probe softly but firmly for the hot pulsating aching boil that was Nathan's fury. And at last Nelson would utter those three naked uncompromising words he was to repeat so many times: "*Kin you kill?*" Then Nathan's own words would pour out in a savage, strangled rush all wet and garbled with hatred: "Shit, man, kin I *kill!* I mean, man, git me a ax, I *kill* awright! I chops de dick an' balls off'n a white man an' you *see* how I kin kill!" And at that moment—as with Daniel and Davy and Curtis and Stephen and Joe and Jack and Frank and so many more—a recruit was born into my great cause.

Yet if the enlistment of zealous young Negroes was central to our activity at that time, it was equally important that we guard against treachery. As for our killers, the enthusiasts, the trustworthy converts—of these by midsummer I counted a committed two dozen, all tough, stalwart, desperate young men around whom the other Negroes would rally as we swept the countryside. On pain of death, each of them had been sworn to the profoundest secrecy. I had had the opportunity to speak to them in private, one by one, either behind the market or at my woodland sanctuary, where they were

brought on a Sunday by Sam or Nelson. I was impressed by
the ardor of these plowboys and pig tenders and woodcutters;
the idea of freedom had stirred and inflamed their hearts, the
prospect of a long and dangerous journey made them quiver
with excitement. For them the threat of death as a penalty
for betrayal was a needless flourish, since they were quite
beside themselves with joy at the bloody adventure in the
offing, and would not (except inadvertently, which became
my nagging fear) have given away their magnificent secret
for all the world. These young men were safe, captured,
within the fold. What kept me at an agonized pitch of tension
was not the fear of treachery among the faithful ones, but
apprehension that through a careless murmur or slip of
tongue my great scheme would come to the attention of some
obsequious coon of a house nigger who, wringing his hands
and asweat with lubricious intent, would hurry to Old Massah or Ole Mistis with the tidings. For if I was touched to my
very roots by this revelation that there were, after all, Negroes proud and furious enough to stake their flesh and souls
on this gamble for liberty, my own pride was somehow
diminished by the certain knowledge that there existed other
Negroes, and many of them, who to gain no more than a plug
of tobacco or a couple of fishhooks or half a pound of stew
beef would tattle away their own mother's life. Indeed, that
summer I lived cheek by jowl with one of these in the stable
quarters at Mrs. Whitehead's—with Hubbard, an obese and
chocolate-colored toady, a lard-haunched mincing flatterer
with an artful tongue who at the faintest hint or flicker of
trouble could be expected to croon his suspicions into Miss
Caty's ear. It was Hubbard, and others like him living in
proximity to any of my men in houses up and down the
county, that gave me nightmares and grounds for my most
piercing disquiet.

But as the warm days passed with their blue skies and
sweet smell of hay and as summer reached its zenith, I be-

came more and more confident of success. So far as anyone could tell, the secret was kept; both the white people and the Negroes went about their customary business—building barns, haying, chopping corn and cotton, cutting timber, making wheels and money. Toward the end of my hire at Mrs. Whitehead's—on that "Mission Sunday" I have earlier described—I managed to gather my inmost followers around me at a service preached by Richard Whitehead at his church. During the parley we held down by the creek afterward, while the white people were interring one of their number in the graveyard (some pox-stricken infant—among the favored last, it struck me at the time, to be spared the disagreeable events to come), I was able to impart to the group my final plans for the campaign.

I had long pondered the strategy of my assault, and had come up with the conclusion that to assemble my force in one place was not only disadvantageous but virtually impossible —the sudden gathering together of so many Negroes would surely be noticed and would arouse suspicion or alarm. No, my attack had to be one of accretion and rising momentum, a snowball-like accumulation of forces whereby the spearhead group (in this case, myself and my inmost four) must be joined by single individuals prepared and waiting at the various homesteads as we swept through the county on our serpentine way toward Jerusalem. Each of the Negroes, then, of the twoscore or more who had committed themselves to me would be "spotted" in this or that house, along the route—almost always at the place he belonged to anyway— and there would stand ready to take up arms against his master as soon as we appeared—my fine black hellion then participating in the slaughter and continuing on with us to the next objective where still another black killer, or several, would be waiting. Such a scheme required timing and coordination, and to this end I delegated to each of my inmost four the task of riding herd on and closely instructing a "troop" of five or six of the others; he must keep in touch with his little troop as much as possible during the intervening weeks while he drubbed into them incessantly the idea of secrecy and made certain that each man—on that fateful August Monday now hovering near—would be at his station. If all went well, I calculated that from our first midnight strike at Travis's until our capture of the armory in Jerusalem the time elapsed would be thirty-six hours.

And I felt that all *would* be well.

That Sunday as I dismissed my followers with a prayer, my spirit was filled with a strange exaltation and with a sense of the imminence of glorious victory. I knew that my cause was just and, being just, would in its strength overcome all obstacles, all hardships, all inclement turns of fortune. I knew too that because of the noble purpose of my mission even the most cowed and humbled of Negroes would divine its justice, and I foresaw legions of black men everywhere rising up to join me. Black men all over the South, all over America! A majestic black army of the Lord!

> *Blessed be the Lord my strength, which teacheth my*
> *hands to war, and my fingers to fight:*
> *My goodness, and my fortress; my high tower and my*
> *deliverer; my shield . . .*

Yet no sooner than I was about to leave Mrs. Whitehead's and go back to Travis, when a frightening and, indeed, almost unprecedented incident took place—something which, because of the sudden enmity and distrust for Negroes it was bound to stir up among many of the white people, caused me to fear that my entire mission would be thrust into jeopardy, or ruin.

What occurred had to do with Will—Sam's fellow slave at Nathaniel Francis's. While submitting to one of his owner's periodical beatings, Will had finally snapped, perpetrating what for a Negro was the gravest of deeds: he had struck

Francis back. Not only that, he had struck Francis savagely enough (with a lightwood fagot wrenched from a barnyard stack) as to have broken Francis's left arm and shoulder. Then Will lit out for the woods, and had yet to be found. In certain ways the episode—when I first heard of it—caused me a mixture of feelings. On the one hand, I felt a distinct relief that Will was gone. I feared his mania, his unfocused hatred and madness, and I passionately wanted him to have nothing to do with my campaign of destruction, sensing that I could in no way control or govern him. I knew that he was obsessed with the idea of raping white women—something I could not abide. His assault upon Francis and his flight to the woods—provided he was gone for good—was thus for me the resolution of a minor but nagging problem. Yet I was appalled. For at the same time, such a violent act, even though well provoked and not entirely unheard of, was rare and shocking enough so as to make it likely that an atmosphere of suspicion would close in upon Negroes in general. The gossip would get started: *God durned niggers gittin' so they hit back.* I was deeply afraid that with such feelings prevalent, our Negroes would become unsettled by the overall mistrust and lose heart for the venture or—even worse—would under this new pressure somehow give away our great secret.

As at other houses in the vicinity, tumult reigned at Mrs. Whitehead's when the news came of Will's atrocity. It was noon on a Friday, and I was hitching up the buggy in order to take Miss Margaret to her friend's house down-county— she was to spend the weekend—when word was brought by two melodramatic-looking white men on horseback, sagging with sidearms and rifles. A posse was being organized to track the black bugger down, one man shouted to Richard from the saddle. "Git a gun, preacher," he cried, "and come along!" The sweating, stamping horses filled the barnyard with a cloud of dust; one of the men listed sideways, grinning, already inebriate with brandy and the thrill of the chase. "That air nigger," called the other, "we goin' have to shoot him down!"

I watched Richard disappear inside the house. There was something incongruous about the idea of this delicate and enervated man of God in his lethal pursuit through the swamps of a demented unarmed black runaway, but soon he emerged from the house with a musket and a pistol, prim lips vengefully set as he adjusted a beaverskin hunting cap at a rather rakish tilt over his brow. One of the other Negroes had saddled the fat gelding. Trailing her son with a look of pale concern, Miss Caty clutched her hands together while entreaty charged her voice: "You *must* take care, Boysie! A darky like that is like a mad dog!" And now Margaret's three married sisters, just arrived for a summer's visit, spilled out from the house with gingham skirts ballooning on the wind; they also began to implore their brother to watch out for his safety, and as he climbed aboard his bovine steed they uttered little chirps and squeals of alarm. "Do be careful, Boysie dear!" Miss Caty cried, clinging to his hand. Then the three little grandchildren scampered from the kitchen to wave their uncle on his way, while at the same instant, like some grotesque harbinger of all in black folk gone emasculate forever, the egregious house nigger Hubbard wiggled out on sloping ladylike hips to add his blessing to the chorus of Godspeeds. "You take good care ob yo'sef, massah," he gabbled unctuously, his hoarse caution a fawning echo of Miss Caty's own. "Dat Will he some mean nigger, I knows! Will jes' a *mad dog*, massah, an' dat's de troof!" He resembled nothing so much as some asinine fat mammy, and I could have seen him dead on the spot. Only Margaret remained detached from the scene. I glimpsed her at the doorway of the house, where she lingered among the shadows, a look of solemn annoyance engraved upon her pretty face. Then as Richard, murmuring, "Don't worry, Muvva," pressed a brave kiss upon Miss Caty's outstretched knuckles and wheeled about to join the other men, Margaret's annoyance deepened; she made a grimace of disgust and, turning, vanished from sight.

And, "Such stupid folderol!" she was saying soon after, as we rode southward toward the Vaughans'. "I mean all those guns and everything, and chasing down this poor darky Will who's probably just half crazy with fear and everything, out there in the swamps. And they'll probably shoot him! Oh, it's just terrible!" She paused for an instant; out of the corner of my eye I saw her wipe a fleck of dust from her nose. Descending, my eyes caught a glimpse of the fabric of her skirt, drawn tight across her lap, jiggling to the rhythm of the buggy, while even closer to me was her hand, white as milk glass, blue-veined, twirling the bone handle of her parasol. "I mean of course he shouldn't have done what he did," she went on, "striking Mr. Francis back like that. But honestly, Nat! Every single solitary soul in this county knows about Mr. Francis, and how he treats his darkies. They all think it's just terrible what he does to them. I know Mama does. And look at her! I should hardly blame Will for striking him back like that. Wouldn't you have struck Nathaniel Francis back if he'd abused you so much like that? Just wouldn't you, Nat?"

Now I sensed her eyes full upon me even as I escaped looking back at her, and connived in my mind at a way to answer that question which she alone among all the white people I had ever talked to would have been artless enough to ask. Such a question no Negro should be forced into a position to answer, and because it was asked in such a spirit of sympathy and innocence I resented her for it, now, somehow all the more. I was unable to refrain from stealing a glance again at the twin soft ridgelike promontories where her skirt drew tight across her thighs, the wrinkled valley of taffeta between, the stiff round bone twirling ceaselessly in the porcelain hand. I sensed her eyes again, the saucy tilt of a dimpled chin, her face turned, poised, waiting. I struggled for an answer.

"I mean just *wouldn't* you, Nat?" she repeated, the girlish voice whispery and near. "I mean, I'm only a female, I know, but if I were a *man* and a darky and I was abused like that by that horrible old Nathaniel Francis, I'd just hit him right back. Wouldn't you?" "Well, missy," I replied, choosing a tone of humility, "I don't rightly know as how I would. That way you might just end up dead." I paused, then added: "But I guess Will he just had about more than he could stand. And by and by when you have more than you can stand you sort of go crazy and hit back before you even know it. And I reckon that's just what Will done with Mr. Francis. But I'd be mighty careful about retaliating against a white mastah, I would indeed, missy."

She said nothing then, and when she spoke finally her voice was grave, pensive, filled with a kind of ample, questing, hurtful sorrow I had never before heard, or overheard, in a white person so young. "Oh *me*, I don't know!" she sighed, and the sound rose from deep within her. "I just don't know, Nat! I just don't know why darkies stay the way they do—I mean all ignorant and everything, and getting beaten like that Will, and so many of them having people that own them that don't feed them properly or even clothe them so that they're warm enough. I mean so many living like animals. Oh, I *wish* there was some way that darkies could live decently and work for themselves and have—oh, real self-regard. Oh, guess what, Nat, let me tell you something!" Her tone changed abruptly, the quality of lament still there but now edged with indignation.

"I got in the most terrible fight with this girl at the Seminary named Charlotte Tyler Saunders. She was one of my very best friends and still is, but we got into this terrible fight in May just before school was over. Well, the fight was over darkies. Because you see this girl Charlotte Tyler Saunders's father owns, oh, just *quintillions* of darkies on this plantation up in Fluvanna County and he's in the legislature in Richmond and whenever the thing comes up there about emancipating the slaves he always gives these big long boring speeches about it that Charlotte Tyler finds in the *Gazette* and reads to the other girls. I mean he's all against emancipation and he says all these things about how darkies are irresponsible and have no morals and are *bestial* and lazy and how you can't teach them and all that balderdash. Well, this time I'm talking about she'd just finished reading this speech that her father gave and, I don't know, Nat, I just sort of finally exploded. And I said, 'Well listen, Charlotte Tyler Saunders, I don't intend any disrespect to your father but that is simply folderol because it just isn't so!' And *oh*, she got mad at me, and said, 'It *is* so, any person with a grain of sense and eyes to see *knows* it's so!' And I was almost crying then, I was so mad, and I reckon I was almost screaming. And I said, 'Well, listen to me, *Miss* Charlotte Tyler Saunders, I happen to know that where I live in Southampton my mother hires a darky slave who is almost as intelligent and refined and clean and religious and profoundly understanding of the Bible as Dr. Simpson'—Dr. Simpson is principal of the Seminary, Nat—'and not only that, my *erstwhile* friend'—I was positively almost screaming—'if you want my humble opinion, and I'm *certain* that I'm the only girl in school who thinks so, but *my* humble opinion is that the darkies in Virginia should be *free!*' "

After a pause, Margaret said: "Oh, she made me so angry! And the thing is, Nat, she is *au fond* a very kind, sweet, considerate girl. *Au fond* means 'deep down' in French. It's just that some people—" She broke off with a sigh, saying: "Oh, I don't know. Sometimes life is so complicated, isn't it? Anyway, Nat," she concluded slowly, "that darky I was talking about was you. I mean, it really *was*."

I made no reply. Her closeness, her presence stifled me, even now as the summer air flowed past my face, wafting toward me her odor—a disturbing smell of young-girl-sweat

mingled with the faint sting of lavender. I tried to inch myself away from her but was unable to, found instead that I
could not avoid touching her, nor she me, elbow lightly kissing elbow. With a longing that made me wet beneath the
arms I ached for the ride to be finished, even as I realized
that we had half an hour more to go. I watched the horse's
black tail ripple and flourish, and the brown rump glistening.
Along the rutted road the buggy wheels counted off the
hillocks and humps in a steady clatter of iron on stone. We
were riding through a deserted part of the county where
fields of broom and briar and sedge and yellow mustard became interspersed with patches of dappled woodland. It was
country I knew well. There were no dwellings here, no
people—only a decrepit fence or, far off in an empty
meadow, the shattered hulk of an ancient barn. The air was
clear, the sun dazzling bright; grand pinnacles and peaks of
summer clouds sent across the fields racing shadows shaped
like gigantic hands. Again I smelled the warm girl-sweat,
sensed her presence, soap, skin, hair, lavender. Suddenly,
despite myself, the godless thought came: I could stop now
and here, right here by the road in this meadow, do with her
anything I wished. There's not a soul for miles. I could throw
her down and spread her young white legs and stick myself in
her until belly met belly and shoot inside her in warm milky
spurts of desecration. And let her scream until the empty
pinewoods echoed to her cries and no one would be the
wiser, not even the buzzards or the crows . . . The sweat
poured down my sides beneath my shirt. Then I uttered a
silent prayer, and furiously thrust the thought out of my
mind as one thrusts away the very body and spirit of Satan.
How did I dare think such disastrous thoughts with my great
mission so near? Even so, I still could not help but feel my
member swollen and pulsating underneath my trousers. My
heart was pounding. I prodded the horse on with a snap of
the reins.

And again the whispery voice in my ear: "I mean Charlotte Tyler really tries to be a very religious person—that's the thing. That's why I can't understand really religious people holding such views. I mean, look at Mama! And *Richard,* for pity's sake! And every *one* of my sisters! And that Charlotte Tyler Saunders—*au fond* she professes to believe in love when, honestly, I don't believe she has the faintest *inkling* of what the Bible teaches about love. I mean all those beautiful teachings of John about love and how you shouldn't fear it. Fear and torment. Oh, you know, Nat, that verse that speaks about *torment.* How does it go?"

"Well, missy," I replied after a moment, "you must mean the verse in the first epistle that says: *There is no fear in love; but perfect love casteth out fear: Because fear hath torment. He that feareth is not made perfect in love.* That's how it goes."

"Oh yes!" she exclaimed. "And he said: *Beloved, let us love one another: for love is of God; and every one that loveth is born of God, and knoweth God.* Oh, it is the simplest thing in the world, is it not, Nat—the perfect Christian love of God, and of one another, yet how many people shun that blessed grace and live in fear and torment? *God is love,* John said, *and he that dwelleth in love dwelleth in God, and God in him* . . . Could anything be more simple or easy or plain?"

On she prattled in her whispery voice, love-obsessed, Christ-crazed, babbling away in an echo of all the self-serving platitudes and stale insipid unfelt blather uttered by every pious capon and priestly spinster she had listened to since she was able to sit upright, misty-eyed and rapt and with her little pantalettes damp with devotion, in a pew of her brother's church. She filled me with boredom and lust— and now, to still at least the latter emotion, once and for all, I let her constant rush of words float uncaptured through my mind, and with my eyes on the horse's bright undulating rump, concentrated on a minor but thorny problem that was facing me at the very outset of my campaign (This concerned Travis—I should say, rather, Miss Sarah. I had resolved on a mercilessly intransigent course of action when it came to killing the white people, determined that not a single soul—no matter how friendly our relations had been—would be spared the ax or the gun. To contemplate otherwise might be fatal, for if I allowed my heart to soften in the case of one person, it would be all too easy for such clemency to overtake me with another, and another, and still another. I had granted only one exception to this rule—Jeremiah Cobb, that stern and tormented man whose encounter with me will be remembered. Now, however, despite my efforts to thwart a fondness for her in my heart, I could not help but feel that Miss Sarah—who had never regarded me with anything but kindness and who during my last illness nursed me with a motherly, sisterly, clucking solicitude—should escape the blade of my wrath. I had no qualms about the others of the house, including Travis, who although decent enough stirred in me few fraternal reverberations; the others, especially young Putnam, I heartily wished to see removed from their existence. About Miss Sarah's fate, however, I suffered already painful guilt and misgivings, and I felt that if in some devious fashion or other I could contrive to make sure—perhaps through subtle ministerial urging—that she, a good Baptist, was shouting hallelujahs at that Carolina camp meeting on the night of my attack, out of harm's way with her infant child—Yet was that any answer? Because then she would only return to a scene of grievous devastation—) I was pondering this difficult matter, greatly troubled and suddenly despondent, when Margaret Whitehead gave a little gasp, clutched my sleeve, and said: "Oh, Nat, stop! Please stop!"

A passing wagon or cart, hours before, had run over and crushed a turtle. Margaret had spied it from her side of the buggy and she insisted—with another tug at my sleeve—that we climb down and help it, for she had seen that it was still alive. "Oh, the poor *thing*," she whispered as we viewed the little beast. The black and brown mosaic of the turtle's shell had been split down the center from side to side, a pale bloody paste oozed out of the fissure and from a spiderweb of minute fracture marks that grooved the surface of the shell. Yet, indeed, the turtle still lived; it wiggled feebly and hopelessly with its outstretched legs and craned its long leathery neck and remained immobile, dying, jaws agape and hooded eyes mossed over in some dim reptilian anguish. I touched it lightly with my toe.

"Oh, the poor thing," Margaret said again.

"Ain't nothing but a turtle, missy," I said.

"Oh, but it must suffer so."

"I'll put it away," I replied.

She was silent for a moment, then said softly: "Oh yes, do."

I found a hickory branch at the side of the road and smote the head of the turtle hard, a single time; its legs and tail quivered briefly, then relaxed with a soft uncurling motion, the tail drooped, and it was dead. When I threw the stick into the field and turned back to Margaret, I saw that her lips were trembling.

" 'Twasn't nothin' but an old turtle, missy," I said. "Turtle don't feel anything. He's pretty dumb. They's an old nigger sayin' about animals that goes, 'They that doesn't holler doesn't hurt.' "

"Oh, I know it's silly," she said, composing herself. "It's just—oh, suffering things." Suddenly she put her fingers to her forehead. "I'm kind of dizzy. And it's hot. Oh, I wish I could have a sip of water. I'm so thirsty."

I kicked the turtle into the ditch.

"Well, they's a brook that runs along back in those trees there," I said. "Same brook that goes by yo' mama's place. It's fit to drink here, I know, missy. I'd fetch you some water but I don't have a thing to carry it in."

"Oh come, we'll walk," she replied.

Her spirits brightened again as I led the way across a scrubby parched field toward the stream. "I'm really very sorry that I spoke of Charlotte Tyler Saunders in that fashion," she said cheerfully behind me. "She's really just the sweetest girl. And so talented. *Oh*, did I ever tell you about this masque that we wrote together, Nat?"

"No, missy," I replied, "I don't believe so."

"Well, a masque is a sort of a play in verse—you spell it with a *q-u-e* on the end—and it's quite short and it has to do with elevated themes—oh, I mean things of the spirit and philosophy and poetical matters and such like. Anyway, we did this masque together and it was performed at the Seminary last spring. It was *quite* some success, I can tell you that. I mean after it was performed, do you know, Dr. Simpson told Charlotte Tyler and me that it was the equal of dramas he had seen performed up North on the stages of Philadelphia and New York. And Mrs. Simpson—that's his wife—told us that rarely if ever had she seen a performance that was so affecting and imbued with such lofty ideals. Those were her words. Anyway, this masque that we wrote is called *The Melancholy Shepherdess*. It's laid in first-century Rome. In one way it's very pagan but at the same time it exemplifies the highest aspirations of Christian belief. Anyway, there are these five characters. At the Seminary they were all played by girls, naturally. The heroine is a young shepherdess who lives on the outskirts of Rome named Celia. She is a very devout Christian. The hero is the young manor lord whose name is Philemon. He's very handsome and everything, you see, and *au fond* he's very kindly and good but his religion is still quite pagan. Actually, the truth is that his religion is animistic . . ."

As the dry field gave way to a patch of woods I could hear water splashing in the brook. The sunlight dimmed out as we entered the grove of trees; a ferny coolness enveloped me, there were pine needles underfoot and I smelled the sharp bittersweet odor of rosin. The closeness, the stillness, the seclusion here created once more a voluptuous stirring in my blood. I turned now to guide her by my glance, and for an instant her eyes met mine unflinchingly, not so much coquettish as insistent—inviting, daring, almost *expecting* my gaze to repose in her own eyes while she prattled blissfully on. Although as brief and fleeting as the space of a blink, it was the longest encounter I could remember ever having with a white person's eyes. Unaccountably, my heart swelled in my throat in a quick ball of fear. I turned away, swept with lust again, hating her guts, now driven close to distraction by that chattering monologue pitched at a girlish whisper which I no longer bothered to listen to or to understand. Years and decades of pine needles made a buoyant sweet-smelling carpet sibilant beneath our feet. I paused to dislodge a pine branch that lay across our path, then rose, and she gave a little murmur of surprise as the fullness of her breast bumped the flesh of my arm in soft collision. But she paid it no notice, continued talking while we walked down toward the stream. I was oblivious of her words. The place where her breast had met my arm was like an incandescence, tingling; again I was smothered by remorseless desire. Insanely, I found myself measuring the risk. *Take her,* a voice said. *Take her here on this bank by this quiet brook. Spend upon her all afternoon a backed-up lifetime of passion. Without mercy take your pleasure upon her innocent round young body until she is half mad with fright and pain. Forget your great mission. Abandon all for these hours of terror and bliss* . . . I felt my virile part stiffen again beneath my trousers, and I was suddenly and absurdly torn between fear that she might see my state and an impulse to expose it to her—oh God, forget it, forget it! Never could I remember having been so unhinged by desire and hatred. Trying to settle my emotions I said in an uncertain voice, too loud: "There's the water!"

"Oh, I'm so *thirsty!*" she exclaimed. Fallen trees made a

little rapids here, and the water foamed over the logs cool and green. I watched as she knelt by the brook and brought pale cupfuls of water up to her face in the curved hollow of her hands. *Now,* the voice said, *take her now.*

"Oh, that's better!" she said, drawing back. "Don't you want some, Nat?" And without waiting for an answer, went on: "Anyway, Nat, after this wicked Fidessa kills herself in remorse, then Philemon takes his sword and kills Pactolus, the evil old soothsayer. I played Philemon in our performance and that part was such fun, I mean with wooden swords and all. Then Philemon is converted to Christianity by Celia and in the very last scene you see them as they plight their troth. And then there are these last lines, I mean what is known on the stage as curtain speeches. That's where Philemon holds his sword up in front of Celia like a cross and says: *We'll love one another by the light of heaven above . . .*"

Margaret rose from her knees and turned, standing at the edge of the brook with her arms outstretched to the air, transfigured as if before a crowd of onlookers, her eyes half closed. "Then Celia says: *Oh, I would fain swoon into an eternity of love!*

"Curtain! That's all!" she said brightly, proudly, looking toward me. "Isn't that a wonderful masque? I mean it has a very poetical, religious quality, even if I do say so myself."

I made no reply, but now as she moved from the side of the stream she tripped, gave a little cry, and for the briefest instant fell against me, clasping my arms with her still-wet hands. I grabbed her about the shoulders—only as if to prevent her falling—and as quickly let her go, but not so quickly that in the intervening space I did not smell her skin and her closeness and feel the electric passage across my cheek of strands of chestnut-colored hair. During that moment I heard her breathing and our eyes met in a wayward glint of light that seemed to last much longer than any mere glance exchanged between two strangers journeying of a summer afternoon to some drowsy dwelling far off in the country.

Could it be, too, that I felt her relax, go the faintest bit limp, as she slumped against me? This I would never know, for swiftly we were apart; a cloud passed over the day, bringing shadows and a breeze which teased the loosened, wanton edges of her hair. The flicker of an instant then, no more, but she was frozen in an attitude of stiff, still death. As the wind rose there was a clatter in the trees like the noise of cataclysmic strife, and I was suddenly—without reason—inconsolable with an emptiness such as I have never known.

Then she trembled as if with a chill, saying gently, "We'd better hurry back, Nat." And I, walking beside her now, replied, "Yes, missy," and this was the last time—but for one—that I ever looked into her face.

We were ready. I knew that the exodus of many of the Baptists of the county to their camp meeting down in Carolina would commence on Thursday the eighteenth of August, and they would not return until the following Wednesday. And so for close on to a week Southampton would be deprived of a large portion of its white population, and the armed enemy would be considerably fewer both in Jerusalem and the outlying countryside. I hit upon Sunday night as the time to begin my assault, largely on the advice of Nelson, who pointed out with his usual shrewdness that Sunday nights were habitually the nights when Negroes went hunting for coon or possum, at least during the leisurely month of August; those evenings always resounded until dawn with a great commotion in the woods—hoots and shouts and the yapping of dogs—and so our own disturbance would be less likely to attract notice. Furthermore, it would be simply easier to assemble on Sunday, normally the Negroes' free day. Seizing an early advantage by slaying all at Travis's, equipping ourselves with his several guns and two horses, we should then be able to proceed along the lower loop of the great "S" I had laid out on the map and (after invading the properties in between and slaughtering all therein) arrive sometime the next day at the middle of the "S" and thus at what I had long since termed my "early objective"—Mrs. Whitehead's home with its rich store of horses, guns, and ammunition. I would have by then a goodly body of troops. Including the Negroes I had "spotted" at the intervening houses (plus two of Miss Caty's boys, Tom and Andrew; them I had easily recruited during my final stay), I calculated that upon leaving Mrs. Whitehead's our force should number more than a score, apart from another four or five whom out of instinct I had not trusted enough to take into my earliest confidence but who I expected would join us when we appeared. Provided that we took the most extreme care to prevent anyone from escaping and raising an alarm, we should be able to sweep the rest of the country and arrive, triumphant, in Jerusalem by noon of the second day, our force swollen into the many hundreds.

Late that Sunday morning my four inmost followers gathered themselves for a final barbecue in the dense woodland ravine beyond my sanctuary. At the last moment, the night before, I had sent Hark up the road to the Reese farm with instructions for him to tell one of the Reese Negroes, Jack, to join the barbecue and so become a member of our initial striking force. I had felt the need for a strong arm to augment our first blow, and Jack fitted the requisite details—weighing well over two hundred pounds and by luck boiling at a high pitch of resentment and wrath: only one week before, Jack's woman, a butter-skinned, almond-eyed beauty, had been sold to a Tennessee trader scrounging quite openly he allowed to planter Reese (and within Jack's hearing), "for likely-looking pussy for gov'mental gentlemen in Nashville." Jack would go with me to the far ends of the earth; certainly he would make quick work of Reese.

All morning and most of the afternoon I withdrew from

my followers, remaining near my sanctuary, where I read from my Bible and prayed for the Lord's favor in battle. The weather had become sultry and close, and as I prayed a single locust shrilled somewhere amid the trees, playing like an incessant tormented fiddle-string on my eardrums. After my long prayers I set fire to my tabernacle and stood aside from the clearing as the pine logs which had for so many years sheltered me went up in blue smoke and a roaring and crackling of flames. Then when the ashes had cooled I knelt amid the ruin and made a final prayer, beseeching God for his protection in the coming struggle: *The Lord is my light and my salvation; whom shall I fear? The Lord is the strength of my life; of whom shall I be afraid?*

It was just after I had risen from my knees that I heard a rustling in the underbrush behind me and turned to see the demented, murderous, hate-ravaged, mashed-in face of Will. He said nothing, merely looked at me with his bulging eyes and scratched at his naked black scarred belly below which a pair of gray jeans hung in tatters. I was seized by reasonless fear.

"What you doin' here, boy?" I blurted.

"I seed de smoke. Den I done seed dem niggers down dere in de gully," Will replied coolly. "Dey done gib me some barbecue. I heered dem talkin' 'bout startin' a ruction an' killin' de white folks. When I ax Sam an' Nelson if'n I could jine up dey tol' me to ax you."

"Where you been all these yere weeks?" I asked. "Nat Francis see you an' he'll shoot you dead."

"Don' *shit me* 'bout no Nat Francis," Will retorted. "I shoot *him* now!"

"Where you been?" I repeated.

"Aroun'," he replied. "All aroun'." He shrugged. His eyes caught the light in disks of malign fire, and I felt anew the old dread his presence always caused me, as if I had been suddenly trapped like a fly in the hatred he bore toward all

mankind, all creation. His woolly head was filled with cockle-
burs. A scar glistened on his black cheek, shiny as an eel cast
up on a mud bank. I felt that if I reached out I could almost
touch with my fingertips the madness stirring within him,
feel a shaggy brute heaving beneath a carapace of scarred
black skin. I turned away.

"You git on out of here," I said. "We don' need no more
men."

Abruptly, in a single bound from the underbrush, he was
at my side. He brandished a knobbed fist beneath my chin.
"Don' *shit* me, preacher man!" he said. His voice was the hiss
of a cornered cat. "You try an' shit me, preacher man, an' you
in *bad* trouble. I isn't run in de woods all dis yere time fo'
nothin'. I'se tired of huckaberries. I gwine git me some
meat now—*white* meat. I gwine git me some dat white
cunt too." For weeks he had hidden in the woods, grubbing
for berries and nuts and earthworms—even carrion—stealing
an occasional chicken in between times of pursuit by white
men and dogs; he had lived like an animal and now, streaked
with mud, stinking, fangs bared beneath a nose stepped upon
and bent like a flattened spoon, it seemed to me that he *was*
an animal—a wicked little weasel or maddened fox—and the
blood ran chill in my veins. I felt that he might at any moment leap for my throat. "You shit me, preacher man," he
said hoarsely, "an' I fix yo' preacher ass! I knock you to yo
fuckin' black knees! I isn't gwine hang out in de swamp no
mo' eatin' huckaberries. I gwine git me some *meat*. I gwine
git me some *blood*. So, preacher man, you better figger dat
Will done jined de ruction! You maybe is some fancy talker
but you isn't gwine talk Will out'n dat!"

(*After this I saw in the night visions, and behold a beast
dreadful and terrible, and strong exceedingly; it devoured
and brake in pieces . . .*)

Even as he spoke I knew that I was on the verge of
capitulating to him, backing down. I was, to be sure, fearful

of him, afraid that I could not control him or bend him to my will; and it was this instinctive mistrust that had caused me months before to eliminate him from my plans. At the same time, it was clear now that if I could channel his brutal fury and somehow keep him in check he would make a potent addition to our striking force. All the privation in the woods had not weakened him but rather had lent to his sinewy body furious zeal and strength; the muscles along his purplish black arms quivered and jumped with murderous power. I saw the vicious scars implanted upon his flanks by Francis's lash and suddenly, though without spirit for the move, I relented.

(*Then I would know the truth of this beast, which was diverse from all the others* . . .)

"Awright," I said, "you can jine up with us. But let me tell you one thing good, nigger. *I* is the boss. *I* runs this show. When I says jump there, you jump right *there*, not in no still or cider press and *not* in no haystack, neither. You ain't goin' to spread no white woman's legs, not on this trip you ain't. We got a long way to go and a pile of things to do, and if the niggers start a-humpin' every white piece in sight we ain't goin' to get half a mile up the road. So brandy and women is *out*. Now come on."

In the ravine my followers, together with the new recruit Jack, had finished the last remnants of their barbecue. Pig bones littered the ground around the ashes of a fire, still smoldering. The five men were reclining amid the cool ferns that rimmed the ravine; they had been talking in soft voices —I heard them as I came down the path with Will—but at my approach they arose and stood silent. Ever since the spring, when I revealed my plans, I had insisted that they pay this deference in my presence, explaining to them patiently that I wished for no obeisance, only absolute obedience; it should not have surprised me, as it did, that they so readily complied—endless years of servility had done their abrasive work. Now as they stood waiting among the afternoon shadows I approached them with an upraised hand and said: "The first shall be last."

"An' de last shall be first," they replied, more or less together.

"Report from the First Troop!" I commanded. I used the form of order I had adopted after hearing drills of the mounted militia outside the Jerusalem armory. The First Troop was Henry's responsibility. Because of Henry's deafness I had to repeat the command again, whereupon he stepped forward and said: "First Troop dey all ready. Nathan an' Wilbur bofe is waitin' at de Blunts' place. Davy he waitin' at Mrs. Waters's. Joe he all ready too down at Peter Edwards's. Joe he done got him a bad case of de quinsy, but he put him a hot flannel roun' his th'oat an' he say he 'spect he gwine be all right time we gits dere."

"Report from the Second Troop!" I said.

The Second Troop, a body of six, was Nelson's. "All my niggers is ready an' rarin' to go," he said. "Austin say he could maybe sneak away from de Bryants' dis evenin' an' jine us at Travis's roun' 'bout nightfall. If'n he can, he gwine bring Bryant's horse."

"Good," I said, "more they is at first the better." Then: "Report from the Third Troop!" Just as I gave this command a tremendous belch broke loose from one of my company, followed by another belch, and I turned quickly to see that it had come from Jack. With a brandy bottle clutched against his black chest he was swaying in a delicate circular motion; his thick lips parted in a self-absorbed grin and he regarded me through eyes misted over with a dreamy film—the gaze oddly studious although utterly blank. In a flood of rage I knocked the brandy bottle from his hand.

"No mo' of *that*, nigger!" I said. "Applejack is *out*, you hear? I catch yo' black mouth at a bottle again and you goin' to get clobbered fo' good. Now *git* on back over there in the trees!"

As Jack sidled away sheepishly, weaving, I called Nelson aside into a small stand of slash pine—a dark place with spongy ground underfoot, swarming with gnats. "Listen!" I said angrily in a low voice. "What's gone wrong with you, Nelson, anyways? You supposed to be my right arm, an' now look what's done happened already! 'Twas *you* been sayin' all along we got to keep the niggers away from the stills and presses! 'Twas *you* been warnin' about drinkin', an' now here you let this yere big black clown get pissy-eyed drunk right in front of yo' nose! What'm I goin' to *do*? If I can't depend on you for a simple thing like that, then we done lost the war before it ever gits goin'!"

"I sorry," he said, licking his lips. His round middle-aged stolid face with its graying stubble and its look of depthless oppression suddenly sagged, became hurt and downcast. "I sorry, Nat," he repeated, "I guess I jes' done forgot 'bout all dat."

"Man, you can't *'low* yo'self to forget," I insisted, boring in hard, "you my chief lieutenant, you know that, you an' Henry. If y'all can't help me keep these niggers in line, then we might as well run up the white flag right now."

"I sorry," he said again, abjectly.

"Awright," I went on, "forget all that now. Just mind from now on to keep them niggers out'n them stills. Now listen here, one last time. Give me the plan for Travis's so we git it straight with no trouble. Remember, we uses the broadax an' the hatchet. Cold steel. No noise. No shootin' till I give the word. We start shootin' too soon an' they be on top of us before daybreak."

"You right about dat," he declared. "Anyways—" I listened as he outlined for my satisfaction, one last time, our plan of attack on Travis's house. "—Den you an' Henry goes

in to get Travis an' Miss Sarah, dat right?" he was saying.
"Sam goes to git Miss Maria Pope—"

"Only she ain't there," I put in.

"How come?" he said.

"She done gone up to Petersburg on a visit, this very day,"
I explained with some regret. It was true: the no-account
biddy had had supernatural luck.

"Mm-*huh*," Nelson sighed, "too bad 'bout dat. Sam sho
would of fixed dat ol' bitch's wagon."

"Anyway, she gone," I said. "Go ahead."

"Well den," he continued, "I 'spect it best dat Sam stay
with you, ain't dat right? An' me an' Hark an' Jack goes up to
de attic an' gits Putnam an' dat othah boy. Dis while you
takin' keer of Travis. Meanwhiles, Austin he in de barn sad-
dlin' up dem horses. What 'bout Will, Nat? Whar he figgers
in?"

"Nem'mine 'bout Will," I replied. "We'll use him as a
lookout or somethin'. Nem'mine 'bout Will."

"An' what 'bout dat little baby?" he said. "You done tole
me you was gwine tell us what to do 'bout dat business.
What?"

I had a sinking sensation deep inside. "Nem'mine 'bout
that either," I answered him, "I goin' to git all that straight-
ened out when the time comes. Maybe we jest let that baby
alone, I don't know." I was stung with a sudden, inexplicable
annoyance. "Awright," I told him, "go on now and git on back
with the men. I'll come down with y'all after dark."

After Nelson had gone back through the trees, leaving me
to chew on a piece of pork they had saved for me from their
feast, a mood of anxiety began to steal over me, announcing
itself with a faint numbness in my extremities, an urgent
heartbeat, pain all around the bottom of my stomach. I
started to sweat, and I laid the joint of pork aside, uneaten. I
had many times prayed to the Lord to spare me this fear, but
now it was plain that, unheeding, He was going to allow me

to suffer anyway this griping sickness, this clammy apprehension. The waning summer day was humid and still. I could hear nothing except for the gnats' feverish insensate humming around my ears and a muffled snatch of talk from the Negroes in the ravine. I wondered suddenly if the Lord had also permitted Saul and Gideon and David to endure this fear before their day of warfare: did they too know this demoralizing terror, this tremor in the bones, this whiff of imminent, hovering death? Did they too taste the mouth go dry at thought of the coming slaughter, sense a shiver of despair fly through their restless flesh as they conjured up images of bloodied heads and limbs, gouged-out eyes, the strangled faces of men they had known, enemy and friend, jaws agape in yawns of eternal slumber? Did Saul and Gideon and David, armed and waiting on the eve of the battle, feel their blood change to water in everlasting fright and then long to sheath their swords and turn their backs upon the strife? For an instant panic seized me. I arose as if to flee headlong through the pines, to find some refuge in the distant woods where I would be hid forever beyond the affairs of God and men. *Cease the war, cease the war,* my heart howled. *Run, run,* cried my soul. At that moment my fear was so great that I felt that I was even beyond reach or counsel of the Lord. Then from the ravine I heard Hark's laugh, and my terror subsided. I was trembling like a willow branch. I sat down on the ground and addressed myself to further prayer and contemplation as the shades of evening drew glimmering in . . .

An hour or so after nightfall—at around ten o'clock—I rejoined my men in the ravine. A full moon had risen to the east, something I had anticipated for months and was in keeping with my plans. Since I was confident that we would be on the offensive throughout all the first night (and with good fortune the second night too), the moon would favor us rather than the enemy. For added illumination I had torches made of lightwood stakes and rags soaked in a gallon cask of camphene—turpentine mixed with grain alcohol—that Hark had stolen from the wheel shop. These torches would be used indoors and with care on the march, whenever the moonlight failed us. Our initial weapons were few and simple: three broadaxes and two hatchets, all carefully honed on Travis's grindstone. As I made it clear to Nelson, for purposes of stealth and surprise I wished to avoid gunfire at least until the first daylight, when our assault would have gained a safe momentum. As for the rest of the weapons—guns and swords —the houses along the way would keep us supplied until we reached Mrs. Whitehead's and her gun room, a veritable arsenal. Our enemy had supplied us with all the instruments of his own destruction: now in the ravine Sam lit one torch with a lucifer match from a handful he had stolen from Nathaniel Francis. A ruddy light washed across the grave black faces of the men, flickered out at my command as I raised my hand and pronounced a final word of damnation upon the enemy: *"Let the angel of the Lord chase them, let them be as chaff before the wind."* Then in the moonlight their faces receded into shadow and I said: "All right. *Now.* We commence the battle."

In silence and in single file—Nelson leading, I close at his heels—we came out of the woods and into the cotton patch behind Travis's wheel shop. One of the men coughed in the darkness behind me and at that instant two of Travis's cur dogs set up a yapping and howling in the barnyard. I whispered for quiet and we stood stock-still. Then (having foreseen this too) I motioned for Hark to go ahead before us and hush up the dogs: he was on good terms with them and could put them at ease. We waited as Hark stalked across the moonlit field and into the barnyard, waited until the dogs gave a friendly whimper and fell silent. The moon in an opalescent hush came down like dust, like dim daylight, exfoliating from the shop and the barn and sheds elongated shadows—black sharp silhouettes of gable, cornice, roof-

beam, door. It was hot and still. There was no sound from the
woods save for the katydids' high-pitched *cheercheer-cheer-
cheer* and the peeping of crickets among the weeds. In the
flat blazing yellow of the moonlight Travis's house slum-
bered, dark within and still as the halls of death. Nelson suddenly laid a hand on my arm and whispered: *"Look dar."*
Then I saw Hark's huge outline detach itself from the shadow
of the barn, and still another, angular and tall: this would be
Austin, the last member to join my striking force. Twenty-five
or so, he had nothing against his present owner, Henry
Bryant, who had treated him amiably, but felt nothing for
him either and had sworn that he would gladly kill him. He
had, however, once gotten into a vicious fight with Sam over
a yellow girl in Jerusalem and I only hoped that their enmity
would not flare up now again.

I signaled for the other men to follow me and we proceeded in Indian file across the cotton patch, clambered quietly over a stile, and met Hark and Austin in the lee of the
wheel shop, out of sight of the house. We were now eight. As
I gave my keys to Nelson and whispered instructions to him
and Sam, I could hear Travis's hogs grunting sleepily in their
pen. Now while Sam and Nelson stole into the shop for a ladder, I told Austin to go to the stable and saddle up Travis's
horses, bidding him to work as silently as he could. He was a
tall, lanky field hand with a mean black skull-shaped face,
agile and quick despite his height, and very powerful. On the
way over through the woods from Bryant's his horse had
flushed a skunk and he stank to heaven. No sooner had he
gone off to the stable than Sam and Nelson returned with the
ladder. I joined them in walking across the yard to the side of
the house while the other four moved noiselessly ahead in
front of us to their station in the shrubbery around the front
porch. The skunk stench lingered, hot in the nostrils. The two
cur dogs ambled along with us beneath the ladder; their bony
flanks were outlined in sharp moonlit relief, and one dragged

a game leg. A faint breeze sprang up and the skunk odor was obliterated. The air was filled with the rank fragrance of mimosa. I caught my breath for an instant, thinking of the time so long ago when I had played with a boy named Wash in a mimosa-sweet glade at Turner's Mill. The brief reverie, burst like splintered glass. I heard the ladder make a faint *tap-tapping* as they set it against the side of the house and quickly I tested it for balance, gripping it tight by a chest-high rung, then without a word began my climb up the side of the house, past the newly whitewashed clapboard timbers that hurt my eyes in a calcimine lunar glare. Even as I reached the open upper hallway window with its fluttering curtains I heard from the main bedroom a stertorous rasping sound, deep-throated, half-strangled, and recognized it as Travis's snore. (I remembered Miss Sarah's "Land sakes alive, Mister Joe does make a racket but you jus' do learn to live with it after a bit.") I heaved myself silently over the sill into the dark hallway, into the very bosom of the cavernous snoring noise that muffled the sound of my feet as they struck the creaking floor. I was all aslime with sweat beneath my shirt, my mouth had the dry bitter taste of a walnut shell. It's not I who's doing this, I thought abruptly, it is someone else. I tried to spit but my tongue scraped at the roof of my mouth as if against plaster or sand. I found the stairs.

Down on the first floor at the foot of the stairs I lit a candle with a lucifer match, meeting as I did the black wonder-struck face of the servant boy Moses, who had been aroused from his tiny cupboard beneath the stairway by the sound of my feet. His eyes rolled white with alarm. He was stark naked. "What you doin', Nat?" he whispered.

"Just never you mind," I whispered in return. "Go back to sleep."

"What time hit?" he whined.

"Hush up," I replied. "Go to bed."

I removed two rifles and a sword from their rack at my

elbow and then crossed to the front door, where I unhooked the inside latch and let the others enter, one by one, from the front porch. Will was last. I put a restraining hand against his chest. "You stay here at the door," I told him, "Be on the lookout if anybody comes. Or tries to get out this way." Then I turned to the others and said in a low voice: "Nelson and Hark and Jack up to the attic and at them two boys. Sam and Henry stay with me." The six of us mounted the stairs.

In the many weeks since that night I have wondered more than once what passed through Travis's sleep-drowned senses when with such violence and rude suddenness we flung ourselves into his presence and made clear those designs which even he, a forbearing and lenient master, must have considered a nightmare possibility but long since put away from his thoughts as one puts away all ideas of remote and improbable ruin. For surely in the watches of the night, like all white men, he must from time to time have flopped over with a sick groan, thinking of those docile laughing creatures down at the rim of the woods, wondering in a flash of mad and terrible illumination what might happen *if*—*if* like gentle pets turned into rampaging beasts they should take it into their hearts to destroy him, and along with him all his own and dearest and best. *If* by some legerdemain those comical simpleheads known for their childish devotion—so affecting along with their cunning faults and failings—but never known for their manhood or their will or their nerve, should overnight become transformed into something else, into implacable assassins, let us say, wild dogs, avenging executioners—what then would happen to this poor frail flesh? Surely at one time or another Travis, like other white men, had been skewered upon such disquieting fancies, and shuddered in his bed. Just as surely his pathetic faith in history had at last erased these frights and apprehensions from his head, allowing him more often sweet composure and pleasant dreams—for was it not true that such a cataclysm had never

happened? Was it not fact, known even to the humblest
yeoman farmer and white-trash squatter and vagabond, that
there was something stupidly inert about these people, something abject and sluggish and emasculate that would forever
prevent them from so dangerous, so bold and intrepid a
course, as it had kept them in meek submission for two centuries and more? Surely Travis put his trust in the fragile
testimony of history, reckoning with other white men that
since these people in the long-recorded annals of the land had
never risen up, they never *would* rise up, and with this faith—
rocklike, unswerving as a banker's faith in dollars—he was
able to sleep the sleep of the innocent, all anxieties laid to
rest. Thus it may have been disbelief alone that governed
his still-drowsing mind, and no recollection of past fears,
when he shot upright in his bed next to Miss Sarah, cast his
eyes at my broadax in a gaze of dull perplexity, and said:
"What you all think you're doin' in here?"

The sharp piney odor of camphene stung in my nose. The
air was blurred with greasy smoke. By the light of the torch
that Henry held aloft I could see that Miss Sarah too had
risen up in bed, but the look on her face was not one of
puzzlement, like her husband's, but of naked terror. Instantly
she began to moan, a castaway whimper low in the lungs,
barely audible. But I turned back to Travis now, and in doing
so I realized with wonder that this was the first moment in all
the years I had been near him that I had ever looked directly
into his eyes. I had heard his voice, known his presence like
that of close kin; my eyes had a thousand times glanced off
his mouth and cheek and chin but not once encountered his
own. It was my fault alone, my primal fear but—no matter.
Now I saw that beneath the perplexity, the film of sleep, his
eyes were brown and rather melancholy, acquainted with
hard toil, remote perhaps, somewhat inflexible but not at all
unkind, and I felt that I knew him at last—maybe even now
not well but far better than one knows another man by a

pair of muddy trousers viewed from the level of the ground, or bare arms and hands, or a disembodied voice. It was as if by encountering those eyes I had found the torn and long-missing fragment of a portrait of this far-off abstract being who possessed my body; his face was complete now and I had a final glimpse of who he truly might be. Whatever else he was, he was a man.

All right, man, I thought.

With this knowledge I raised the broadax above my head, and felt the weapon shiver there like a reed in a savage wind. "*Thus art thou slain!*" I cried, and the ax descended with a whisper and missed by half a foot, striking not Travis's skull but the headboard between him and his wife. And at that moment Miss Sarah's soft moan bloomed into a shriek.

In this way I inaugurated my great mission—*Ah Lord!*—I who was to strike the first blow. It seemed as if all strength had left me, my limbs were like jelly, and for the life of me I could not pry the blade of the broadax from the imprisoning timber. Murmuring a prayer, I struggled with the haft. Travis in the meantime, with a terrified bellow, had escaped from the bed and in the sudden dawning of fright, weaponless and with his exit blocked by three Negroes and the bed itself, had become overmastered by raw panic and was trying to find his way out through the wall. "Sarah! Sarah!" I heard him wail. But she could not help him. She shrieked like a demented angel. *My God,* I thought, as I worked at the ax handle; in a fog of senseless deliberation I commenced to catalog the miscellany of homely bedroom artifacts that by torchlight swarmed at the rim of my sight: gold pocket watch, blue hair ribbon, pitcher, faded slate-gray looking glass, comb, Bible, chamber pot, portrait of a grandmother, quill pen, glass of barley water half full. "Shit!" I heard Sam say behind me. "Shit! *Kill* dat fuckin' bastid!" With a squeal of sprained timber I yanked the blade from the oak, raised it up, swung again at Travis, still clawing at the wall, and—incredibly, impossibly—missed once more. The outside of the blade glanced lightly from his shoulders and the ax handle itself made a deft little pirouette in my hand, twinkled from my grasp, and slid harmlessly to the floor. Half deafened by Miss Sarah's screams, I reached to retrieve the ax; as I bent down I saw that Travis, regaining charge of his senses, had wheeled about and now stood with his back against the wall and clutched a pewter vase in hand, prepared to defend himself. His gaunt work-worn face was the hue of his white nightshirt —but at last how brave he was! Ready for anything, he had joined the battle. In his strong woodsman's hands the flimsy vase seemed as lethal as a bludgeon. His head moved from side to side in a wary, dangerous rhythm like that of a bobcat I had once seen cornered by a pack of dogs. *"Kill* him!" I heard Sam roar behind me. But *I* was not ready.

I had laid my fingers on the haft of the ax again—dismayed at my irresolution and clumsiness, trembling in every bone—when there now took place that unforeseen act which would linger in my mind during whatever remaining days I was granted the power of memory. Just as I saw it happen I knew that it would be part of my being wherever I went, or whatever I was or became through my allotted time, even in the serene pastures of ancient age. For now as if from the outer dark, from nowhere, and with a silence that was a species of mystery in itself, Will hurled his body into the narrow space between myself and Travis, and his small black shape seemed to grow immense, somehow amorous, enveloping Travis's nightshirted figure in a brief embrace, almost as if he had joined him in a lascivious dance. There were no words spoken as Will and Travis met thus in the torchlight glare; only Miss Sarah's scream, rising now to an even higher pitch of delirium, informed me of the true nature of this anxious coupling. So quickly that it took a moment for me to realize that the flash of light I glimpsed was from one of the hatchets, honed to an exquisite edge. I saw Will's arm go skyward,

all black resistless sinew, and come down, go up again, and
down, up and down once more, then he jumped backward
and away, parted company with this companion he had so
intimately clasped, and it was at that instant that Travis's
head, gushing blood from a matrix of pulpy crimson flesh,
rolled from his neck and fell to the floor with a single bounce,
then lay still. The headless body, nightshirted, slid down the
wall with a faint hissing sound and collapsed in a pile of
skinny shanks, elbows, knobby knees. Blood deluged the
room in a foaming sacrament.

"*Dar now, preacher man!*" I heard Will howling at me.
"If'n you cain't do it, *I* do it! *Das* de way us rock dem white
fuckahs! Shut yo' face, white cunt!" he cried to Miss Sarah,
then to me: "Does you git her, preacher man, or does I?"

I had no power of speech—though I tried to move my
lips—but it made no difference anyway. Will had just begun,
his lust was so voracious as to be past all fathoming.
Before I could make a sign he had absolved me from the
choice. The initiative had become his alone. "Git on aside,
preacher man!" he commanded; despite myself I did so, and
in a single leap he was across the bed and astride the screaming, squirming fat woman, friendly soul, who had not been
able to go to that camp meeting after all. Once again the act
was done with prodigious speed and intensity; again in its
absolute devotion and urgency it was as if by his embrace this
scarred, tortured little black man was consummating at last
ten thousand old swollen moments of frantic and unappeasa-
ble desire. Between Miss Sarah's thrashing, naked thighs he
lay in stiff elongate quest like a lover; his downward-seeking
head masked her face and mostly hid it—all but for the tangled tresses of her hair and the pupil of one eye, wildly quivering, which cast me a glint of lunatic blankness even as the
hatchet went up again, and down, and chopped off her
scream. Then unimaginable blood spewed forth and I heard
the inhabiting spirit leave her body; it flew past my ear like a

moth. I turned away as the hatchet made a final *chunk-chunk* and became still. I thrust aside Henry and Sam (can it really be that I was trying to escape?) and reached the open door. As I gained the threshold I saw the black boy Moses standing with a candle, mouth agape, rigid and transfigured as if in a sleepwalker's dream. Oddly like music, a horn blow, the voice of a Negro cried out upstairs—surely it was Hark—a jubilant sound; there was the rough scuffling of something being dragged, a creaking of attic timbers, and the blanched, hacked, bleeding corpses of Putnam and the Westbrook boy came clumpety-clumping down the steep steps together like huge loose-limbed dolls hurled by an angry child, drenching Moses's bare feet in vermilion. Streams of blood past all comprehension lay across the walls and timbers of the evening, blood like all the billows and deeps of the oceans of the world. *"Ah my God!"* I thought, half aloud. *"Hast Thou truly called me to this?"*

Suddenly Hark plunged with thundering footsteps down the attic stairs, and his eyes glittered in the torchlight, wearing an expression of serene joy. He vaulted the two bodies in a bound. A servant of servants was Hark no more; he had tasted blood. The lost and grieving father had become a killer of men.

"Hot damn!" I heard him say.

"Let's git out of here!" I called, controlling my voice. "Let's git movin' on!"

And even as I spoke I felt my wrist being impaled upon agonizing pain. At almost the same instant I looked down and began to force open the jaws of Moses, who, driven quite mad by all he had witnessed, had sunk his teeth into the nearest flesh at hand.

One afternoon in my cell in jail just before my trial I remember Mr. Thomas Gray saying to me in that half-distraught, half-choked tone his voice achieved when he was at the highest point of his own disbelief: "But the butchery, Reverend, the senseless *slaughter!* The blood of so many of the *innocent!* How are you able to justify all that? That's one of the things the people want to know most of all. That's what I'd like to know, by God! *I!*"

A bitter November wind had swept through the cell. My ankles were cold and numb from the chains. When I failed to answer him right away, he went on, slapping the folded paper notes to my confessions against his thick haunch. "I mean, *God Almighty,* Reverend, these items defy civilized belief, some of 'em! Lissen here. *Item.* Taken from your own sworn testimony. After you've left the Travis house, leaving behind four slain, you suddenly recollect the little infant—a less than two-year's-old babe sleepin' in his cradle. You tell me you *was* goin' to spare the child but suddenly you have a second thought about it. So you say out loud, 'Nits breed lice!'—there's a delicate sentiment, I'll vow, Reverend, for a man of the cloth—and you send Henry and Will back to the house an' they take that pore pitiful little babe and dash its brains out agin the wall. That's an item that truly defies civilized belief! Yet it's as true as true can be. Right from your own lips. An' you still persist in sayin' that you feel no guilt over such a ghastly item. You *still* can claim that you feel not the slightest pang of remorse."

After another long hesitation, during which I carefully considered my words, I said: "That's right, Mr. Gray. I fear I would have to plead not guilty to everything, because I don't feel guilty. And try as I might I simply can't feel—as you put it, sir—a pang of remorse."

"*Item.* Them two boys you all killed at Mr. William Williams's in the fodder field, afternoon of the first day. Them two little boys, both of 'em not yet ten years old. You mean to tell me you can feel no remorse over that?"

"No sir," I replied calmly, "no, I feel no remorse."

"Then goddammit—*item!* Them ten innocent schoolchil-

dren slaughtered at the Wallerses' place, later in the day. *Ten
little children!* You mean to tell me that now, after all these
here months, your heart ain't touched by the agony of an
event like that? That you don't feel guilt over butchering a
helpless and defenseless little group like that?"

"No sir," I said, "I don't feel anything. I'd like to add,
though, if I may, sir, that those people at the Wallerses' wasn't
entirely defenseless. They wasn't all just children. Those
white men there put up quite a fight against us. They done a
lot of shootin' back. That's where a couple of my men got
their first wounds." I paused, then added: "But even aside
from that I don't feel any guilt."

As I spoke I saw that Gray was glaring at me, and I
wondered just how much of the truth I was telling him might
find its way into those confessions of mine that he would
eventually publish. I assumed not much, but it no longer
mattered to me. My weariness was as bitter and as aching as
that November wind that swept through the cracks of the
cedar wall and froze my bones, chilled the chains that
shackled my feet. I pointed out that we had seen one young
girl of fourteen or so escape screaming into the woods at the
Harris plantation late during the first afternoon, and re-
minded him that he himself had told me that this plucky lass,
all breathless and hysterical, had come running to warn the
people at the Jacob Williams place, two miles to the north.
Not only did her flight result in Williams's eluding our retribution (notably that of Nelson, whose slave he was and who
longed to settle accounts) but caused Williams himself to
ride off early and alert people up-country in big estates like
the Blunts' and Major Ridley's. It was at those places that we
met our most fierce resistance. And not long after this there
appeared on the scene mounted troops from three counties,
cutting off our entry into Jerusalem and our capture of the
armory, when we were but a short mile or so from the bridge
and the county seat.

Gray said nothing for a while. Then at last he drew a deep breath and the air whistled from his throat in a sigh. "Well, Reverend, I'll have to hand it to you," he said in a gloomy voice, "for what you set out to do, if you wanted slaughter, you done a pretty complete and satisfactory job. Up to a point, that is. I reckon even you didn't know the actual statistics, hiding out until now like you done. But in the three days and nights that your campaign lasted you managed to hasten fifty-five white people into early graves, not counting a score or so more fearfully wounded or disabled—*hors de combat,* as the Frenchies say, for the rest of their natural lives. And only God knows how many poor souls will be scarred in their minds by grief and by terrible memories until the day they part this life. No," he went on, breaking off a black wad from a plug of chewing tobacco, "no, I'll have to hand it to you, in many respects you was pretty thorough. By sword and ax and gun you run a swath through this county that will be long remembered. You did, as you say, come damn near to taking your army into this town. And in addition, as I think I told you before, you scared the entire South into a condition that may be described as well-nigh *shitless.* No niggers ever *done* anything like this."

There was nothing to say.

"Well, you was a success, all right. Up to a point. Mind you"—he jabbed a brown-stained finger at me—"*up to a point.* Because, Reverend, basically speaking and in the profoundest sense of the word you was a flat-assed *failure*—a total fiasco from beginning to end insofar as any real accomplishment is concerned. Right? Because, like you told me yesterday, all the big things that you expected to happen out of this just didn't happen. Right? Only the little things happened, and them little things when they was all added up didn't amount to a warm bottle of piss. Right?"

I felt myself shivering as I gazed downward between my legs at the plank floor and at the links of cold cast iron sagging like a huge rusting timber chain in the chill dim light. Suddenly I felt the approach of my own death, and with a prickling at my scalp, considered that death with mingled dread and longing. My hands trembled, my bones ached, and I heard Gray's voice as if from a broad and wintry distance.

"*Item*," he persisted. "By the U. S. census of last year there were eight thousand niggers in this county, all chattel, not counting around fifteen hundred niggers that were free. Of this grand total of ten thousand plus or minus whatever, you fully expected a good percentage of the male population, at least, to rise up and join you. Anyway, that's what you have said, and that's what the nigger Hark and that other nigger, Nelson, before we hung him, *said* you said. Let's figure that, oh, maybe a little less than half of the nigger population of the county lives along the route you traversed toward Jerusalem. Lives within earshot of your clarion call, so to speak. Counting on the bucks alone, that's one thousand black people who might be expected to follow your banner and live and die for Niggerdom, and this is only if we figure that a pathetic fifty per cent of the eligible males joined you. Not including pickaninnies and old uncles. One thousand niggers you should have collected, according to your plans. One thousand! And how many actually did join you? Seventy-five at the most! *Seventy-five!* Reverend, I ask you, what kind of a miser'ble-assed percentage is that?"

I made no reply.

"*Item*," he said again. "The item of drunkenness and general unmilitary conduct among your so-called troops. This you can't deny in spite of the picture I'm sure you'd love to present to the world of a majestic military force in full, ordered, disciplined panoply—elegant soldier boys in bully ranks and files. But we've got too much testimony *au contraire*. What you had pure and simple was not an army but a draggledy mob of drunken black ruffians who couldn't keep out of them stills and cider presses and thus in true nigger fashion contributed further to your downfall. Why, Major Claiborne, who ran the Isle of Wight militia, told me that when he broke you up there at Parker's field fully a third of your troops was staggerin' aroun' drunker'n hoot owls, some of 'em so pissy-eyed grogged up that they didn't know the butt-end of a gun from the barrel. I ask you, Reverend, is that any way to run a proper revolution?"

"No," I said, "that was bad, I admit. That was one of the worst things that went wrong. I gave orders about that, but when my troops grew in size—when there was a lot of us instead of just a few—why, I somehow lost control over them. I just couldn't keep an eye on them all at once and I—" But then I fell silent. Why try to explain anything now? Gray was right. Despite a measure of triumph, despite the single short mile that finally separated us from our goal—a nearness to Jerusalem so tantalizing that I could still feel in my flesh the remembered thrill of almost-victory—despite everything we had nearly achieved, in the end we failed beyond all hope or salvage. As he said, I had not been able to govern the boisterous black riffraff, so many of them only half grown, that had rallied behind me; neither I nor Nelson nor Henry nor anyone had been able to prevent those callow hare-brained recruits from plundering the liquor cellars, just as we had been hard put to keep them from raiding attics for fancy clothes or ransacking smokehouses for hams or plunging away on horseback in the wrong direction or, more than once, with black fingers unacquainted with guns, almost shooting off their own feet or hands. *But, Mr. Gray, I found myself wanting to say, what else could you expect from mostly young men deaf, dumb, blind, crippled, shackled, and hamstrung from the moment of their first baby-squall on a bare clay floor? It was prodigious that we come as far as we did, that we nearly took Jerusalem* . . . But I said nothing, recalling only that moment in the forenoon of the second day when at some pillaged ruin of a manor house far up-county I watched a young Negro I had never seen before, outlandishly garbed in feathers and the uniform of an army colonel, so drunk that he could barely stand, laughing wildly, pissing into the hollow mouth of a dead, glassy-eyed white-haired old grandmother still clutching a child as they lay sprawled amid a bed of zinnias, and I said not a word to him, merely turned my horse about and thought: It was because of you, old woman, that we did not learn to fight nobly . . .

"Last but not least," Gray said, "*item*. And a durned important item it is, too, Reverend, also attested to by witnesses both black and white and by widespread evidence so unimpeachable as to make this here matter almost a foregone conclusion. And that is that you not only had a fantastic amount of niggers who did *not* join up with you but there was a whole countless number of other niggers who was your active *enemies*. What I mean in simple terms, Reverend, is that once the alarm went out, there was niggers *everywhere*—who were as determined to protect and save their masters as you were to murder them. They was simply livin' *too well!* All the time that you were carryin' around in that fanatical head of your'n the notion that the niggers were going to latch on to your great mission, as you put it, an' go off to some stinkin' swamp, the actual reality was that nine out of ten of your fellow burrheads just wasn't buyin' any such durn fool ideas. Reverend, I have no doubt that it was your own race that contributed more to your fiasco than anything else. It just ain't a race made for revolution, that's all. That's another reason that nigger slavery's goin' to last for a thousand years."

He rose from his seat across from me. "Well, I got to go, Reverend. I'll see you tomorrow. Meanwhile, I'll put down in my deposition to the court which precedes your confession that the defendant shows no remorse for his acts, and since he *feels* no guilt his plea will be that of 'not guilty.' Now, one last time, are you *sure* you feel no remorse at all? I mean, would you do it again if you had the chance? There's still time to change your mind. It ain't goin' to save your neck but it'll surer'n hell look better for you in court. Speak up, Reverend."

When I made no reply to him he left without further word. I heard the cell door slam shut and the bolt thud home in the slot with its slippery chunking sound. It was almost night again. I listened to the scrape and rustle of fallen leaves as the cold air swept them across the ground. I reached down to rub my numb and swollen ankles and I shivered in the wind, thinking: Remorse? Is it true that I really have no remorse or contrition or guilt for anything I've done? Is it maybe because I have no remorse that I can't pray and that I know myself to be so removed from the sight of God? As I sat there, recollecting August, I felt remorse impossible to know or touch or find. All I could feel was an entombed, frustrate rage—rage at the white people we had killed and those we had failed to kill, rage at the quick and the dead, rage above all at those Negroes who refused us or fled us or who had become the enemy—those spiritless and spineless wretches who had turned against us. Rage even at our own minuscule force, which was so much smaller than the expected multitude! For although it ravaged my heart to accept it, I knew that Gray was not wrong: the black men had caused my defeat just as surely as the white. And so it had been on that last day, that Wednesday afternoon, when after having finally laid waste to twoscore dwellings and our force of fifty had rallied in the woods to storm Major Ridley's place, I had caught sight for the first time of Negroes in great numbers with rifles and muskets at the barricaded veranda, firing back at us with as much passion and fury and even skill as their white owners and overseers who had gathered there to block our passage into Jerusalem. (The alarm had gone out at least by the morning of the day before, our schedule was disastrously upset, and we had met resistance everywhere for many hours. The Ridley place, which straddled the road into town, was

now an ominous fortress yet it had to be taken—and quickly:
it was our last chance—if we were to break through and dash
the last mile on horseback, seizing Jerusalem before it became an armed camp.) Far up on the veranda of the old
stately brick house now barricaded by wagons and crates and
hogsheads I could see twenty-five or thirty Negroes owned by
the white gentry near town—coachmen, cooks, some field
hands maybe but I could tell from what they wore mostly
gardeners and house nigger flunkies, even a clutch of ban-
dannaed yellow kitchen girls passing ammunition. I heard
the voice of Major Ridley above the steady fusillade of gunfire
—"That's the spirit, boys!" he cried to the defenders, black
and white alike. "That's the spirit! Fire away, lads! Lay on the
lead! We'll turn the rascals back!"—and the volleys swelled
tempestuously down upon us with a noise like the continual
crackle of lightning, ripping twigs and leaves from the green
summer trees.

Then I recall Hark saying to me as we crouched behind the
great stump of a felled oak, shouting above our own rifle fire:
Look at dem black fuckahs shootin' at us! And I thought,
lying to myself: Yes, they're black but they've been forced,
dragooned by white men who have threatened them with
their very lives. Negroes would not fire back like that of their
own free will, at least not in those numbers. And all this I
kept thinking desperately even as I signaled and we charged
the house (but far within I knew better: had not pitifully less
than a hundred joined us? When I had expected hundreds?
Had not I with my own eyes seen fifty more Negroes flee at
our approach all along the way, scattering to the woods?)—
our men now moving on foot and crouched in a ragged
skirmish line behind hedged and sun-dappled boxwood and
maple trees. Each of us was mercilessly exposed, the force
not outnumbered but outpositioned and outgunned in a lopsided uphill assault, and intimidated nightmarishly less by
white men now than by the sight of a horde of housebound

and privileged town and up-county Negroes sending coolly aimed gunfire into our black ranks. At last we had to fall back and disperse into the woods. I saw my men streaming off in panic everywhere. Unmounted horses burst for the meadows. My mission had become totally shattered, blown apart like gunpowder on the wind. Then the ghastly final mortal mischief. Two of my men had made it to within twenty yards of the veranda and then were both killed as I watched: one of these was Will, raging to the end with a sublime fury beyond mere valor, beyond even madness; the other was my old great Henry, who, lacking ears to judge the whereabouts of danger, caught a musket ball in the throat. He fell like a dead tree.

Hark too had fallen wounded far behind me as we made our withdrawal down the slope. I got up from where I had stumbled to go back for him but he was too near the veranda; as he struggled from the lawn with a hand clutched to his bloodied shoulder I saw three bare-chested Negroes who were dressed in the pantaloons of coachmen charge from the house under covering fire and kick him back to earth with booted feet. Hark flopped about in desperation but they kicked him again, kicked him with exuberance not caused by any white man's urging or threat or exhortation but with rackety glee, kicked him until I saw droplets of blood spray from his huge and jagged wound. Then they dragged him past one of the barricade wagons and underneath the veranda and two of the Negroes kept aiming booted kicks at his shoulder even as they disappeared from sight. I fled, escaped then. And I remember feeling sick with rage and with the knowledge of defeat, and later that night after my troops dissolved forever (the twenty of us who remained in a final fire-fight with a dozen mounted Isle of Wight County militia along the rim of humid twilit woods, some of my men too weary, some too demoralized or drunk—*yes, Gray was right* —to refrain from slipping away once and for all into the trees, thereupon to steal back home, harboring wild hopes that in the confusion their adventure with me might not have been noticed) and I too lit off alone, hoping against hope that I could find Nelson or Austin or Jack and regroup and swim across the river for a three- or four-man attack by stealth on the armory—but knowing even as night came down over the woods and the voices of white men hallooed in the dark and the drumming of far-off cavalry hooves echoed from the roads that such a hope trembled on lunacy—an accusation kept howling somewhere in the black defeated hollow of my brain: *It was the niggers that beat you! You might have took Ridley's. You might have made Jerusalem if it wasn't for those bootlickin' black scum of white men's ass-suckin' niggers!*

The following morning after I had slept for the first time in days, alone just as sunrise shimmered up cool and hazy over the pinelands, I sneaked out of the woods in search of food and soon happened upon the Vaughans' place where Nelson's troops had slain four people. Kitchen fires were still smoldering from the day before, the spacious white house lay deserted and still. As I crept past the chicken shed and into the barnyard I heard a grunting and a snuffling noise, and saw two razorback wild hogs devouring the body of a man. It must have been the overseer. The corpse was parted from its head and I knew that the last face the man had ever seen had been that of Will. I watched the hogs rooting at the man's intestines for a moment and I was without feeling; the iniquitous mud-smeared beasts may as well have been feeding upon slops or offal. Yet after I had taken some food from the plundered, littered kitchen and had prepared a sack of bacon and meal to help me through the first part of my flight to the woods, I was afflicted by fear and uneasiness. It had been my custom for many years, as I have said before, to spend part of this hour of the day in prayer and meditation, but when I went back to the border of the woods and knelt there to ask God's guidance in the coming time of solitude—

to request that He show me the ways and necessities for my salvation now that my cause in His name was irrevocably lost—I found to my terrible distress that for the first time in my life I was unable even to think. Try as I might, I could not cause a prayer to pass my lips. The God I knew was slipping away from me. And I lingered there in the early morning and felt as alone and as forsaken as I had ever felt since I had learned God's name.

And so while I sat shivering in the November wind I listened to the sounds of late afternoon welling up from the town, and the rage withered within me and died away. Again the emptiness and desolation returned: the same ache of loneliness that had not really left me once since that morning at the edge of the woods and during the long weeks I had hidden out in my little swampland cave—the same inability to pray. And I thought: Maybe in this anguish of mine God is trying to tell me something. Maybe in His seeming absence He is asking me to consider something I had not thought of or known before. How can a man be allowed to feel such emptiness and defeat? For surely God in His wisdom and majesty would not ordain a mission like mine and then when I was vanquished allow my soul to be abandoned, to be cast away into some bottomless pit as if it were a miserable vapor or smoke. Surely by this silence and absence He is giving me a greater sign than any I have ever known . . .

I rose wearily from the cedar plank and hobbled the length of the chain to the window. I gazed out into the fading light. Faint from the end of the rutted dirt road, by the water's edge, I heard the sound of a mandolin or a guitar and the voice of a young girl singing. Sweet and gentle, from some white, delicate throat I would never see, the song floated up along the river shore on a breath of wind. Bright pinpoints of snow flickered through the dusk and the music mingled in my spirit with a lost fragrance like that of lavender.

"She is far from the land where her young hero sleeps . . ." Tenderly the voice rose and fell, then faded away, and another girl's voice called out softly—"Oh, Jeanie!"—and the sweet lavender smell persisted in my memory, making me stir with longing and desire. I thrust my head into my hands and leaned against the cold bars, thinking: No, Mr. Gray, I have no remorse for anything. I would do it all again. Yet even a man without remorse, in the face of death, may have to save one hostage for his soul's ransom, so I say yes, I would destroy them all again, all—

But for one . . .

It had been as early as that first hour after leaving the Travis house that I began to fear that Will might actually seize control from me and disrupt my entire mission. I was not then so much afraid that he would dominate close followers like Henry or Nelson or Hark; they were safely under my influence and leaders in their own right. But as the night progressed and as we picked up new men at the half-dozen places which lay on our winding route between Travis's and Mrs. Whitehead's, Will's crazy, deafening rivalry for leadership was something I could not dismiss any more than I could fight down my panic over my own inability to kill. Had not Joshua with his own sword slain the King of Makkedah? And with his own bow had not Jehu killed Joram on the field of battle? I felt premonitions of disaster. I knew I could not expect men to rally around me and to fight with bravery if I myself was unable to draw blood.

Yet after my appalling failure to dispatch Travis and Miss Sarah, there were two more separate occasions when in full view of my followers and recruits I had tried to bring death with my sword, two times when I had raised the glittering blade over some ashen white face, only to have it glance away with an impotent thud or miss by such an astonishing space that I felt that the blow had been deflected by a gigan-

tic, aerial, unseen hand. And each time it had been Will—
shouting taunts at me, jabbering, "Step aside, preacher man!"
—who had shouldered me out of the way and with baleful
and amorous and remorseless skill, broadax bloody and
gleaming, performed the execution. Nor was I able to repri-
mand or control him in any way. His insatiate appetite for
blood was in the eyes of others, too, awesome beyond understanding; to dispense with Will even if I was able would be to
chop off my right hand. All I could do when he ordered me to
step aside would be to do just that, and stepping aside, hope
that the others might not notice the sick humiliation in my
eyes or see me when (as I did once after watching Will's ax
cleave the skull of a young planter named William Reese) I
stole off to puke my guts up for minutes in the woods.

Mist the color of pearl hung over the countryside several
hours past dawn when a dozen of us stopped to have breakfast of bacon and fruit in the woods near Mrs. Whitehead's.
The sun had begun to burn off the haze, cloaking the day in
muggy heat. During the night we had successfully attacked
six homesteads and plantations, and seventeen white people
lay dead. Of these, Will had accounted for seven; the rest
were apportioned among Hark, Henry, Sam, and Jack. No
one had escaped our ax and sword, and thus no one had
survived to raise the alarm. The surprise we had effected was
stunning and complete. Our campaign so far had been perfectly silent, perfectly lethal. I knew that if we were by now
blessed by good fortune to negotiate the upper loop of the "S"
with as much thoroughness and quiet, murderous precision as
we had managed so far, we might not have to risk using
gunfire at all until we were very close to Jerusalem. Our
present force had grown, as I had expected, to eighteen; nine
of these men now had horses—including four magnificent
Arabian stallions we had taken from the Reese plantation.
We were bountifully supplied with swords, broadaxes, and
guns. Two young Negroes who had joined us at the Newsom

place were drunk and clearly terrified, but the remainder of the new recruits flexed themselves and strutted about beneath the trees in fighting mettle. Yet I was still restless and troubled. In desperation I wondered if ever a commander had been beset by such a wicked dilemma—his authority, his very being, threatened to its roots by the near-mutinous insolence of a subaltern whom he could not afford to lose, much less send away. Partly in an effort to free myself momentarily from Will's deranging presence, but also because the place was an objective in my plans, I had just before dawn sent Will and four others under the command of Sam to sack the Bryant estate, which lay three miles or so off to the east. Sam had of course grown up with Will at Nathaniel Francis's, and once or twice they had run off together; I thought that for a while at least, Sam might be able to control him and in the process calm him down. At the Bryant place there were half a dozen people who must be put to death, several recruits to get, and a number of swift, gallant quarter horses that would be invaluable for surprise attacks. Because of the isolation of the estate I told Sam that they could use guns. It should be easy work. We waited in the hushed hot woods for this group to rejoin us before we set out in full strength on the next stage of our attack.

I did not feel at all well; the long siege of vomiting that overcame me at the Reese place had left me sweaty and queasy and weak, with racking recurrent spasms of pain in my stomach. A catbird squawked and chattered close by in the woods. *Hush up!* my mind cried. It had become fearfully hot—the sun glowering down already through a canopy of haze no longer milky-pure but leaden, oppressive, hostile. Trying to conceal from the rest of the men the tremors that had begun to shake my body, I ate no bacon or peaches but withdrew alone with my map and plans into a clump of trees. I left Nelson and Henry in charge of the troops. A creek ran nearby and as I made brief notations of our progress on the map I heard the men watering the horses with the copper buckets that were part of our plunder. There was an air of excitement and high spirits among the Negroes in the clearing. I could hear their laughter; even though some were drunk, I wished that I might share their swagger and boisterousness, wished I could still the trepidation gnawing at the inside of me, slow the anxious beating of my heart. Finally I offered up a prayer, asking the Lord to strengthen my resolve as he had done with David, and some of the sickness and vertigo went away. When Sam's troops reappeared in the clearing at about half past eight I felt partially revived and I rose and strode out to greet them. Those six had now become ten—several mounted on the Bryants' dashing quarter horses —I could see by the sumptuous new leather boots which Sam wore that their errand had been successful in more ways than one. I had not actively discouraged a certain amount of looting; it was plain that to try and forbid any one of this disinherited and outcast army from grabbing baubles and trophies and plums would be like attempting to prevent a newly uncaged pigeon from seeking the air. At the same time I was determined to enforce limits: we must *not* be encumbered, we must *not* be impeded, and when I saw that Will had carried off from the Bryant place an enormous gilt-framed wall mirror I knew that it was now or never again—I had to call him down at once.

As I walked toward the group I could tell that Will had made himself both hero and cynosure of the mission. Face and hands streaked with blood as he swung about in the saddle, he wore a blue jacket whose shoulders glittered with the epaulets of an army colonel, and an officer's braided cap rode piratically on his head, bobbing about as he harangued the new field-hand recruits with a triumphant jabber of disconnected words and sounds: "De axes you gotta keep shahp, man!" he crowed. "Shahp as piss-ice, das what! If'n de ax ain' *shahp* de red juice don' run! Das right! Das how come I got de mirrow, so's I can *see* how *shahp* is de ax!" The men and boys around him howled with laughter. They were flecked with dry strings of gore on pants and boots and bare black arms. They leaned forward toward him from their saddles or, dismounting, gazed up at him with flashing white teeth, in thrall to his mad and singsong apostrophe. The Bryant Negroes, three of whom I had never seen before, were joyously, seraphically drunk, flourishing half-gallon jugs of brandy. The mixture of bloodshed and freedom had set them afloat upon a cloud of delirium, their laughter and hysteria seemed to soar up and blow like a gust of wind through the very trees. To them Will, not I, was the black avatar of their deliverance. One of those boys, a light-skinned lad of around eighteen with rotted teeth, had so lost control of himself in laughter that he had wet his pants in a flood.

"I'se runnin' de show now!" Will cried. "I'se de one dat make de ax sing 'Zip Coon.' Will he de gin'ral now!" He spurred his mount, one of the Arabians, and at the same time checked in his reins and the great foaming stallion like Pegasus leaped skyward with a frenzied scream. "Will he de gin'ral now!" he shouted once more, and as the horse's front legs came down to earth the satanic mirror snared the sun blindingly, threw back a shimmering vista of sky, leaves, earth, and a blur of black and brown faces that whirled in a glassy void, then vanished. "*Whoa* dere, Roscoe!" Will bellowed at the horse, stopping him. "I'se runnin' de show, hawse, not you! I boss ob de ruction!"

"No, *I'se* runnin' the show!" I called then. The Negroes fell silent. "We get that straight right now. You ain't runnin' *no* show. Now drop that mirror on the ground. White people can see that two miles off. I *mean* what I says."

From the saddle he regarded me with haughtiness and disdain. Against all will or desire I felt my heart pounding, and I knew that my voice had cracked, revealing fear. In vain I tried to keep the tremor from coursing visibly along the length of my arms. For a long moment Will said nothing, casting down upon me his contemptuous gaze. Then he stuck out his tongue, red as a slice of watermelon, and made a long, slow, circular licking journey around the edges of his pink lips—a gesture of droll and lunatic derision. Some of the men behind me began to giggle, scuffling their feet in pleasure. "I doesn' *has* to gib you no mirrow," he said in a mincing, surly voice. "An' I isn't *gwine* gib you no mirrow. So stick dat in yo' ass, preacher man!"

"Drop that there mirror on the ground!" I commanded him again. I watched him tighten his grip on the haft of his broadax—naked threat—and panic swept over me in an icy wave. I saw my whole mission burnt to ashes in the fire of his madman's insensate eyes. "Drop it!" I said.

"Preacher man," he drawled, rolling his eyes comically at the new men, "preacher man, you jes' better step aside an' let de *ax* man run de show. 'Cause, preacher man, less'n you can handle de ax you cain't handle de army." And he gave a vicious yank upward on the thick blood-drenched haft of the ax and pulled the mirror tightly, possessively against the saddle. "Preacher man"—and his voice became a snarl—"less'n you kin make de *ax* sing a tune you is *all done*."

I do not know what might have happened if at that point Nelson had not intervened, bringing to a halt this confrontation which had so nearly broken me. Perhaps my other close followers would have rallied to my aid and we would then have proceeded onward in much the same fashion as we had planned. Perhaps Will might have cut me down on the spot, then in demented command ridden off with the others to chaos; surely they could not have gotten far without my knowledge of a strategic route, and my mission would have been set down as a "localized disturbance" involving "a few disgruntled darkies" rather than the earthquake it truly became. Whatever, Nelson rescued the situation by donning at the critical moment the mantle of authority which—in Will's eyes, at least—I lacked or never had the right to own. I cannot explain his method, his charm's workings. It might have been Nelson's older age and manner—that methodical, muscular, laconic, self-assured air of experience he carried, his quality of brawny discretion and worldly wisdom: these were fatherly attributes in a way, and through some alchemy they had gained Will's loony respect if not his fear. Hardly before I was aware that he had come between us, I heard Nelson's voice and saw him reach up and clutch the bridle of Will's horse. "Slow down dere, sweet," he said sharply. "Nat he *do* run de show! Now slow down, sweet, and drap dat mirrow on de ground!" It was the tone one uses in addressing a likable but headstrong child—a voice not so much enraged as vexed, cross, severe, unmistakably meant to be obeyed. It cut through to Will like a hickory stick—"Drap it!" he again commanded, and the mirror slid from Will's fingers and toppled unbroken to earth.

"Nat he *still* de gin'ral," Nelson rasped, bristling as he glared upward. "You better study 'bout dat, sweet, or me an' you's really gwine hab a *rookus!* Now you jes' *cool off* yo' black head!" Then he turned and lumbered back to the cooking fire beneath the trees, leaving Will briefly chastened, sulky-looking, and abashed.

Yet although this crisis had been disposed of, I could not rest easy. I was sure that Will's frightening competition for power had not been buried by the stand-off but simply deflected, put aside, and his bitter, contemptuous words—thrown at me, a challenge—had made me all the more panicky over the knowledge that I was unable to kill. Of the others of my force, only Nelson had failed to spill blood, and he not through any reluctance but because he had simply lacked the occasion. And as for the rest—Henry and Sam and Austin and Jack, my closest followers: was it only my imagination that caused me to feel in their manner toward me a coolness, to sense in the way they had spoken to me in the last hours a new-found suspicion and mistrust, a withdrawal, as if by failing to perform, even as ritual, that act which each of *them* had done I had somehow begun to lose a sure grip upon my rights and the respect due me as a commander? Certainly in days and weeks past I had never pretended that I would shirk this duty. Had I not told them so many times: *To draw the blood of white men is holy in God's eyes?* Now in my impotence and irresolution I felt beleaguered not only by Will's obscene jibes and threats but by fear that even those closest to me might abandon faith in my leadership if I persisted in this womanish failure to strike down white flesh. Heat blazed upon the clearing, still another catbird screeched in the humming woods. Dizzily, I stole off to retch dry spasms in the bushes. I felt mortally sick and the aching self beneath my skin pulsed and burned with fever. But at nine o'clock or thereabouts I returned to the clearing to assemble the company. And in this condition—shivering, ill, nearly torn apart by frights and apprehensions that I never thought God would permit—I was by providence hurried toward Margaret Whitehead, and our last meeting . . .

To Richard Whitehead on his path toward the hogpen, standing alone beneath the hot morning sun in a patch of green cotton, our approach likely conjured up that of the hosts of Armageddon. Twenty Negroes and more in a jagged line— all mounted, light glistening from ax and gun and sword—who burst from the distant woods in a cloud of dust which, obscuring us at the same time that it revealed our relentless purpose and design, must have appeared to him borne from the hellish bowels of the earth: the sight was surely a re-enactment of all the fears and visions of black devils and heathen hordes that had ever imperiled his Methodist sanctity. Yet he too, like Travis, like all the others lulled by a history which had never known our kind before, was doubtless touched with disbelief at the same time that a portion of his mind grappled with the horror—and who knows but whether this was not the reason that he stood rooted to the ground like a cotton plant, his bland divine's sun-pink face uptilted to the sky in vague bewilderment as we drew closer, perhaps hoping that this demonic apparition or vision or whatever, the result of undigested bad bacon or troubled sleep or August heat or all three, would go away. But the *furor!* The *noise* of pounding hooves and clanking steel and the panting lungs of horses and the hoots and harsh whispers of breath, closer now, from those grinning nigger faces! Merciful Lord! Such noise was a part of no apparition; besides, it was becoming almost intolerable! He seemed to raise his hands as if to stop up his ears, rattled a little in the legs, made no other motion, stood immobile and perplexed even as the two outriders, Hark and Henry, enveloped him on either side, and slackening pace only long enough to take aim, struck him dead with two swift hatchet chops to the skull. From the house I heard a woman shriek.

"First Troop!" I cried. "Secure the woods!" I had just seen the new overseer, a man named Pretlow, and his two young white helpers jump from the steaming still and streak for the woods, the boys running, Pretlow astride a crippled barrel-bellied mule. "Git after them!" I cried to Henry and his men. "They won't git far!" I wheeled and shouted to the others: "Second and Third Troops, take the gun room! On to the house!"

Ah God! At that moment I was overcome again by such dizziness that I pulled in my horse and got down instantly and stood there in the hot field, leaning with my head against the saddle. I shut my eyes; needlepoints of red light floated through the dark, my lungs were filled with dust. When the horse stirred, I rocked as if in a rowboat. Across the field screams of terror came from the house; one stricken female cry, prolonged and wavering, ceased with shocking suddenness. I heard a voice nearby, Austin's, and looked up to see him riding bareback one of the stallions, with a Bryant Negro seated behind. I gave the other boy my mount and told them both to join the troop chasing Pretlow and his helpers at the edge of the woods. I stumbled, fell to my knees, rose quickly.

"You's sick, Nat, isn't you?" said Austin, peering down.

"Go on," I replied, "go on!" They galloped off.

On foot now I skirted Richard Whitehead's corpse lying face down between two rows of cotton. I walked unsteadily, following along the old familiar log fence which I myself had helped build, separating field and barnyard. My men in the house, in the stable, and in the barn, were making a barbaric racket. Still more screams erupted from the house: I remembered that Mrs. Whitehead's summer-visiting daughters were home. I clambered over the fence, nearly falling. As I grabbed for the post, I glimpsed the gross old house nigger Hubbard, at gunpoint, being forced into a wagon by Henry and another: captive eunuch, he would not go with us willingly, but tied up in the cart with other pet collected coons, would surely go. "Lawd, sweet Lawd!" he boohooed to the skies as they shoved him up into the wagon, and he sobbed as if his heart would perish. At that moment I rounded the corner of the oxen barn and looked toward the porch of the house. There deserted of all save those two acting out their final tableau—the tar-black man and the woman, bone-white, bone-rigid with fear beyond telling, pressed urgently together against the door in a simulacrum of shattered oneness and heartsick farewell—the porch seemed washed for an instant in light that flowed from the dawn of my own beginning. Then I saw Will draw back as if from a kiss and with a swift sideways motion nearly decapitate Mrs. Whitehead in a single stroke.

And he had seen me. "Dar she is, preacher man, dey's one left!" he howled. "An' she all your'n! Right by de cellah do'! Go git her, preacher man!" he taunted me in his wild rage. "If'n you cain't make de *red juice* run you cain't run de *army!*"

Soundless, uttering not a word, Margaret Whitehead rose up and scrambled from her hiding place beyond the sheltering wall of the cellar door and fled me—fled me like the wind. Fleet and light she ran, after the fashion of a child, with bare arms stiffly outstretched, brown hair tied with a bow and tossing this way and that above a blue taffeta dress, pressed to her back in a sweaty oblong of deeper blue. I had not caught sight of her face and realized it was she only when, disappearing around the corner of the house, the silk ribbon which I had seen before fell from her hair and rippled briefly on the air before fluttering to earth.

"Dar! She gone!" Will roared, gesturing with his broadax to the other Negroes, who had begun to straggle across the yard. "Does you want her, preacher man, or she fo' me?"

Ah, how I want her, I thought, and unsheathed my sword. She had run into the hayfield, and when I too rounded the corner of the house I thought she had slipped away, for there was no one in sight. But she had merely fallen down in the waist-high grass and as I stood there she rose again—a small and slender figure in the distance—and resumed her flight toward a crooked far-off fence. I ran headlong into the field. The air was alive with grasshoppers: they skimmed and flickered across my path, brushed my skin with brittle momentary sting. I felt the sweat streaming into my eyes. The sword in my right hand hung like the weight of all the earth. Yet I gained on Margaret quickly, for she had tired fast, and I reached her just as she was trying to clamber over the rotted pole fence. She made no sound, uttered no word, did not turn to plead or contend or resist or even wonder. Nor did I speak —our last encounter may have been the quietest that ever was. Beneath her foot one of the poles gave way in crunching powdery collapse and she tripped forward, bare arms still outthrust as if to welcome someone beloved and long-unseen. As she stumbled thus, then recovered, I heard for the first time her hurtful, ragged breathing, and it was with this sound in my ears that I plunged the sword into her side, just below and behind her breast. She screamed then at last. Litheness, grace, the body's nimble felicity—all fled her like ghosts. She crumpled to earth, limp, a rag, and as she fell I stabbed her again in the same place, or near it, where pulsing blood already encrimsoned the taffeta's blue. There was no scream this time although the echo of the first sang in my ears like a far angelic cry; when I turned aside from her fallen body I was troubled by a steady soughing noise like the rise and fall of a summer tempest in a grove of pines and realized that it was the clamor of my own breathing as it welled up in sobs from my chest.

I lurched away from her through the field, calling out to myself like one bereft of mind. Yet hardly had I taken a dozen steps when I heard her voice, weak, frail, almost without breath, not so much voice as memory—faint as if from some distant and half-forgotten lawn of childhood: Oh Nat I hurt so. Please kill me Nat I hurt so.

I stopped and looked back. "*Die*, God damn your white soul," I wept. "Die!"

Oh Nat please kill me I hurt so.

"Die! Die! Die! Die!"

The sword fell from my hand. I returned to her side and looked down. Her head was cradled against the inside of her arm, as if she had composed herself for sleep, and all the chestnut streaming luxuriance of her hair had fallen in a tangle amid the hayfield's parched and fading green. Grasshoppers stitched and stirred in restless fidget among the weeds, darting about her face.

"I hurt so," I heard her whisper.

"Shut your eyes," I said. I reached down to search with my fingers for a firm length of fence rail and I could sense once more her close girl-smell and the fragrance of lavender, bitter in my nostrils, and sweet. "Shut your eyes," I told her quickly. Then when I raised the rail above her head she gazed at me, as if past the imponderable vista of her anguish, with a grave and drowsy tenderness such as I had never known, spoke some words too soft to hear and, saying no more, closed her eyes upon all madness, illusion, error, dream, and strife. So I brought the timber down and she was swiftly gone, and I hurled the hateful, shattered club far up into the weeds.

For how long I aimlessly circled her body—prowled around the corners of the field in haphazard quest for nothing, like some roaming dog—how long this went on I do not recollect. The sun rose higher, boiling; my own flesh was incandescent, and when at the farm I heard the men call for me their voices were untold distances away. By the edge of the woods I found myself seated on a log, head in my hands, unaccountably thinking of ancient moments of childhood—warm rain, leaves, a whippoorwill, rushing mill wheels, jew's-harp strumming—centuries before. Then I arose again and resumed my meaningless and ordained circuit of her body, not near it yet ever within sight as if that crumpled blue were the center of an orbit around whose path I must make a ceaseless pilgrimage. And once in my strange journey I thought I heard again her whispery voice, thought I saw her rise from the blazing field with arms outstretched as if to a legion of invisible onlookers, her brown hair and innocent school gown teased by the wind as she cried: "Oh, I would fain swoon into an eternity of love!" But then she vanished before my eyes—melted instantly like an image carved of air and light—and I turned away at last and went back to join my men.

All day after that we swept north through the countryside. Despite certain unforeseen halts and delays, our advance was everywhere successful. The Porter place, Nathaniel Francis's, Barrow's, Edwards's, Harris's, Doyle's—each was overrun, and each was the scene of ruthless extermination. We missed laying hold of Nathaniel Francis himself (much later I learned from Hark that he had been away at the time in Sussex County), and so it was one of the lesser ironies of our mission—and a source of bitter disappointment to both Sam and Will—that almost the only white man in the county who owned a truly illustrious reputation for cruelty to Negroes escaped the blade of our retribution. His ending would have had a quality all its own. Such are the fortunes of war. By early afternoon I had regained my stability and composure; my strength came back, I felt immeasurably better and took heart and vigor from our rapid gains. Under the influence of Nelson—but also because of my actions at the Whitehead place—Will had become somewhat more subdued, and I felt that finally he was under a semblance of control. By late afternoon there was no one who was white left alive along the twenty miles we had traveled.

Even so, our work of death was not absolutely exhaustive, not complete, and I am far from sure that this was not the ruination of my mission, since it took but a single soul to raise the alarm. And I must admit to a failing on my own part which may have caused more than anything else the fact of the resistance we began to encounter the following day and which slowed us to a fatal pace. For as I told Gray, late that afternoon just before twilight at the Harris farm we had seen a young white girl of fourteen or so flee to the woods, screaming her terror as she rushed into the haven of a grove of juniper trees. And Gray himself had established that it was this girl who had managed to reach the Williams place near dark, allowing that fortunate man to hide his family and his slaves and to ride off north, spreading the alarm. In turn it had been that alarm which may or may not (I cannot be certain) have given the enemy their ultimate advantage and tipped the balance against us. What I failed to confide to Gray is that it had not been "us" who had seen her but I alone, rocking weary in the saddle as dusk descended and my men killed and ransacked and looted the Harris house. I heard her faint frantic cry, saw a flicker of color as she vanished into the darkening thicket of trees.

I might have reached her in a twinkling—the work of half a minute—but I suddenly felt dispirited and overcome by fatigue, and was pursued by an obscure, unshakable grief. I shivered in the knowledge of the futility of all ambition. My mouth was sour with the yellow recollection of death and blood-smeared fields and walls. I watched the girl slip away, vanish without a hand laid upon her. Who knows but whether we were not doomed to lose. I know nothing any longer. Nothing. Did I really wish to vouchsafe a life for the one that I had taken?

Part

IV

"IT IS DONE..."

✦ ✦ ✦ ✦ ✦ ✦ ✦ ✦ ✦ ✦ ✦ ✦ ✦

Surely I Come Quickly . . .

Cloudless sunlight suggesting neither hour nor season glows down upon me, wraps me with a cradle's warmth as I drift toward the river's estuary; the little boat rocks gently in our benign descent together toward the sea. On the unpeopled banks the woods are silent, silent as snowfall. No birds call; in windless attitudes of meditation the crowd of green trees along the river shore stands drooping and still. This low country seems untouched by humanity, by past or future time. Beneath me where I recline I feel the boat's sluggish windward drift, glimpse rushing past eddies of foam, branches, leaves, clumps of grass all borne on the serene unhurried flood to the place where the river meets the sea. Faintly now I hear the oceanic roar, mark the sweep of sunlit water far-near, glinting with whitecaps, the ragged shoulder of a beach where sea and river join in a tumultuous embrace of swirling waters. But nothing disturbs me, I drowse in the arms of a steadfast and illimitable peace. Salt stings my nostrils. The breakers roll to shore, the lordly tide swells back beneath a cobalt sky arching eastward toward Africa. An unhurried booming fills me not with fear but only with repose and slumbrous anticipation—serenity as ageless as those rocks, in garlands of weeping seaweed, thrown up by the groaning waves.

Now as I approach the edge of land I look up for one last

time to study the white building standing on its promontory high above the shore. Again I cannot tell what it is or what it means. Stark white, glittering, pure as alabaster, it rests on the precipice unravaged by weather or wind, neither temple nor monument nor sarcophagus but relic of the ages—of all past and all futurity—white inscrutable paradigm of a mystery beyond utterance or even wonder. The sun bathes its tranquil marble sides, its doorless façade, the arches that sweep around it, revealing no entry anywhere, no window; inside, it would be as dark as the darkest tomb. Yet I cannot dwell on that place too long, for again as always I know that to try to explore the mystery would be only to throw open portals on even deeper mysteries, on and on everlastingly, into the remotest corridors of thought and time. So I turn away. I cast my eyes toward the ocean once more, watch the blue waves and glitter of spume-borne light approaching, listen to the breaking surf move near as I pass, slowly, in contemplation of a great mystery, out toward the sea . . .

I come awake with a start, feeling the cedar plank cold beneath my back, the leg irons colder still—like encircling bands of ice. It is full dark, I can see nothing. I rise up on my elbows, letting the dream dwindle away from my mind, fade out—this one last time, and forever—from recollection. The chains at my feet chink in the morning's black silence. It is bitterly cold but the wind has died and I no longer shiver so; I draw the remnant of my ragged shirt close around my chest. Then I tap with my knuckles against the wall separating me from Hark. He sleeps deeply, his breath a jagged sigh as it rattles through his wound. *Tap-tap.* Silence. *Tap-tap* again, louder. Hark awakes. "Dat you, Nat?"

"It's me," I reply, "we go soon."

He is quiet for a moment. Then he says, yawning: "I knows it. Lawd, I wish dey would git on wid it. What time it is you reckon, Nat?"

"I don't know," I say, "they must be a couple hours more."

I hear the heavy thump of his feet and the sound of his chain-links clinking together, then the noise of a bucket scraping across the floor. Hark chuckles faintly. "Lawd me, Nat," he says. "Wisht I could move about. Hit hard enough to pee lyin' down in de daytime, at night I cain't hit dat bucket in no way." I hear a noisy spatter and splash and Hark's laughter again, low in his throat, rich, amused at himself. "Ain't nothin' mo' useless dan a twofifty-pound nigger dat cain't hardly move. Did you know, Nat, dey gwine hang me all roped up in a *chair*? Leastwise, dat's what dat man Gray done said. Dat sho' is *some* way to go."

I make no reply, the sound of flowing water ceases, and Hark's voice too falls still. Somewhere far off in the town a dog howls on and on without lull or respite, a continuous harsh lonely cry from the bowels of the dark morning, touching me with dread. *Lord,* I whisper to myself in anguish, *Lord?* And I clench my eyelids together in a sudden spasm, hoping to find some vision, some word or sign in the profounder darkness of my own mind, but there is still no answer. I will go without Him, I think, I will go without Him because He has abandoned me without any last sign at all. Was what I done wrong in His sight? And if what I done was wrong is there no redemption?

"Dat God durned dog," I hear Hark say. "Lissen at him, Nat. Dat sho de sign of somepn, awright. Lawd, dat dog done barked right on th'ough my dreams jes' now. Dreamed I was back home at Barnett's long long time ago when I was jes' a little ole thing 'bout knee-high to a duck. An' me an' my sister Jamie was gwine fishin' together down in de swamp. And we was walkin' along underneath dem wild cherry trees, jes' as happy as we could be, talkin' about all dem fish we was gwine catch. On'y dey dis yere dog a-barkin' at us an followin' us th'ough the woods. An' Jamie she done kep' sayin', 'Hark, how come dat dog make all dat holler?' An' I say back to Jamie, 'Don' bothah 'bout no dog, don' pay dat ole dog no nem'mine.' Den you done knock on de wall, Nat, and now here dat *same* dog a-barkin' way off in de road, and here *I* is, an' dis mornin' dey gwine hang me."

Then behold I come quickly . . .

I drowse off dreamless for a time, then I wake abruptly to see that morning approaches with the faintest tinge of pale frosty light, stealing through the barred window and touching the cedar walls with a glow barely visible, like ashes strewn upon a dying fire. Way off in the lowlands across the river, somewhere among the fields and frosty meadows, I hear the sad old blast of a horn as it rouses up the Negroes for work. Nearer there is a tinkle and a rustle, barely heard; the town stirs. A single horse passes *cloppetyclop* over the wooden bridge, and far away in the distance a cock crows, then another, and they cease suddenly; for a moment all is still and sleeping. Hark again slumbers, the air whistles from his wounded chest. I rise and make my way to the end of the chain, shuffling in a sideways motion toward the window. Then I lean forward against the freezing sill, and stand motionless in the still-encompassing dark. Against the rim of the heavens, high above the river and the towering wall of cypress and pine, dawn begins to rise in light of the softest blue. I raise my eyes upward. There alone amidst the blue, steadfast, unmoving, fiery marvel of brightness, shines the morning star. Never has that star seemed so radiant, and I stand gazing at it and do not move though the chill of the damp floor imprisons my feet in piercing icebound pain.

Surely I come quickly . . .

I wait for minutes at the window, looking out at the new day which is still dark. Behind me I hear a noise in the tiny corridor, hear Kitchen's keys jangling, and see against the walls a lantern's ruddy orange glow. Footsteps scrape on the floor with a gritty sound. I turn about slowly and find that it is Gray. But this time he does not enter the cell, merely stands outside the door as he peers in, then beckons me with his finger. With clumsy trouble I move across the floor, chain dragging between my feet. In the lantern light I see that he is clasping something in his hand; when I draw closer to the door I can tell that it is a Bible. For once Gray seems quiet, subdued.

"I brung you what you asked for, Reverend," he says in a soft voice. So composed does he seem, so tranquil, so gentle are his tones, that I almost take him for another man. "I done it against the will of the court. It's my doing, my risk. But you've been pretty fair and square with me, all in all. You can have this solace if you want it."

He hands the Bible to me through the bars of the door. For a long moment we gaze at each other in the flickering light and I have a strange sensation which passes almost as quickly as it comes, that never have I seen this man in my life. I say nothing to him in answer. At last he reaches through the bars and grasps my hand; as he does so I know by some strange and tentative feeling in his hasty grip that this is the first black hand he has ever shaken, no doubt the last.

"Good-bye, Reverend," he says.

"Good-bye, Mr. Gray," I reply.

Then he is gone, the lantern flame fades and dies out, and the cell again is filled with darkness. I turn and place the Bible down gently on the cedar plank. I know that I would not open it now even if I had the light to read it by. Yet its presence warms the cell and for the first time since I have been in jail, for the first time since I gazed into his irksome face, I feel a wrench of pity for Gray and for his mortal years to come. Again I move to the window, inhaling deeply the wintry morning air. It tastes of smoke, of burning apple wood, and I am flooded with swift shifting memories, too sweet to bear, of all distant childhood, of old time past. I lean against the sill of the window, and gaze up at the morning star. *Surely I come quickly . . .*

Then behold I come quickly . . .

And as I think of her, the desire swells within me and I am stirred by a longing so great that like those memories of time past and long-ago voices, flowing waters, rushing winds, it seems more than my heart can abide. *Beloved, let us love one another: for love is of God; and everyone that loveth is born of God, and knoweth God.* Her voice is close, familiar, real, and for an instant I mistake the wind against my ear, a gentle gust, for her breath, and I turn to seek her in the darkness. And now beyond my fear, beyond my dread and emptiness, I feel the warmth flow into my loins and my legs tingle with desire. I tremble and I search for her face in my mind, seek her young body, yearning for her suddenly with a rage that racks me with a craving beyond pain; with tender stroking motions I pour out my love within her; pulsing flood; she arches against me, cries out, and the twain—black and white—are one. I faint slowly. My head falls toward the window, my breath comes hard. I recall a meadow, June, the voice a whisper: *Is it not true, Nat? Did He not say, I am the root and the offspring of David, and the bright and morning star?*

Surely I come quickly . . .

Footsteps outside the door jar me from my reverie, I hear white men's voices. Again a lantern casts a bloom of light through the cell, but the half-dozen men go past with thumping boots and stop at Hark's door. I hear jingling keys and a bolt slides back with a thud. I turn and see the outline of two men pushing the chair past my door. Its legs bump and clatter on the plank floor, there is a heavy jolt as its arms strike against the doorjamb of Hark's cell. "Raise up," I hear one of the men say to Hark. "Raise yore ass up, we got to rope you in." There is silence, then a creaking sound. I hear Hark

begin to moan in pain. "Easy dar!" he cries out, gasping.
"*Easy!*"

"Move his legs," I hear one of the white men order another.

"Grab him by the arms," says someone else.

Hark's voice becomes a wail of hurt and wild distress. The
sound of bumping and shoving fills the air.

"*Easy!*" Hark cries out, sobbing.

"Push him down!" says a voice.

I find myself hammering at the walls. "*Don't hurt him!*"
I rage. "Don't hurt him, you white sons of bitches! You've
done hurt him enough! All his life! Now God damn you don't
hurt him no more!"

Silence descends as the men cease talking. In a long
drawn-out breath Hark's wail dies away. Now I hear a hurried sound of snapping ropes as they tie him into the chair.
Then the white men whisper and grunt while they strain beneath the weight of their burden and lift Hark out into the
hallway. Shadows leap up and quiver in the lantern's brassy
radiance. The white men shuffle in furious labor, gasping
with the effort. Hark's bound and seated shape, like the
silhouette of some marvelous black potentate borne in stately
procession toward his throne, passes slowly by my door. I
reach out as if to touch him, feel nothing, clutch only a handful of air.

"Dis yere some way to go," I hear Hark say. "Good-bye,
ole Nat!" he calls.

"Good-bye, Hark," I whisper, "good-bye, good-bye."

"Hit gwine be all right, Nat," he cries out to me, the voice
fading. "Ev'ythin' gwine be all right! Dis yere ain't nothin',
Nat, nothin' atall! Good-bye, ole Nat, good-bye!"

Good-bye, Hark, good-bye.

The edge of dawn pales, brightens; stars wink away like
dying sparks as the night fades and dusty sunrise begins to

streak the far sky. Yet steadfast the morning star rides in the heavens radiant and pure, set like crystal amid the still waters of eternity. Morning blooms softly upon the rutted streets of Jerusalem; the howling dog and the crowing roosters at last are silent. Somewhere behind me in the jail I hear a murmuration of voices; I sense a presence at my back, I feel the approach of gigantic, unrelenting footfalls. I turn and retrieve the Bible from the cedar plank and for one last time take my station by the window, breathing deeply in the apple-sweet air. My breath is smoke, I shudder in the cold newborn beauty of the world. The footsteps draw near, suddenly cease. There is a rattle of bolts and keys. A voice says: "Nat!" And when I do not answer, the same voice calls out: "Come!"

We'll love one another, she seems to be entreating me, very close now, *we'll love one another by the light of heaven above.* I feel the nearness of flowing waters, tumultuous waves, rushing winds. The voice calls again: "Come!"

Yes, I think just before I turn to greet him, *I would have done it all again. I would have destroyed them all. Yet I would have spared one. I would have spared her that showed me Him whose presence I had not fathomed or maybe never even known. Great God, how early it is! Until now I had almost forgotten His name.*

"Come!" the voice booms, but commanding me now: *Come, My son!* I turn in surrender.

Surely I come quickly. Amen.

Even so, come, Lord Jesus.

Oh how bright and fair the morning star . . .

The bodies of those executed, with one exception, were buried in a decent and becoming manner. That of Nat Turner was delivered to the doctors, who skinned it and made grease of the flesh. Mr. R. S. Barham's father owned a money purse made of his hide. His skeleton was for many years in the possession of Dr. Massenberg, but has since been misplaced.

—Drewry, *The Southampton Insurrection*

✦ ✦ ✦

And he said unto me, It is done.
I am Alpha and Omega, the beginning and
the end. I will give unto him that is
athirst of the fountain of the water
of life freely. He that overcometh shall inherit
all things; and I will be his God and
he shall be my son.

✦ ✦ ✦

ABOUT THE AUTHOR

A native of the Tidewater region of Virginia, William Styron grew up not far from Southampton County, where Nat Turner's revolt took place. The story of Nat Turner was the subject of the first novel that the author wanted to write, and he has maintained a special interest in American Negro slavery ever since. He has written three other novels, *Lie Down in Darkness, The Long March,* and *Set This House on Fire.*

CENTRAL WYOMING COLLEGE